Nigel Cawthorne is the author of *Military Commanders*, and *Vietnam – A War Lost and Won*. His writing has appeared in over a hundred and fifty newspapers, magazines and partworks – from the *Sun* to the *Financial Times*, and from *Flatbush Life* to the *New York Tribune*. He lives in London. His son, **Colin Cawthorne** helped to compile the first-hand accounts that make up this anthology.

THE MAMMOTH BOOK OF
THE
MAFIA

EDITED BY NIGEL AND COLIN CAWTHORNE

ROBINSON

RUNNING PRESS
PHILADELPHIA · LONDON

ROBINSON

First published in the UK by Robinson, an imprint of Constable & Robinson Ltd, 2009

Reprinted by Robinson in 2017

5 7 9 10 8 6

A CIP catalogue record for this book
is available from the British Library.

UK ISBN: 978-1-84529-958-3

Robinson
An imprint of
Little, Brown Book Group
Carmelite House
50 Victoria Embankment
London EC4Y 0DZ

An Hachette UK Company
www.hachette.co.uk

www.littlebrown.co.uk

First published in the United States in 2009 by Running Press Book Publishers
A member of the Perseus Books Group

Books published by Running Press are available at special discounts for bulk purchases in the
United States by corporations, institutions and other organizations. For more information, please
contact the Special Markets Department at the Perseus Books Group, 2300 Chestnut Street, Suite 200,
Philadelphia, PA 19103, or call (800) 810-4145, ext. 5000, or email special.markets@perseusbooks.com.

US Library of Congress number: 2008944128
US ISBN 978-0-7624-3720-7

10 9 8
Digit on the right indicates the number of this printing

Running Press Book Publishers
2300 Chestnut Street
Philadelphia, PA 19103-4371
Visit us on the web!
www.runningpress.com

Printed and bound in Great Britain by CPI Group (UK) Ltd., Croydon CR0 4YY

Papers used by Robinson are from well-managed forests and other responsible sources

MIX
Paper from
responsible sources
FSC® C104740

Contents

Acknowledgments

The editor would like to thank all those who made this book possible by letting us reprint the extracts listed below:

Anna Kotopoulos from St Martin's Press for use of "The Odyssey", "The Grand Inquisition" and "The Castellammarese War" from *A Man of Honour: The Autobiography of Joseph Bonanno* (André Deutsch, London, 1983) © Joseph Bonanno and Sergio Lalli 1983; Mike Hamilburg from Simon and Schuster for "Drugs, Guns and Swindles" from *Blood Oath* (Simon and Schuster, New York, 1994) © George Fresolone and Robert J. Wagman 1994; Mellisa Brant of the Perseus Book Group for use of "Pontiac Trans Am" and "Chevy Corvette Convertible" from *Born to the Mob* (Running Press, London / Philadelphia 2004) © Frankie Saggio and Fred Rosen 2004; I would also like to thank Mellisa for the use of "Fat Tony Wants Him Dead" from *Contract Killer: The Explosive Story of the Mafia's Most Notorious Hitman Donald "Tony the Greek" Frankos* (Thunder's Mouth Press, New York, 1993) © William Hoffman and Lake Headley; Blanche Brown and David Grossman for "The Bonannos" from *Donnie Brasco* (New American Library, New York, 1987) © Joseph D. Pistone and Richard Woodley 1987; from Sterling Lord Literistic

for chapter 11 of *Casino* (Transworld, London, 1996) ©
Nichola Pileggi; Catherine Trippett of the Random House
Group Ltd for use of chapter 1 from *Excellent Cadavers:The
Mafia and the Death of the First Italian Republic* (Pantheon
Books, New York, 1995) © Alexander Stille 1995; and I
would also like to thank Catherine for her help in securing
"The Earlier Battles with Bandits" from *The Last Struggle
with the Mafia* (Mondadori, Milan, 1932) © Cesare Mori
1932; Alicia Torello for "Little Man" and "Double Jeopardy"
from *For the Sins of My Father: A Mafia Killer, His Son, &
the Legacy of a Mob Life* (Broadway Books, New York, 2002)
© Albert DeMeo 2002; I'd also like to thank Alicia for
"Entertainers and the Mob" and "Assassination Squads"
from *My Life in the Mafia* (Doubleday, New York, 1971)
© Vincent Teresa 1971; Ailsa Morrison of Mainstream
Publishing for "Murder for Hire" and "The Enforcer" from
The Ice Man (St Martin's Griffin, New York, 2007) © Philip
Carlo 2007; [for use of "The Godfather: The Way Things
Ain't" and "Gallo and Colombo: The Way Things Are"
from *Joey The Hitman: The Autobiography of a Mafia Killer*
(Pocket Book Inc., New York, 1975 © David Fisher; [for
use of chapters 9, 10 and 11 of *The Last Testament of Lucky
Luciano* (Little, Brown and Company, New York, 1974) ©
Martin A. Gosch and Richard Hammer 1974; Julia Gayner
for "The Making of a Made Guy" from *The Last Mafioso:
The Treacherous World of Jimmy Fratianno* (Times Books,
New York, 1981) © Ovid Demaris 1981; Rohini Janda at
Harper Collins for "The 'Illustrious Corpses'" and "The
Second Mafia Wars" from *Mafia Wars: The Confessions of
Tommaso Buscetta* (Fontana Press, London, 1988) © Tim
Shawcross and Martin Young 1998; I would also like to
thank Rohini for use of chapters 10 and 15 from *Underboss:
Sammy the Bull Gravano's Story of Life in the Mafia* (Harper
Collins, London, 1998) © Peter Maas 1998.

Every effort has been made to trace the original copyright holders of the following without success; the editor and publishers would be pleased to hear from any claimants to the legal copyright of:

Chapters 4 and 5 of *The Canary That Sang,* also published as *The Valachi Papers: The First Inside Account of Life in the Cosa Nostra* by Peter Maas (Putnam, New York, 1968).

Introduction

The origins of the Mafia are obscure, though fearsome Sicilian gangs have been around for centuries. They seem to have arisen during the Middle Ages when Sicilians fought to rid themselves of a series of foreign invaders – Saracens, Normans and, later, the Spanish. The Mafia boss turned *pentito*, or informant, quoted in these pages, Tommaso Buscetta – once known as the "Godfather of Two Worlds" – claimed that the organization he served for forty years originated as a secret society which took an oath to protect the people of Sicily from Catalan marauders in the fifteenth century.

Sicily's gangs took advantage of the political upheavals of the nineteenth century and came to prominence during Italy's Risorgimento – the struggle to unify the country and throw off foreign domination. They fought to overthrow Sicily's Bourbon rulers and, in 1860, threw in their lot with Italy's liberator Giuseppe Garibaldi. However, the Sicilians did not like being ruled by the Italians any more than by the Bourbons and continued in their old ways. Later gangs were hired by absentee landlords to protect their lemon groves and estates from bandits. But as they grew strong, they turned against the landlords, extorting money from them. As the population had long been alienated from their rulers, this new indigenous force – the Mafia – laid down its own law. This was based on the *omertà* – a savage code of honour that meant that mafiosi never, under any circumstances, turned to the authorities to settle a grievance. Victims and their families had the right to avenge any wrong, while anyone breaking the code of silence would be dealt with by the Mafia itself.

Mafia rule became increasingly organized when, in the late 1800s, various "families" in western Sicily joined together in a loose confederation. They enforced a brutal code. Death was the punishment for any infringement and corpses were mutilated as a warning to others. A corpse with a missing tongue signified that the victim had violated the *omertà*. A body with a hand chopped off was a petty thief. One with the severed genitals stuffed into its mouth meant that the dead man had "dishonoured" the wife of a *compagna* member.

There is some dispute over the origin of the name Mafia. According to the *Encyclopaedia Britannica*, the small private armies that guarded absentee landlords' property were known as *mafie*. Others say that the word comes from the Sicilian adjective mafiusu whose origin is, again, uncertain. In 1863, the Sicilian actor Giuseppe Rizzotto wrote a popular play called *I Mafiusi di la Vicaria* – "The Beautiful People of Vicaria" – though the characters were Palermo street thugs and the setting, Vicaria, was the city's central prison. The play was such a success that he added two acts and put on a new production called simply *I Mafiusi* – mafiusi being the plural of mafiusu. Already, the word mafiusedda was used as a term of admiration in the waterfront district of Palermo called the Borgu, or the "Hamlet", while mafiusu meant fearless, enterprising, and proud, but pejoratively it also signified a bully. These days mafiusu means "swagger", but can also be translated as "boldness, bravado".

The word mafiusu itself is thought to derive from the Arabic slang word mahyas, meaning "aggressive boasting, bragging", or marfud meaning "rejected". Alternatively, it might derive from the Arabic word mu'afah, meaning "exempt from the law", or mahfal, meaning "a meeting or gathering". Then, in Norman-French there is the verb se méfier, which means "to beware". In the Tuscan dialect, the word maffia means "misery". In the Latin there is vafer meaning "shrewd", then there is the proper name Maufer, which the medieval Knights Templar used to refer to the "God of Evil".

Giuseppe Bonanno – or "Joe Bananas", boss of one of the "Five Families" of New York – has a more colourful theory about the origins of the Mafia and its name, remembered from his childhood in Sicily, which he recorded in his autobiography *A Man of Honour*:

In my grandfather's time, Sicily was under the dominance of the Bourbon dynasty, a royal family of Spanish and French ancestry. Italy itself was like a jigsaw puzzle with the pieces owned by various powers.

Because of this patchwork of foreign domination and internal weaknesses, Italy was the last major country in Europe to be unified under a native ruler. The unification movement was spearheaded by King Victor Emmanuel II and his brilliant prime minister, Cavour. It could not have been accomplished, however, without the leadership and inspiration of the Italian patriot Giuseppe Garibaldi.

Garibaldi catalysed the unification movement by enlisting a volunteer army to liberate Sicily. These volunteers, a motley crew of idealists and zealots, wore a distinctive garb and became known as the Red Shirts. In 1860 Garibaldi's enthusiastic band, some 1,000 strong, landed in Marsala on the west coast of Sicily.

Although the Red Shirts were vastly outnumbered by the Bourbon army, they had the backing of the populace. Men of my Tradition, such as my grandfather, sided with Garibaldi in order to overthrow the hated Bourbons. The ranks of the Red Shirts also swelled with Sicilian youngsters, the picciotti, the young ones.

You can imagine what a stirring tale this made when I heard from my elders how, for example, during one famous victory Garibaldi tricked the Bourbons into believing the Red Shirts were more numerous than they actually were. The picciotti gathered cattle and sheep from the countryside and herded the animals in front of the enemy at a distance. The animals raised such a cloud of dust that the Bourbon soldiers, thinking a huge army was marching toward them, fled before the battle even started.

With the invaluable aid of the local insurgents, most of them men of my Tradition, Sicily was liberated, paving the way for the unification of Italy. But if Garibaldi and the men of my Tradition collaborated in ousting the Bourbons, they did so out of different impulses.

Garibaldi wanted to forge an Italian national state, which had never existed. (Some wags insist that it does not exist today.) However, the local insurgents were mainly interested in a little more freedom to run their own affairs. The men of my Tradition knew that as far as Sicily was concerned, nothing changes basically. They had gotten rid of the House of Bourbon only to make themselves subject to the House of Savoy. One ruler departs, another takes his place.

The concept of nationhood never stirred them deeply. It was a vague concept that required men to give their highest loyalty to an abstract entity, the nation, rather than to their families, which were flesh and blood. It would require young men to fight foreign wars on behalf of the national state, to fight strangers from whom one had never received a personal affront or injury, to fight people one didn't even know.

Sicilians are among the most idealistic people on earth, but they are not abstract. They like things on a human scale. Even in the smallest business transactions, they like to deal with each other man to man, eyeball to eyeball. It is no different when they fight. They take fighting very personally. They believe in personal, not abstract, honour.

In this regard, the story of the Sicilian Vespers bears repeating. The story describes another insurrection, this one when the island was under French domination. During Easter week of 1282, while the people of Palermo were making their way to evening worship (vespers), agents of the treasury waited outside the churches to apprehend tax debtors. The agents handcuffed and dragged many citizens to jail, publicly shaming them by slapping their faces – an intolerable insult.

As it happened, a young lady of rare beauty, who was soon to be married, was going to church with her mother when a French soldier by the name of Droetto, under the pretext of helping the tax agents, manhandled the young lady. Then he dragged her behind the church and raped her.

The terrified mother ran through the streets, crying – Ma fia, ma fia!

This means "My daughter, my daughter" in Sicilian. The boyfriend of the young lady found Droetto and killed him with a knife.

The mother's cry, repeated by others, rang out through the streets, throughout Palermo and throughout Sicily. "Ma fia" soon became the rallying cry of the resistance movement, which adopted the phrase as an acronym for Morte alla Francia, Italia anela – "Death to France, Italy cries out".

This was the version of the Sicilian Vespers story as told to me.

Scholars now consider parts of the story to be legend or folklore. That may be true, but so what? The important element of the story is not its factual veracity, but the Sicilian spirit which it exemplifies. It speaks to me to this day of the living ideals of personal honour, personal justice and personal dignity.

The years between the unification of Italy and World War I have been described as the golden age of my Tradition. The new rulers were willing to tolerate or make accommodations with men of my Tradition in exchange for their political support.

Although they acted separately in pursuit of their own goals, men of the old Tradition, as a group, composed a sort of shadow government which existed alongside the official government. In the western part of Sicily, where the old Tradition was strongest, "men of honour", as they were called, flourished as they never had and probably never will again. The rustic culture of the island condoned the activities of these "men of respect". The king of Italy might rule the island, but men of my Tradition governed it.

These men usually came from the middle class. Some or them owned land. Some of them had a monopoly (or were trying to acquire one) in a particular business enterprise. No matter how they made their living, however, they usually had influence or control over jobs. This gave them leverage to influence votes for politicians. One could also turn to these men for solutions to personal problems, for the redress of wrongs. They assisted friends in need and were implacable toward enemies.

To be sure, some of these men abused their power or perverted it for personal gain. But the Tradition I am describing would have never endured without the backing of the people. And it had the people's support because, in the main, the Tradition worked in practice.

"Men of honour" were essential to Sicilian society in their capacities as brokers, facilitators and arbiters. But to serve as a middleman, a "man of respect" needed more than personal courage. He needed friends, in all places and at all levels. His effectiveness depended on his network of friendships.

To deal effectively with city hall, for example, one had to have a friend there. Consequently, if someone asked a favour from a "man of honour", let us say to expedite some legal papers, he could tell the supplicant:

– Rest assured, you shall have your papers tomorrow. I have a friend in city hall and he will do me this favour.

By performing such favours, large and small, the "man of honour" made himself indispensable.

If, for example, someone asked the "man of honour" to recover a stolen ring, the "man of honour" needed some connection among bandits and brigands in order to negotiate for the return of the ring.

The "man of honour" handled such a task realistically and with aplomb. He could not very well charge up the hills and shoot every bandit in sight. There were too many bandits in Sicily for that. First of all, he would ask for a marginal sum of money from the man whose ring was stolen. Then, through his connections in the demi-monde, the "man of honour" would find out who stole the ring and buy it back for a sum less than its actual worth. He also kept part of the money from the ring's owner as a commission. As a result, the owner got his ring back, the bandit made money and the "man of honour" performed a favour and got a commission.

Those who did such favours were variously referred to as "men of honour", "men of respect" or "men of order". Such men were also said to be "qualified" – they were qualified in all aspects of life, qualified to deal with all types of people. Usually, these men used diplomacy, astuteness and friendly persuasion; sometimes, however, they resorted to violence.

Joe Bananas considered himself to be a "man of honour" and believed that he was misunderstood. Some even thought that he had broken the code of silence – the *omertà* – himself by writing his autobiography, but he felt he needed an opportunity to explain himself.

. . .The greatest regret of my life is that I never pushed myself to master the English language. This has proved to be a terrible disadvantage. My lack of fluency in English, for example, had forced me to be more taciturn with journalists than I perhaps would like to have been, on occasion. I know I come off poorly in interviews. Since I have a limited English vocabulary, I'm forced to simplify my thoughts. Consequently, I come off sounding crude, or needlessly obscure. My frustration is such that to avoid making a fool of myself I would rather say "no comment" and let it go at that.

Lastly, in deciding whether to write a book of my life, I always had to consider what impression such a book would make on the ordinary reader. Would the reader believe what I had to say? Would people make fun of me? Would people be interested? Oh, I knew there was interest in the sensational aspects of my life, but would people be interested in my insights about honour, family, trust? How could I possibly convince people there was another Joe Bonanno than the "Joe Bananas" they read about in the newspapers?

I am misunderstood. I had every reason to suppose that my book would be misunderstood as well. The overwhelming majority of Americans just plain don't understand what my Tradition is all about. One of their ill-informed notions concerns the so-called code of silence – *omertà*.

Many people reading this book undoubtedly believe that in writing it I have violated the code of silence and thus have broken a cardinal rule of my Tradition.

Omertà comes from the word *omu* or *omo* – which means "man". In my Tradition, *omertà* has come to describe the "manly" behaviour of someone who refuses to get his friends in trouble. In the hands of the police, a captive from our Tradition ideally should remain silent. He should not co-operate. Such a man is willing to face even death rather than betray his friends to the authorities or to his rivals.

Omertà in my Tradition is a noble principle. It praises silence and scorns the informer. Try as you might, there's no complimentary way of describing an informer. All the terms are pejorative: stool pigeon, spy, rat, tattler, quisling, snitch, fifth-columnist, betrayer. It's probably true that all cultures and all languages recognize informers, no matter what side they're on, to be unsavoury types.

Informers are universally scorned because they are the sort of people who betray their friends to save their own skins. In order to save himself, the informer is willing to get others in trouble. The informer is willing to talk. This is unmanly behaviour.

Omertà is an injunction against allowing yourself to be the instrument of another man's downfall.

My Tradition has had its share of rotters. Informers such as Joe Valachi, Vincent Teresa and James Fratianno don't deserve to be called *omu*. They are louses. They bargained for their lives or their creature comforts by co-operating with the authorities, who used them for their own purposes. When a man betrays his friends, as these men did by "singing" to the cops, he betrays himself.

Out of these men's co-operation with the police came forth books: *The Valachi Papers, My Life in the Mafia, The Last Mafioso*, to name a few. All these books are bad, not so much for their inaccuracies and pretensions as for their insincerity. The books were written under duress of one form or another, most often to please the authorities. None of these men would have ever squawked about his life if he hadn't been in prison and if he hadn't had something to gain.

Omertà, however, doesn't mean that a man can't say what he feels, which is what I'm doing. I am under no coercion to write. What I say in this book about my friends or enemies I have already said to them in person. Never in my life have I provided information that would send anyone to jail. This book is not an exception.

I do not accuse others, and I do not apologize for myself. My object is to unmask. I do not judge conduct on the basis of legal innocence or legal guilt. I talk in terms of what is right and what is wrong, who is weak and who is strong, what makes me laugh and what makes me cry.

Having despaired of writing a book, I rejected all overtures. The matter languished. Then something quite startling, you might even say miraculous, happened. I began to write all on my own – to maintain my sanity.

Within these pages is a selection of writings from others who have broken the *omertà* for their own reasons. However, this only applies to American mafiosi. Although Bonanno was born and, later, educated in Sicily, his career as a criminal was confined to the United States. Despite the mass trials that are devastating the Sicilian mafia, the *omertà* still holds in Italy.

The Mafia in Sicily

Sadly, few mafiosi are well-educated men and their grasp on the history of the Mafia, outside their own direct experience, is tenuous. However, the American author and journalist Alexander Stille has devoted much of his career to the study of Italy, its politics and the Mafia. In 1995, he published the book Excellent Cadavers, *which covers the events leading up to the crackdown on the Sicilian Mafia in the 1990s following the bloodthirsty reign of Corleonesi boss Salvatore "Totò" Riina. The book is dedicated to the memory of two murdered anti-Mafia prosecutors, Giovanni Falcone and Paolo Borsellino. Setting the scene, Stille tells how the modern Sicilian Mafia came into being.*

The history of the Mafia and of the modern Italian state begin together. Soon after Garibaldi and the troops from the northern region of Piedmont invaded Sicily in 1860 and united it with the rest of the new Italian nation, they encountered the problem of rampant crime. In the chaos that followed the war of unification, bandits terrorized the countryside, murdering government troops, while criminal bands tried to control the sale and renting of land, placing their own men as guards on the lush gardens and groves in and around Palermo. The northern Italians were struck by the Sicilians' refusal to co-operate with the new government, the stubborn silence of even innocent victims, their tendency to take justice into their own hands. The word "Mafia" entered the Italian vocabulary at this time to describe the peculiarly tenacious kind of organized crime the northern Italians found deeply embedded in Sicilian life.

Unlike bandits or common thieves who live outside respectable society, most mafiosi continued to work at regular jobs, using force or the intimidating power of the organization to extort advantage from others. Many of the early mafiosi were armed guards or administrators who ran Sicily's great rural estates for their absentee landlords in Palermo. Traditionally, the mafioso put himself in the role of intermediary, keeping the peasants in line and guaranteeing that the harvest would be brought in, while using his control of the land to extract concessions from the landlord. In a place where government has never been particularly effective or well liked, mafia groups usurped many of the functions of the state–administering justice, settling disputes and dividing up resources. Although mafiosi have often cultivated the image of being modern-day Robin Hoods who rob the rich and give to the poor, they have always been dedicated to the task of self-enrichment, never hesitating to use violence and murder in defence of their own interests.

Centuries of corrupt and brutal government by foreign conquerors taught most Sicilians to regard government with suspicion and hostility. Justice was frequently administered not by rule of law but by the private armies of Sicily's feudal landlords. The mafia draws on a code of behaviour – the refusal to co-operate with police authorities, the preference for private rather than public justice, even the practice of extortion – that can be traced back centuries. While it has its cultural roots in feudal Sicilian life, the Mafia, as a form of organized crime, appears to be a product of modernity, of the new freedom and opportunity of unified Italy. There was little room for organized crime in the highly static world of feudalism, where the landowners had a virtual monopoly of both economic resources and the use of violence. The break-up of the great feudal estates and the expansion of trade opened up possibilities for the lower classes to participate in the confused grab for wealth that followed unification. With no tradition of law or public administration to fall back on, violence or the threat of violence became the easiest way to gain a leg up on the competition. As Paolo Borsellino once observed: "The desire to prevail over the competition, combined with a lack of a credible state, cannot bring about a normal marketplace: the common practice is not to do better than your rivals but to do them in."

Crime in Sicily reached such epidemic proportions that in 1874 it became the subject of an enormous national debate. The conservative government proposed emergency police measures to regain control of the island, which prompted [Italian politician] Leopoldo Franchetti's trip to Sicily two years later. In the end, the question brought down the government and brought the Left to power for the first time in Italian history. Public order in Sicily was restored through a typically Italian compromise between Mafia and government that set the pattern for the future. The Mafia helped police track down and arrest the bandits who were the most obvious threat to public security, and in exchange the government allowed the Mafia to continue its own more subtle form of economic crime. This ability to co-opt and corrupt public authority has characterized the Mafia from its beginning and has guaranteed its impunity for more than 130 years of history. The advent of democracy and the expansion of voting rights gave organized crime new opportunities to acquire political influence. By controlling substantial blocks of votes, Mafia groups helped elect politicians who, in turn, helped them.

Even in Franchetti's day, the disastrous consequences of this compromise were evident. "Italy, annexing Sicily, has assumed a grave responsibility," he wrote. "The Italian government has the obligation to give peace to that population and to teach it the meaning of the law, and to sacrifice any private or political interest toward that aim. Instead we see Italian ministers of every party setting the example by engaging in those 'interested transactions' that are the ruin of Sicily, by recognizing and negotiating with those local powers they ought to try to destroy in order to get their help at election time. The chief of police in order to obey his superiors ends up imitating them and thus forgets the purpose of his mission . . . While the *carabinieri* [Italian military police] and army soldiers are marching up hill and down dale under the rain and snow, the chief brigand is passing the winter peacefully in Palermo – and not always hidden . . . People scheduled to be arrested are warned even before the warrants have been signed and the troops who come to arrest them find them gone three or four days earlier."

It was not until Mussolini's Fascist regime that a first serious, if bloody, attempt to suppress the Mafia was made. Between 1924 and 1929, Mussolini's "Iron Prefect", Cesare Mori, conducted mass arrests, surrounded and besieged entire towns, took hostages and destroyed property and livestock in order to track down suspected criminals. To some extent, the campaign was a success: according to government figures homicides in the province of Palermo dropped from 278 to only 25 in 1928. Grateful landowners wrote letters to Mori in which they reported that after being "freed" from the Mafia the value of their land had skyrocketed, with rents doubling, tripling and in some instances increasing by 1,500 per cent. But if he appeared to reduce criminal activity, Mori did little to cut the social roots of the Mafia. His campaign of terror, by using brutal and illegal tactics and indiscriminately arresting hundreds of innocent people along with the guilty, turned mafiosi into persecuted victims who enjoyed popular sympathy. The fact that the regime also used the operation to eliminate some of its own political opponents further undermined its credibility. Moreover, as the rent figures show, the chief beneficiaries appear to have been the landowners. By contrast, agricultural wages dropped by some 28 per cent during the late 1920s and early 1930s. The Fascists appeared not so much to have eliminated the mafiosi as to have replaced them by acting as the new enforcers for the Sicilian landowning class. After Mussolini recalled Mori in 1929, saying his mission had been completed, the regime had to pretend that the Mafia no longer existed and ignored signs that the mafiosi were cautiously coming back out of the woodwork.

With the fall of Fascism and the liberation of Sicily by Allied troops during the Second World War, the Mafia was ready to emerge in full force. There is a widespread belief in Italy that the Allied landing was prepared with help from the Mafia, which was then rewarded with important positions of power. According to this theory, the American government contacted the Sicilian-American gangster Lucky Luciano, who enlisted the co-operation of his Sicilian counterparts to pave the way for a rapid Allied victory.

While colourful (and politically useful), the story appears to have little basis in fact. But, as with many legends, there is a grain of truth. Naval Intelligence did contact Lucky Luciano for information about German saboteurs in the docks of New York. But Luciano, who had left Italy as a boy, denied any role in the Sicilian landing: "At home, I didn't have any contacts," he said. After the war, either as a quid pro quo or as an expedient attempt to rid themselves of known criminals, the United States deported Luciano and some forty other American mafiosi back to Italy where they used their American experience to help modernize organized crime.

The Allied occupation undeniably gave new oxygen to the Mafia. Anxious to exclude both Communists and Fascists from power, the occupying Anglo-American army – whether knowingly or unknowingly – installed several prominent mafiosi as mayors of their towns. (An Italian-American mafioso, Vito Genovese, managed to become interpreter for the American governor of Sicily, Colonel Charles Poletti, during the six months of military occupation.) Criminal elements succeeded in infiltrating the Allied administration, often with the help of Italian-American soldiers. They managed to smuggle supplies from military warehouses and ran a flourishing black market in such scarce commodities as food, tobacco, shoes and clothing. While this black market trade may have involved the corruption of low- and middle-level officials, there is nothing to suggest that it was part of a strategy conceived in Washington. The Pentagon and the Roosevelt administration, in fact, registered their alarm about the situation in Sicily. As in the period after the Italian battle of unification, the aftermath of World War II was a time of chaotic freedom and economic expansion which the Mafia exploited ably.

Determined to avoid the persecution it had suffered under Fascism, the Mafia made a concerted effort to assure itself political protection in the new post-war order. At first, many mafiosi backed the new movement of Sicilian separatism, helping to organize its small guerrilla army. But when the cause of separatism faded and other parties, such as the Christian Democratic Party, emerged, Mafia bosses shifted their allegiances. With the Italian Left seemingly on the brink of power, the new parties accepted Mafia support as a bulwark against communism.

Between 1945 and 1955, forty-three Socialists or Communists were murdered in Sicily, often at election time. On 20 April 1947, the united Left (Communists and Socialists) won an impressive 30 per cent of the vote in Sicily against the 21 per cent of the Christian Democratic Party. Ten days later, when Communist farmers of Porrella della Ginestra gathered to celebrate May Day and their electoral victory, the criminal band of Salvatore Giuliano opened fire on the crowd, killing eleven people.

The killings took place in the new chill of the Cold War. That year, the United States announced the Truman Doctrine, stating its commitment to fight Communist expansion throughout the world. Indeed, on the day of the massacre of Porrella della Ginestra, Secretary of State George Marshall sent a telegram to the US ambassador in Rome, expressing alarm over the rise of the Communists (especially in Sicily) and the need to adopt new measures to reinforce anti-Communist, pro-American elements. Until that time, the Communists (along with all other anti-Fascist parties) had participated as equal partners in the government with the Christian Democrats – an arrangement of which (as Marshall's telegram makes clear) the United States strongly disapproved. As a result of this pressure, the Christian Democrats kicked the Communists out of the government. With the fate of democratic Europe at stake, and Stalin swallowing up entire nations whole, the excesses of local thugs in rural Sicily seemed a minor problem.

The decision to enlist the Mafia's help in Sicily was a quite conscious one, as one of the founders of the

Sicilian Christian Democratic Party, Giuseppe Alessi, acknowledged openly many years later. While personally opposing this local pact with the devil, Alessi was outvoted by others who viewed it as a practical necessity. " 'The Communists use similar kinds of violence against us, preventing us from carrying out public rallies. We need the protection of strong men to stop the violence of the Communists,' " Alessi quoted one of his colleagues as saying. "I was in the minority and the 'group' entered *en masse* and took over the party." (Despite his dissent, Alessi shared a rather rosy view of the "honoured society" prevalent at that time: "It was another kind of Mafia, not the kind of violent organized crime we see today," he said.)

"The DC decided to accept the Mafia's support to reinforce itself in the struggle against communism," said historian Francesco Renda. "If one doesn't understand this, it's impossible to understand everything that happens afterwards. The people who made this choice were not criminals, nor were they joining with low-level criminals. They were allying themselves with a force that had historically played this role in Sicily. All this was justified in the name of the Cold War. The Mafia was ennobled by being given the role of the military arm of a major political force, something it had never had in the past. Naturally, the Mafia then drew on the power of the government and became not only a political and social force but an economic force and that's when the real adventure began."

The perpetrators of the Porrella della Ginestrra massacre, Salvatore Giuliano and his criminal band, roamed freely around the Sicilian countryside for seven years, giving newspaper interviews, meeting with politicians and even the chief prosecutor of Palermo. "The only people unable to find Giuliano were the police," declared a court sentence issued several years later. In 1950, when his presence had become a national embarrassment, the Mafia helped wipe out Giuliano's band, presenting the bandit's corpse to police. "Bandits, police and Mafia are one and the same, like Father, Son and Holy Ghost," said Gaspare Pisciotta, Giuliano's cousin, whose betrayal was key in the outlaw's final capture and death. Shortly after his trial in 1954, Pisciotta was himself mysteriously poisoned in Palermo's Ucciardone prison when someone put strychnine in his coffee.

The Mafia's valuable role as intermediary in capturing Giuliano and other bandits was openly praised by Italian judges of the period. In 1955, Giuseppe Guido Lo Schiavo, a member of Italy's highest court, wrote an outright defence of the Mafia: "People say the Mafia does not respect the police and the judiciary: it's untrue. The Mafia has always respected the judiciary and justice, has bowed before its sentences and has not interfered with the magistrate's work. In the persecution of bandits and outlaws . . . it has actually joined together with the police."

Well-known Mafia bosses with lengthy criminal records were all accorded places of honour in the Christian Democratic Party. And it was not uncommon for prominent politicians to appear as honoured guests at the christenings, weddings and funerals of major Mafia figures. In Sicily, being known as a friend of a mafioso was not a sign of shame but of power.

Mafia bosses could move blocks of votes and the politicians turned to them at election time, as is clear from a letter written in 1951 by a Sicilian member of parliament, Giovanni Palazzolo, of the Liberal Party, to the Mafia boss of Partinico.

Dearest Don Ciccio,
The last time we saw one another at the Hotel delle Palme (in Palermo) you told me quite correctly that we needed a bright young member of the Regional

Parliament from Partinico who was a friend and would be accessible to our friends. My friend Totò Motisi has all these requisites and I have decided to help him with all my strength. If you help me in Partinico, we will make him a member of parliament.

The letter's recipient was Francesco Coppola, known as Frankie "Three Fingers" Coppola in the United States, where he had served a long prison sentence until he was freed and deported to Italy along with Lucky Luciano after the war.

In the 1950s, after land reform helped break up the last great feudal estates (a process that the Mafia worked to its own benefit), agriculture in Sicily diminished in importance and hundreds of thousands of unemployed peasants emptied the countryside for the growing cities. Many headed for Palermo, the new capital of the Sicilian region. In order to undercut the separatist movement, the government in Rome had granted Sicily special autonomy, including the right to have its own parliament and regional government in Palermo. While failing to fulfil the promise of greater self-determination and dignity for the Sicilian population, the new arrangement provided an extra layer of bureaucracy, thousands of jobs to be distributed to political cronies, and control over millions of dollars in government funds with seemingly limitless possibilities for corruption and patronage. So much so that many Sicilians referred to their regional representatives simply as *i novanta ladroni*, "the ninety thieves", there being ninety seats in the local parliament.

With the flow of both people and money toward the new regional capital, the city experienced a massive building boom known as "the Sack of Palermo". Real estate developers ran wild, pushing the centre of the city out along Viale della Libertà toward the new airport at Punta

Raisi. With hastily drafted zoning variances or in wanton violation of the law, builders tore down countless Art Deco palaces and asphalted many of the city's finest parks, transforming one of the most beautiful cities in Europe into a thick, unsightly forest of cement condominia.

Developers with close Mafia ties were not afraid to use strong-arm tactics to intimidate owners into selling or to clear the way for their projects. One of the most important buildings of the great Sicilian architect Ernesto Basile was razed to the ground in the middle of the night, hours before it would have come under protection of the historic preservation laws. In the period from 1959 to 1964, when Salvatore Lima and Vito Ciancimino were, respectively, mayor and commissioner for public works, an incredible 2,500 of the 4,000 building licences issued in the city of Palermo went to three individuals whom the Italian parliament's anti-Mafia commission has described as "retired persons, of modest means, none with any experience in the building trade, and who, evidently, simply lent their names to the real builders".

The expansion of the new city was accompanied by the gradual abandonment and decay of the old. Already damaged by bombs during the Second World War, the centre of Palermo was gradually reduced to a wretched slum, through a deliberate policy of neglect. There was little money to be made in the old centre because of zoning restrictions: throwing up cheap high-rise apartments was much more lucrative than patiently restoring seventeenth- and eighteenth-century structures. Many areas were left for months or years without gas, electricity or hot water, forcing residents to move out into the new housing projects. Even neighbourhoods that had not been bombed during the war began to look as if they had been. Palermo gained the distinction of not only having a Department of Housing, but a department of *edilizia pericolante* or "collapsing housing" – a disgrace that continues to this day.

The residents of the city centre dropped from 125,481 to 38,960 between 1951 and 1981 – a period in which the population of Palermo as a whole nearly doubled. Many of the great monuments of Palermo – the onion-domed Arab mosques-turned-Christian churches, the Norman palaces, the Renaissance fountains and baroque churches – stand next to empty, rubble-strewn lots or abandoned buildings with broken windows. Those who remained behind were generally the city's poorest and most wretched, prepared to put up with Third World conditions not unlike those of the bidonvilles of Cairo or Rio de Janeiro.

The story of Mafia power in Palermo can be told in terms of real estate – block by block and building by building – a legacy that is reflected both in the cheap construction and infernal congestion of the "new" city and the total degradation of the old. The changes it wrought were so fundamental that almost no one was immune. The Falcone and Borsellino families were no exception.

Born respectively in 1939 and 1940, Giovanni Falcone and Paolo Borsellino grew up during this period of transformation only a few blocks apart in an old, dilapidated neighbourhood of Palermo near the seaport known as La Kalsa. For centuries the area had been one of the most elegant in the city. In the eighteenth century, the poet Goethe admired the striking axial views created by Palermo's criss-crossing avenues, along which the city's aristocracy rode in carriages for the daily *passeggio* in order to see and be seen. The Falcones lived on Via Castrofilippo, in a house once inhabited by a city mayor, Falcone's great-uncle. Paolo Borsellino and his family lived nearby on Via della Vetriera, next to the family pharmacy. As boys, Falcone and Borsellino played soccer together in Piazza Magione. The neighbourhood had come down a bit since Goethe's time, but it had retained some of its elegance, and remained a healthy mix of professionals and day labourers, aristocrats and fishermen, businessmen and beggars.

The Borsellinos' house on Via della Vetriera was declared unsafe and the family was forced to move out in 1956. The family pharmacy (run at the time by Paolo's mother and now by his sister, Rita, and her husband) remained, while the neighbourhood crumbled around it. Homeless squatters occupied their old building and, forced to live without light or heat, partially destroyed it in a fire. During the sack of Palermo, the Falcones' own house was earmarked for demolition to make way for a road. Falcone and the rest of his family haunted the offices of various city officials, carrying photographs of the palace's frescoed ceilings in hopes of convincing them of the building's historic and artistic value. The building was destroyed in 1959, although the road it was supposed to make room for was never built – a testament to the blind and irrational urban planning of the period. Both families had little choice but to join the exodus to the anonymous dormitory community on what had been the outskirts of town.

It is probably not an accident that the two prosecutors who wound up together on the front line against the Mafia came from Palermo's small but solid professional middle class. Falcone's father was a chemist, Borsellino's a pharmacist. The middle class in Sicily – as in the rest of Italy – was perhaps also the part of Sicilian society that had been the most receptive to the values of patriotism and nationalism promoted by the new Italian state and emphasized even more energetically during Fascism. "Our family was very religious and very attentive to the idea of civic duty," said Maria Falcone. "We grew up in the cult of the Fatherland. Mamma's brother died at age eighteen in the First World War, falsifying his birth certificate so he could volunteer for the army at age seventeen. My father's brother died at age twenty-four, as a career air force official. Hearing about these relatives as children developed in us, and in Giovanni, a love of country above all. 'They served the Nation!' my father would say with reverence."

The family went to church every Sunday and, for a time, Giovanni served as an altar boy. Giovanni's mother showed few outward signs of affection but communicated a very Sicilian idea of manhood: "She would often repeat to him that boys never cry, because she wanted him to grow up to be a strong man," Maria said. Giovanni's father was more affectionate but remained the stern patriarch typical of the fathers of that period. "He taught us to work and to do our duty," Falcone once said. "He was a man of strong moral principle, serious, honest, extremely attached to the family . . . He slapped me only once during my childhood. It was during wartime when I broke a bottle of oil. Someone who didn't live through those times wouldn't understand. A bottle of olive oil at that time was a treasure. My family was not rich, we lived on a modest state salary." In this somewhat austere, frugal household, Falcone's father was proud of the fact that he had never treated himself to a coffee at a café.

Falcone's parents were not politically active. "They had a rather uncritical view of Fascism, they were loyal, law-abiding citizens," said Maria Falcone. As a boy he had been infatuated with a phrase of the Italian patriot Giuseppe Mazzini, "Life is a mission and duty is its highest law." In fact, Falcone considered a career in the military, spending one year at the Italian naval academy, before returning to the University of Palermo to study law.

At the university, Falcone drifted away from his family's Catholicism and became interested in communism. "Our studies – particularly with Giovanni and me – brought us to a decidedly critical attitude toward Fascism, as with any form of absolutism," said Maria Falcone. The Italian Communist Party, while not breaking with the Soviet Union, had long distinguished itself as the most independent and democratic Communist Party in the West. Falcone never became a party member.

Paolo Borsellino grew up with the same "cult of the Fatherland". He, too, had two uncles who had served in the army. Although they had not been killed, both had been taken prisoner in Africa during the Second World War. Both had worked for a year in the Italian colonies in Africa during Fascism and had moved back to Palermo after the war. Because his father had died when Paolo Borsellino was only twenty-two, his uncles assumed a more important role in his life. One of them, Francesco (Zio Ciccio), lived with the Borsellinos for many years. "When these uncles talked about experiences in Africa he fell under the spell of these stories," says his sister, Rita. In fact, to the end of his life, Paolo Borsellino's study in Palermo was full of African masks and artifacts brought back from Somalia by his uncle. "Paolo had this great thirst for learning; completely on his own initiative he went to city hall to trace the origins of our family," says his mother, Maria Pia Lepanto Borsellino. He also made a very elaborate and carefully designed family tree of Italy's royal family, the Savoy. This would not have been unusual twenty years earlier, but by the time Paolo Borsellino was growing up, Italy had abolished the monarchy and the Savoy were living in exile, compromised by the Fascist regime. But he was named Paolo Emanuele Borsellino, after King Vittorio Emanuele, and was born in 1940, when the Savoy family still held the Italian throne. "He was passionately interested in history, he wanted to know about Fascism, he joked about being a supporter of the Bourbons [the Spanish monarchy that ruled Sicily and southern Italy before Italian unification]," his sister, Rita, said.

When Borsellino was at the University of Palermo, he joined a neo-Fascist student group. While this fact became the source of some scandal in later years, Fascism in the Sicilian context had a specific meaning: for better or worse, the Fascist regime was the only Italian government that had made a serious effort to wipe out the Mafia. In a land where the rule of law has generally been feeble or non-existent, Borsellino dreamed of a State with a capital "S". In fact, Mafia witnesses have testified repeatedly that the two parties they were strictly forbidden to support were the Fascists and the Communists. So that while starting at opposite ends of the political spectrum, Falcone and Borsellino were attracted by the two political forces that seemed the most uncompromising towards what was worst in Sicilian life.

Growing up, both Borsellino and Falcone had direct experience of the Mafia. Borsellino often recalled envying a schoolmate of his who bragged about an uncle who was a mafioso. Both prosecutors had classmates who ended up as mafiosi. Because the Kalsa is a port area, it is filled with both sailors and smugglers of contraband goods. As a boy, Falcone used to play ping-pong with Tommaso Spadaro, who became known as the "King of the Kalsa", a major smuggler of contraband cigarettes and, later, of heroin. "I breathed the odour of Mafia from the time I was a boy, but at home my father never talked about it," Falcone said. "It was a forbidden word." (When Falcone later prosecuted Spadaro as a mafioso, the boss could not resist reminding Falcone of how badly he had beaten him at ping-pong.)

Falcone and Borsellino became friends again while at the University of Palermo and both decided to join the magistrature. In the early years of their careers, both men left Palermo to take jobs in the Sicilian provinces, Borsellino in Agrigento and Monreale, Falcone in Lentini and Trapani. Borsellino returned to Palermo in the early

1970s and Falcone arrived in 1978, taking a job with the bankruptcy court. Borsellino was working as a prosecutor in one of the two principal prosecutors' offices, the *Ufficio Istruzione*, or investigative office. By the time they became magistrates, Falcone's and Borsellino's early political enthusiasms were greatly tempered and became the subject of joking and teasing between them. "*Camerata* Borsellino," Falcone would say, mimicking the standard form of address between members of the Fascist Party.

Like Falcone, Borsellino never joined any political party in order to avoid any appearance of partisanship in his work as a magistrate. "He refused numerous offers to become a political candidate by both the Socialists and the MSI (Movimento Sociale Italiano, the neo-Fascist Party)," said Giuseppe Tricoli, an activist in the MSI and a friend of Borsellino's from his university days. " 'No one should ever have any doubts about my motives, that I do what I do in order to gain notoriety for myself,' " he told Tricoli.

Their middle-class origins – the fact that their parents worked in professions that did not especially interest the Mafia – may have protected Falcone and Borsellino when they became prosecutors. Mafia witnesses have testified that the organization did not extort small shopkeepers (like pharmacists) in the 1950s and 1960s. Members of the Palermo upper class – wealthy landowners or businessmen – were much more likely to be on familiar terms with the Mafia, either as victims or accomplices. Some simply paid protection to be left alone, others decided to use the power of Cosa Nostra by having a mafioso as a partner in a business deal, a land sale or a development project. Many noble families participated happily in the Sack of Palermo, eager to make a quick profit by selling or developing their old estates. In fact, some prosecutors from the Palermo upper crust found themselves under pressure from friends and relatives to go easy on this defendant or not to explore the interconnections between common criminals and respected, "legitimate" businessmen. Falcone and Borsellino did not belong to any of the exclusive social clubs frequented by some of their colleagues. Even if a magistrate went purely to pass an evening playing bridge, he could very well rub elbows with someone whose name might turn up in a police report or investigation. (Michele Greco – the notorious Mafia boss known as "the Pope" – was a member of a fashionable gun club; when some members began to grumble about his presence, the club suffered a robbery that many interpreted as a warning.) Both Falcone and Borsellino led highly restricted social lives among a small circle of close friends and colleagues. They declined invitations to most social occasions and always inquired closely to find out who would be present at any event they were supposed to attend. The most innocuous-seeming event could provide an occasion for the Mafia to contact or compromise a prosecutor by having him shake hands with or be seen with a person of dubious reputation.

When Falcone returned to Palermo in 1978, he was undergoing an intensely difficult personal crisis. His wife, Rita Bonnici, chose to remain in Trapani, announcing that she was leaving him for another man. To make matters worse, the other man was one of Falcone's superiors, the chief judge of Trapani, making the affair a hot topic of gossip in the courthouses of Trapani and Palermo. In Sicily, where the word *comuto* (cuckold) is reserved for the lowest forms of human life, the collapse of his marriage was a scalding humiliation and a personal loss that left Falcone smarting for years. He never discussed his first marriage with his friends and told his two sisters that he would never marry again. Instead he threw himself into his new job at the bankruptcy court, mastering a new area of the law and the intricacies of the economic life of Palermo.

At the time, a general Pax Mafiosa reigned in the city. There had been virtually no major Mafia killings in recent years, which led some people (in good faith as well as bad) to declare that the Mafia no longer existed. There had been no major Mafia prosecutions in several years. The Mafia war of the early 1960s had led to the parliament's anti-Mafia commission and to a series of massive Mafia trials mounted by the Palermo magistrate Cesare Terranova. While Terranova had correctly identified all the major bosses of the Sicilian Mafia, the cases all ended in disastrous failure. The culture of *omertà* (silence) and the intimidation of witnesses and judges were so great that the government's cases rarely held up in court.

Many pre-eminent scholars at the time insisted that the Mafia, if it existed, was not an organization but an anthropological phenomenon, a set of values and attitudes common in Sicily. The stories of initiation rites, highly structured Mafia "families", with *capi* (bosses) and *consiglieri* (counsellors), were nothing more than the fantasy of Hollywood and the sensationalist press, they said. More attentive observers noted that the relative calm indicated something quite different, a harmony among the city's Mafia clans that meant that they were going happily about their business with little or no opposition.

In fact, all the men whom the anti-Mafia commission had denounced as the pillars of the Mafia system in Palermo were still in place. Vito Ciancimino – the former barber of Corleone – continued to pull the strings at Palermo city hall. All of the important municipal contracts continued to be steered to Count Arturo Cassina, accused of subcontracting out much of the work to Mafia firms. The island's taxes were collected by the private monopoly of the Salvo family, long suspected by police of being mafiosi themselves. Salvatore Lima, the mayor who presided over the Sack of Palermo, was now a member of parliament, and his political mentor, Giulio Andreotti, was prime minister, thus placing Lima at the centre of power in Rome.

Despite the apparent calm, a small number of police officials and prosecutors knew that all was not what it seemed. Deputy police chief Boris Giuliano had begun to notice suitcases full of drugs and money moving back and forth between Palermo and New York. Rather than disappearing, Mafia business was booming as never before. Moreover, a series of mysterious kidnappings, murders and disappearances taking place in the Sicilian countryside indicated indecipherable rumblings within the obscure world of Cosa Nostra.

Meanwhile, the rest of the country was preoccupied with what seemed like much more pressing and more important problems – the right to divorce and abortion, terrorism, the rise of the Italian Communist Party, Italy's place in the international struggle between East and West. From the mid-1970s forward the headlines of the daily papers were dominated by terrorist bombings, kneecappings and killings. The Italian Communist Party had gained 34.5 per cent of the national vote, just a point less than the ruling Christian Democratic Party and the two had begun to share government power in an arrangement known as "the historic compromise". In March 1978, the Red Brigades kidnapped former prime minister Aldo Moro, one of the architects of the new alliance between Christian Democrats and Communists.

Throughout that spring, the nation was so caught up with the Moro kidnapping that it barely noticed when the Mafia peace was briefly interrupted on the morning of 30 May, and a group of killers murdered Giuseppe Di Cristina, the boss of Riesi, a town in eastern Sicily. Although the crime was committed in broad daylight on a crowded Palermo street, there were no witnesses. There were, however, a few intriguing clues. In Di Cristina's pocket, police found a

$6,000 cheque from Salvatore Inzerillo, the Mafia boss in whose territory Di Cristina had been killed, and the private telephone numbers of Nino and Ignazio Salvo, the fabulously wealthy Christian Democrat businessmen who had the concession to operate Sicily's private tax collection system.

Although his case was ignored, Di Cristina had left investigators a gold mine of valuable information. Only a few days before his death, Di Cristina held a secret meeting with police in a deserted farmhouse in order to tell them of his imminent assassination, identify his potential killers and alert police to the scourge that was about to afflict both the Mafia and Sicily during the coming years. Di Cristina provided police with a rare view inside the closed world of Cosa Nostra at its highest levels. He described a widening split between the traditional, "moderate" Mafia and the crude and violent interlopers from the town of Corleone and their allies. The Corleonese Mafia – under the leadership of Luciano Leggio in the 1960s – had distinguished itself for its homicidal ferocity. Leggio – an ignorant former field guard – had grown into a charismatic Mafia leader by showing his ruthless determination to eliminate anyone who stood in his way, often with his own hands and the long knife he carried with him. After Leggio's arrest in 1974, his place was taken by two of his lieutenants, who gave nothing away, in ruthlessness, to their boss. "Salvatore Riina and Bernardo Provenzano, nicknamed 'the beasts' because of their ferocity, are the most dangerous men that Luciano Leggio has at his disposal," Di Cristina told police. "They are personally responsible for at least forty murders each . . ." Most dangerous of all, he added, was Salvatore Riina, "because [he is] more intelligent" than Provenzano. While the "traditional" Mafia, represented by Palermo bosses such as Stefano Bontate, Gaetano Badalamenti, Salvatore

Inzerillo and Di Cristina himself – favoured a conciliatory attitude toward public officials, the Corleonesi preferred confrontation and violent intimidation. Against the wishes of the Mafia's governing body, the Commission, the Corleonesi had murdered retired police colonel Giuseppe Russo, a tenacious investigator. They had carried out a series of kidnappings in Sicily – a practice the rest of the Mafia frowned on.

At the end of this secret confession, Di Cristina acknowledged that his life was in imminent danger: "In the next week, I'm expecting a bullet-proof car some friends are sending me. It costs about 30 million lire [nearly $40,000 at the time]. You know, Captain, I have many venial sins to my credit and a few mortal ones, as well."

None of Di Cristina's warnings were heeded. Just as he had predicted, the investigation into his own murder concentrated on the better-known members of the "traditional" Mafia. Police issued an arrest warrant for Di Cristina's friend and ally, Salvatore Inzerilla, on whose territory Di Cristina had been killed – falling into the trap Salvatore Riina had prepared.

The military offensive of the Corleonesi that Di Cristina predicted came, tragically, to pass. On 21 July 1979, Mafia killers gunned down Boris Giuliano, the vigilant police officer who had shown too much interest in the suitcases travelling between Palermo and New York. In September, the Corleonesi made good on their threat to kill Cesare Terranova, the member of the parliament's anti-Mafia commission who had returned to rake over the investigative office of the Palermo Palace of Justice. And just four months later, on 6 January 1980, they murdered Piersanti Mattarella, the president of the Region of Sicily, the most important Christian Democrat politician on the island, because he had tried to clean up the lucrative market of government contracts, heavily polluted by Mafia interests. The season of excellent cadavers had begun. The emerging new Mafia was sending a clear message that anyone who dared stand up to Cosa Nostra – even the president of the Region – would meet with instant death.

During this period, Falcone was given the opportunity to move from the bankruptcy court to join his friend Borsellino at the investigative office, the Ufficio Istruzione of Palermo. (At that time, there were two distinct prosecutors' offices within the Italian judicial system: the Procura della Repubblica initiated criminal proceedings against a defendant, then passed the case on to the Ufficio Istruzione to be investigated and prepared for trial. The Procura della Repubblica would then review the evidence and present the case in court.) The investigative office was run by a tough Communist prosecutor, Rocco Chinnici, who was determined to pursue the strong anti-Mafia stand promised by his predecessor, Cesare Terranova, who had been murdered before he could even take office.

On the night of 5 May 1980, three Mafia killers shot and killed police captain Emanuele Basile, who had taken up the drug investigations of Boris Giuliano. The following day, Palermo police ordered the arrest of some fifty-five members of three different Mafia families in Palermo, the Inzerillo, the Spatola and the Di Maggio, accused of running a massive international heroin ring together with the Gambino crime family in New York. The arrests constituted one of the biggest anti-Mafia operations in more than a decade. The case quickly became mired in controversy. The two assistant prosecutors to whom the case had been assigned in the Procura della Repubblica of Palermo refused to validate the arrest warrants against the Palermo clans. The head of the office, Gaetano Costa, while acknowledging that the evidence against some of the defendants was preliminary, insisted it was important for the office to show it was not afraid to keep important mafiosi in jail. The two young prosecutors, who had evidently told the defendants' lawyers that their clients would soon be out on bail, were reluctant to break their word. Costa and his assistants argued heatedly, while a crowd of journalists and defence lawyers waited expectantly in the hallway outside. In the end, Costa was forced to take the bold and unusual step of signing the arrest warrants himself. When the meeting broke up, one of the assistant prosecutors apparently said to the Mafia lawyers waiting outside. "He signed them, not us," leaving Costa in an exposed, vulnerable position.

Immediately afterward, the Spatola-Inzerillo heroin case – with its already long trail of blood – was transferred to the investigative office, where it reached the desk of Giovanni Falcone – his first big Mafia prosecution in Palermo.

Giovanni Falcone was killed in May 1992 when a bomb hidden in a trench beside the motorway leading to Palermo International Airport blew up as he drove by. The assassination was organized by Salvatore Riina. Less than two months later, Paolo Borsellino was killed by a car bomb in the Via D'Amelio in Palermo. Five policemen were killed in the incident. Salvatore Riina is now serving life for sanctioning the murders of Falcone and Borsellino, and other killings. Palermo International Airport has been renamed Falcone-Borsellino Airport.

A Man with Hair on His Heart

*Soon after Benito Mussolini came to power as prime minister
of Italy in 1922, he told a meeting of southern Fascists: "I have
the power to solve . . . even the problem of Italy's* Mezzogiorno*"
– that is, the southern part of Italy that includes Sicily and
Sardinia. "It is my most fervent aspiration to do so." His aim
was to crush the Mafia and other criminal organizations to
bring the whole country under the leadership of Rome. However,
the people of Sicily did not welcome outside interference and
during Mussolini's early years in power the Fascists made
little progress asserting their power there. Then in June 1924,
he appointed a new prefect of Trapani on the west of the island.
His name was Cesare Mori and he had instructions to wipe
out the Mafia. He had been in Sicily before. In his book* The
Last Struggle with the Mafia *he described methods he used.
These were honed during his early brushes with the* latitanti
*– "fugitives from justice" – as he outlined in this chapter "My
Earlier Battles with Bandits".*

I have been engaged in chasing *latitanti* since my earliest
years, and I could tell many stories of the chase. But I
will only tell two which are characteristic because of their
attendant circumstances.

In May 1916, I was ordered to go to Sicily from which I had been absent for a year, in order to assist in a special service which was being organized with the aim of remedying the deplorable state of public safety in the four western provinces of the island. These had been very sorely tried by the intense activity of numerous criminals and, in particular, by the audacity of two armed bands: one of these, the Carlino band, working on foot, consisting of three young *latitanti* who had been joined by some free criminals, had been for many months troubling the southern part of the province of Caltanissetta, with their centre at Riesi; and the other, the Grisafi band, working on horseback, consisting of five regular bandits who were often joined by other *latitanti*, had been for years plaguing the western part of the province of Agrigento and the neighbouring districts of the provinces of Palermo and Trapani, with its centre at Caltabellotta. When I reached Palermo, I was given direction of the police services in the provinces of Caltanissetta and Agrigento, so that the chase of both bands fell within my competence.

After staying some days at Palermo to organize my personnel, I went to Caltanissetta, where everything, both people and country, was new to me. I set to work by concentrating particularly on the Carlino band, round which terror had created a quite impenetrable veil of mystery and some rather baseless legends. A few months before there had been added to the various murders committed by the band, that of a brave *carabiniere* [military policeman] who, surprised by the bandits at daybreak while he was going from Riesi to the distant railway station to spend a few days' leave in his own village, had fallen after a gallant fight with muskets. After this tragic episode, the police had redoubled their energies, combing out the country by general drives in force or by special operations, guided by the rare and vague information which they sometimes managed to procure – information that was always inconclusive in spite of the large price that the Government had put on the leader's head.

All this, however, though it undoubtedly showed courage and determination on the part of the police, only produced the very same inconvenient state of things that had led to so many failures: it troubled the waters, and so assisted the hunted men. The system of congesting the countryside with armed men and of keeping them continually on the move is not the best adapted for hunting down *latitanti*. On the most favourable hypothesis it can only result in driving the quarry outside the district that is being searched. It is wrong to suppose that by multiplying the number of movements of the police one increases the probabilities of a chance meeting with the *latitanti*. In reality, exactly the opposite occurs: the greater the force and the more it moves about, the easier it is to see and, therefore, the less likelihood it has of lighting on the quarry. The battle with the *latitanti* is rather like that of love: *vince che fugge*, or he who can keep out of the way wins. That sounds a paradox, but it is true. To know how to keep out of the way is, in this field, the best way of being there at the right moment: to know how to remain inactive is the best way of being able to act when action is necessary. Eight days' inactivity for an hour's action; a month's absence for five minutes on the spot: that is the way to do it. One prepares for a bandit-hunt by letting the local sediment settle; it is carried on by stealth and concluded by surprise.

When one has made up one's mind to act in earnest, the neighbourhood should be left absolutely quiet. Only thus can it be clearly scrutinized and all the psychological and material data be collected which it is necessary to know for the direction and development of the action. From a hundred to three hundred men on foot or on horseback moving about the district make this difficult: a few men are enough, and one alone is best, with his head screwed on the right way, his heart in the right place and his nerves of steel. Two ends are attained in this way: the bandits, not being disturbed, not only stay where they are but are lulled into security and allow their movements to be more easily seen; and the structure and nature of the protective system that aids them is revealed. This is of capital importance, since according to the character, quality, behaviour and family position of the bandits, the reasons for their *latitanza* and their subsequent interference in all kinds of local activities and interests, the difficulties created by the protective system that surrounds them vary in kind. They may be of a passive kind, born simply of fear, or of an active nature inspired by a hundred considerations, not excluding sentimental or even – formerly – electoral ones. It is clear that, once all these factors have been observed and closely scrutinized, the subsequent action, of stealth and surprise, will at least be based on rational lines.

To come back to the particular instance I am speaking of, a few days after my arrival, I learnt that Carlino and Co. were taking advantage of the frequent absences of the police on their usual operations in the country to come into the village at night and stay there roystering with women of ill-repute. I paid special regard to this, as it seemed to me to correspond perfectly with the unbridled, dissolute character and the youth of the bandits. About three weeks passed, and then one of the usual pieces of information came in. The band had been seen going about in full warpaint on a steep mountain that rises about fifteen kilometres from Riesi. I did not believe it. I was gradually coming to the conclusion that the former reports of that kind, which had regularly been followed by unsuccessful operations, were of doubtful origin, that is, that they were put about by friends of the bandits to entice the police away from certain points and concentrate them in other

places where there was nothing to find. Something told
me that this fresh piece of information, which had come
in an apparently urgent and circumstantial form, was
of that kind, and had the same origin, perhaps with the
aim of testing the probable direction in which I, the new
commander, should take action. There was nothing to
prove this: it was only an inner voice that came from some
twist of my sub-conscious mind – a voice that has spoken
to me more than once, and to which I have always listened.
Perhaps what is called good luck is simply due to this
inner voice, in so far as sudden intuitions sometimes lead
to unexpected successes, though involving the illogical
dismissal of more carefully thought out plans. However
that may be, I listened to it again. And what followed was
typical of its results.

I need not say that as soon as this new information was
received, I was warmly recommended to undertake one of
the usual operations – a sudden concentration of force by
night to surround the foot of the incriminated mountain
completely, and a subsequent enveloping movement by
pushing the whole force up the slopes to the top of the
mountain. If the bandits were there, as had been reported,
they would be unable to escape. It was mathematically
certain: but – were they there? I asked that question,
and I was answered on all sides that they certainly were.
"There is too much certainty," I thought: "so the bandits
are somewhere else." So I enthusiastically agreed to the
proposed operation, and gave orders that almost the whole
of the armed force of which I disposed should take part in
it. It would take four days to carry out.

Meanwhile, on my own account, on the afternoon of
the third day, when the heat of the mountain would be
just at its height, I got on my horse and left Caltanissetta
unobserved with three men by the lonely road that
leads through the open country to Riesi. As I reached

the neighbourhood of Riesi it was getting dark. A long and dense procession of peasants, almost all mounted on horses, mules or donkeys, and wagons of every kind was pouring, as it did every evening, from the fields to the village in a dense cloud of dust, through which, in the growing dusk, men and animals took on indistinct and nebulous shapes. The peasants, their eyes swollen with the sun, dust, fatigue and sleep, went along in a dull and dreamy silence. My men and I scattered and worked our way into the long column; I adapted myself to its lounging pace, its sleepy appearance and its dumbness, and, under convenient cloak of dust, horse-flies and the reek of horses, I got into the village quite unobserved, though I had never been there before and did not know one stone of it from another. When it reached the houses, the long column split up as each man went his way into the lanes. I followed one lane at a venture, and caught a glimpse of the police station. Naturally I went past it, and, cautiously followed by my three men, I halted at a lonely and deserted corner from which, favoured by the darkness which the few street lamps did not make less thick, I went quietly and alone, like one of the inhabitants, to the police station: and my men joined me there a little later, they having been able to stable their horses in the barracks without arousing suspicion in the general confusion of the returning peasants.

My main object was therefore attained, since the chief thing was to get into the heart of the position unobserved. Half an hour had not gone by when news came to the office where I was, that the *latitanti* Tofalo and Carlino had come into the village a short time ago mingled with the same column of peasants in which I had come in, that is to say from the direction immediately opposite to that of the mountain which at that moment was occupied by the police force. It was quite obvious: profiting by the absence of the armed force which had been attracted away by false information, the *latitanti* had come to the village to make a night of it undisturbed. But where? In such places, it is true, the women of ill-repute are so few and so notorious that they are all known and may be counted on the fingers. Thus, the women with whom the bandits usually went were known, but nobody in the police could tell me where they assembled. And Riesi is not so small a place that one can find one's way about it easily without knowing it, especially at night. Meanwhile, so as not to give the alarm, it was absolutely indispensable that the whole of the police (twenty-five men) who were present in the village, with their leaders and officers, should remain still and indoors. Towards midnight, the streets being deserted and silent, I decided to act.

A police official had been able to find out that the two low women who were friends of the bandits were absent from their houses. That confirmed the idea that the bandits were in the village with them. By a process of exclusions and inductions founded on a few timid words murmured by people living near, I was able at last to locate the place where the meetings were probably held and, after a quick and silent inspection, the block of buildings in which the meeting-place must be. It was a block made of a long row of hovels, consolidated into a single construction, in the heart of a populous quarter; and not even the police agents of the place knew its internal plan, its arrangement and the ways of possible communication between the hovels. It was no use losing time in conjecture or plans of operation: the thing was to find out if the bandits were there and to act at once.

With a part of the force I surrounded the whole block on the outside: with the rest I went up to the first house in the row and demanded admission. The door was opened without hesitation. There was nobody there except the small family of peasants who lived there. While the police officials and men were finishing the inspection of the premises and asking a few questions, I went out into the street. I was slightly disappointed, and I leant against the rather rickety door of the hovel next door to the one I had left, and exchanged a few words with one of the officials. Suddenly, as I was speaking, I distinctly heard behind the door against which I was leaning the stamp of an animal's hoof. At that time and in such a place animals were never left alone. Where an animal was shut up somebody else was sure to be shut up too. After having knocked at the door repeatedly without effect, I called: "Open the door."

Dead silence. I was now sure I was right. "Open the door," I repeated, "or I'll have it broken in."

A silence of the grave. Turning to some of the police agents who had come out of the house and were standing round, I said: "Break in that door."

Hardly had I uttered the words than two musket shots were fired from behind the very door. The bullets slapped against the wall opposite without hurting anybody. This visiting card left no doubts and demanded an immediate and adequate reply. My men, dashing to one side and lying down, returned the fire and the battle opened very furiously. When the first fury had spent itself, I made sure that the blockade round the block of houses was such as to prevent all flight or surprise on the part of the bandits, and I took every possible means to give the greatest possible effect to our own fire. In my ignorance of the number of the *latitanti* that I had to deal with, and also of the internal arrangements of the place they were in, and in the impossibility of picking out a target behind that door which, rickety and weak as it was, though it allowed a free passage to the bullets of both sides, gave the bandits a certain view of their target while it completely hid ours. I decided to maintain my assault at the highest intensity so as to clear up the situation as quickly as possible. So, there, in the darkness of the night, in the radius of a few yards, a desperate and deadly battle went on between unknown adversaries firing blind and sudden volleys. Although our fire was rather oblique and low owing to the narrowness of the street, and though my men (being completely exposed) had to fire prone, the old door was gradually splintering to bits, so that I saw the moment approaching for a sudden rush that should carry the door, the bandits and everything with them. The bandits, however, in spite of the fire of three of my men which was sweeping the door and its surroundings from loopholes made, after the first exchanges, in the wall of the house opposite, had obviously found a position out of range of our fire; they kept up wild and intermittent firing from the now enlarged cracks in the door, showing how alert and well provided with ammunition they were. The village, awakened by the noise of the firing, kept within doors, in silence and in darkness. But it was summer, and dawn was quickly approaching. At the first streak, as soon as it was light enough for me to see the position, I descried an opening at the back of the block which led to a little staircase giving access to a room above that in which the bandits were. I immediately occupied it and had the floor pierced with an iron bar, thus making a loophole in it in spite of the shots which the *latitanti*, guessing my intention, concentrated on the hole from below. The position of the bandits was now tragic. Under fire from the front, from the flank and from above, and reduced to taking cover beneath a flight of stairs from which they could not possibly fire except for honour's sake, they lost heart and, as they afterwards confessed, thought of surrendering, but could not make up their minds to do so for fear of losing their lives. I was now determined to carry the place with a rush.

Just at that moment Carlino's mother and an uncle of his, who were certainly aware of the dangerous position the bandits were in, came to me and asked if they might make an attempt to induce Carlino and his companions to surrender before the fight ended in inevitable tragedy. I thought I could not reject the mother's request, so I gave her five minutes in which to make the attempt. I ordered a ceasefire, and shouted to the *latitanti* that if they did not surrender in five minutes, I would resume firing till they were all killed. Then Carlino's mother, taking cover behind the angle of the house, called "*Figghiu!*" (son), and Carlino replied with an equally loud cry "*Matre!*" Some brief motherly exhortations followed, till the bandits shouted that they surrendered and asked for their lives to be spared. I answered that they must throw down their arms and come out into the open. They obeyed immediately.

They were the *latitanti*, Carlino and Tofalo, with two free criminals as their companions. Two loose women were with them. They were armed with Mauser muskets, automatic pistols of the most modern kind, long claspknives and sword-bayonets, besides having field-glasses. They had fired about 300 rounds between them, and still had 200 rounds in reserve. Carlino and Tofalo confessed that, with another bandit who had left them a few days before, they had murdered the *carabiniere* I mentioned above, besides committing another fourfold murder, an act of attempted homicide which failed, and about twenty offences of blackmail. Their two companions swore they were as innocent as doves.

Having cleared matters up in the province of Caltanissetta, I went on to that of Agrigento, where the state of things was rather different. The *latitante*, Grisafi, a mountain-dweller of thirty-six years of age, originally a shepherd, who commanded the armed band there, was a consummate bandit. Fierce and cautious, most redoubtable, up to all the tricks and stratagems of guerrilla warfare, and protected by a thick net of local favour strengthened by terror, he had been a *latitante* for quite twelve years; and he had set up in the western part of the province a kind of special domain over which he ruled absolutely, interfering in every kind of affair, even the most intimate, making his will felt in every field, including the electoral field, and levying tolls and taxes, blackmailing and committing crimes of bloodshed without stint. Some thirty murders were put down to him, besides an unending series of crimes. Perhaps he had not committed so many: possibly he had committed more: certainly he was ready to go on committing them. They called him *Marcuzzo* (little Mark), but he was a man of thews and muscles, inclined to stoutness.

Aided not only by his boldness but by constant good luck, and being a good shot, he had always succeeded in escaping from the toils of the police; he had escaped unhurt from several conflicts and had sometimes inflicted loss on his pursuers. Not long after I came to the province of Agrigento, during a raid on the southern part of the province of Palermo, he had run into a group of five police agents with his whole band. Instead of opening fire, as was his wont, he had beaten a hasty retreat over the gentle slope of a small hill, disappearing from view over its shoulder. The police agents had immediately rushed in pursuit, but in their zeal they had not thought of the trap laid for them. Instead of coming on in open order, they had kept close together. Grisafi and his companions were waiting for them on the other side of the slope: and a well-aimed volley caught the pursuers full at their first appearance on the skyline, killing two brave men. For some time, too, Grisafi had had such a reputation for being uncapturable that the country folk began seriously to believe that he was *maato* (bewitched). The thing was ridiculous, as well as being very regrettable, and it had to be put an end to at once, not only for reasons of duty, but also for those of prestige.

I took on the job, and, with a small party of young and brave officials, including a *carabiniere* officer, I pitched some tents on a beach at Sciacca, a charming and hospitable little town, in whose rocky hinterland there rise, about twenty kilometres away, three typical rocky peaks, immediately overhanging the picturesque village of Caltabellotta, Grisafi's native place. According to my system, I told my assistants that the probabilities of success would be in direct proportion to the tangible proofs we could give of inactivity, indolence and ineptitude. It was my idea, in fact, that as soon as we succeeded in being regarded as a useless party of more or less stupid idlers, we should have a nine to one chance of success.

After the end of Carlino and Co., my arrival in the province of Agrigento had aroused some anxiety. I was told that, a few days after my arrival, the Grisafi band, which apparently numbered nine men at that time, had been reduced to six. Three of the bandits had preferred to go off on their own affairs. After a little time had elapsed another bandit had gone away, owing to some dispute with the leader, and the band had been reduced to five – Grisafi, his brother, the two brothers Maniscalco and a certain Santangelo. At that rate there was the risk that the famous band would disappear into thin air, and I wanted to capture it, not to break it up. By capturing it entire, I cut the evil at the root: by forcing it to disband I accomplished nothing; or worse, I simply dissolved the evil in the neighbourhood. It was necessary, therefore, to reassure them as to my intentions by some thoroughly stupid action.

Sciacca, among other things, is famous for its hot springs, for its mullet and its soles. So I and some of my subordinates suddenly found ourselves affected with rheumatic pains and took a strict course of treatment for them – morning baths, reaction, lunch of mullet, afternoon sleep, digestive promenade, dinner of soles, a game of cards, another little walk and so to bed. We did it all openly, in the local hotel, with revolting persistence and entire want of shame. Every now and again we took an innocent little ride in the neighbourhood, and that was all.

Nobody, of course, knew that by night, in our little rooms that were tightly closed against all intrusions, the work of study and preparation was busily going on. And people began to ask if we had come to Sciacca to take the water cure or to catch the Grisafi band. I was really glad when I heard this. Meanwhile the police force at my disposal remained concentrated at certain places specially selected, so that, while apparently scattered and distant, it was really in complete readiness and quite handy. The Grisafi band, which had eyes everywhere, became reassured and remained quietly on the look-out, awaiting events, in the district between Sciacca and Caltabellotta.

It was then that I began to send out my men, cautiously, one by one, without any preparation and on the most bureaucratic excuses, into the various places that had been the scenes of the bandits' crimes, in order to collect – without raising the alarm and so without any official formality – all possible current news on the past activities of the band and especially the necessary indications for identifying their habitual and occasional helpers, whether voluntary accomplices or compelled by fear. There was need for haste because, if the game went on too long, it would be found out. Their work was carried out quickly and quietly with as good results as could possibly be obtained in such conditions: and feverish activity, all night long, reigned in the little bedrooms of the Sciacca hotel.

Now, if in the province of Caltanissetta a certain number of helpers bound simply by terror or bonds of complicity had grown up round the Carlino band, insufficient to hinder seriously the action of the authorities, the network of assistance that had been drawn round the Grisafi band had grown wide, thick and strong in the course of time. The whole system was welded together by complicity in crimes, fear of reprisals, terror, espionage on behalf of the bandits, conflicting interests and equivocal alliances for the most varied ends, to an extent that made it almost impenetrable. To attempt victory by trying to circumvent it would have been an arduous task, and would in any case have created a danger in our rear. If we wanted to get at the band, we had to confront it, annihilate and finish it off at a blow, all in one piece and with all its ramifications. We had to arrest simultaneously all Grisafi's helpers and keep them under arrest till the bandits were caught.

The idea in itself had not the attraction of novelty; for over and over again attempts to capture *latitanti* had been marked by the arrest more or less *en masse* of their helpers; but just because it had been abused, the manoeuvre, against which high-class *latitanti* always took precautions, had become particularly difficult. And in this case, through a complication of special circumstances, the difficulties of the operation were immense. But it would undoubtedly dismay and confuse the bandits, if such an assertion of will and power occurred after so many years of inaction, and would at the same time draw the neighbourhood to our side owing to the immediate rise in the prestige of the State. In its concrete effects it would isolate the bandits in a more or less neutral environment which would allow us to get direct contact with them, and mean their certain capture. But it would be necessary to gain complete and accurately timed success: even a partial failure would be disastrous. And there was no time to be lost.

One night, therefore, by sudden simultaneous action in different places, I made an attempt to arrest all the helpers we had identified and against whom – at my own request, which had been kept secret – the judicial authorities had issued warrants of arrest: 357 persons in all, of whom ninety were in Caltabellotta alone. The attempt succeeded perfectly and without incident. But there was one amusing thing. The officials found in the possession of Grisafi's old father, who was among the arrested persons, some scrip of a national loan that was being subscribed at the time, an obvious fruit of his son's labours. When asked to explain how he got it, the old man with a quiet and patriotic smile answered that he too had done what he could for his country. This extensive and unexpected action, not least on account of the standing of some of the arrested persons, made a profound impression and produced the effects that I had foreseen. There was only one thing that I feared, namely, that the band would be dissolved in view of the turn affairs had taken.

But this did not happen. On the dawn of the third day after the arrests, a large black flag, fixed to a mast on the highest of the three peaks overlooking Caltabellotta, appeared fluttering in the keen mountain breeze. In this way the band asserted its presence and its intentions. And now, our mutual positions being unmasked, the fight became openly declared, close and uninterrupted.

I have already said that one bandit, owing to a dispute with Grisafi, had left him a little while after my arrival in the province of Agrigento. There were some indications of his presence in a district adjacent to that held by the band to whom, perhaps, he thought of giving the benefit of his assistance. A brave police official undertook to deal with him, and one night, with a party of police and *carabinieri*, he succeeded in surprising and surrounding him. A violent conflict ensued. The bandit finally surrendered, but one gallant soldier was killed and the official, seriously wounded in the chest, had to be taken hurriedly to the local *carabinieri* barracks. The populace, who had begun to take heart after the arrests, became a little depressed. I immediately intervened, and over the bloodstained remains of the poor *carabiniere* who had heroically fallen in the name of duty I made a solemn, public declaration that the end of the famous band was decided, sure and close at hand. The Mafia took care to answer on the band's behalf.

A few days after the *carabiniere*'s funeral, a criminal of the neighbourhood died of natural causes in prison, and the Mafia arranged to make his funeral the occasion of an imposing demonstration, summoning all its members from all the villages of the district to the function. The funeral procession with its brass bands was to march through the principal street of the place, pass in front of the barracks of the *carabinieri* and under the windows of the very room where the wounded official was still lying and halt at the cemetery where was the still fresh grave of the poor *carabiniere*. Although it was secretly prepared, the plan leaked out and came to my knowledge, so I took up my position on the main street, which I had patrolled. At a given moment the hearse arrived at the entrance to the village. After a short halt to form the procession, as had been arranged, the funeral cortège advanced along its prearranged route. At the sides of the road, and in front of the houses and shops, little groups of curious observers, especially countrywomen and girls, were standing waiting. I too stood waiting, till the procession reached the place where I was standing. First came the priest, then the hearse, then the group of relations and intimate friends. I made no movement. But when I saw, a few paces behind this group, a band playing a raucous dirge and a dense body of people who wanted to make the funeral an excuse for making a demonstration of their presence and their intimidating power, which was an insult, I came forward and stopped them. Two words were enough: "Go away!" and a point of the hand to the direction they had come from. Perhaps my voice roused some obscure echo in their consciences, for they turned about like one man and went off in a twinkling with their band.

In the other direction the hearse, preceded by the holy symbols of the Christian faith, and followed by the group of mourners, went on slowly and silently to its destination in the sad majesty of death which levels all, the bad and the good, before human pity and Divine mercy. I went off to the barracks. As I went by, there arose from the groups of women and girls who had been waiting to see the funeral a murmur of brief phrases: *ci vuolia* (that's what was wanted), *'un se ne putia cchiù!* (it was too much to put up with!) *buono!* (good!) and *binirittu!* (bless you!) That was enough for me. It is needless to say that, like the arrest *en masse* of the helpers, the episode of the funeral had some repercussions both near and far, with some due exaggeration and apposite comment. But I had been too long accustomed to such repercussions and comments to pay much attention to them.

We were now really at close quarters. The Grisafi band preferred to remain on the heights where it undoubtedly had a place of refuge. I attempted a sudden enveloping movement, and the band was caught in it. Grisafi himself, after his capture, confessed this to me, and he added that more than once on that day he had us within range from the peak on which the band was posted, but that he had not fired – very kind of him! – so as not to attract in his direction all the parties of police by which he saw himself surrounded. However, during the night, the bandits got away by impenetrable tracks only known to themselves.

But we at last found their base refuge: a cave high up in the hills which one reached through a hole in the rock that could not be singled out at a distance. Beyond the hole which formed its entrance, the cave broadened out into a large space, fitted as a stable for horses and provided with a fine manger of cement. Beyond the stable the cave gradually narrowed, funnel-wise, for a sufficient length to provide sleeping places for the men, and it ended in a kind of chimney in which had been cut rough steps, which came out in the open across a small and unsuspected rocky pinnacle. The effect of this discovery was at once apparent. Two days later five horses were found abandoned and wandering about in the country round Sciacca. These horses belonged to the bandits, for whom their mounts had now become an embarrassment. Naturally I pretended to have understood nothing and to believe that it was a case of cattle-stealing. I protested loudly at the audacity of cattle-thieves and I sent out circular telegrams to find out where the theft had taken place. On the other hand, during the two nights following, I had each of the horses mounted in turn by a police agent and left free to go where it would, so that from the direction that the animal invariably took I was able to draw precious conclusions as to the direction in which the police should move. It was the moment to come to grips.

The Grisafi band, now on foot and without support, moved very little and, owing to the fewness of the houses where it could take refuge, had necessarily to go round the caves. From certain vague information, moreover, I knew that it was keeping near the town with the strange intention of making a nocturnal incursion and giving us a "serenade" under the windows of our quiet hotel. One day, late in the afternoon, I learnt with comparative certainty that the band would be found that same night in a certain cave looking on the sea, a few kilometres from Sciacca. The indications as to the exact topographical position of the cave were rather vague, but there was no time to make sure of them. It was obviously a perfect night for the enterprise: it was the middle of January and the weather was beastly.

That night, the police officials and men having assembled, I left for the place in question, guided by an old police agent belonging to the place, whom I had suddenly called in at the last moment. When we came to the neighbourhood of the cave, we found that it was a kind of huge platform from the edge of which steep and rocky slopes led down to the sea, and the bandits' cave opened off one of these. It was pitch dark, there was a hurricane of wind and the rain came down in torrents. I halted the party on the high ground and, accompanied by one or two officers and the old guide, I began to go down a kind of footpath to reconnoitre the place and the way to it, my companions muttering low curses against the band at every fresh squall of rain. At a certain point our path, which went straight down to the sea, crossed another that ran parallel to the beach. According to the indications I had we ought to have gone to the right: but our old guide – who had not yet been told the object of our expedition, but had evidently guessed it – said the path stopped to the right, and that we must turn to the left. I was not convinced, but he stuck to his opinion. A short turn in both directions did not clear up the doubt; and a false move might have alarmed the band and sent it flying heaven knows where. It was still the dead of night and we had not been seen by anyone. So I went back to the high ground, collected all my men and went cautiously back to the town, where I sent them all to bed, though I kept the old guide under lock and key so that he should not come into contact with anybody.

Next night I repeated the attempt. I blockaded the position according to my own principles and advanced at dawn. I had been right. The old guide had not been deceitful, but he only knew the place from hazy recollections of his far-off youth. The cave was found: a real fortress very well furnished with provisions. But the bandits were not there. There were fresh traces of them, namely, a strip of paper hung on the wall with dabs of shaving soap on it. Evidently the band had gone out on some expedition, and now that we had arrived would not come back to that place. But it would be within range. So I went back to the town and openly moved some of my men to places some way off so that the band should not go away.

Two days passed: and on the morning of the third day I heard that by night I should get information of the band's new place of refuge. I said nothing to anyone, so that the expression of ill-concealed commiseration at our recent disappointment should stay on everybody's face; but I had a strong party of police sent cautiously down towards the town from a village near by and concealed it a few hundred yards from the houses in a tunnel of a branch railway line then being constructed. By evening I knew that the band was in a country cottage about 800 yards as the crow flies from the town, on the opposite lip of a deep valley that runs to the west of the town and immediately below it. But the indications were not enough to ensure the certain success of a surprise, which was also made very difficult because our advance on the cottage would inevitably rouse all the watchdogs in the numerous habitations which were scattered all over the small tract we should have to pass through. I still said nothing. We had dinner as usual; we played our usual game of cards and had our little walk; then we went – to bed. Only then did I tell them all to stay in their rooms, in the dark, dressed and in readiness.

As for me, having somewhat disguised myself, I went out unobserved a little later, and in a short time got further indications as to the position of the cottage, its configuration and the way to it. Of its internal arrangement I learnt nothing. One useful thing I found out was that the cottage had a rustic courtyard in front of it surrounded by a high wall with a big, strong door. At the back it had a balcony looking on the town and particularly favourable for the bandits' fire. I went back to the hotel, and a little after midnight I assembled all my men under the tunnel, where the force remained waiting for an hour or two.

To discount the inevitable alarm that would be given by all the dogs it was necessary that the encirclement of the cottage should take place in dead silence, with the utmost rapidity and with mathematical precision. But nobody knew its position, and in the thick darkness that wrapped the countryside it was extremely difficult to find one's way. I formed four squads, commanded by excellent police officers and two officers of the *carabinieri* who were voluntarily joined by a young cavalry lieutenant who was doing police duty in the district; and I assigned them the task of surrounding the cottage at not more than thirty yards' distance, allotting to each squad the side of the cottage it was to face.

The orders were to march quickly and silently, to reach all positions simultaneously, each squad to extend opposite the side of the house allotted to it, immediate communication to be established between all so that there should be no gaps, especially between one squad and the next, and to wait without moving from their posts on any pretext whatever. If anybody came out of the cottage, they were to fire but not move. If they were fired at from the cottage, they were to reply but not move. I said I would give final orders on the spot according to circumstances. Having assigned a particular route to each squad, so that all should reach their positions on the four sides simultaneously, I sent them off at short successive intervals, according to the distance they each had to travel. When the last squad had moved off I also went towards the place. It was a short march; it was a very dark night, as

I have said: so that everything should have been favourable to surprise.

Suddenly, however, dogs began loudly barking in front of us, and the barking spread to our flanks and accompanied our footsteps. The men ducked their heads as though under a shower of hail and, muttering low curses against the friend of man, quickened their pace. I was highly annoyed, the famous cottage being too near for the bandits not to have heard the dreadful noise. Nevertheless, I did not lose heart. A few minutes later the squads were at their posts, extended in an unbroken line round the cottage. My men found some cover behind clumps of cactus, trees or bits of tumbledown wall, but most of them lay in the open. The squad in front of the balcony was entirely without cover. It was half past two in the morning when our wait began.

Many minutes had not gone by when the big door of the yard was opened cautiously to let a man out. The squad in front opened fire, just one round. The door shut with a bang, and the man who came out disappeared into the darkness. A few moments later a sudden volley was fired from the balcony at the back. The squad below it replied and there followed a rapid exchange of heavy fire. The band evidently wanted to test the position. So, to scatter any illusions or hopes on their part, I shouted to the force: "Fire from all sides!" when I could make myself heard. A heavy discharge struck the cottage on every side: the bandits now knew what they were up against.

A long pause followed on both sides. I had no interest in continuing to fire while the thick darkness still prevented our even seeing the windows. It was enough to hold on to the position. At daybreak I should have light to see my way. The bandits, however, did not take the same view. Being under cover, they began firing again with the evident intention of provoking reply from us, so that they could accurately single out our positions one by one. With this end in view they pushed some rolled-up mattresses out on to the balcony so that, standing behind them, they could bring their fire further forward. The fight went on in this way, with shots on both sides rather wildly aimed in the dark and with sudden volleys till dawn.

At the first streak of dawn the *latitanti* ceased fire. They were obviously having a council of war. I took advantage of this to inspect my men and give each of them orders for the decisive action: but I was seen, and fire was opened again. I was moving along the posts in front of the yard door when, in the thick of a clump of cactus near the wall of the yard, I saw the outline of two boot soles. On my order two agents seized them and pulled vigorously. It was a man – the one who had come out of the door in the night shortly after our arrival. He was a peasant, the tenant of the surrounded cottage in which he lived with his wife. Half-dead with fear, he told us that three days before Grisafi and his complete band had suddenly turned up and ordered him with dire threats of death to give him and his men food and lodging. He had had to obey and had been even compelled to go down to the town several times on errands for the bandits, while his wife was kept as a hostage. The afternoon of the preceding day he had been told to go to the town to see what I was doing. He had come, had watched me, and when he had seen me go quietly back to the hotel with my officers and go to bed, he had come back to the cottage to say that all was quiet in the town and that I was snoring hard.

This had so reassured the bandits that, while keeping their clothes on, they laid themselves down to sleep the sleep of the just. The barking of the dogs had awakened them, but had not roused their suspicion; the first suspicions had come from the noise my men had made in surrounding the house. One of them, the poor man added, had said it was probably only some animals got loose; but Grisafi, collecting the whole band with muskets loaded, had gone down, placed himself behind the door of the yard and told him to go out and see what was up. So he had had to go out. Greeted by our first volley, the poor fellow had been forced to take a lightning decision between two courses – either to go back into the yard with the probability of being killed by the bandits on the suspicion of treachery or to go on with the probability of being killed by the police on a contrary suspicion. "In my awful doubt," he said, "I had a sudden inspiration: to pretend to be killed. I threw myself motionless on the ground in the clump of cactus from which you have just dragged me."

We heard afterwards from the bandits themselves that, after the volley that had greeted the owner's exit, they had pretended to shut the door, but had remained behind it in the hope we would rush in. When this hope failed, they had shut and bolted the door and had gone out on to the balcony and opened fire from it to see if they were really surrounded.

It now became light, and after the householder's declaration, the situation was now perfectly clear. The cottage looked like a small fortress, and it was no easy thing to get into it. So we should have to force the bandits to move. Having, therefore, assigned to each of my posts its particular target, i.e. some opening in the house, door, window or balcony, I ordered fire to be reopened simultaneously, so that a hail of bullets was poured into the house from all sides. The bandits made a vigorous reply on all sides, and the fight raged fiercely in full view of the population who, attracted by the noise of the firing, were growing every moment thicker on the opposite slope of the valley. The· curiosity and interest of the public were so great that the town authorities had to make certain groups move on, because some shots from the bandits on the balcony, aimed high, had come among them.

Suddenly, as I was looking up, I distinctly saw one of the bandits crawling out of the window of the dovecot and up on the roof of the house to get to the top and find a better field of fire there. I pointed him out at once and a violent volley went in his direction. The bandit got off unhurt, but one of our bullets broke an arm of a small stone cross that stood at that place on the roof: and the bandit saw this. The bold attempt had meanwhile put my men's backs up and our fire was resumed more hotly than ever. On the other hand, none of us was under any delusion. It was remembered that the bandit Torrigiami, formerly, when surrounded by the police, had first fought gallantly and then committed suicide rather than surrender; and it was thought that Grisafi was of the same mettle. But that was not so. The more savage such men are, the more cowardly.

All at once, as we were still keeping up a hot fire, loud shouts came from inside the cottage: "*N'arrénnemu! N'arrénnemu!*" (we surrender). I was surprised and, suspecting some trick, I replied in a loud voice: "I don't accept!" and turning to my men I shouted: "Continuous fire!" Another hail of bullets penetrated the house at every opening, and the shouts of surrender became desperate. I ordered fire to cease and went to the closed door of the yard, ordering the bandits to lay down their arms, to open the door and come out with their hands up, and giving them two minutes' grace, after which I should break down the door and rush the house by storm without answering for their lives. The two minutes went by in silence: then, quickly breaking in the door, I went into the yard with my officers and men, resolved to put my threat into execution. As we rushed in, however, at the top of a flight of steps that went from the yard to the house Grisafi, followed by his four companions, appeared unarmed and with his hands up. It was the end of a reign!

The bandits had excellent military muskets, both 91s and Mausers, the best revolvers, *armes blanches*, field-glasses and a large store of ammunition, much of it with explosive bullets which were particularly dear to Grisafi. I asked him at once why, having lost nobody by death or wounds and still having so much ammunition, he had decided to surrender. He looked at me and made no answer. And at that moment, in the eyes of the man who had shed so much blood and caused so much terror for the last twelve years, I saw the frightened look of a bull that is being led to slaughter.

I shall never forget the scene of the captured band's bringing into the town. Right from the immediate neighbourhood of the cottage the road was lined by parties of onlookers which gradually turned into a large crowd. For a good part of the way the sullen group of bandits went by in a silence of almost overwhelming incredulity. Suddenly the crowd gave tongue. There was such a shout of joy and liberation as I shall never forget. The bandits turned pale and cast down their eyes. Later on, however, one or two of them came to notice again. In fact, some months later, in the big prison at Palermo, Grisafi procured a revolver somehow and killed his prison-companion, the bandit Calla, on account of some old grudge. A little later Santangelo, who had succeeded in escaping, came back to the district of Sciacca, killed two people and then disappeared.

When Mori returned to Sicily in 1924, the Mafia had moved decidedly upmarket. They had benefited from the turmoil created by the First World War. According to a pamphlet called "The Underworld in Sicily and the Fascist Response" that was serialized in a Trapani newspaper in 1923:

They used to be called "*lu zu Vincenzo*" or "*lu zu Andrea*", but today they are pompously known as "Don Vincenzo" or "Don Andrea", wholesale merchants now knights of the Crown of Italy. Janissaries, friends and shoddy clients follow them around *en masse*. What services they render is not clear; but we do know that their so-called warehouses, and their great farms and farmhouses are frequented by foul brutes who in the country wear leggings, coarse clothes, and caps like a cyclist's, pulled down at an angle over their foreheads. But in town they sport luxury clothes and often go around in carriages and even in cars.

The author of that pamphlet was a fan of Mori who had "restored peace to the island with his strategic arrests" and said that peasants spoke of him in gratitude as their "saviour". He was, of course, still famous for his nine-hour shoot-out with Paolo Grisafi. Stories of his bravery circulated. He was called "a man with hair on his heart", and was said to go about disguised as a monk when on the track of criminals. Within days of arriving in Trapani, Mori wrote to Mussolini, saying:

A new feature of the situation is the attitude of the old Mafia, many members of which (above all through unbridled exploitation of specific circumstances during the war) have now reached a comfortable economic position. Through self-interest they have grown conservative and law-abiding; they have withdrawn, or are tending to withdraw, from active life, and have assumed the curious garb of law and order fanatics. But others have remained at their stations and are fighting tooth and nail to preserve their power and

prestige against the steady advance of the new
Mafia. This . . . sprang up in the immediate post-
war period as a reaction to, and rebellion against,
the inflexible and persistent domination of the old
Mafia. But it has the same characteristics . . . as
the old Mafia, except that its reflexes are quicker
and its actions more aggressive.

*After attempting to purge the Fascist Party in Trapani
of Mafiosi, Mori was appointed prefect of Palermo the
following year. He then began a series of mass arrests,
saying: "I am fully convinced that strong measures against
the Mafia can cause no serious political harm. Quite the
contrary in fact."*

*As well as rounding up hundreds of suspects in the
villages of the Madonie inland, his men kept certain night-
spots under surveillance. They seized elegantly dressed
young men who frequented the bars of Palermo and drove
ostentatiously along the city's most fashionable streets on the
grounds that their wealth was ill-gotten.*

*The most infamous operation in the crackdown was the
Siege of Gangi in January 1926. Mori sent his men out into
the hills around the village of Gangi. A notorious gangster's
stronghold, it was built into the side of a hill and many
of the houses had two entrances, one on the ground floor,
the other on the first, so it was easy to escape if the house
was raided. There were also hideouts behind walls, under
floors or in attics, skilfully constructed by a local handyman
named Tofanella. Mori swamped the area with* carabinieri,
leaving the latitanti *no choice but to give themselves up. The
first man to do so was Gaetoni Ferrarello, who had been
wanted for over thirty years. He emerged from hiding on
the morning of 2 January, walked to the house of Baron
Li Destri on the central square and presented himself to*
questore *Crimi, who Mori had sent to head the operation.*

According to the newspaper, Ferrarello flung his stick on the table and said slowly: "My heart trembles. This is the first time I have found myself in the presence of the law. I am giving myself up to restore peace and tranquillity to these tormented people." After shaking hands with the local police and officials, he was led away.

But Mori did not just want to capture the mafiosi, he wanted to humiliate them. "I wanted to give the population tangible proof of the cowardice of criminals," he wrote in his memoirs. The police were told to enter the houses of wanted men at night, when they were asleep. Their cattle were slaughtered and the meat sold at cut-price to local merchants. If men could not be found, their wives and children were taken hostage – women complained of maltreatment. Their fierce sense of honour then forced their menfolk to surrender. In 1926 alone, there were 5,000 arrests in the region of Palermo, making a mountain of paperwork. Eleven thousand men were behind bars when Mori left Sicily in 1929, claiming that the Mafia had been eradicated. He was wrong.

The Black Hand

The Mafia in America

It was pure hubris for Cesare Mori to imagine that he could stamp out the Mafia, even using the most draconian methods afforded him by the Fascist state. It had already spread beyond his jurisdiction. By the 1890s there were criminal gangs operating in any American city that contained a sizeable Italian population. As early as 1878, a gang of Sicilian immigrants was operating a flourishing extortion racket among the Southern Italian residents of San Francisco. They called themselves "*La Maffia*". The San Francisco *Examiner* described them as "a neat little tea party of Sicilian brigands . . . a villainous gang" whose objective was "the extortion of money from their countrymen by a system of blackmail, which includes attacks on character and threats to kill". Their activities were curtailed when the body of a Sicilian immigrant called Catalani was found near Sausolito. Evidence pointed to Salvatore Messino, Iganzi Trapani, Rosario Meli and Giuseppe Bianchi. They were arrested and, eventually, convicted – but not of murder, only of robbing Catalani prior to his death.

In 1881, a young detective named David C. Hennessy was investigating the high rate of homicide in New Orleans. His investigations led to the Mafia boss Giuseppe Esposito, a Sicilian bandit who led "a band of seventy-five cut-throats" who specialized in kidnapping and extortion. He was arrested and deported as he was wanted by the Italian authorities. Soon after, Hennessy was dismissed from the force. However, after a victory by reformers in an election in 1888, he was appointed police chief. Under his leadership, the police began investigating violence on the New Orleans waterfront involving Italian immigrants. They discovered two rival Mafia gangs – the Provenzanos and the Matrangas – were fighting for control. The Provenzanos were arrested and tried for an attack on the Matrangas. They were convicted, but granted a second trial after evidence of perjury was uncovered. The Provenzanos believed that Hennessy favoured the Matrangas and threats were made on his life. Shortly before the new trial, Hennessy was assassinated using the traditional Mafia method – the blast of a shotgun. His last words were said to be: "The Dagos did it." Hundreds of Italian immigrants were arrested and nineteen were indicted. Allegations spread that the Sicilian Mafia were trying to take over the city. When those indicted were acquitted there was a riot. A mob stormed the jailhouse and six of the accused Italians were lynched, along with five other co-defendants who had not even been tried yet. Italy broke off diplomatic relations. There was even talk of war.

However, this did not stop the influx of Italians. Early in the twentieth century, New York became the second biggest Italian city after Naples. One quarter of the population – more than half a million people – were Italian. Bewildered by the new land and its strange language, the new immigrants flocked to the Little Italies of New York, Philadelphia, Chicago, New Orleans and other cities. In many cases, people moved *en masse* from the towns and villages of Italy to set up new communities together in America. They brought with them their old loyalties and some from the south their old vendettas.

Mafiosi often entered the US on false papers, which the Italian authorities had been only too happy to supply to get rid of them. Many had good reasons to travel to America as restrictions imposed on ex-convicts in Italy were debilitating. After leaving an Italian prison the convict would be placed on *Sorveglianza Speciale* – "Special Surveillance" – meaning strict night curfew, no employment without permission from the police, regular reports to the local police station, a ban on carrying weapons and a ban from frequenting all drinking places. Criminals on the run also made their way to the United States. Once they arrived in America they found that the underworld was already overpopulated with Irish and Jewish ne'er-do-wells. At first, they could not penetrate the established gangs. But they could always prey on their own community.

Plunged into poverty, facing poor living conditions, prejudice and even lynching, the law-abiding immigrants soon realized the Promised Land they had dreamt of was, in fact, a nightmare. In their closed communities they found themselves living in a microcosm of the stratified society they had left behind in Europe. Sicilians, particularly, clung on to their distrust of the law and authority. Mafiosi exploited this fact and turned to their traditional occupation – extortion. They preyed on bankers, barbers, contractors and merchants, fellow Italians who already understood the ways of the Mafia.

On 3 August 1903, Nicolo Cappiello, a prosperous contractor living in Brooklyn, received a letter that read:

If you don't meet us at Seventy-second Street and Thirteenth Avenue, Brooklyn, tomorrow afternoon, your house will be dynamited and your family killed. The same fate awaits you in the event of your betraying our purposes to the police.

The note was adorned with three black crosses surmounted by a skull and crossbones, and signed *"Mano Nera"* – "Black Hand". When Cappiello ignored the letter, he got another two days later. It read:

> You did not meet us as ordered in our first letter. If you still refuse to accede to our terms, but wish to preserve the lives of your family, you can do so by sacrificing your own life. Walk in Sixteenth Street, near Seventh Avenue, between the hours of four and five tonight.

This one concluded with the line: "Beware of *Mano Nera*". When Cappiello ignored this letter too, several men visited his house. Some were old friends. Others claimed to be agents of the Black Hand. They told him that a price of $10,000 had been put on his head, but if he handed over $1,000 they would do their best to persuade the blackmailers to spare his life. Cappiello delivered the money on 26 August, but within a few days four men returned for an additional $3,000. Convinced that the gang intended to rob him of his entire fortune – which amounted to around $100,000 – bit by bit, he went to the police. Five men – three friends and two Black Handers – were arrested, tried and convicted. The case was complicated by the fact that the extortion racket had begun as a plot by Cappiello to ensnare his nephew-in-law whom he considered had disgraced his family by eloping with his niece. Nevertheless, the name "Black Hand" stuck.

Cappiello and the extortionists were Neapolitan and Brooklyn was largely the province of the Camorra, Naples' equivalent of Sicily's Mafia. Until then, the newspapers had written about the criminal activities of *La Società Cammorristi*, the *Mala Vita* and the Mafia. But in 1903 the New York *Herald* and Italian-language *Bollettino della Sera* began to use "Black Hand" as a catch-all term for all Italian criminal gangs as, for some time, respectable Italian-Americans had petitioned them not to bandy the name "Mafia" around as it applied only to a small band of Sicilian thugs. The other newspapers soon followed suit – as did the extortionists who preyed on other Italian immigrants.

Letters demanding money were regularly adorned with a crudely drawn Black Hand symbol. On 24 May 1911, Tano Sferrazzo of 307 East 45th Street in New York City received one. It read:

> Various men of my society as you know well will demand some money because we need it in our urgent business and you finally have never consented to satisfy us to fulfil your duty. Therefore today finishes your case. In a few words I will explain the matter. You must know that in cases of this kind as your own when they are handled by useless persons the matter can be easily dropped or in other words neglected, but in your case we are men of high society and of great importance, and therefore the matter cannot be dropped, or in other words we cannot neglect this matter because the society will inflict a severe penalty. Therefore today talking with the chief, I have decided that you must do your duty otherwise death will take you and you must not worry over it because these are our rules, so you are warned which road do you wish to choose. Do what you please, it is immaterial to us. Money or death. If you want to save your life, tomorrow 25 May at 10pm take the Third Avenue train, go to 129th Street, walk towards Second Avenue. Walk as far as the First Avenue Bridge that leads you to the Bronx, walk up and down the bridge for a while; two men will then present themselves and will ask you, where are you going? To them you will give not less than $200.
>
> Signed Black Hand

Sometimes the extortionists were apprehended. This letter appeared as an exhibit in the trial of Salvatore Romano, who had been indicted along with Antonio Lecchi and Pasquale Lopipero at the Court of General Sessions in New York on 22 September 1911.

Other letters were more straightforward:

If you have not sufficient courage you may go to people who enjoy an honourable reputation and be careful as to whom you go. Thus you may stop us from persecuting you as you have been adjudged to give money or life. Woe upon you if you do not resolve to buy your future happiness, you can do from us by giving the money demanded . . .

Or:

This is the second time that I have warned you. Sunday at ten o'clock in the morning at the corner of Second Street and Third Avenue, bring three hundred dollars without fail. Otherwise we will set fire to you and blow you up with a bomb. Consider this matter well, for this is the last warning I will give you.

> I sign the Black Hand

Black Hand gangs also appeared in Pittsburgh. On 27 May 1908, Mr G. Satarano received a letter, saying:

You please you know the company of the Black Hands. I want you to send $2,000, all gold money. You will find some friend to tell you about it. Send it to head man, Johnstown. We don't want you to tell no person that talks too much. If you report about this letter we will kill you. We will kill you with a steel knife. You and your family. Give me money right away, for I want to use it. And remember, keep it quiet.

Black Hand

That same year, an Italian-American in Philadelphia also received a threatening letter, which read:

You will never see Italy again if you do not give $1,000 to the person that pinches you after he salutes you. (I say one thousand.) Carry it with you always and remember I am more powerful than the police and your God.

Black Hand

And in St Louis, another immigrant received a letter:

Dear Friend,
   This is your second letter. You did not answer or come. What have you in your head? You know what you did in Brooklyn and that you went to Italy and then returned to Dago Hill [St Louis's Italian quarter] to hide yourself. You can go to hell to hide but we will find you. It will be very bad for you and your family if you do not come to an understanding. So come Thursday night at ten o'clock. If you do not come we will cut you up in pieces. How will that be, you dirty false face. So we will wait for you. Best regards, good bye.

Under these words were two pictures – one of a man in a coffin; the other a skull and crossbones. There was also a postscript: "So this will be your appearance if you do not do as we tell you. The way the blood flows in my veins is the way the blood will flow from your veins."

Most people paid up. Italian immigrants felt that American law had no understanding of their situation and no power to help them. They knew that the threats in

Black Hand letters were likely to be carried out if they did not pay up. Many Italians were armed. According to an official at Ellis Island, the clearing station for immigrants, two-thirds of all male immigrants landing were carrying knives, revolvers or blackjacks. And there was no law permitting the immigration authorities to disarm them. The police said: "Ninety-five out of every one hundred Italians are armed with some sort of deadly weapon."

However, the New York Police Department did take the situation seriously. They set up a special Italian squad under Detective Sergeant Giuseppe "Joe" Petrosino. An immigrant from Salerno region, Petrosino had dealt with extortion rackets earlier in his career with the NYPD. In 1902, he accompanied prosperous wholesale tailor Stephen Carmenciti, who lived on East 103rd Street in the Italian neighbourhood of East Harlem in Manhattan, to a rendezvous to pay $150 to an extortion gang calling itself the "Holy House". Two Holy House members – Carmine Mursuneso of East 106th Street and Joseph Mascarello of East 107th Street – were arrested. However, they were acquitted when Carmenciti refused to testify, fearing for the safety of his family.

Petrosino rose to prominence in 1903 when the corpse of a man with seventeen stab wounds was found stuffed in a barrel in a vacant lot at East 11th Street and Avenue D, near Little Italy on Manhattan's Lower East Side. His throat had been cut so savagely that his head was nearly severed from his body. His severed genitals had also been cut off and stuffed in his mouth. This was reminiscent of a murder the previous year when the partially dismembered body of a Brooklyn grocer named Giuseppe Catania had been found in a sack on the beach at Bay Ridge, Brooklyn. The murderers had not been found, but the motive had been traced back to a criminal trial in Palermo some twenty years before when Catania's testimony had sent

a number of men away for a twenty-year stretch. The
murders had plainly been gangland affairs and the bodies
were left where they would be found as a warning.

The body in the barrel was not immediately identified.
However, Petrosino believed that he had seen the victim
before at the trial of Italian counterfeiter Giuseppe De
Priemo. The detective travelled to Sing Sing to see him.
When De Priemo saw a photograph of the dead man,
he immediately identified him as his brother-in-law
Benedetto Madonia. The victim had been a member of a
counterfeiting gang who had been in hiding in Buffalo, upstate New York. He had recently visited De Priemo with a
man named Tomasso Petto – better known as "Petto the
Ox" – and was on his way to New York City to get their
share of the loot.

A pair of gloves found near the barrel bore the label
of a Buffalo store – Petto had also been holed up in the
city. According to De Priemo, his brother-in-law always
carried a watch with distinctive markings "on the neck".
Pawnshops were checked and the watch was found in one
of them. The man who had pawned the watch for one
dollar was identified as Petto. When the police went to
question Petto in the Prince Street Saloon, Petto pulled
a stiletto. They grappled him to the ground. Once he was
restrained, they searched him and found another knife,
a pistol and the pawn ticket for the watch. Petto denied
murdering Madonia, or getting the watch from him. He
had obtained it, he said, from an Italian named "John"
whose last name he did not know, though he said they
had been friends for three years. As he neither wanted or
needed the watch, he had pawned it.

According to the Secret Service – which was then part
of the US Treasury – Madonia had been the agent for the
counterfeiting ring. It was his job to distribute the forged
bills to dealers around the country. Some of the money

had gone missing. Suspected of double-dealing, Madonia had been put to death.

The leaders of the gang were Ignazio Saietta – aka "Lupo the Wolf" – and Giuseppe Morello. Petto was the gang's heavy. Physically strong but not very bright, Petto could not resist stealing the only valuable – and traceable – item in Madonia's possession. He went on trial for murder, but went free after Madonia's wife, son and brother-in-law refused to testify against him. He left New York and went to Scranton, Pennsylvania, where he became involved in various "Black Hand" activities. In August 1904, he was implicated in the kidnapping of Morello gang member Vito Laduca, though no charges were ever filed. The following year, he was found dead outside his home in Wilkes Barre, Pennsylvania. There were sixty-two stab wounds in his body. Giuseppe De Priemo – then out of jail – was suspected, but no arrests were made and Petto's murderer was never found.

Another man involved with the Lupo-Morello gang was Don Vito Cascio Ferro. When he first travelled to New York in 1901 he was already a seasoned criminal. It was said that he was the first mafioso "of respect" to set foot in America and was feted in Sicilian-American criminal circles. Living with his sister Francesca in an apartment on 23rd Street before finding his own place at 117 Morgan Street, he introduced the extortion method known as *u pizzu*, from the Sicilian expression *fari vagnari u pizzu*, which means "to wet one's beak" or, colloquially, "to wet your whistle" – traditionally a glass of wine or other light refreshment offered in recognition of a service rendered. The principle was simple. Instead of asking for a large amount that risked bankrupting the victim, it was better to ask for smaller amounts that the victim could afford, then return later for more money. Don Vito decreed that no one who could afford it was to escape paying the *Onorata Società u pizzu* for its protection. Ferro was suspected of involvement in the murder of Madonia. The charges against him blocked his application for citizenship. To escape arrest, he fled to New Orleans, then back to Sicily, leaving Lupo and others to continue the Black Hand's collection of *u pizzu*. Ferro took with him, it is said, a photograph of Joe Petrosino which he carried always in his wallet.

Despite the formation of the Italian Squad and Petrosino's campaign against the Black Hand, extortion remained rife in New York City. Then two plain-clothed policemen were killed by a young man who had just arrived from Palermo. This prompted a citywide sweep for Italians carrying concealed weapons. The county coroner who first considered homicide cases – himself an Italian – received a letter signed by 200 Italian women, protesting that Italians were being picked on. It was the Sicilians to blame, they said:

> The Sicilian is a blood-thirsty man. He belongs to the Black Hand. He exercises blackmail, is a dynamiter and, by blood, a coward ... We must suppress the immigration from Sicily. Then you will see if the Italians in America will not be mentioned any more criminally.

The problem was that most New York policemen, who were traditionally Irish, could not tell the difference between a Sicilian and an Italian.

However Petrosino's Italian Squad did have its successes. During the round-up, it arrested Enrico Erricone, "Generalissimo of the Camorra", who was deported back to Italy to stand trial and Petrosino was hailed by the newspapers as the "Italian Sherlock Holmes". It was reported that this caused "an enormous sensation among the members of the Neapolitan Camorra" and that "the Black Hand condemned Petrosino to death".

They continued undeterred. A 6.30pm on 23 January 1908, a bomb went off outside the bank of Pasquale Pati & Sons at 240 Elizabeth Street, between Houston and Prince Streets, in the heart of Little Italy. It blew out the windows scattering $40,000 in gold and bills displayed there to show that the bank was solvent across the street. Usually there was $30,000 on display, but recently Pati had upped the amount when several other Italian banks had got into trouble. Pasquale's son Salvatore was injured by flying glass, but managed to recover most of the money. Pati's neighbour Paolo Bononolo, who owned the building at 242 Elizabeth Street adjoining the bank, thought the bomb was directed at him as he had received several Black Hand letters. He owned a tenement at 512 East 13th Street which adjoined a house where a bomb had gone off in the early hours of the morning two days before. Petrosino dismissed this as the Black Hand rarely make mistakes and, after fervent denials, Pati admitted that he had received Black Hand threats some time before, but ignored them. He then locked up the money that had been in the window and hired a special policeman to guard the building at night.

After the bombing, a meeting was called at 178 Park Row, above the offices of the *Bollettino*. Taking their cue from the White Hand Society formed to combat the Black Hand in Chicago in November 1907, those attending set up the Associazione de Vigilanza e Protezione Italiana. The editor of *Bollettino*, Frank L. Frugone, became president and it soon had over 300 members. It did no good. On 1 February, the Senna Brothers grocery store at 244 Elizabeth Street was blown up. Three nights later a bomb exploded in the hallway of La Sovoia restaurant and saloon at 234 Elizabeth Street. The bar was blown over, collapsing on waiters and customers. Then on 26 March, the bombers hit Bononolo's bank at 246 Elizabeth Street. The bomb blew a hole in the wall of Bononolo's quarters, burying Bononolo's wife and two daughters under the debris. Though their clothes were blown off, they were uninjured except for a few scratches and bruises. All the windows in the building above were smashed and the tenants ran out into the street where crowds were crying, "*Mano Nero!*"

Bononolo told the police: "This has happened because I did not heed their warnings. For five years, scarcely a month has gone by when I have not received one or more Black Hand letters. They asked for sums ranging from $1 to $1,000, but nothing ever happened, and recently I had paid no attention to their threats. This is to warn me. Next time I shall be killed."

Even so Bononolo was refused permission to carry a pistol. Meanwhile Pati had armed himself. He had made representations to the Mafia that he should be left alone, due to his connections to the Camorra. But Black Hand warnings had been given. They would not be withdrawn and Pati was still to consider himself a target. When men arrived at the bank to collect money, Pati and his son, along with a half a dozen friends, shot and killed one of them. Pati was congratulated by the police as "a brave man and the first of his race to face the Black Hand issue squarely". Then he secretly relocated, for fear of Mafia reprisals, it was said. However, it was later discovered that, after Lupo the Wolf had first made threats against Pati, there had been a run on his bank. The man shot was actually an innocent depositor. When Pati disappeared, he made off with the rest of the bank's money. Four years later, the police were still looking for him, but for the moment he was hailed as a hero. Perhaps more of a hero was Pietro Caropole of New Jersey, who killed one member of the Black Hand and wounded another, and in 1908 was still holding his ground, despite new death threats.

In Chicago, the White Hand Society had gained the support of the city's leading Italian-language newspapers, *L'Italia* and *La Tribuna Italiana Transatlantica*, as well as the Italian ambassador in Washington and the Italian minister of foreign affairs in Rome. Its organizers declared "war without truce, war without quarter" against the Black Hand and looked forward to the day when there would be *Mano Bianca* groups "in all the cities that contain large Italian colonies, which suspect the existence of mafiosi or Camorristi in their midst". Indeed, White Hand Societies sprang up in Pittsburgh, Baltimore and other cities. They had some early successes. Rich Pittsburgh merchants and pillars of the White Hand Giuseppe Sunseri and E. Bisis, along with friends of Baltimore Black Hand victim Joseph Di Giorgio, joined battle with the Black Hand in the Pennsylvania Railroad yards on 9 December 1907. In an exchange of gunfire, Sunseri was wounded, but he killed one of his assailants, Philip Rei.

By January 1908, the White Hand claimed they had driven ten of the worst Italian criminals out of Chicago. However, the *Mano Nera* fought back. On 28 February, the president of Chicago's White Hand Society, Dr Carlo Volini, received a letter telling him:

> The supreme council of the Black Hand has voted that you must die. You have not heeded our warnings in the past, but you must heed this. Your killing has been assigned and the man waits for you.

Volini told reporters that he was unafraid. "They may kill me," he said, "but the cause I live for will go on." However, Volini was not killed, but support for the *Mano Bianca* began to ebb away. Italian immigrants had little faith that the White Handers could be any more effective than the authorities in stemming the power of the *Mano Nera*.

But in New York, Petrosino pressed on. In July 1908, his men arrested a man they claimed to be the Black Hand's principal bomb-maker and raided a saloon on East 11th Street they said was the gang's headquarters. It did no good. Only a few days later a letter appeared in *The New York Times*. It read:

> My name is Salvatore Spinelli. My parents in Italy came from a decent family. I came here eighteen years ago and went to work as a house painter, like my father. I started a family and I have been an American citizen for thirteen years. I had a house at 314 East Eleventh St and another one at 316, which I rented out. At this point the "Black Hand" came into my life and asked me for seven thousand dollars. I told them to go to hell and the bandits tried to blow up my house. Then I asked the police for help and refused more demands, but the "Black Hand" set off one, two, three, four, five bombs in my houses. Things went to pieces. From thirty-two tenants I am down to six. I owe a thousand dollars interest that is due next month and I cannot pay. I am a ruined man. My family lives in fear. There is a policeman on guard in front of my house, but what can he do? My brother Francesco and I do guard duty at the windows with guns night and day. My wife and children have not left the house for weeks. How long can this go on?

Dynamiting was a favourite Black Hand method of enforcement. There was a great deal of construction work going on in New York at the time and dynamite had recently replaced blasting powder for blasting foundations or subway tunnels in Manhattan's solid rock substrate. Workmen used to make off with used sticks as there was a profitable black market among extortion gangs. As late as 1917, long after strict laws controlling the sale and use of dynamite had been introduced, the police commissioner warned that the "workmen at the 14th Street subway are getting away with two or three sticks of dynamite daily".

There was a lively debate about the origin of the name "Black Hand". There was, of course, the famous Black Hand gang in Serbia, who assassinated Archduke Franz Ferdinand, precipitating the First World War. However, that Black Hand had not been formed until 1911. Journalist Lindsay Denison, writing in *Everybody's Magazine* in September 1908, said that the Black Hand had been "a secret society which fought the government and the church" in Spain during the Inquisition and "the secret societies of Southern Italy were its heirs". The president of the United Italian Societies of New York, Gaetano D'Amato, said that the name had been used again in Spain in the 1860s by a society of thieves and murderers who styled themselves protectors and guardians for the downtrodden against persons of wealth. He also said that the term was first used in the United States "some ten years ago . . . probably by some Italian desperado who had heard of the exploits of the Spanish society, and considered the combination of words to be high-sounding and terror-inspiring".

Denison replied that "a false report was raised in Spain" during the 1870s and 1880s that it had been revived. The story, Denison said:

> . . . lingered in the brain of a [New York] *Herald* reporter, and one fine day he attempted to rejuvenate waning interest in a puzzling Italian murder case by speculating as to the coming to life of the Black Hand among Latin immigrants in America. The other newspapers seized on the idea eagerly, and kept it going . . .

Denison went on to speak of the organized sections of the Black Hand:

It is not possible to speak certainly of the way in which the spoils of their plots are divided. It seems most likely that the "divvy" is governed by the generosity of the head "bad-man" and the risks taken by the members accumulating the loot. The worst and greediest scoundrel in the plot takes all he dares. Most of the rest goes to the men who made the threats. Half of what the chief takes goes "higher up". There are at least two or three old graduates of South Italian crime, who never sully their Hands with the commission of actual crimes nor trouble their minds to plan them, though occasionally the big chief or one of his nearest lieutenants may drop in on an Italian banker and ask for a thousand dollars or so. He gets it, quick. He doesn't have to make any threats; the appearance of his face in the place is a threat . . . The very names of the Black Hand's big chiefs are names of terror.

The success of the Black Hand methods caused the idea to spread all over the country. The Pittsburgh police were credited with "the break up of the best organized blackmailing bands in the history of the Black Hand". One of their raids produced evidence that they had "stumbled upon a huge society combining the worst features of the Mafia and Camorra". They had found "carefully written by-laws, with a definite scale of spoil division and with many horrible oaths". Then on another raid they found what appeared to be a "school of the Black Hand", two young Italians had "actually been practicing with daggers on dummy figures". However, further investigation revealed that the Pittsburgh band was in fact the alliance of the three or four local Black Hand gangs and no connection with New York Black Handers was ever made.

Lieutenant Petrosino learnt of a new, more sophisticated extortion method that was spreading through the community. A shopkeeper in Elizabeth Street told him that three men had entered his shop and said they knew he had received Black Hand letters. They offered him protection from the Black Hand threats for a small, regular fee. Many of the Black Hand bombers slowly turned into fatherly "protectors" who integrated themselves openly into society. The anonymous terrorist had become a known face in the community and the protection racket had started.

In the summer of 1908, Raffaele Palizzolo, a Mafia chief and long-time deputy for the city of Palermo in the Italian parliament, visited New York. Despite – or, perhaps, because of – having been tried for murder three times, he was acknowledged as "the political boss of Palermo; indeed, the uncrowned king of Sicily".

Although Palizzolo was greeted as an honoured guest by the Italian community, Petrosino shadowed him. In fact, Palizzolo's power was waning in Sicily and his visit to New York was a fund-raiser. He posed as an enemy of the Black Hand and the Mafia. Nevertheless, stories that he was the "king of the Mafia" began to circulate. The close attention of Petrosino inhibited Palizzolo's freedom of action and he headed home sooner than planned. According to the New York Mayor George B. McCellan, on leaving, Palizzolo shook his fist at Petrosino, who had followed him to the pier, and shouted: "If you ever come to Palermo, God help you."

During 1908, New York Police Commissioner Theodore A. Bingham kept a record of all crime relating to the Black Hand. The summary read:

Black Hand cases reported : 424
Arrests : 215
Convictions : 36
Discharges : 156
Pending : 23

<u>Bomb outrages reported</u> : 44
Arrests : 70
Convictions : 9
Discharges : 58
Pending : 3

The Black Hand had become such a problem that a new undercover squad had to be formed. On 20 February 1909, the *New York Times* ran a story on the new force:

NEW SECRET SERVICE
TO BATTLE "BLACK HAND"

Italian Merchants Said to Have Raised Fund
for Bingham's Detective Force.

PETROSINO IS IN CHARGE

Identity of New Sleuths Kept
as a Profound Secret –
Italian Government Will Co-operate.

Police Commissioner Theodore A. Bingham finally has his secret service. It is a secret in every sense of the word, since no one at 300 Mulberry Street [formerly police headquarters] except Lieutenant Petrosino and Bingham himself knows its membership. Substantial funds for the maintenance of the Secret Squad have been made available to the Commissioner, but this is all he will say. He refuses to discuss their source, confining himself to the assurance that it is not public money. It is generally believed that the money was contributed by a number of prosperous Italian merchants and bankers across the city, aroused by the wave of extortions in recent years.

Petrosino was quoted as saying:

> There is only one thing that can wipe out the Black
> Hand, and that is the elimination of ignorance. The
> gangsters who are holding Little Italy in the grip of
> terror come chiefly from Sicily and Southern Italy,
> and they are primitive country robbers transplanted
> into cities. This is proved by their brutal methods. No
> American hold-up man would ever think of stopping
> somebody and slashing his face with a knife just to take
> his wallet. Probably he would threaten him with a pistol.
> No American criminal would blow up a man's house
> or kill his children because he refused to pay fifty or
> a hundred dollars. The crimes that occur among the
> Italians here, are the same as those committed at one
> time by rural outlaws in Italy; and the victims, like the
> killers, come from the same ignorant class of people. In
> short we are dealing with banditry transplanted to the
> most modern city in the world.

The only way to thwart the Mafia was to cut it off at its roots,
Petrosino said. He had to go to Sicily. On 20 February 1909,
The New York Times reported that Petrosino had been given
a roving commission to wipe out the Black Hand and had
disappeared from police headquarters. The police would
only say that he was on vacation, which no one believed. In
fact, he had been in Washington making arrangements for
his trip with the State Department and the Secret Service.
He returned briefly to New York, where he consulted with
Commissioner Bingham, then disappeared again. The
Herald reported that he was on his way to Italy and Sicily,
"where he will procure important information about Italian
criminals who have come to this country".

Petrosino had left the country secretly on 9 February
under an assumed name. However, the purser on the Italian

liner *Duca di Genova* recognized him. Arriving in Genoa on 21 February, he headed to Rome carrying a letter of introduction from the State Department to Ambassador Lloyd C. Griscom and a list of Italian criminals then resident in the United States. Petrosino believed that around 5,000 Italians in New York had Old World criminal records. In his twenty-six-year career, he had already succeeded in deporting more than 500 Italian criminals to serve jail sentences they had eluded by emigrating.

However, when Petrosino arrived in Rome, the US embassy was closed for Washington's birthday. Roaming the streets he met the editor of *L'Araldo Italiano*, a New York Italian-language newspaper, who was in Italy to cover the aftermath of the earthquake that had hit Messina on 28 December 1908. On 5 February, *L'Araldo* had published a story about Petrosino's forthcoming departure, giving his itinerary and wishing him well in his mission. Together they went to a restaurant where they bumped into Giovanni Branchi, the former Italian consul general in New York who Petrosino knew well.

The following day, the embassy was open again and Petrosino got to see Ambassador Griscom who arranged for him to visit Giovanni Giolitti, the Italian minister of the interior, and Francesco Leonardi, the head of the national police. However, he did not actually get to meet Signor Giolitti, only his secretary to whom he explained his "study trip" on international crime. Police Chief Leonardi was more helpful, furnishing him with a letter of introduction to his subordinates, ordering them to give Petrosino all possible help. Apparently, Petrosino did not disclose that the actual purpose of his mission was to set up a spy network so he could keep tabs on the comings and goings of Mafiosi.

Petrosino then made a short visit to Padula, his home town, where his brother showed him an Italian paper that carried a reprint of the *Herald* story. His secret mission, it seems, was not so secret any more. On the train to Naples, he was recognized by a captain in the *carabinieri*. From Naples, Petrosino took a steamer to Palermo, arriving there on the morning of 28 February.

He registered at a hotel under a false name, then called the US consul, William H. Bishop. Bishop was the only person he confided his plans to, though he said he had informers in Palermo. He went to a bank and opened an account in his own name so that he could have his mail directed there. After that, he went to the courthouse and started collecting the criminal records of the men on his list to find out which ones were wanted.

For nearly a week, Petrosino moved around Palermo and the surrounds alone. Then, carrying a letter of introduction from Bishop, he visited Police Commissioner Baldassare Ceola. At that point, he was checking to see whether the passports carried by Italian criminals entering the United States were valid, making it plain that he did not trust the local authorities. Ceola offered him a bodyguard, which he refused. On 11 March, Petrosino told Bishop that he was going to Caltanissetta to check the records in the courthouse there. He said that he would be back in Palermo the following day as he had an important appointment at nine in the evening.

However, Petrosino was already growing wary. He wrote in his notebook: "Have already met criminals who recognized me from New York. I am on dangerous ground."

The following day, after he had made copies of the material he had collected, he made a fresh note, concerning: "Vito Cascio Ferro, born in Sambuca Zabut, resident of Bisaquino, Province of Palermo, dreaded criminal." After lunch at a café, where he was seen talking briefly with two men, he went to the Piazza Marina. A few minutes later shots were heard. Petrosino's dead body was found near the Garibaldi Gardens in the centre of the square.

News of Petrosino's assassination caused a sensation in New York. Reporters besieged police headquarters for details. The Italian community were particularly upset, fearing they might be blamed. The *Bollettino* said:

> We will answer to the attack that the Black Hand are not all Italians and that the assassins are not all Sicilians, among whom are many honourable people deserving of respect and esteem. The assassins of Petrosino are wild beasts capable of the most terrible crimes. They have no country, no religion, no family, and no civilization.

Il Telegrafo said:

> The assassination of Petrosino is an evil day for the Italians of America, and none of us can any longer deny that there is an organized Black Hand Society in the United States. The agents of the Society in Sicily were evidently aware of Petrosino's coming, and they prepared to kill him accordingly.

L'Araldo said that it was time for Italians to take action "to prevent the spreading of that criminality which had brought so much unjust discredit on the name of the Italians in the United States", while *Il Progresso* ran the Petrosino murder on its front page for several days and carried a reprint of a *New York Journal* editorial calling for greater police protection for Italians, in both English and Italian.

Petrosino's body was shipped home to New York. An estimated 250,000 people turned out for his funeral.

The procession was led by Mayor McClellan and Police Commissioner Bingham, but was made up largely by "men of Italian birth" according to the New York *Sun*, "who testified by their presence to their esteem for this valuable peace officer and their approval of the work he did."

But the popular acclaim of Petrosino did little to dent the power of the Black Hand. A few weeks later, Pioggio Puccio, who had helped organize the funeral and a benefit at the Academy of Music for Petrosino's widow, was shot and killed on his doorstep at East 75th Street in Manhattan. The benefit itself was not a great success as "the majority of those who promised to take part at the last moment sent excuses". Almost everyone involved with the benefit, including Puccio, received threatening letters. Soon after an Italian grocer on Spring Street received a letter demanding money which said: "Petrosino is dead, but the Black Hand still lives." He took it to the police. Days later, the tenement where he lived was burnt down with the loss of nine lives.

The fate of Giuseppe Petrosino surprised no one in Palermo. An article in the Sunday *New York Times* by "A Veteran Diplomat" said: "Petrosino's murderers will never be brought to justice. It is just as well that the people of New York should resign themselves to the fact."

In Sicily, Bishop, the American consul, felt that he was being "delayed and hindered" by the authorities in his own efforts to investigate the murder. However, pressure was brought to bear on Commissioner Ceola, who had been trying to purge his force of Mafia influence. In April, he issued a report calling for the indictment of fifteen men, including Vito Cascio Ferro who, since his return from the US, had risen to become the *capo di capi* in Palermo. His system of collecting *u pizzu* had been extended to those outside commerce. Everyone – lawyers, landowners, civil servants – paid this "tax" to the Mafia one way or another. Even lovers had to give *"a cannila"* – "candle" – tribute, which allowed the man to walk up and down beneath his sweetheart's window.

Also on the list were Antonio Pasananti and Carlo Costantino, two men who had been involved in the barrel murder case in New York and had returned unexpectedly to Sicily a few days before Petrosino arrived. They were already in custody. Cascio Ferro was picked up a few days later.

However, Cascio had a cast-iron alibi supplied by the Honourable Domenico De Michele Ferrantelli who had been elected to the chamber of deputies in the general election held a few days before the murder. In the election, Palizzolo had been soundly defeated after backing Francesco Nitti. Ferrantelli was a supporter of Giovanni Giolitti, the minister of the interior and now premier. His administration was later described by historian Gaetano Salvemini as "the prime ministry of the underworld".

After submitting his report, Commissioner Ceola was summoned to Rome and sacked. The suspects were freed on bail. Two years later, when people's attention was taken up with the forthcoming war with Turkey over Libya, all charges were dismissed.

Don Vito Cascio Ferro's criminal career continued to flourish until 1929, when he fell foul of Mussolini. Unwilling to compromise with the Fascists, he was arrested by Cesare Mori on trumped-up charges of smuggling. The trial was short. Throughout Don Vito maintained a disdainful silence, which he broke only to rebuke his counsel for making certain statements that "clashed with his principles and authority". At the end of the proceedings the president of the court asked him whether he had anything to add. He looked the judges straight in the face and said: "Gentlemen, since you have been unable to find any evidence for the numerous crimes I really have committed, you are reduced to condemning me for the only one I have not."

In prison he was treated with respect by the other inmates. He was able to help needy prisoners and their families by providing for them from the ill-gotten gains of other prisoners. He also arranged sizeable dowries for the daughters of certain prisoners. It was even said that he managed to get the dowry of the daughter of a leading Fascist in Caltanissetta transferred to the daughter of one of his fellow prisoners.

Much of the respect given to Don Vito came from the one and only murder he did admit to – that of Giuseppe Petrosino.

"In my entire life," he said, "I killed only one person and that I did disinterestedly."

That day, Don Vito had been invited to lunch by Deputy Ferrantelli. In the middle of the meal, Cascio Ferro absented himself for a short time, borrowed his host's carriage, drove to the Piazza Marina where he waited outside the Palazzo Steri, the seat of the Courts of Justice. When Petrosino arrived, Don Vito despatched him with a single shot, got back in the carriage and returned to Ferrantelli's house to finish lunch. Later, when Cascio Ferro was charged, Ferrantelli testified that he had been in his home all the time and Don Vito walked free.

For Don Vito, killing Petrosino personally was a matter of honour. Although other candidates have been put up, it is now widely accepted that Cascio Ferro pulled the trigger – while Passananti and Costantino were on hand to set him up.

"Petrosino was a courageous enemy," Don Vito said. "He did not deserve a dirty death at the hands of just any hired killer."

In the Vicaria, in one of the passages leading to the infirmary, Don Vito carved the motto: "*Vicaria, malatia e nicissitati si vidi lu cori di l'amicu*" – "In prison, sickness or need, one finds the heart of a true friend." For many years, these words gave comfort to inmates and warders alike.

It is not known how Don Vito died. According to anti-Mafia journalist Michele Pantaleone, he died "of a broken heart after a few years". Officially he died in 1945 at the age of 83. However, Petrosino's biographer Arrigo Petacco believes he died in 1943, after the Allied invasion of Sicily.

"Fascism had collapsed, the Allied armies were moving north along the peninsula and the Flying Fortresses were attacking without respite," said Petacco. "So the prison authorities had ordered the evacuation of the penitentiary of Pozzouli, which was too exposed to bombardment. In a few hours all the inmates were moved except one; Don Vito, who was *forgotten* in his cell. He died of thirst and terror in the gloomy, abandoned penitentiary, like the villain in some old serial story."

For many years afterwards it was an honour to occupy Don Vito's prison bed. Other inmates treated it with respect. Later it would be occupied by another famous Mafioso – Don Calogero Vizzini, better known as Don Calò, who lent Mafia assistance to the Allied invasion.

While the Mafia continued to flourish on both sides of the Atlantic, the Black Hand suffered irreversible setbacks. The Secret Service rounded up the Lupo-Morello gang. Convicted of counterfeiting, Lupo the Wolf was sentenced to thirty years. His brother-in-law Giuseppe Morello got twenty-five. Both sentences were to be served in the new Federal penitentiary in Atlanta. Twelve smaller fry were sentences to shorter terms. The two- and five-dollar bills had been printed in Salerno and shipped over in boxes supposedly containing olive oil, olives, cheese, wine, macaroni, spaghetti and other Italian produce. They were sold for 30 or 40 cents each to agents who then distributed them around the country. Both Lupo and Morello were paroled in 1922 in time to benefit from Prohibition.

While Lupo and Morello and much of their gang were in jail, Giosue Gallucci became "King of Harlem's Little Italy" and was thought to be worth $500,000. However, shortly before 10pm on 7 May 1915, Gallucci left the family bakery at 318 East 109th Street and walked to the coffee shop he had just bought for his son Luca. Four men then entered the shop and fired at the Galluccis. Giosue was hit in the neck and stomach; Luca in the stomach. There were fifteen customers in the coffee shop, mostly friends of Gallucci. They returned fire but the assailants escaped. When the police arrived they arrested everyone in the coffee shop. Giosue Gallucci died that evening in hospital. Luca, who had managed to stagger back across to the family home, survived until the following day. Their bodyguard, Joe Nozzaro – known as Joe Chuck who always wore a steel vest – was found under a trolley car on 16 March 1917. There was a bullet hole in his chest and one in his right shoulder. The body had been dragged 100 feet by the car before it stopped and it took half an hour to disentangle it. The police said that he was "one of fifty or more men whose lives were sacrificed in a long-standing feud which it had been hoped ended on 7 May 1915, when Gallucci and his son Luca were murdered".

It was the Morellos who benefited most from the death of Gallucci. The gang was run by brothers Nicolo and Antonio Morello and half-brothers Vincenzo and Ciro Terranova while Giuseppe was away. Other members of the family included the ambitious Giuseppe "Joe the Boss" Masseria and Umberto "Rocco" Valenti. It was also to become a breeding ground for future leaders of New York's "Five Families" such as Charles "Lucky" Luciano, Frank "the Prime Minister" Costello, Vito Genovese and Giuseppe "Joe Adonis" Doto.

Lucky Luciano

Salvatore Lucania

Organized Italian racketeering became a national force in the US in the 1920s with Prohibition. Along with prostitution and gambling, there was now a new illicit commodity that millions of Americans craved – alcohol. It brought gangsters riches and respectability beyond their wildest dreams. Until then the underworld had been monopolized by the Irish, Jews and, to a lesser extent, Poles. Now Italian racketeers seized the chance to move into the big time. Even before Prohibition, thousands of home distilleries had been operating in Italian immigrant neighbourhoods. This gave them a head start when it came to bootlegging.

By the end of the decade, despite the publicity given to Alphonse "Scarface Al" Capone, a vain, podgy little man named Giuseppe "Joe the Boss" Masseria had emerged as the most powerful single figure in Italian crime. In a power struggle within the Morello gang, Masseria gained the reputation of being "the man who can dodge bullets" after surviving two assassination attempts unscathed. In retaliation, he organized the assassination of his rival Umberto Valenti and did a deal with Pietro Morello, making Masseria Mob boss while Morello remained chief strategist. Allied with Al Capone in Chicago and Bronx crime boss

Tom Reina, Masseria sought to take over completely in New York. Ranged against him were the Castellammarese, immigrants from the Sicilian town of Castellammare del Golfo, who had settled across the eastern seaboard. Although widely dispersed, they remained fiercely loyal to their New York chief Salvatore Maranzano. A student of the works of Julius Caesar, Maranzano had been sent to the US in 1925 by Sicily's Mafia boss Don Vito Cascio Ferro to bring the American Mafia under his control.

Masseria himself was from Masala, less than thirty miles from Castellammare. He set out to eliminate Maranzano, as well as other Castellammarese leaders such as Joe Bonanno and Joseph Profaci in Brooklyn, Buffalo's Stefano Magaddino and Joseph Aiello in Chicago. But Maranzano knew what was coming and set up a meeting with Tom Reina in an attempt to get him to switch allegiance.

He also put out feelers to the leader of a group of young turks named Charles "Lucky" Luciano. Born Salvatore Lucania in the village of Lercara Friddi, Sicily, in 1896, he had emigrated to the United States with his family at the age of nine. They settled in the Lower East Side of Manhattan. At the age of ten, he was already involved in mugging, shoplifting, burglary and extortion. One of the Jewish kids he tried to extort protection money from at school was Maier Suchowljuansky. Born in Grodno, then in Russia, in 1902, he had moved to New York with his family in 1911 and anglicized his name to Meyer Lansky. Lucania and Lansky became firm friends, along with Lansky's younger sidekick who was Benjamin "Bugsy" Siegel.

Lucania's attendance at school was sporadic and he was sent to a special school for truants in Brooklyn. On his release, he got a job as a delivery boy for a milliner, his only legitimate job. In 1916, he was caught carrying heroin concealed under the hat bands and was sentenced to a year in jail, where he changed his name to Charlie as the diminutive of his given name "Sal" invited homosexual assaults.When he was released, he formed a gang with Meyer Lansky, Bugsy Siegel, Frank Costello, Joe Adonis and Vito Genovese. Together they began robbing banks, pawnshops and money lenders on the Lower East Side. Then America entered the First World War. Lucania was called up, but had no intention of serving.

"I wasn't afraid of going to war because I'd get killed or nothin' like that," he said. "But I knew goddamn well that if I went to Europe, by the time I came home it would be the end of me when it came to my outfit."

He avoided being drafted by deliberately contracting gonorrhoea. He lived to regret it.

"If I'd known the way it was gonna be like to get cured," he said, "I'd rather have run around the trenches in France with a bunch of krauts shootin' at me. I had to get treatments every other day for over a year by some doctor down on 10th Street ... And what a treatment. He put a rubber tube with some kinda solution in it all the way up my pecker, and then he'd follow this with a round metal bar I think he called a 'sound'. He told me it'd help make the cure permanent so that my pecker would never close up again."

At the beginning of Prohibition, Lucania's gang went into the bootlegging business. They were financed by Arnold Rothstein, whose mythic reputation included the unfounded claim that he had fixed the 1919 World Series, and veteran gangster Johnny "The Fox" Torrio – aka The Brain – the man who had originally set Al Capone up in business. Lucania's gang, the Seven Group, soon attracted the attention of New York's two Mafia bosses, Giuseppe Masseria and Salvatore Maranzano. Both wanted a share of his bootlegging business. Charlie sided with Masseria and became his chief lieutenant, directing bootlegging, prostitution, the distribution of narcotics and other rackets.

In 1928, he was arrested for robbery under the alias Luciano. As the police found that name easier to pronounce that Lucania, he adopted it. But to avoid further brushes with the law, Luciano withdrew from front-line crime and concerned himself with overall planning.

"It was like, if you're the head of a big company, you don't have every guy who works on every machine comin' up to you and askin', 'Hey, boss, what colours should I use on the cars next year?'" he said.

However, he would not tolerate failure. There were penalties.

"Some guys got their fingers broke or their knuckles cracked or maybe had their heads busted," he said. "They hadda learn how to do it the right way the next time."

In the late summer of 1929, Luciano and Masseria had a falling-out over a large shipment of Scotch, worth nearly a million dollars. They met in Luciano's suite in the Barbizon Hotel to discuss the matter as Luciano recalled in his memoir The Last Testament of Lucky Luciano:

"Joe, we got a deal. We shook hands. You're not in the whisky. We shook hands." The repetition was to remind Masseria of the inviolate Sicilian code of the handshake.

"The whisky belongs to me," Masseria shouted as he turned and strode to the door. "And if I want to, I drink it all myself. I break the handshake."

Within minutes after Masseria had departed, Siegel, Torrio and Adonis had joined Luciano and Costello. Lansky and Genovese were summoned, and within a half-hour, the seven sat down to a council of war.

To agree to Masseria's demand did not even merit discussion. Masseria was enraged at the moment, but given a little time, Luciano was certain, he would ease up, at least partially and at least from this open hostility. But Masseria had thrown down a challenge to Luciano and his independence, one he could not completely back away from. Luciano might be able to stall Masseria, but only for a time.

Could Luciano afford an open conflict with Joe the Boss? He was not, at that moment, strong enough, not even in combination with his partners in the Seven Group. They could count on a hundred soldiers; Masseria had perhaps five hundred.

"I noticed that Lansky was pretty quiet. We was like Mutt and Jeff by this time, and I could almost read his mind. So I said to him, 'What're ya thinkin' about, Little Man – Maranzano?' "

Lansky nodded. "That's right. We've all been so busy we've been losin' track of what's really goin' on. This thing between Masseria and Maranzano's gonna bust open any day and there'll be a real war, not the penny-ante stuff. Charlie, we have to pick the winner now, and then go with him."

"There you go again," Siegel said, "always tryin' to beat the odds. What the fuck do you think you are, some guy with a crystal ball? Between Masseria and Maranzano, it's not even six to five. Go ahead, wise guy, you pick the winner."

"I picked the winner a long time ago," Lansky said. "Charlie Luciano. All we have to do is eliminate the two roadblocks and from then on, Charlie sits on top. That's what we want, isn't it?"

Luciano and his friends were convinced they had time to develop their plans, to choose the most propitious moment to put them into operation. Not so Tom Reina, who had come to a similar decision but was certain he had to move rapidly. The word of his meeting with Maranzano had got back to Masseria, he discovered, and knowing Joe the Boss's reaction to any dealings with the enemy, he decided to seek the protection of Maranzano immediately. A few days after the Barbizon confrontation, Luciano received a call from his friend Tommy Lucchese, requesting an urgent meeting at a Turkish bath on upper Broadway where Lucchese had arranged for them to have the privacy of the steam room. Lucchese told Luciano that the switch was imminent. "So now I knew that Maranzano was gonna call Masseria's hand and there was gonna be all-out war.

"I told Tommy to send out the word to Maranzano that I would finally agree to meet with him." To set up the arrangements, Lucchese chose a Maranzano lieutenant named Tony Bender. "He was pretty good at workin' both sides of the street and gettin' away with it." At the beginning of October 1929, Bender brought back the word that Maranzano was agreeable to a conference, to take place on Staten Island, a neutral territory controlled by Joe Profaci, another Maranzano lieutenant but an old friend of Luciano's from childhood. "I agreed to go, on the condition that Maranzano and I would come alone, and that's the way it was set up. I figured that in spite of everythin', Maranzano wanted me with him bad enough so he'd live up to his word."

Just after midnight on 17 October, Genovese picked up Luciano at the Barbizon. "He tried to keep me from goin' alone; he even said he'd like to hide in the back under a blanket, but I told him to forget it." Luciano drove himself to the Staten Island Ferry, rode across, and then went to a shipping pier about a half-mile away.

"Maranzano was already there, waitin' for me. I got out of the car, we shook hands and he put his arm across my shoulder like he always did, and said, 'I'm so glad to see you again, bambino.' We walked inside this big building on the pier. It was empty and dark. We found a couple boxes and sat down. There was a couple minutes of horseshit talk and then Maranzano said, 'Charlie, I want you to come in with me.'

"I said, 'I been thinkin' about it.' "

"'Good, good,' Maranzano replied. "'You know, I always wanted you before and now is a good time for us to shake hands.'"

"'Yeah, I guess it is.'"

"'But tell me, Charlie, why did you make that terrible mistake and go with Giuseppe? He's not your kind. He has no sense of values.'"

"'Yeah, I found that out.'"

"'Now you have thought better of that decision?'"

"'That's why I'm here.'"

"'Good. We will work it out together. It is a delicate matter and we will solve it. As I always said before, you will be the only one next to me. But, Charlie'" – at this point, Luciano remembered, as he reconstructed the events of that night, Maranzano's voice and manner lost their velvet and became sharp and dictatorial. "I have a condition."

"What is it?"

Maranzano stared at him, his eyes flat, his voice emotionless. "You are going to kill Masseria."

This, Luciano thought, was no condition at all, and he said, "Well, I've been thinkin' about that, too."

"No, no, you don't understand, Charlie. I mean you. You, personally, are going to kill Giuseppe Masseria."

That condition, Luciano immediately realized, was a trap. In the tradition-laden Sicilian underworld, one cannot kill the leader personally and then succeed to his throne; the killer cannot expect more than a secondary role in the new hierarchy and more likely he can expect to be killed himself in revenge.

"You're crazy." He had hardly got the words out when something smashed against his skull and he blacked out.

"When I come to, I felt somebody splashin' water in my face, and I was tied up and hangin' by my wrists from a beam over me, with my toes just reachin' the floor. There was some flashlights shinin' at me and I could make out maybe a half-dozen guys with handkerchiefs coverin' their faces, so that I couldn't tell who anybody was." Later, he said he was convinced that Tony Bender was behind one of these masks, though Lucchese told him he was wrong. "I could make out Maranzano. He was standin' near me and didn't say a word. But I could tell what he was thinkin', and I just said, 'I ain't gonna do it.' So he gave a signal and those pricks without the guts to show who they was began to work on me. They did a pretty good job, with belts and clubs and cigarette butts – until I passed out again.

"I don't know how long I was out or when I came to, but this time my hands felt like they was on fire. Because when I looked up I saw that I was practically hangin' by my thumbs." The more Luciano was beaten and tortured, the more stubborn he became, and the more determined that if he survived, which at that moment he very much doubted, he would make certain that Maranzano's days would be short. The beating continued; Maranzano watched silently, occasionally calling a pause as he stepped forward to say, "Charlie, this is so stupid. You can end this now if you will just agree. It is no big thing to kill a man, and you know he is going to die anyway. Why do you have to go through this, Charlie? Why are you so stubborn? All you have to do is kill him, kill him yourself. That you must do, kill him yourself. But, Charlie, I promise you, if you do not do it, then you are dead."

Luciano remembered later that the repetition of Maranzano's demands, the almost ritual aspect of the beating, gave him a sudden spurt of strength and he lashed out with his feet, catching Maranzano in the groin. Maranzano doubled over, fell to the ground, and began to scream with pain and rage: "Kill him! Kill him! Cut him down and kill him!" But before that could be done, Maranzano himself staggered to his feet, grabbed a knife one of his men was holding and slashed Luciano's face, severing the muscles across his right cheek to the bone. Luciano would bear the scars to his death, and would forever have a slightly drooping right eye that gave him a sinister look.

As Maranzano slashed at Luciano again, opening a long gash across his chest, one of the masked assailants took out a gun and aimed it at Luciano. Suddenly Maranzano calmed, snapped, "No! Let him live. He'll do what has to be done or we will see him again."

"Somebody cut me down and I felt like every square inch of me had a knife in it. I couldn't even move. But I never passed out completely. A few of the guys picked me up and threw me into the back of a car and about three or four minutes later they tossed me out on the road like I was a sack of potatoes. I must've laid there for a good fifteen minutes before I could crawl to a little streetlight down the block. It was about two in the mornin'. Then I passed out."

A few minutes later, a police car cruising along Hylan Boulevard in Staten Island spotted Luciano lying in the street, picked him up, and drove him to the hospital. It took fifty-five stitches to close his wounds. "I don't think there was a part of me that didn't have marks or that wasn't covered by bandages." To add to his indignity, the Staten Island police, when Luciano refused to give an explanation of what had happened, booked him on the charge of grand larceny, for the theft of a car. The charge was quickly dismissed.

Until he related this story in 1961, Luciano had never given a satisfactory explanation of that October night. He once told a story, and soon dropped it, that he had been "taken for a ride" by a gang of masked men who had beaten him and then thrown him out on the road in exchange for a promise to pay them 10,000 dollars. In his refusal to talk about that night, rumours spread; that he had been kidnapped by a rival gang at the corner of Broadway and 50th Street, beaten as a warning to stop encroaching on its territory, and then dumped on Staten Island; that he had been seized at that Broadway corner by Maranzano's men and rescued at the Staten Island Ferry by Lansky and Siegel, who found him badly battered and who then left him on Staten Island to create a mystery; that he had been assaulted by federal agents who discovered him waiting for a narcotics or whisky shipment on Staten Island; and that he had been beaten by a cop, the father of a girl he had made pregnant.

All Luciano himself would ever say was, "I'll take care of this in my own way."

Still the rumour spread and was credited by many that he had been taken for a ride and had returned, perhaps the only gangster in history to survive that experience. People began to talk about his good luck, that he was "Lucky" Luciano; the nickname stuck.

As far as Luciano himself was concerned, it was not the press or the world at large that gave him that nickname; it was Meyer Lansky. When he came back from Staten Island, still battered and forced to spend some days in bed in seclusion, Costello and Lansky visited him. To them he related the entire story of the beating. "I guess I'm just lucky to be alive."

"Yeah," Lansky replied, "lucky. That's you – 'Lucky Luciano'."

"Lyin' in bed, I had a little time to think over what happened. For a coupla days I couldn't understand why the fuckin' bastard went to all that trouble and then let me live. Finally, I figured it out, Masseria was guarded like the Philadelphia Mint; nobody could get close to him unless you was part of the outfit. Maranzano knew that because he tried a couple times and come up empty. That meant he had to have somebody close to Joe. So why should Maranzano knock me off when I'm the logical guy he needs? But it was typical of the Sicilian touch of 'Mister Julius Caesar', that if I knocked off Masseria personally, that would be the end of my so-called career as a top man."

Looking back on the event more than thirty years later, Luciano was able to be a little philosophical. "In a way, I don't blame Maranzano, because maybe he knew – or maybe he didn't know – what I was plannin'. But if he did, then he should've killed me. For three days every time I even moved my pinky, it hurt so bad I could hardly stand it. That's the only time in my life I ever took narcotics. Joe A. used to come twice a day and shoot me full of morphine. Whenever I got one of them shots, I'd figure out a new way to bump off Don Salvatore Maranzano."

It was late October before Luciano was ready to leave his suite at the Barbizon. On the 28th, Lansky and Costello stopped by late in the morning, and the three strolled through Central Park in the glow of the Indian summer. They talked about the troubled pregnancy of Lansky's wife, Anna, which was making him distraught. They talked about the stock market, which was sliding faster than the ticker tape could keep track. "None of us guys was in the market. What the hell, we didn't have to be. But Meyer was very interested in what was goin' on and he said, 'If we're smart, we'll hold on to all our cash. When the bottom falls out of the market the whole fuckin' country's gonna need money and they'll pay through the nose for it. We'll have the garment district by the balls; they won't be able to live without us.' "

Costello pointed out that it wasn't just the garment industry that would need them. They would be indispensable to the politicians and the police: "Every one of them idiots has been playin' the market, tryin' to make the big scene. The funny thing is they're all gamblin' with our free money. Yesterday, around noon, Whalen [Police Commissioner Grover Whalen] called me. He was desperate for thirty grand to cover his margin. What could I do? I hadda give it to him. We own him."

Into this talk of national economics and its impact on them, Luciano suddenly brought up the names of Masseria and Maranzano. "Screw them," Lansky said. "Knockin' off Joe and Maranzano is the easiest thing in the world; all we've gotta do is figure it out like Charlie says: make 'em kill each other."

"It was one of the few times I ever heard Lansky really laugh, one that comes up from the belly. He really enjoyed the idea of playin' checkers with two big shots. Even Frank laughed, and for him that was almost unbelievable."

The next day, 29 October, catastrophe overtook the United States. The stock market, which had been falling chaotically every day, crashed carrying with it fortunes and hopes. Fear and despair settled like a shroud over the nation, and it would be years before they lifted. The decade-long boom of the Roaring Twenties was over; the Great Depression had begun.

The world of the bootleggers and the racketeers was not unaffected. "One day, everybody was buyin' cases of booze. And the next day they was glad to have enough dough to buy a pint. Every angle of our business was hit. Like by a tornado. The jewellery heists that Adonis loved didn't mean a thing no more. All them rich broads was out of diamonds; they had everything in hock. Costello's slots still did some business, but it was down to less than half. The only place where we didn't have a drop-off was in Harlem and wherever the numbers was runnin'. The little guy who was sellin' apples still wanted to put a few pennies on a number, prayin' he'd hit somethin', not a big bundle, just somethin'. So what happened was that pennies became the backbone of our dollars, our bread and butter. On the other stuff, we took a bath along with the other losers."

With the crash, Luciano and his friends became convinced that Prohibition would soon die, that repeal was only a matter of time. "The public won't buy it no more," he told his close allies. "When they ain't got nothin' else, they got to have a drink or there's gonna be trouble. And they're gonna want to have that drink legal." It was necessary, they decided, to begin to plan for ways to get into the legal whisky business when that day came. At the same time, they decided to re-examine their whole operation in light of the country's economic crisis, to see if it might be necessary to get out of some rackets and to put extra effort into others.

One thing they knew; they had some time. On the eve of the crash, Luciano had been caught in the middle. His ambitions and his very life had been threatened by both Maranzano and Masseria; both were issuing ultimatums and he could not satisfy both and still live, yet he was determined to satisfy neither. But the pressure now eased, for both the gang lords were too concerned with putting their own businesses into shape in the aftermath of that black week in October, and too busy with their own intensifying rivalry, to devote themselves to the Luciano problem.

In the course of the daily meetings at his apartment, Luciano and his friends realized that in a time of no hope the man who could provide some hope, no matter how ephemeral, some escape, no matter how temporary, would not lack for clients. Such hope could be found in the bottle, in games of chance and in other rackets.

Vito Genovese had another plan to provide the public with escape. Despite Luciano's admonitions, he had not ceased dealing in narcotics. Now he wanted to expand. The profits, he said, were so much greater than in anything else and once a sale was made, the customer was hooked and he had to keep coming back for more. Luciano was just as convinced that narcotics led only to trouble; he knew that from his own experience. "I kept tryin' to argue Vito out of it, but he wouldn't listen. Maybe I should've thrown him out, but you can't just throw a guy like that out cold. Especially not after all the things Vito done for me."

In Genovese, Luciano had a sure gun, and at that moment he needed all the guns he could find, guns that were trustworthy and unquestioning. So he told Genovese, "I don't wanna know nothin' about it. If you wanna do it, do it; anybody you wanna do it with, do it with. But don't tell me about it. I don't want it and I don't wanna know about it. Just remember, Vito, if you get in trouble with that stuff, you'll have to bail yourself out."

If Luciano, then, ruled out narcotics, he ruled, in a bigger way than ever, in favour of the old idea of usury. The bankers were extremely chary about lending what little money they had, and so potential borrowers had to look elsewhere. Elsewhere meant the underworld, which had amassed millions of dollars in cash during Prohibition – for it did little else than cash business. Within a year after the crash, so fast did their shylocking business grow that millions of dollars had been put into the street in the form of usurious loans. With companies failing at a disastrous rate, it became senseless to wreak physical violence on the defaulting borrower. So more and more companies in the garment industry, meat-packing, milk, trucking and other industries vital to the city's economic life began to fall under Mob control, to be used as legitimate fronts for illicit activities.

Luciano himself, in these days, had his money out on the street not merely as a loan shark. As the economic panic worsened, some of his society and Wall Street friends, with no little trepidation, came to him for help, prepared to receive it at exorbitant rates. But since they were friends, Luciano was generous. "I wanted to prove to them guys that even a gangster had a heart and was willin' to help a friend out of a spot. I loaned lots of 'em whatever they needed, and I charged 'em like I was a bank – two or three per cent interest." Some never repaid, and Luciano merely shrugged off the losses.

While loan-sharking preyed on the need to borrow, gambling in its various forms played on the dream of a windfall. The numbers racket took a sudden upsurge beyond the expectations of Luciano, Lansky, Costello and the others; Costello's slots, after a letdown, began to regurgitate a never-ending stream of nickels, dimes and quarters. Betting on everything and anything seemed to be the passion of those who had nothing but hope that a bet would pay off.

The nationwide betting syndicate that had been seeded by Moses Annenberg in Chicago now flourished. If people wanted to bet on horses, they didn't care about going to the track; what they wanted was to place their bets and get the results as soon as possible. A national telephone wire service, which could bring the results into every bookmaking parlour, was necessary. "I always thought of Annenberg as my kind of guy," said Luciano. He had provided Annenberg with the goon squads to seize and hold prime corners in Manhattan when Annenberg, as circulation director at the time for Hearst, had led the *Daily Mirror* into New York to challenge the *Daily News*. "And I used to think of the *Mirror* as my newspaper."

When Annenberg developed the racing wire, Luciano was a prime customer and a prime backer. "The new racin' wire had been worked out with the telephone company; to this day that high-class corporation knows that it's the heart of the biggest gamblin' empire in the world. As far as Annenberg was concerned, he never could've operated without us. He needed us and we needed him. It was a good thing all around."

So, while the nation around him was falling deeper into depression, Luciano's star continued to rise. Even his family was coming at least partially to terms with his activities. "My old man never really changed. I have to be honest, sometimes he knew me better than I knew myself. But he got tired of tryin' to tell my mother that I'd always be in the rackets. To keep peace, he finally learned how to shrug it off. That Christmas of 1929 was the nicest one we had all through the years up to that time. Everybody was together and for the first time I actually sat down to dinner with my whole family and nobody talked about me bein' a truant or gettin' out of the can or nothin'. There wasn't even no mention of the marks on my face, but every once in a while when my mother would walk past where I was sittin' at the table, she'd sort of run her hand over my cheek where Maranzano knifed me and I could see that she was cryin' to herself. Outside of that, it was all very happy and for a fast few hours I almost wished I had a nine-to-five job, like the rest of the crumbs. Then I looked out the window and I seen my Cadillac parked at the kerb and I knew that I'd never give that up."

But moments of calm and a time for major involvement in his own business could not last long. Soon the pressures began to mount. His friend Tommy Lucchese came to see him one day with disturbing news. The negotiations between Reina and Maranzano had reached a climax, and Reina was about to make his move and take Lucchese with him. "This was gonna put us in one lousy spot. Lepke and Lucchese was doin' great in the moneylendin' business and they had a guy with them named Abe Reles who was doin' a lot of the enforcin' for them. And Tommy said if we could put together a big enough kitty – I mean millions in cash – we could control everythin' in the district. So if Tommy's break with Masseria come too soon, it was gonna fuck up the whole combination that I put together in the garment district. Lucchese would be part of Maranzano's outfit and Lepke was still, through me, with Masseria. I told Lucchese to see if he could keep Reina from makin' the move too soon so we could have enough time to set up the garment district with a good foundation."

But there was to be little time. Soon after the new year of 1930 began, Masseria told Luciano he finally had complete proof of Reina's impending treachery; he ordered Luciano to devise a plan to stop Reina. "I have to prove to every punk who's in our outfit," Masseria said, "that there's only one boss in the city of New York and only one head of the brotherhood in America – and that's Don Giuseppe Masseria. If I close my eyes to Reina, then Maranzano will win this war without firing another shot. You must keep Reina with me and I don't care how you do it, but do it."

It was a delicate assignment; Luciano called his friends together to discuss it. They met early in January on a fishing boat off Oyster Bay, Long Island, on a cold, snowy night. Along with Luciano there were Adonis, Costello, Genovese, Siegel and Lucchese. Lansky was unable to attend. His wife, Anna, was seriously ill as a result of her pregnancy; with a premature delivery imminent, she became nearly hysterical whenever Lansky left the house. "How the hell could I ask Meyer to leave Anna? So we went on without him."

The following day, 15 January, Anna Lansky gave birth to a son, who was named Bernard after a favourite Lansky uncle. The delivery was difficult and the child was born a cripple. Anna Lansky suffered a breakdown as a result, seeing the physical defect of her child a Judgment from God on both her and Lansky. Distraught at his wife's outbursts at him and over the birth of a crippled child, Lansky fled from New York in the company of a good friend, Vincent "Jimmy Blue Eyes" Alo, holed up in a Boston hotel for several days drinking himself into oblivion before coming to some kind of terms with his tragedy, and then returned to pick up his life back in New York.

Even without Lansky, the decisions were made. "Tommy Lucchese showed up at last and he brought some very bad news. He'd had dinner with Reina a couple of hours before and he'd learned somethin' that Masseria didn't tell me – that Masseria was plannin' to knock off both Joe Profaci and Joe Bananas [Joseph Bonanno], who was Castellammarese, with Maranzano. If he done that and Reina could be persuaded to stay with Masseria, maybe it would keep everybody else in line. We all agreed then that there was no way to stop the war, and the only thing we should think about was how we could win it.

"That's when we suddenly realized we had to switch our old plans around – that Masseria had to go first instead of Maranzano. Now, when you're dealin' with a Sicilian, you gotta think Sicilian or you ain't got a chance. So I tried to put myself into Masseria's head and figure out why he wanted to keep Reina alive while he was plannin' behind my back to knock off Joe Profaci and Joe Bananas. That's when it got very clear. Masseria would make it look to Maranzano like I had masterminded the hits on those two big shots who was on his side and at the same time I was workin' to keep Reina from goin' over to him. The result would be that Maranzano would come after me with everythin' he had.

"The minute I explained it, Bugsy Siegel said, 'We're always wastin' time. You Italian bastards are forever chewin' it over and chewin' it over until there's not a fuckin' thing to swallow. There's only one way to go – we gotta knock off Reina as soon as possible and Tommy's gotta pass the word on to Maranzano that it was a hit from Masseria. And we gotta make sure nothin' happens to Profaci and Bananas.'

"That's the way we set it up. I picked Vito for the job, with instructions that Reina hadda get it face-to-face, accordin' to the rules. I really hated to knock off Tom Reina, and none of my guys really wanted to neither. Reina was a man of his word, he had culture, and he was a very honourable Italian. He practically ran the Bronx except for what Dutch Schultz was doin' with beer and meat, and he had control of the whole ice racket, which was pretty important when you figure that seventy-five per cent of the city didn't have electric refrigerators and was usin' ice. But he hadda be eliminated so I could keep on livin' and keep on movin' up."

Luciano learned that every Wednesday night, Reina had dinner with an aunt on Sheridan Avenue in the Bronx. On 26 February 1930, Genovese was waiting outside that house about eight o'clock in the evening. When Reina emerged, Genovese called to him. "Vito told me that when Reina saw him he started to smile and wave his hand. When he done that, Vito blew his head off with a shotgun."

The suspicion was immediate and widespread, as Luciano and his friends had hoped, that Masseria had ordered the killing and that it had been carried out by one of his assassins, Joe Catania. Masseria compounded the suspicion when he summoned Reina's top lieutenants – Gaetano "Tom" Gagliano, Tommy Lucchese and Dominic "The Gap" Petrilli – to announce that he was taking over and appointing Joseph Pinzolo as boss of the Reina family interests. "I always thought Masseria was a stupid pig, but I honestly didn't believe that he was that stupid, to expect Reina's top guys to swallow all that. As big a shit as Masseria was, he didn't hold a candle to Pinzolo. That guy was fatter, uglier and dirtier than Masseria was on the worst day when the old bastard didn't take a bath, which was most of the time."

Pinzolo immediately tried to emulate his master in dealing with Reina's lieutenants. Outwardly, they offered few objections, though their dissatisfaction was barely disguised and they carried many of their complaints to Luciano. He was, after all, a close friend to all three, particularly to Lucchese and Petrilli – he had got his nickname, "The Gap", when, as a child, two of his front teeth had been knocked out in a fight. "I sent him to my own dentist on Columbus Circle, and he fixed up the Gap's mouth with a bridge. Girls used to laugh at him and he had a hard time. After that, he become a real ladies' man and from that minute on, if I asked him to jump off a buildin' he would've done it." As Pinzolo became more arrogant, the three lieutenants began to plot his elimination, and in September, Lucchese asked Pinzolo to meet him at an office he maintained on Broadway near Times Square. Lucchese left Pinzolo alone to check out some receipts and, as Lucchese later told Luciano, Petrilli entered and put two shots into Pinzolo's head, right to his face, according to the rules.

"Nobody mourned, not even Masseria. He told me afterwards, 'The hit on Pinzolo was a good thing. Now maybe Lucchese and the rest of them guys will stop squawkin'.' The whole thing was dropped right then and there and Pinzolo didn't even get the regulation funeral."

While the plot against Pinzolo was maturing, Tom Gagliano picked up the negotiations Reina had started with Maranzano. Early in the summer, accompanied by Joe Adonis, he met Joe Profaci at Peter Luger's, a famous Brooklyn steak house. As Luciano was told soon afterwards, "When Adonis, Profaci and Gagliano came out of the restaurant, Maranzano was sittin' in the back of Joe A.'s car with Joe Bananas, waitin' for 'em. That's where and how the deal was made for the Reina family to make a secret switch to Maranzano.

"While this was goin' on, I talked privately to [Albert] Anastasia. I knew I could count on him and I knew he would kill for me. When I told Albert what the plan was, he grabbed me in a bear hug and kissed me on both cheeks. He said, 'Charlie, I been waitin' for this day for at least eight years. You're gonna be on top if I have to kill everybody for you. With you there, that's the only way we can have any peace and make the real money. But I gotta warn you, you gotta get rid of Pete Morello before anybody else – take my word for it; you don't know him like I do – because this guy can smell a bullet before it leaves the gun. You'll never knock off Joe the Boss unless you get Morello outa the way.' "

Pietro "The Clutching Hand" Morello was a veteran gunman and Masseria's constant bodyguard and shadow. His elimination was, indeed, a necessity, and Luciano handed that assignment to Anastasia and Frank Scalise. On 15 August 1930, the two trapped Morello in his loan-sharking office in East Harlem and gunned him down. "There was another guy with him in the office, and he hadda get it too. Later on, I found out that his name was Pariano and he was a collector for Masseria. Albert told me that when he and Scalise walked in, Morello was countin' receipts, and they grabbed the dough after they knocked him off; it come to more than thirty grand."

Unaware of the Luciano–Anastasia involvement, Masseria was convinced that the murder of Morello had been committed at Maranzano's orders and he bought the rumours that the gunman was a hired import from Chicago. He immediately sought revenge, and it was to

Chicago that he turned to exact it. There Masseria was supported by Capone, while Maranzano was receiving both moral and financial support from Capone's bitter enemy, Joseph Aiello. "To make sure the job was done right, Masseria sent Al Mineo to Chicago to handle things." Aiello was machine-gunned to death on a Chicago street. The police blamed Capone mobsters for the killing.

On 5 November 1930, Maranzano retaliated. Three of his gunmen had been holed up in a Bronx apartment overlooking the residence of top Masseria aides in hopes of catching Joe the Boss in a crossfire if and when he paid a visit. That afternoon, Masseria, indeed, showed up, accompanied by his number two and three leaders, Steven Ferrigno and Al Mineo. Maranzano's gunmen opened up, killing both Mineo and Ferrigno. But Masseria still seemed impervious to bullets; he escaped unharmed.

The climax to the Castellammarese War was rapidly approaching. Soldiers on both sides were in hiding, gunning for each other on sight. A climate of fear had been created, diverting time and attention from the real business of the underworld, making money out of the rackets. If the war continued, public attention would focus sharply on the underworld and would lead to a severe crackdown. Once more, Luciano met with his friends at Oyster Bay. This time, Lansky was present. The time had arrived, it was decided, to put their plans into operation. Word was promptly sent to Maranzano that Luciano was now prepared, "for the good of everybody", to do what Maranzano had demanded more than a year before on Staten Island. "I knew the time for this was absolutely perfect. Masseria's luck was holdin' good, and Maranzano couldn't get within a mile of him. He'd have to have me, and nobody else but me, to settle this thing once and for all. If I was gonna negotiate, this was the time to move."

Through Tony Bender, a meeting was arranged. "Maranzano knew goddamn well, after what happened on the pier, I wasn't gonna give him the right time when it come to pickin' the place. I finally made the meet at the Bronx Zoo. I had Tommy Lucchese, Joe A. and Bugsy Siegel with me; I wanted to have a Jew so Maranzano would know he couldn't pull the 'exclusive Sicilian' crap again. He had Joe Profaci and Joe Bananas with him. It was late in the afternoon when we met in front of the lion cage. I said to him, 'I hope you appreciate that the lion is supposed to be the king of the animals.' That done it. Maranzano laughed, and his belly started to shake like jelly. He put his arm around me, but before he could open his mouth, I said, 'Maranzano, there's somethin' I been wantin' to tell you for a long time. My father's the only one who calls me bambino.' Jesus, you might think I hit him. He stopped smilin' and he really got sore.

"He said somethin' like that he couldn't understand why I should resent it, that didn't I understand that he could look on me like his own son. I said, 'After what happened between us last year, I'll never look on you as my old man, so let's stop that horseshit and get down to business. If we work everythin' out, then we'll be friends. That's it.' "

Everything was, indeed, worked out. Maranzano guaranteed the personal safety of Luciano and his friends and followers once the Masseria murder had been accomplished and peace restored. He guaranteed that he would not interfere with Luciano's business or that of Lansky and Siegel, Adonis or Costello. "And he agreed to get rid of all that exclusive Sicilian crap when I pointed out to him that it was crazy and didn't mean a fuck." When the agreement had been struck, Maranzano pointed to Luciano's face and expressed a regret that he had been provoked into doing such a thing. "Never mind. I'm ready to forget it. Let's look ahead," Luciano said.

Maranzano, reverting to his papal attitude, stretched out his hands and placed them on Luciano's shoulders. "Whether you like it or not, Salvatore Lucania, you are my bambino."

Spring had come to New York, and 15 April 1931 was a beautiful warm and sunny day. That morning at nine o'clock, Luciano and Masseria were alone at one of Joe the Boss's headquarters, on lower Second Avenue in downtown Manhattan. Masseria leaned back and listened as Luciano outlined the blueprint for the murder of a score of Maranzano's lieutenants, a bloodletting that would bring complete victory to Masseria. "I must've talked for a couple of hours and old Joe was beamin' and laughin' like he could just taste Maranzano's blood out of a gold cup. Finally, he leaps out of this leather chair about twice as big as he was and he starts to do a dance in the middle of the office. The only time I ever seen anythin' like it was in the newsreels durin' the war when they showed Hitler doin' a dance like that when he beat France. It reminded me of Masseria – two fruitcakes in search of a brain."

About noon, Luciano suggested that, the day being so pleasant, they drive out to Coney Island for a leisurely lunch to celebrate the impending victory. "I could see Masseria's eyes start to shine the minute I mentioned this great food and when I was makin' the arrangements over the phone, I swear I could see the spit droolin' out of his mouth, because I ordered enough food to stuff a horse."

Luciano and Masseria reached the Nuova Villa Tammaro in Coney Island shortly after noon, and the restaurant's owner, a friend of Luciano and many other mobsters, named Gerardo Scarpato, showed them to a table in a corner of the crowded restaurant. Never a big eater, Luciano ate slowly and sparingly, sipping a little red wine. Masseria gorged himself on antipasto, spaghetti with red clam sauce, lobster Fra Diavolo, a quart of Chianti. He was still eating when most of the other diners had departed. He still had ahead of him cream-filled pastry and strong Italian coffee. "It took him about three hours to finish that meal."

Just before three-thirty, the last customers had gone and so had most of the help. Luciano and Masseria were the last patrons. Luciano suggested that they relax for a while and play a game of Klob, a Russian-Hungarian two-handed card game that Masseria had learned from Frank Costello. Masseria hesitated for a moment, then agreed to a short game, reminding Luciano that there was still work to be done back at headquarters. Scarpato brought a deck of cards to the table and then left, saying that he was going for a walk along the beach.

They had played only a single hand, had just dealt the cards for a second, when Luciano got up from the table and told Masseria he had to go to the men's room. Masseria relaxed, enjoying a second bottle of wine.

As soon as the lavatory door closed behind Luciano, the front door of the Villa Tammaro opened. The car that Luciano had driven from Manhattan had been followed at a discreet distance by a black limousine, driven by Ciro Terranova and carrying Vito Genovese, Joe Adonis, Albert Anastasia and Bugsy Siegel. Those four burst into the restaurant, pulled out pistols, and began firing at Joe the Boss. More than twenty shots ricocheted around the room, six smashing directly into Masseria, who slumped over the table, face down, his blood staining the white tablecloth; in his right hand dangled the ace of diamonds.

Even before silence returned, Genovese, Adonis, Anastasia and Siegel were out the door and into the waiting car, its motor still running. But Terranova was so shaken that he was unable to put the car in gear. Siegel pushed him away, took the wheel himself, and sped off. The killing had taken less than a minute; there were no witnesses.

And Luciano? He emerged from the lavatory, took a look at the dead Masseria, called the police, and waited for them to arrive. "When the cops come, naturally they wanted to know whether I seen what happened. I said no, I didn't, and I didn't have no idea why somebody would want to kill Joe. They asked me where I was when it happened – and every newspaper printed that I said, 'As soon as I finished dryin' my hands, I walked out to see what it was all about.' That's an absolute lie. I said to them, 'I was in the can takin' a leak. I always take a long leak.'"

Masseria was given the funeral befitting his status. His body lay in state for some days, and then was followed to the cemetery by cars laden with flowers and limousines filled with mourners. When it was over, Luciano took Genovese aside, the first opportunity that they had to talk about the events at Coney Island. "How did it go?"

Genovese smiled. "The old man would've been proud of it."

A Man of Honour

Giuseppe Bonanno

Giuseppe Bonanno was Salvatore Maranzano's chief of staff during the Castellammarese War. Born in Castellammare del Golfo in Sicily in 1905, he emigrated to the US with his parents when he was one. They settled in Brooklyn. However, when Joe was six, his parents returned to Sicily after the family's business interests were threatened by a rival family. His father and mother died there, while Joe was still young. Orphaned at fifteen, he enrolled in the nautical college in Palermo, but was expelled for anti-Fascist activities. When Mussolini's Prefect Cesare Mori began his crackdown, a warrant was issued for the arrest of Bonanno. He and his cousin Peter Magaddino were forced to flee, arriving in America illegally via Cuba. Back in Brooklyn, Bonanno stayed with his uncle Peter Bonventre, a barber, and went to work for the local Mafia, nominally under the leadership of Nicolo Schiro, where he quickly rose in the ranks. However, at the beginning of the Castellammarese War, Joe "the Boss" Masseria sought to assert himself in Brooklyn. He demanded a $10,000 tribute from Schiro, who paid up and went into hiding to be replaced by Maranzano. Bonanno predicted that, under the guidance of Masseria's chief strategist Pete Morello, Joe the Boss would hit Bonanno's cousin Vito Bonventre, a wealthy bootlegger and the only

Castellammarese rich enough to finance the War. He was gunned down outside his home. While Bonanno remained loyal to Maranzano throughout the Castellammarese War, he sympathized with the American-born "young turks" under Lucky Luciano, realizing that the day of the "Moustache Petes" – as they called the Sicilian-born old-timers – was fast drawing to a close. When the war was over and Maranzano was dead, Bonanno was awarded what was left of Marannzano's crime family and married the sister of Mob boss Frank Labruzzo. He ran what became the Bonanno family – one of the Five Families of New York – until 1969 when he retired to Tucson, Arizona. He died of heart failure at the age of 97 in 2002. Bonanno is thought to be the model for Don Vito Corleone in Mario Puzo's novel The Godfather. *In his own book,* A Man of Honour, *he recalled his involvement in the Castellammarese War.**

Maranzano was ready.

He shunned his home and office. No one, except those closest to him, knew where he would be from one day to the next. He designated several places, most in New York and one in Long Island, as "safe houses" where he and his personal staff would find shelter, food and supplies. No one knew ahead of time in which of these houses Maranzano would spend the night.

Maranzano divided his "army" into squads and designated a leader over each group. Each "soldier" pledged to totally obey his squad leaders. Only these group leaders knew who the other group leaders were and their whereabouts.

He also established an extensive system of supplies. Some people were responsible only for supplying our hideouts with food and equipment. Others were responsible only for delivery of ammunition.

Maranzano and his personal staff rode in armoured cars. These cars, two Cadillacs outfitted especially for us in Detroit, had special metal plates on the sides and bullet-proof windows. Maranzano's Cadillac was always preceded by the other Cadillac. Sometimes a third car would ride behind his car, making it nearly impossible to ambush our leader.

If anyone was foolhardy enough to attack our vehicles, we were more than capable of defending ourselves. We carried pistols, shotguns, machine guns and enough ammunition to fight the Battle of Bull Run all over again.

Maranzano would sit in the back seat of his car with a machine gun mounted on a swivel between his legs. He also packed a Luger and a Colt, as well as his omnipresent dagger behind his back.

Just as the President of the United States has his Secret Service men, the King of England his palace guards and the Pope his Swiss guards, so did Maranzano have his personal bodyguards and staff.

We called ourselves "the boys of the first day" because we were with Maranzano from the start.

During the war, I acted as Maranzano's chief of staff. Needless to say, I didn't attain that position by being a spectator. I had to prove myself by undertaking dangerous missions. Most of the time, people had to go through me first before they could see Maranzano. Maranzano could entrust me with a diplomatic mission, in addition to entrusting me with military assignments. I rode in Maranzano's car, in the front passenger seat.

Maranzano's driver was Charlie DiBenedetto. Charlie had a quick mind and a fluent tongue. Born in America, he was the best English speaker among us. If a policeman stopped our car for some reason, you could count on Charlie to talk his way out of it. Like the rest of us, Charlie could handle a gun without embarrassing himself.

The lead escort car would usually contain Gaspar DiGregorio, Bastiano Domingo and Vincent Danna. Gaspar was a deliberate and fussy soldier, almost the opposite of what he was in normal life. For example, before an engagement, Gaspar would usually take the longest of all of us in selecting a firing position. He would examine and reject several covers before finally choosing one that met his stringent standards concerning line of sight.

Gaspar's snail's pace would usually spur Bastiano to make some wisecrack:

–Whenever you're ready, Gasparino. Take your time. If the rest of us start without you, it doesn't mean we don't like you . . .

Bastiano, or Buster, was the quickest to set up and the best shot among us. He could shoot from any angle and from any direction. His specialty was the machine gun, with which he was a virtuoso.

Vincent we referred to as "Doctor". He and I had been school cronies in Castellammare, where Vincent's father was a pharmacist and his uncle was a doctor. Medical know-how seemed to run in the family. Vincent acted as a sort of medic for us, in addition to being a sharpshooter.

We also had a sixth musketeer among us, Joe Stabile. Joe owned one of the homes we used as a safe house. A sharpshooter extraordinaire, Joe volunteered for many missions. We were all tall, except for Joe, who was short. Once during the pandemonium of a street brawl in which he took part, Joe escaped arrest by crawling between the legs of a cop.

To keep track of enemy movements, Maranzano utilized taxi drivers, among whom he had many friends. Hacks roam the streets at all hours. They make excellent spies.

Within our Family, only a minority were combatants. The majority were non-combatants such as bakers, butchers, undertakers, masons, doctors, lawyers and priests. They all pitched in, helping us out with their special skills. We all saw nothing wrong in us Sicilians settling our differences among ourselves.

In order to chip away at Masseria's support in New York City and elsewhere, Maranzano would stress that the war was not only to defend the honour of Castellammare but also to free everyone else from servitude and slavery to Masseria.

Maranzano's challenge to Masseria soon had its effect on the fence straddlers. In private, Tom Reina of the Bronx expressed admiration for Maranzano, the only one who had the guts to stand up to Joe the Boss. An informant within Reina's Family relayed these sentiments to Reina's *paesano* from Corleone, Peter Morello. And Morello reported it to Masseria.

Early in 1930, Tom Reina was shot to death in the Bronx. As he had done in Detroit, Masseria quickly backed one of his own supporters to take charge of the Family. In this case, Masseria endorsed Joe Pinzolo to become the new Father. In the meantime, Gaetano Gagliano, a member of the Reina Family, formed a splinter group within the Family in open opposition to Masseria and Pinzolo. Gagliano's group attracted Tommy Lucchese, Steve Rondelli, John DiCaro and others.

At the same time that Maranzano was trying to draw defectors from Masseria's side, he also had to extirpate quislings within our own Family.

After Cola Schiro went into hiding, Masseria had supported Joe Parrino to become the new Father of the Castellammarese clan. That tactic failed when we elected Maranzano as our leader. Parrino was a despicable sort. For a chance at becoming Father, Parrino was willing to serve a tyrant. He was also willing to overlook the slaying of his brother, who was shot with Gaspar Milazzo in Detroit. Joe Parrino was shot to death in a restaurant.

The inability of Masseria to gain a foothold in the Castellammarese Family in Brooklyn and the erosion of his influence in the Reina Family were minor setbacks. Masseria still reigned supreme. His chief adviser, Morello, felt so safe that he openly went to his office every morning. The Castellammarese were thought to be in disarray and on the defensive. No one expected them to strike.

Maranzano used to say that if we hoped to win the war we should get at Morello before the old fox stopped following his daily routines, as Maranzano had already stopped doing. Once Morello went undercover, Maranzano would say, the old man could exist forever on a diet of hard bread, cheese and onions. We would never find him.

Morello never got a chance to go on such a severe diet. He went to his Harlem office as usual one morning, along with two of his men. All three were shot to death.

Masseria had lost his best man, the brains of his outfit. "The Clutch Hand" was gone.

At the outbreak of the war, Maranzano had sent Al Capone a message warning him not to meddle directly in the New York conflict. Although Capone had supplied Masseria with money, Capone was too busy fighting Aiello and his supporters to do anything else. Until the end of summer in 1930, therefore, Capone had not sent any reinforcements to Masseria.

After Morello's death, however, Masseria leaned on his allies all the more. In exchange for Capone's more direct help, Masseria went ahead and accepted Capone, the Neapolitan, into our Sicilian orbit.

In September of 1930, Maranzano received a tip that some of Capone's people were to arrive in New York, perhaps as many as a dozen men, reinforcements for

Masseria. They were supposed to rendezvous in an office building on Manhattan's Park Row. We didn't know how reliable the information was, but just to play safe Maranzano prepared a welcome for Capone's men.

The rendezvous was supposed to be held in a spacious office room. A locked door separated this large room from a smaller adjacent room. Maranzano's plan was for me, Bastiano Domingo and Charlie DiBenedetto to hide in the small room and wait for our out-of-town visitors. At the proper time, we were to kick down the door and welcome everyone to the Volcano. We loosened the door hinges ahead of time.

For this mission we needed "fresh" machine guns – weapons that could be abandoned on the spot and not traced to any of us individually.

On the day of the ambush, Charlie went to pick up the machine guns. I waited for him in the park in front of City Hall, which borders Park Row. City Hall is located just about at the entrance to the Manhattan side of the Brooklyn Bridge. After picking up the weapons, Charlie was supposed to pick me up. Buster was going to meet us outside the Park Row building.

It was a Thursday. I remember that because every Thursday a band would play on the park pavilion in front of City Hall. I listened to the band that pleasant afternoon, idly watching the office workers and strollers.

It had been almost a year since the Wall Street stock market crash. The economic boom of the 1920s was over. Prohibition itself had but a short time to run. Franklin Roosevelt was governor of New York and being mentioned as a Democratic candidate to run against President Herbert Hoover. I supposed most people were worried about the hard times ahead.

Uppermost on my mind, however, besides my immediate mission, was winning the war and getting back to my sweetheart, Fay Labruzzo. After not having seen her for nine months, I had impetuously gone to her house late one night. I told Fay how much I had thought of her and declared she had grown lovelier during my absence. Her father wanted to hear all the news about the war. Don Calorio said he would like to meet Maranzano one day. I couldn't take a chance on staying very long . . .

I abandoned my reveries when I saw Charlie's car pull up to the kerb. I dashed to the car, but I had barely opened the door and sat down when I heard the bark of policemen:

–Hold it, you two. You're under arrest.

Since I didn't have a gun permit, the first thing I did was take my pistol off me and stash it under the seat. When I looked up, police detectives had us surrounded.

Buster watched the arrest from across the street but was helpless.

The detectives, as I later found out, were homicide investigators working on a machine-gun slaying unrelated to the Castellammarese War. In the course of their investigation, they had staked out a suspected machine-gun supplier. By coincidence, this was the same man who was getting us our machine guns from Detroit. When the police saw Charlie's car entering and leaving the building, they followed the car to Park Row. When I got in the car, they decided to apprehend both of us. They thought they had stumbled on a lucky break, but they didn't know who we were or what the machine guns were for.

Charlie and I were driven a short distance to New York City police headquarters on Centre Street. Inside the car, police found one pistol, three machine guns and about six hundred rounds of ammunition. At my preliminary interrogation, I told the police that I was listening to the band music at the park on my day off from work. I was about to take the trolley car across the bridge to Brooklyn when I saw my friend Charlie and decided to catch a ride with him.

I was then left alone in a room for about half an hour. Charlie and I had been segregated and I didn't know what was happening to him. I couldn't imagine how the police had found out about the machine guns. Had someone snitched on us? What were the police after? I was in the dark and totally on my own.

Presently, two tall and hefty detectives came in my room and began taunting me:

–Oh, so you're the guy with the machine guns.

I didn't say anything. Without warning and with no trace of emotion, the two policemen began working me over. They punched me, kicked me, kneed my head and threw me on the floor. They struck me repeatedly until I was nearly unconscious. Then they raised me from the floor and flopped my bruised body on the chair next to the solitary table in the room. They left.

Two other detectives entered shortly thereafter. One of them said,

–What's happened here?

He took off my jacket and used it to wipe my blood off the floor. I started to mumble a reply when his colleague grabbed the chair from under me and crashed it across my shoulders and neck. I passed out.

It must have been around midnight when I received my next visit. This time, three detectives entered the room. Two of them didn't say anything. The third did all the talking. He wore eyeglasses.

–I just came on duty, he said, and I'm sorry for what happened. It's not right. If I was here this wouldn't have happened.

He identified himself as a captain. He had a suave, even-tempered manner.

–How do you feel? You want anything?

It hurt to talk. I shook my head sideways, my lips curling derisively.

–It's my duty to question you, the captain with the eyeglasses continued. What I want to know first is your name. What's your name?

–Joseph Bonanno.

–What work do you do?

–I'm learning how to be a barber.

–And where do you live?

–4009 Church Avenue, Brooklyn.

–What's your name?

–Joseph Bonanno.

–You're lying.

–I'm telling the truth.

–So why do you have two names?

The captain was referring to the two licences I carried. One was my driver's licence, which was under the name of Joseph Bonanno. When I went to work for my Uncle Vito Bonventre, the baker, I took out a chauffeur's licence because I had to drive trucks. The chauffeur's licence was under the name Giuseppe Bonventre. The name Bonanno didn't mean anything to the police. However, my distant cousin Vito Bonventre (with the same name as my uncle the baker) was known to the police as a "mafioso" and a leader of the Castellammarese clan in Brooklyn. Since his death was publicized, police also knew that Vito Bonventre had been slain in what they described as gang warfare. The police figured that I was a Bonventre and that Bonanno was an alias. If my name was Bonventre, as they thought, they assumed that I also was mixed up with gang warfare and I could provide the police with valuable information. In nabbing me and Charlie, the police thought they had found a way into the maze of Sicilian warfare current in New York. It seemed like a big break for them.

–My name is Joseph Bonanno.

The Captain looked down on me dubiously. Unknown to me, while I had been unconscious, police had questioned my Uncle Peter Bonventre, whose address, 4009 Church Avenue, was on my driver's licence. Before the war my uncle and I had agreed that if anyone ever asked him who I was he should say I was his apprentice barber.

–What's your uncle's name? the detective said.

–Bonventre.

–Then your name is Bonventre.

–My name is Joseph Bonanno.

The captain said he wanted to help but that my replies were beginning to agitate him.

–How can I help you if you don't co-operate? he said. Don't you realize you could go to prison for a good long time?

The telephone rang. Its shrill jingling seemed to irritate every nerve in my body. The captain answered and mainly listened to the person at the other end. Periodically, the captain would alternately say,

–Ah huh . . .. Right. . . . Ah huh . . .. I see.

He hung up and turned to me.

–You know what that was about? the captain said. That was about your friend Charlie. He's a nice boy, that Charlie. He's going to tell us . . . everything.

The captain circled me, giving me time to absorb this information. Although I didn't know how Charlie was being treated, I had to believe that Charlie was not going to betray me, just as he had to have faith I wouldn't betray him. Silence and trust were virtues inculcated into us by our Tradition. And yet, since we were both young, we had never really been tested. Would we live up to our principles under actual duress?

As it turned out, Charlie was undergoing a somewhat easier test of his manhood than I was. While I was being pummelled unconscious, Charlie was leading police on a wild goose chase.

Charlie, the glib musketeer, had told police he was from Buffalo on a visit to New York City. A friend of his in Brooklyn, Charlie told police, had lent him his car for the day. Charlie said he drove the car to Manhattan, went sightseeing and paid quick visits to several places, including the building being observed by the police. On the way back to Brooklyn, Charlie told police, he noticed a friend in the park at City Hall and stopped to give him a ride.

Charlie swore he didn't know anything about the machine guns that police had found wrapped in a blanket on the floor by the back seat. Those guns must have been there all along. Charlie said when he picked up the car he hadn't even looked at the back seat. The first time he saw the guns, Charlie told the police, was when the police searched the car.

Why don't we go to your friend in Brooklyn? the police told Charlie. Okay, Charlie replied, anything to please the police.

Once they drove to Brooklyn, Charlie pretended to be lost. He said all the apartment buildings in Brooklyn looked alike. And the streets in Brooklyn were confusing. After all, he was from Buffalo. On and on they drove, and around and around, never finding their destination.

I didn't find out about Charlie's escapades until later, of course.

At the time, the captain wanted me to think that Charlie was co-operating with the police. The captain even received a second call about Charlie.

–That was from the Empire Street station, the captain said after the second call. Charlie's taking us to see his friend in Brooklyn. Charlie's a real nice boy. He doesn't want to spend his life in prison. You know what Charlie told us? He told us you know everything. You see, you're ruined.

–I'm tired, captain, I said in my first voluntary statement of the night. I want to say this one last time. My name is Joseph Bonanno, my address is 4009 Church Avenue . . .

Before I could continue the captain mimicked me, saying,

–4009 Church Avenue. 4009 Church Avenue. From now on I'm going to call you Mr 4009.

The captain began pacing. I was weary and becoming defiant.

He was weary and reaching the threshold of his patience. His face looked sterner. Time for him to drop the nice-guy pose. In an angry, loud voice, the captain said:

–Charlie's going to go free and you're going to jail. Do you hear me? We're going to send you away!

I didn't answer, having decided to ignore him from then on. But the captain made it difficult to do that. He suddenly took out his gun and pointed it directly in front of my lips. The man was bluffing, but a nervous twitch of his finger and it would have been all over for me.

–Are you going to talk? the captain demanded, putting the tip of his pistol in my ear.

I had now reached the point where I almost didn't care what happened as long as these police stopped tormenting me. If I was going to die, I told myself, I was going to die without giving my captors any satisfaction.

–Go ahead, I shouted, shoot.

He slammed the butt of his revolver on my nose. On impact, my nose felt as if it were flying across the room while my face was trying to pull it back. My rage made me forget everything but retaliation. I struck with my fist, landing flush in the captain's eye. The lens of his eyeglasses shattered and blood oozed out of his eye socket. After my fist landed, my leg instinctively shot up and I kicked him in the groin.

That's all I remember. The other detectives in the room grabbed me. Everything went black.

In the morning, a lawyer hired by Maranzano came to police headquarters and arranged for Charlie and me to be released on bond. But we had to appear later that same day before a magistrate for a hearing.

Charlie briefly took me to a hospital to have my wounds checked.

My face was puffy and bluish. My broken nose canted to the left.

Our lawyer swore up and down that the police would not get away with it. He said we would have our retribution in court. This sort of thing isn't supposed to happen in America, he assured us.

The late morning papers had already printed a story about our arrest. In the articles, I was identified as Joseph Bonventre, alias Joseph Bonanno. Police had told reporters I was suspected of being a machine-gun runner for Al Capone. At that time, because of all the publicity he had received, the public automatically associated machine guns with Al Capone. The allegation that I worked for Al Capone seemed plausible both to the police and to the naive reporter.

To this day, whenever newspapermen search for something to say about me during Prohibition, they refer to me as a gun runner for Al Capone. And although I've just now explained how this error originated – a ludicrous mistake considering that during the Castellammarese War Al Capone was on the *other* side – I'm certain that long after I'm dead reporters will continue to refer to me as a gun runner for Al Capone.

When Charlie and I showed up at the courtroom later that day, I noticed the captain had a black eye and a bandage over his eyebrow. I recognized several other detectives in the courtroom. They all looked serious but slightly disoriented, as if it was the morning after a night of revelry.

Our lawyer wasted no time in telling the judge that during my detainment the night before, the police had assaulted me.

–Tell the court how this happened, the judge instructed me.

–Your Honour, my lawyer doesn't know the true story. He thinks I was beaten. But what actually happened was that while I was being booked last night I accidentally fell down the stairwell and broke my nose.

The magistrate scowled and snuffled.

I never had any intentions of accusing the detectives in court. It wasn't in me to squeal on anyone, not even a cop. What good would it have done anyway? I think everyone in the courtroom realized I was prevaricating.

After my statement, the prosecution huddled and then the state attorneys had a few words with the detectives. By holding my tongue, I let the prosecution off the hook. Theirs was a weak case to begin with. Instead of a celebrity case, they were stuck with two unknowns, me and Charlie. When they understood I wasn't going to make any trouble for them, they realized my silence was contingent upon them not making trouble for Charlie and me. The prosecutor told the judge he wasn't ready to press charges against us.

This unexpected twist made the magistrate very grumpy. He said we were all wasting his time. He told me he didn't believe my story but there was nothing he could do if I didn't speak up. He was forced to dismiss the case.

This ordeal at the hands of the police was one of my proudest moments. I had remained silent in the face of physical danger. I had not betrayed my friends. I had proven to myself that I would not break under pressure.

What's more, because the newspaper accounts referred to me as a gun runner for Al Capone, everyone in my world knew without doubt that I had kept my mouth shut.

My friends, my relatives, and, most important of all, Maranzano praised my valour. I had lived up to the principles of my Tradition. Charlie DiBenedetto also received praise, but it was fainter than mine. After all, I was the one who got the lumps. Charlie didn't even get scratched.

—One of these days, I would tease Charlie, I'm going to give you the beating you missed.

Charlie called me that "one and only notorious gun runner for Al Capone, Joseph Bonventre".

—You expect anyone to believe your real name is Bonanno? Charlie would say. If I had a name like that, I'd change it too.

He would kid me constantly about my broken nose. He would stare at it, reflect and then say,

—I don't know, Peppino. Maybe I should hit your nose from the other side to make it look even.

Indeed, even after it healed, my nose made me look like a pug, and in 1937 I underwent an operation to straighten it out a bit.

Maranzano rewarded Charlie and me with a little rest and recuperation. He had us check into a private sanatorium in Long Island, where we shared a room. Charlie and I were under orders to behave and to enjoy our vacation. The sanatorium food was lousy, lacking all tang or zest. That's what I remember most about the place. Our therapy, such as it was, consisted mainly of alcohol rubdowns administered by young female attendants.

Stool Pigeon

Joseph Valachi

Another of Salvatore Maranzano's soldiers was Joseph "Joe Cago" Valachi. As a boy, Valachi was known for his ability to build makeshift scooters out of wooden crates. This earned him the nickname Joe Cargo, which was later shortened to Joe Cago. As a youth he had made the mistake of joining an Irish gang. This so displeased the Italian underworld that, while he was serving a prison sentence for theft, he was punished by a knife wound that ran under his heart and around to his back, requiring thirty-eight stitches. He got the message and, after he was released, joined the Mafia, starting as a driver. Then with the Castellammarese War, he got his chance to advance his criminal career. He rented an apartment in Pelham Parkway, overlooking that of Steven Ferrigno, one of Joe the Boss Masseria's lieutenants. It was from there that Ferrigno and Al Mineo, another of Masseria's lieutenants, were shot and killed by a team led by an assassin known simply as "Buster from Chicago". Although he was with the two dead men, Joe the Boss once again escaped unscathed. For his participation in these killings, Valachi was "made" – he became a full member of the Cosa Nostra. He then ran a numbers racket, an illegal "horse room", slot machines and a loan-sharking operation. During the Second World War, he made $200,000 out of *selling gasoline on the black market. In 1960, he was convicted for selling drugs and shared a cell in Atlanta Federal Penitentiary with Vito Genovese. Convinced that Genovese was going to have him killed, he beat another prisoner to death with a length of iron pipe. Then he broke the* omertà *and became the first man to admit to membership of the Cosa Nostra. In 1963, he testified before Senator McClellan's committee investigating organized crime. His testimony on the organization and activities of the Mafia were so detailed that the McClellan hearings became known as the Valachi hearings. Although the US Department of Justice banned the publication of his memoirs, they were used by journalist Peter Maas in his 1968 book* The Valachi Papers. *In 1972, the book was made into a movie of the same name with Charles Bronson playing Valachi. After surviving a suicide attempt in 1966, Valachi died of a heart attack at La Tuna Federal Correctional Institution in Texas in 1971. Until Valachi spoke out, the existence of the Cosa Nostra was a thing of rumour. He explained how, in 1930, after the Ferrigno–Mineo assassination, he was picked up by Frank (Chick) Callace, along with two members of his 1929 burglary gang, Salvatore "Sally Shields" Shillitani and Nick Padovano.*

"Chick said, 'Get ready. We're going on a ninety-mile trip.' He knew the way and did all the driving. Besides me, there was also Sally and Nicky. We were a little nervous and didn't do much talking. We had an idea of what was going to happen.

"I never knew where we were when we got there, but the house was what you would call Colonial style. Anyway, it had two storeys and was painted white, and it was in the country. I don't know whose house it was. What I don't know, I don't know. It was night, and I couldn't make out any other houses nearby. I remember when we went in, Chick took us into a little room on the right. The 'Doc' – that's all I know him by; he was with us for a while at the Pelham Parkway apartment – and Buster from Chicago came right in and started bullshitting with us for a minute about this and that. Then me, Sally, and Nicky were left alone. After a time some guy, I forget who, comes to the door. He waves at me and says, 'Joe, let's go.'

"I follow him into this other room, which was very big. All the furniture was taken out of it except for a table running down the middle of it with chairs all around. The table was about five feet wide and maybe thirty feet long. Now whether it was one table or a lot of tables pushed together, I couldn't tell, because it was covered with white cloth. It was set up for dinner with plates and glasses and everything.

"I'd say about forty guys were sitting at the table, and everybody gets up when I come in. The Castellammarese and those with Tom Gagliano were all mixed up, so they are one. I don't remember everybody. There was Tommy Brown – you know, Tommy Lucchese, I never heard anyone call him 'Three-finger' Brown to his face. There was also Joe Profaci and Joe Bonanno and Joe Palisades – real name Rosato – and Nick Capuzzi and Bobby Doyle and The Gap and Steve Runnelli and others too numerous to mention.

"I was led to the other end of the table past them, and the other guy with me said, 'Joe, meet Don Salvatore Maranzano. He is going to be the boss for all of us throughout the whole trouble we are having.' This was the first time I ever saw him. Gee, he looked just like a banker. You'd never guess in a million years that he was a racketeer.

"Now Mr Maranzano said to everybody around the table, 'This is Joe Cago,' which I must explain is what most of the guys know me by. Then he tells me to sit down in an empty chair on his right. When I sit down, so does the whole table. Someone put a gun and a knife on the table in front of me. I remember the gun was a .38, and the knife was what you would call a dagger. After that, Maranzano motions us up again, and we all hold hands and he says some words in Italian. Then we sit down, and he turns to me, still in Italian, and talks about the gun and the knife. 'This represents that you live by the gun and the knife,' he says, 'and you die by the gun and the knife.' Next he asked me, 'Which finger do you shoot with?'

"I said, 'This one,' and I hold up my right forefinger. I was still wondering what he meant by this when he told me to make a cup of my hands. Then he put a piece of paper in them and lit it with a match and told me to say after him, as I was moving the paper back and forth, 'This is the way I will burn if I betray the secret of this Cosa Nostra.' All of this was in Italian. In English Cosa Nostra would mean 'this thing of ours'. It comes before everything – our blood family, our religion, our country.

"After that Mr Maranzano says, 'This being a time of war, I am going to make it short. Here are the two most important things you have to remember. Drill them into your head. The first is that to betray the secret of Cosa Nostra means death without trial. Second, to violate any member's wife means death without trial. Look at them, admire them, and behave with them.'

"I found out later that this was because sometimes in the old days if a boss fell for a soldier's wife, he would have the poor husband killed, whether she liked it or not. Now I was told that this wasn't an everyday thing, but once is enough. Right?

"Mr Maranzano then says, 'Everybody up. Throw a finger from zero to five.' So all the guys around the table threw out their right hand at the same time: Some of them had no fingers out; some had two or three, the limit, naturally, being five. When all the fingers are out, he starts adding them up. I forget what it was. Let's say they came to forty-eight. So Mr Maranzano starts with the first man on his left and keeps counting around the table, and when he got to forty-eight, it fell on Joe Bonanno, also known as Joe Bananas. When Mr Maranzano saw where the number fell, he started to laugh and said to me, 'Well, Joe, that's your *gombah*' – meaning he was kind of my godfather and was responsible for me.

"So Joe Bananas laughs too, and comes to me and says, 'Give me that finger you shoot with.' I hand him the finger, and he pricks the end of it with a pin and squeezes until the blood comes out.

"When that happens, Mr Maranzano says, 'This blood means that we are now one Family.' In other words, we are all tied up. Then he explains to me how one member would be able to recognize another. If I am with a friend who is a member and I meet another friend who is a member, but the two of them don't know each other, I will say, 'Hello, Jim, meet John. He is a friend of ours.' But like if the third guy is just a friend and not a member, I would say, 'Jim, meet John. He is a friend of mine.'

"Now the ceremony is over, and everybody is smiling. I'd say it took about ten minutes. So I move away and leave the chair for the next man, who was Nicky, and there is the same routine. After him it was Sally's turn.

"Then they take the knife and gun from the table, and Mr Maranzano orders the food to be brought in. I didn't see no women, and I didn't go into the kitchen to look. I figured it was no time to be nosing around. The men around the table who were members brought the food in on big platters. First came the spaghetti *aglio ed olio*. Next there was chicken, different kinds of meat, I think also veal. There was a lot of whisky and bottles of wine in those straw baskets, but nobody was drinking much. During the meal Sally, Nicky, and me, being the new members, talked among ourselves – mostly about how great it was to be in the Mob and how we were going to put all our hearts into the 'trouble'.

"After the coffee Mr Maranzano got up and said, 'We're here together because Joe Masseria has sentenced all the Castellammarese to death. At the same time you other guys started at your end because he had Tommy Reina killed without justice. So now we are all one. We're only a few here, but in a month we'll be four or five hundred. We have to work hard. The odds are against us. The other side has a lot of money, but while they're enjoying themselves, we'll eat bread and onions. You all will be placed in different apartments around the city. We will have spotters out on the street. These spotters will have the telephone number of our main headquarters. Headquarters will have each of your numbers. When a call comes in from the Bronx, for instance, that somebody has been spotted, the apartment we have in the Bronx will get a call. And when that call comes, you have to respond as fast as you can. Each of you new members will be placed with someone who knows what the enemy looks like. Of course, you have been given a picture of Masseria. He's the most important one. I also want to tell you that the business at Pelham Parkway has got them confused. They don't know how we found out about the meet they were having, and that's in our favour. Already they don't know who to trust. We must concentrate on getting their main bosses, and we must get Masseria himself. There will be no deal made with Joe Masseria. The war will go on for ten years if we don't get him.' "

Throughout the rest of 1930 and into 1931, the Castellammarese War raged on, and before the bloodletting was over, some sixty bodies would litter US streets. Although nationwide in scope, the crucial battle was waged in New York City between the Maranzano and

Masseria forces . . . Finally two of Masseria's most trusted sidekicks, Charlie "Lucky" Luciano and Vito Genovese, secretly turned against him. In return for their promise to have Masseria killed, Maranzano agreed to halt the war.

Masseria literally never knew what hit him. He was invited by Luciano to dine one afternoon in a Coney Island restaurant called Scarpato's. From all accounts Joe the Boss, surrounded by trusted aides, had a fine time during the meal – the last one he ever ate.

(Case No. 133 of the 60th Squad, New York Police Department, notes that at about 3.30 p.m. on 15 April 1931, Giuseppe Masseria, also known as Joe the Boss, last known residence, 65 Second Avenue, New York City, while sitting in a restaurant at 2715 West 15th Street, in the Coney Island section of Brooklyn, was shot in the back and head by unknown persons who escaped.)

Thus Salavatore Maranzano, always a shadowy figure as far as the police were concerned, became the undisputed chieftain of the Italian underworld in America. His ascension to power also marked the organization of the modern Cosa Nostra:

"Mr Maranzano called a meeting. I was just notified. I don't remember how, but I was notified. It was held in the Bronx in a big hall around Washington Avenue. The place was packed. There was at least four or five hundred of us jammed in. There were members there I never saw before. I only knew the ones that I was affiliated with during the war. Now there were so many people, so many faces, that I didn't know where they came from.

"We were all standing. There wasn't any room to sit. Religious pictures had been put up on the walls, and there was a crucifix over the platform at one end of the hall where Mr Maranzano was sitting. He had done this so that if outsiders wondered what the meeting was about, they would think we belonged to some kind of holy society.

He was just hanging around, waiting to speak, while the members were still coming in.

"Joe Profaci had given me Mr Maranzano's pedigree. He was born in the village of Castellammare and come over here right after the First World War. He was an educated man. He had studied for the priesthood in the old country, and I understand he spoke seven languages. I didn't know until later that he was a nut about Julius Caesar and even had a room in his house full of nothing but books about him. That's where he got the idea for the new organization.

"Mr Maranzano started off the meeting by explaining how Joe the Boss was always shaking down members right and left. He told how he had sentenced all the Castellammarese to death without cause, and he mentioned the names of a half dozen other members and bosses who had suffered the same thing.

"Well, some of these names I didn't know or never ever heard of, but everybody gave him a big hand. He was speaking in Italian, and he said, 'Now it's going to be different.' In the new setup he was going to be the *Capo di tutti Capi*, meaning the 'Boss of all Bosses'. He said that from here on we were going to be divided up into new Families. Each Family would have a boss and an underboss. Beneath them there would also be lieutenants, or *caporégimes*. To us regular members, which were soldiers, he said, 'You will each be assigned to a lieutenant. When you learn who he is, you will meet all the other men in your crew.'

"Then he tells us how we are going to operate, like if a soldier has the need to see his boss, he has to go first to his lieutenant. If it is important enough, the lieutenant will arrange the appointment. In other words, a soldier ain't allowed to go running all the time to his boss. The idea is to keep everything businesslike and in line.

"Next he goes over the other rules. The organization, this Cosa Nostra, comes first, above everything, no matter what. Of course we already know that death is the penalty for talking about the Cosa Nostra or violating another member's wife, but he goes over it again anyway. He tells us now that death is the penalty for telling wives anything about the outfit and also that an order going from a boss to a lieutenant to a soldier must be obeyed or you die.

"Now there are other rules where death ain't the penalty. Instead, you are 'on the carpet' – meaning you have done wrong and there is a hearing to decide your case. The most important one is that you can't put your hands in anger on another member. This is to keep one thing from leading to another. Remember, we are just getting over our trouble, and that's what Mr Maranzano talked about next.

" 'Whatever happened in the past is over,' he says. 'There is to be no more ill feeling among us. If you lost someone in this past war of ours, you must forgive and forget. If your own brother was killed, don't try to find out who did it to get even. If you do, you pay with your life.' "

The table of organization set forth by Maranzano was subsequently adopted by Cosa Nostra Families across the country. And out of this meeting came the five-Family structure in New York City, which still exists. The five bosses initially named by Maranzano to head them were Luciano, Tom Gagliano, Joseph Profaci, Joseph Bonanno, and Vincent Mangano. Valachi can recall only three of the underbosses selected at that time – Vito Genovese in the Luciano Family, Albert Anastasia in the Mangano Family, and Thomas Lucchese in the Gagliano Family. Valachi himself elected to join Maranzano's personal palace guard even though he had entered the Cosa Nostra under the auspices of what was now the Gagliano Family.

The switch, he says, came on impulse. At the meeting Maranzano had announced, "As for those members who have been with me, there is going to be a split. Some of the group will go back to Tom Gagliano, and some will remain with me. If there is anybody who wants to remain with me, whether he was with me before or whether he was not, as long as he was with me during the war, he is entitled to come with me now if he wants to. The ones who want to come with me, just raise your hands."

Annoyed because Gagliano had made no effort to recruit him privately, Valachi, as he puts it, "unconsciously" raised his hand. Then he saw two other Gagliano men, Bobby Doyle and Steve Runnelli, also raise their hands. Almost at once he regretted his move because of his unhappy experience with Runnelli in the Gambino shooting. But when Thomas Lucchese immediately tried to persuade him to change his mind and remain with Gagliano, he felt that to do so now entailed too much loss of face. "Why did you do what you did?" Lucchese demanded.

"Well, you didn't tip me off. I figured I wasn't wanted."

"Let's go see the old man and tell him you made a mistake."

"No," Valachi replied. "It's too late. I won't do anything. I would be ashamed of myself."

On the plus side, however, he could comfort himself with the thought that he would be with Buster from Chicago and that he was at least rid of Salvatore Shillitani, who had decided to remain with Gagliano. Whatever other doubts Valachi might have had disappeared in the excitement of a huge banquet held in Brooklyn to honour Maranzano – in spirit and in cash. As a sign of their obeisance Cosa Nostra bosses throughout the United States purchased tickets to the affair. Even Al Capone sent $6,000. In all, according to Valachi, about $115,000 was collected. As representatives of various Families arrived at the banquet, each threw his contribution on a table. "I never saw such a pile of money in my life," Valachi recalls. Afterwards he began rotating on duty with Maranzano as a chauffeur and bodyguard. But tranquillity in Maranzano's reign was short-lived:

"Mr Maranzano's legitimate front was a real estate company. The offices were in the Grand Central Building at 46th Street and Park Avenue. Around six months after Joe the Boss got his – that makes it around the first part of September – he ordered us not to go into the offices carrying guns, as he had been warned to expect a police raid.

"I didn't like that order. One of the other fellows, I think it was Buster, said, 'What do you mean?'

" 'I don't know,' I said. 'I just don't like the idea. If something happens, we are helpless.'

"He said, 'Talk to the old man about it.'

"Well, I was biding my time to do it, but I was waiting for the right moment. Mr Maranzano wasn't somebody you just started telling what to do. Anyway, a couple of days later I was in the office, and he told me to come by his house in Brooklyn that night. It was on Avenue J, I don't remember the number.

"I got there about nine o'clock. When I went into the living room, he was bent over bandaging a cut on the foot of his youngest son. I'd say the kid was around eight. Mr Maranzano got right to the point. 'Joe,' he said, 'I hear you're wondering why you didn't get a bigger piece of the take from the banquet.' He was right. All I was getting was my expenses and maybe $100 a week. To tell the truth, I was doing a little burglarizing on the side.

"He goes on to say, 'Don't worry. You'll get your share, and more. But we are holding on to the money right now because we have to go on the mattress again.' In other words, he is telling me we have to go back to war. You see, during the Castellammarese trouble we had to take mattresses with us as we were moving from one apartment to another. Sometimes we only had a minute's notice, and so you needed a mattress to sleep on. That is our meaning of going on the mattress.

"I'm still listening as he explains why. He said, 'I can't get along with those two guys' – he was talking about Charlie Lucky and Vito Genovese – 'and we got to get rid of them before we can control anything.' He talked about some others who had to go too – like Al Capone, Frank Costello, Willie Moretti from Fort Lee, New Jersey, Joe Adonis, and Charlie Lucky's friend from outside the Cosa Nostra, Dutch Schultz.

"By controlling things, he meant the Italian lottery, which was very big then, the building unions, bootlegging, bookmaking, all that kind of stuff. Dutch Schultz, who was a Jew boss, had the biggest numbers bank in New York, and Charlie Lucky ran the downtown lottery.

"Gee, I wanted to say, who wants to control everything? You got to remember it's just a few months since we are at peace. All I wanted was to make a good living. But naturally, I dared not say anything.

"Then Mr Maranzano tells me that he is having one last meeting the next day at two o'clock with Charlie Lucky and Vito. This is my chance to bring up the thing about no guns. 'Gee,' I said, 'this is no time to be putting yourself in jeopardy. Suppose those guys know something's in the wind?' Well, he's talking so much about what we are going to do and how big we are going to be, that he don't pay much attention, but finally he tells me, 'All right, call the office at a quarter to two to see if I need you.'

"I went home and spent the night tossing and turning. I got all kinds of reasons to worry. If something happens to Mr Maranzano, I'm finished too. I ain't happy, but I got to go along. All I can do is wait to check in. That afternoon I called the office and this guy Charlie Buffalo, who is one of the members with us, answered the phone and said that everything was fine and that I don't have to go down there. Right after that The Gap comes by – he had stayed with Gagliano, which is another reason why I should have –

and says, 'Hey, I've been looking for you. I got a couple of new girls over in Brooklyn. Let's go over and spend some time with them.'

"I said, 'Good idea. I have nothing to do.' So we went over to Brooklyn and fooled around with the girls until about midnight, and the four of us decided to come back to Manhattan to eat. We went to this restaurant Charley Jones had on Third Avenue and 14th Street. When we are in the restaurant, I notice something funny is going on. First one guy, and then another, is walking in and looking us over. I said to The Gap, 'Do you see what I see?' He says, 'Yes, I don't know what it's about.' Now I go over to Charley Jones. He is no Mob guy, but he has connections and knows a lot. He whispers, 'Joe, go home.'

"That's all I have to hear. I said to The Gap, 'What do you think?' and he says, 'We'll break it up.' So we gave the girls money to get back to Brooklyn. The Gap stayed with Charley, and I drove home alone. On the way up Lexington Avenue I stopped for a newspaper. I just put it down beside me on the seat. I was driving very slow and thinking. I just could not figure out what was going on. It's hard to explain – I was worried, and I did not know what I was worried about. When I got home, I sent my kid brother out to put the car in the garage. Then I sat down in a chair and opened up the paper, and there it was. All about how the old man had been killed in his Park Avenue office that afternoon.

"The story had said that some men pretending to be detectives walked into Mr Maranzano's outer office – it was kind of a waiting room – and lined up everyone who was there against the wall. Then two of the fake detectives went inside, where they shot him and cut his throat. The first thing I remembered was Mr Maranzano telling us not to carry guns in the office as there might be a police raid. Then I read that when the real bulls came, they found

Bobby Doyle kneeling by the old man and had pulled him in as a material witness.

"Now I tell myself no wonder The Gap took me to Brooklyn. He must have known all about it and kept me out of the neighbourhood. You can imagine how I felt."

The murder of Maranzano was part of an intricate, painstakingly executed mass extermination engineered by the same dapper, soft-spoken, cold-eyed Charlie "Lucky" Luciano who had so neatly arranged the removal of Masseria just months before. On the day Maranzano died, some forty Cosa Nostra leaders allied with him were slain across the country, practically all of them Italian-born old-timers eliminated by a younger generation making its bid for power.

Valachi immediately went into hiding ... Doyle was finally released from custody after the Maranzano murder:

"All this time I am waiting for Bobby to come out, and now I find out what happened in the Park Avenue office. He explained to me that they were all sitting around in the outer office when these four Jews walk in and flash badges. I think one was with Dutch Schultz, but the others were really Meyer Lansky's boys. Charlie Lucky could use them because his Family had sided with Lansky in his Jew war with Waxy Gordon. Anyway, Bobby said that what with all the yelling, the old man stuck his head out of the inner office to see what was going on, and one of the fake bulls says, 'Who can we talk to?' and the old man says, 'You can talk to me.' So two of them go in with him, and the other two keep an eye on the crowd.

"A long time after this I met one of the boys who went in with the old man. I met him at a racetrack. His name was Red Levine. I said, 'I heard you were up there.' Levine said, 'Yes, I was there. He was tough.' He told me the idea was to use a knife, so there wasn't any noise, but the old man started fighting back, and they had to use a gun first.

"Naturally Bobby Doyle don't know nothing about this as he was in the waiting room. All he knows is he hears a couple of shots, and this Levine and the other Jew boy come running out and tell everybody to beat it. But Bobby says he ran in to see if the old man still had a chance. That's how come the cops picked him up."

(New York City police records show that at 2.50 p.m. on 10 September 1931 one Salvatore Maranzano, male, white, of 2706 Avenue J, Brooklyn, was shot and stabbed to death in the office of the Eagle Building Corporation, rooms 925 and 926, at 230 Park Avenue. Perpetrators were four unknown men posing as police officers. Cause of death: four gunshot wounds and six stab wounds.)

After the initial purge of the Maranzano "faithful", the massive bloodletting that had racked the Cosa Nostra was largely curbed. Indeed, according to Valachi, Luciano moved swiftly to reduce the special tensions that existed in the New York area by establishing *consiglieri*, or councillors, six men in all, one from each of the five New York Families, and the sixth representing nearby Newark; the function of the councillors was to shield individual soldiers from the personal vengeance of various lieutenants who might have been their targets during the Castellammarese War. The councillors, Luciano declared, had to hear the precise charge against a particular soldier before his death was authorized. If there was a tie vote, any one boss could sit in and break it. While the councillors were as often as not ignored, their formation at least projected an aura of the stability Luciano was bent on achieving.

Luciano also abolished the position of Boss of all Bosses, so dear to Maranzano's heart; the fact of his power was infinitely more important to him than its formal trappings. And the organization of his own Family symbolized, to the naked eye at any rate, the final breakdown of the old Neapolitan versus Sicilian hostility. Luciano came from

Sicily; his number two man, Genovese, was born in Naples. But most important by far was the way Luciano revolutionized the scope and influence of the Cosa Nostra in the US underworld. Shrewd, imaginative, and, above all, pragmatic, he abandoned the traditional clannishness of his predecessors and joined in co-operative ventures with such non-Italian criminal associates as Dutch Schultz, Louis (Lepke) Buchalter, Meyer Lansky, and Abner (Longy) Zwillman. At the same time, however, he carefully maintained the identity of the Cosa Nostra since, for Luciano, peaceful co-existence was merely a step towards total domination of organized crime.

None the less, to consolidate his power base, Luciano immediately had to justify his elimination of Maranzano to Cosa Nostra kingpins elsewhere in the country. "When a boss gets hit," Valachi notes, "you got to explain to the others why it was done." And to his amazement Valachi was told by Genovese that Charlie Lucky desired him to testify personally against Maranzano in Chicago, where Capone, although on the verge of being imprisoned for income tax evasion, was still a force to be reckoned with.

"Why me?" Valachi asked.

"First, because you are known to be close to the old man," Genovese said. "And second, by being one of his soldiers, you gained nothing when he went. So why should you lie?"

Valachi begged off on the ground that he wasn't eloquent enough for such a delicate chore and suggested that a more experienced member, like Bobby Doyle, be sent instead. Actually the battle-weary Valachi, ever cautious, feared that this sort of assignment held unforeseen perils should some new coup be in the making. However ill-founded his misgivings were, he made his point. Genovese agreed, and Doyle, delighted at the status he would gain from the trip, was dispatched to appear before, as Valachi describes them, "our friends in Chicago".

Soon afterward Valachi, in partnership with Doyle, received his first tangible benefit as a member of the Luciano Family. Frank Costello, then a wily Luciano lieutenant, had long since forsaken muscle for political influence to advance his career. New York City was ideal for Costello in those days. Under the dubious reign of Mayor James J. Walker, he had "opened up" the town for slot machines and ran their operation.

Valachi and Doyle approached their own lieutenant, Tony Bender, and asked if there was a chance for them to have a "few machines". Bender took them to the offices of a scrap company on Thompson Street in Greenwich Village which Vito Genovese used as his legitimate front. It happened to be a day when Luciano was present. When the door to the inner office was opened, Valachi suddenly felt himself being pushed in by Bender while Doyle, apparently suffering an acute case of cold feet, stayed outside. Luciano, in the grand manner, spoke not to Valachi, but to Bender: "What's he want?"

"He wants some machines."

As Valachi waited, nervously silent in the great man's presence, he finally heard Luciano say, "Okay, give him twenty."

This did not mean actual machines; Valachi and Doyle would have to finance that themselves. It signified that Valachi was entitled to twenty stickers supplied by Costello. In theory, while slot machines were nominally illegal, any enterprising soul could install one in the rear of a candy store, a pool hall, and so forth. In fact, if a machine did not have a Costello sticker, the colour of which was periodically changed, it was immediately subject to not only Mob action, but police seizure. Once, according to Valachi, a patrolman walking his beat in a Manhattan neighbourhood dumped, for whatever reason, a bottle of catsup down a "protected" machine and was promptly transferred to the far reaches of

Queen's. "Now," Valachi reflects, "it don't take too much to figure who had him sent out there."

It was up to Valachi to place his own machines. He selected the area most familiar to him, East Harlem, and he and Doyle, as soon as they had them suitably installed, were grossing about $2,500 a week. Valachi hired the brother of his former fence, Fats West, to service the machines and pick up the money. Occasionally Valachi would play one of them himself, doubling or tripling its normal take to see if the extra amount was returned to him. Fortunately for young West's health, he turned out to be an honest man.

Valachi derived just as much pleasure, if not profit, from being "recognized as a Mob guy" with connections. His first opportunity along these lines came when old Alessandro Vollero was paroled from Sing Sing after serving fourteen years for the murder of Giro Terranova's brother. [According to Sing Sing records, Vollero was released on 28 April 1933.] Vollero, fearful that Terranova would seek revenge, sent an emissary begging Valachi's help. "The old guy don't know nobody now," the emissary said, "but he hears you're with Vito and them others. Can you straighten things out for him?"

Valachi remembered Vollero with fondness, promised to see what he could do, and discussed the matter with Vito Genovese. At first Genovese was reluctant to get involved in such ancient history – "When the hell did this happen, twenty years ago?" – but eventually he reported that Vollero could stop worrying. When Valachi relayed the good news, nothing less would do than for him to come to Vollero's house for dinner. "It was really something," Valachi says. "He had the whole family lined up to greet me. He called me his saviour. Well, we ate, and it was the last time I saw him. I heard later he went back to Italy and died in peace."

★   ★   ★

Now twenty-six years old, newly affluent and respected, Valachi was ready to get married. His affair with his dance-hall mistress, May, had continued, but he discovered she had been unfaithful to him during his frequent absences in the Castellammarese War. "I told her that I'd stay on with her for a while," he says, "but she could forget about anything permanent."

True love began to bloom for him when he was hiding out in the Reina household and met the dead racketeer's eldest daughter, Mildred. Then twenty-two, she would come up to the attic each afternoon to keep him company. And once out of hiding, he became a frequent visitor in the Reina home. But Mildred's mother, brother, and uncles, as soon as they realized what was happening, did not cotton at all to the idea of Valachi as a prospective bridegroom. Romeo and Juliet had nothing on the tribulations endured by Joseph and Mildred. Before it was all resolved, their romance featured a foiled elopement, an attempted suicide, and, finally, the intervention of Vito Genovese himself:

"When I was in the attic, Mildred would come up the steps through sort of a trapdoor and talk to me. She told me that she had heard a lot about me. I asked her who it was that told her, and she said Charley Scoop, who was a guy I used to sell dresses to when I was out stealing.

"Then after everything was straightened out with Vito about the Maranzano business, I was invited back to the house for supper by her brother. I accepted and brought Johnny D along with me. All through supper Johnny kept kicking me under the table and whispering that Mildred is nuts about me and can't help showing it. When we left, I told Johnny that Mildred was a beautiful girl, all right, but her family looked pretty strict to me, and I better not get mixed up with them. Anyway I figured I didn't know how to act around her as I was only used to hanging around with dancehall girls. I was going to forget the whole thing, but this idea of finally settling down began to get to me. I tried going out with some of the nice girls in the neighbourhood. It didn't work. They all looked bad next to Mildred.

"A couple of days later Bobby Doyle and me started talking about her somehow. Bobby knew the family pretty good. He even knew the old man before Masseria had him killed. Bobby told me that his wife, Lena, was saying that Mildred liked me a lot. 'Oh,' I said, 'Mildred is okay, but that mother she's got is a tough woman, and I think the brother is like the mother. I don't even want to think about her uncles.'

" 'What are you worrying about them for?' Bobby said. 'It's what the girl says that counts.' I said I don't know. After all, my people are from Naples, and they are Sicilian.

"Well, after one thing and another, Bobby's wife tells me that Mildred wants me to speak to her brother about us. I said I wouldn't. Finally Lena says that Mildred is willing to take off with me. By that she means that Mildred was ready to leave home to marry me. At this time I was living at 335 East 108th Street. The building had just been done over, and it had steam heat and hot water, and we had four rooms, so it was a place to stay for a while. I asked Lena how I would know when Mildred was home alone, and she says leave everything to her.

"When she gives me the word, I head for Mildred's home. She is all packed and ready to go, but then her sister Rose says that she has to go, too, or they'll beat her to death. After I heard this, I told Mildred to unpack. I said, 'Okay, I'll talk to your brother.'

"I was amazed when her brother said that it was all right by him to marry her. But the next thing I hear is that Mildred's in the hospital. She had swallowed a bottle of iodine. I found out why. Her brother told her that I didn't want anything to do with her. So now I know how they work. Her brother says okay to me and tells her just the opposite. Lena told me not to go up to the house, as there was a big commotion going on there. I told her maybe I better drop the whole thing, but she says, 'A fine guy you are. Here she's taken iodine for you, and you're talking this way.'

"Well, I went down to see Vito at his office on Thompson Street next to that junkyard he owned and explained the whole mess to him. He told me he would pass the word around that he wants to see Mildred's uncles about it. 'Don't worry,' he said. 'I know what to tell them.'

" 'Will you let me know what happens?' I asked.

" 'Of course,' he said. 'In the meantime, go about your own business and let me handle it. Don't get into an argument with any of them. Don't blow your top, as that's just what they're looking for you to do. I know those girls. They were brought up like birds in a cage. They've never been anywhere. The only place they let them go alone is to a neighbourhood show.'

"In a couple of days Vito called me and said that the Sicilians, meaning Mildred's uncles, had been down. He said he told them that they should keep their noses out of this matter. If they are fit to marry their wives, Joe is fit to marry Mildred. If Joe ain't fit, none of us are fit. Besides, he says, just so they know how he feels about it, he told them that he wants to be my best man. He told them that Charlie knows about it and feels the same way. By Charlie, of course, he meant Charlie Lucky.

"Then Vito said to me, 'I'll do even better for you. I'll go up to the house and talk to the mother. Make an appointment for me.' So I did, and Vito went up there and told her that he took full responsibility for me. That settled it, but the old lady still wasn't ready to make things any too easy. Mildred and me would have to wait six months before the engagement could be announced. She couldn't go out alone with me, and the only place I would be allowed to see her was at home and only on Sunday.

"To tell the truth, I almost gave up. When I would go up there on Sundays, Mildred and me would never have a chance to be by ourselves. After eating, all we could do was just sit there and talk. The old lady or the brother was always around. If Mildred and me got too close sitting on the sofa, they always had some phoney excuse to call her out of the room. I don't know how I lasted until the engagement party. That's when the wedding was set for 18 September 1932. Between the time of our engagement and the wedding, it was the same Sunday business, only now Mildred and her sister Rose were busy lining up bridesmaids, buying clothes, looking at apartments, and all that kind of stuff. Naturally, I was busy taking care of my slot machines.

"The party after the wedding was at the Palm Gardens on 52nd Street, right off Broadway. It was very large and cost close to $1,000 just for the hall. That was big money in them days; you must remember there were a lot of people in the streets selling apples. I got two bands so that everybody could dance without stopping. For food we had thousands of sandwiches and about $500 worth of Italian cookies and pastries. There was plenty of wine and whisky, even though it was Prohibition. I also got twenty-five barrels of beer as a present from one of the boys.

"Now this was when the Maranzano killing and all the trouble before that was still in everybody's mind. There was a lot of friction right under the surface, so I had to weigh the invitations very carefully. But I must say it was a hell of a turnout of people either coming or sending money.

"Vito Genovese couldn't make it to the wedding – I forget why – so he had Tony Bender represent him. But he made it to the party. Tom Gagliano and Tommy Brown were there. Charlie Lucky sent an envelope. Willie Moore,

Frank Costello, Joe Bonanno, and Joe Profaci also sent envelopes. The Raos came in person. Doe from the old group that used to be with Mr Maranzano came, but Buster was dead by this time. Albert Anastasia and Carlo Gambino were there. So was Vincent Mangano, who was a boss then, but now has been missing for a long time. Joe Adonis sent an envelope. John the Bug came. So did Bobby Doyle, Tommy Rye, Frank Livorsi, Joe Bruno, Willie Moore's brother Jerry, Johnny D, Petey Muggins, naturally The Gap, Mike Miranda, and all the boys with Tony Bender, which was my crew. It's impossible to remember everybody's name, but the hall was full.

"After all the expenses of renting an apartment and buying the furniture, even an Oriental rug, we had about $3,800 left over from the envelopes of money we got. The only thing wrong was that the apartment Mildred picked was on Briggs Avenue in the Bronx near Mosholu Parkway – in other words, just a stone's throw from her mother."

Despite this romantic interlude, it was back to business as usual. Soon after his marriage to Mildred, Valachi was handed his first contract to kill since joining the Luciano Family. In the Cosa Nostra a soldier like Valachi was not paid for such an execution; it was simply part of his job. He did not know the victim and was only vaguely aware of the reasons why he had to die. His lieutenant, Tony Bender, relayed the order. The information was fragmentary. The marked man was known as Little Apples, and Valachi never did learn his real name. Bender said that he was about twenty-two years old and frequented a coffee shop on East 109th Street. Bender mentioned in passing that two brothers of Little Apples had tangled with Luciano and Genovese several years before and were slain as a result. Apparently there was some concern that he would now attempt to avenge their deaths. Valachi did not press Bender for details; he really could not have cared less.

When a soldier is given a contract, he is responsible for its success. He can, however, pick other members to help him carry it out. Valachi chose Petey Muggins and Johnny D, both of whom joined the Luciano Family at the same time he did. Then he began hanging out in the coffee shop and eventually struck up an acquaintance with Little Apples. During the next two or three days Valachi would drop in periodically for coffee and more conversation with him. Meanwhile, he scouted out various locations for the killing and finally settled on a tenement a block away on East 110th Street. For Valachi's purpose it was ideal. The ground floor was unoccupied, and there was no backyard fence to hinder a quick exit. His plan was first to station Muggins and Johnny D in the hallway and then to lure Little Apples to the tenement on the pretext that a crap game was going on in an upstairs apartment.

On the night of the hit, Valachi had arranged to meet Little Apples in the coffee shop. "Hey," he said, "let's take a walk. I hear there's a big game going on up the street."

"Great! I got nothing else to do."

According to Valachi, he positioned himself behind Little Apples as they were entering the tenement and suddenly wheeled away. "I heard the shots," he says, "and naturally kept walking down the street."

(New York police records reveal that about 9.20 p.m. on 25 November 1932, a male, white, identified as one Michael Reggione, alias Little Apples, was found in the hallway of 340 East 110th Street. Cause of death: three gunshot wounds in the head.)

Valachi went straight home. "After all," he recalls, "I was just married a couple of months, and I didn't want Mildred to think I was already starting to fool around."

General Mafia

Don Calogero Vizzini

On the night of 9 July 1943, the first of 160,000 Allied troops began landing on the southwest beaches of Sicily. After nearly a full week of fighting that yielded the city of Syracuse and not much more, General George S. Patton was given the task of advancing towards the city of Palermo. The Americans had to travel almost a hundred miles of heavily mined, single-lane highway and some 60,000 Italian troops stood in the way. Yet Patton's men reached Palermo in just four days, with hardly a shot being fired. This lightning strike established General Patton's reputation as America's greatest general of World War II. It was, he said "the fastest blitzkrieg in history" and certainly the least costly. After breaking out of the beachhead, the casualties the Seventh Army suffered were negligible. All this was achieved with the help of the Mafia.

While the British and Canadian forces fought their way doggedly up the east coast of the island, facing an ill-equipped but determined enemy, the Americans had been assigned what seemed to be an even stiffer assignment. They were to take and subdue the central mountainous region. The key point in the German and Italian defensive line was the Mount Cammarata, just west of the towns of Villalba and Mussomelli. There was a mixed brigade of motorized artillery, anti-aircraft guns and 88mm anti-tank guns, plus a squadron of German panzers, including the latest Tiger tanks. The mountain caves and craggy outcrops had been used as a redoubt against invaders since Roman times and it dominated the two roads the Americans must pass down to reach Palermo. In command of the defence force was Lieutenant-Colonel Salemi, who was pessimistic about holding back the Americans, due to lack of air cover. But he was confident that he could delay the advance and make it very costly.

On 14 July 1943, a small American army plane was seen flying low over the small town of Villalba. The plane trailed a yellow banner with a large, black "L" on it. The pilot dropped a nylon bag containing a handkerchief in the same yellow material carrying the same initial "L". It fell near the house of the village priest, Monsignor Giovanni Vizzini, brother of the local Mafia boss. It was picked up by Private Raniero Nuzzolese, an Italian soldier from Bari, who handed it over to Lance-Corporal Angelo Riccioli of the Carabinieri, then stationed in Villalba.

The next day, the plane returned and dropped another bag near the home of Don Calogero Vizzini. This time it had the words *Zu Calò* – "Uncle Calò" – written on it. The bag was picked up by Carmelo Bartolomeo, a servant in the Vizzini household, who delivered it to Don Calò, its intended recipient.

Don Calò was then one of the most powerful Mafia bosses in Sicily, some said the *capo di tutti capi*. Once a lowly Mafioso, Don Calò had established his fortune in 1922, before the Fascists came to power, when he led a band of disgruntled peasants who grabbed land from the absentee landlords. Every peasant got a plot, but Don Calò kept more than 12,000 acres for himself. He managed to survive the Mori crackdown, though he was kept under house arrest for his outspoken opposition to Mussolini.

Then, in 1931, he was exiled, but when he returned in 1937 the whole town turned out to greet him.

When the bag was delivered to Don Calò he opened it and found inside another yellow silk handkerchief with the letter "L" on it. Silk handkerchiefs are a common means of identification between Mafiosi, the equivalent of a password. In 1922, an associate-member of the Mafia in Villalba named Lottò had committed a murder that he made no effort to conceal. This was a breach of all Mafia etiquette. The killing had been ill-planned and he had not sought permission. Arrest and conviction was assured. But to have left a "man of honour" to his fate would have damaged the reputation of the Mafia and resulted in a certain "loss of respect" for Don Calò. So Calò arranged for Lottò to be declared insane. He was confined in the asylum for the criminally insane at Barcellona Pozzo di Gotto, near Messina, an institution that was conveniently under the control of the Mafia. Soon after he arrived there Lottò "died", at least as far as the official records were concerned. A well-ventilated coffin was sent to the asylum to pick up the body and take it for burial – though, once outside the walls, Lottò simply climbed out of the casket. He was then given false documents and sent to the United States. When he arrived in New York, he was greeted by a group of Mafiosi who had been warned to expect him. He identified himself by producing a yellow silk handkerchief with the initial "C" on it. The "C" was for Calò. So when Don Calò received a yellow silk handkerchief with the letter "L" on it, he knew what it meant.

That evening, a young peasant nicknamed Mangiapane set off for the nearby town of Mussomelli carrying a letter from Don Calò hidden in his jacket. The letter read:

Turi, the farm bailiff, will go to the fair at Cerda with the calves on Thursday, the 20th. I will leave on the same

day with the cows, oxen-carts and the bull. Get faggots
for making the cheese, and provide folds for the sheep.
Tell the other bailiffs to get ready. I'll see to the rennet.

It was addressed to *Zu Peppi* – Giuseppe Genco Russo,
the Mafia boss of Mussomeli who would succeed Don
Calò as Sicilians' *capo di tutti capi* – and Mangiapane was
told to swallow the letter if he had a *mala incontratura* –
an "unlucky meeting". Couched in Mafia jargon, the
message informed Peppi that Turi, the *pezzo di novanta*
– leader of ninety – in the district of Polizzo Generosa to
the northeast, would accompany the American motorized
divisions as far as Cerda, five miles from the north coast of
Sicily, while he himself would accompany the main body
of troops – the cows – the tanks – the oxen-carts – and
their commander – the bull. In his absence, Peppi was to
do what he could to provide for the security and comfort
of the Americans. The following morning, Mangiapane
returned with a reply from *Zu Peppi*, saying that Liddu,
his bailiff, has got the faggots ready.

Three days later, with the American front line still thirty
miles from Villalba, a solitary jeep carrying two soldiers and
a civilian made a dash across enemy territory to reach Don
Calò. It too was flying a yellow pennant with a black "L" on
it. Not far from Villalba, it took a wrong turn and ran into
the Italian rearguard under the command of Lieutenant
Luigi Mangano. One of the American soldiers was hit and
toppled out on the road, while the jeep made a quick U-turn
and made off the way it had come. Later Carmine Palermo,
a local villager, approached the fallen soldier. Once he had
ascertained he was dead, he took a leather case from the
soldier. Inside was another nylon bag addressed to Don
Calò. Again it swiftly reached the addressee.

That same afternoon, three American tanks clattered
into the outskirts of Villalba. One hoisted a gold pennant

with the ubiquitous "L" on it. A young officer climbed out of the turret and asked the locals in Italian with a Sicilian-American accent to fetch Don Calò.

In due course, Don Calò arrived. He was wearing, as always, a short-sleeved shirt with braces holding his trousers up over his large round belly. His hat was pulled down almost over his tortoise-shell spectacles and he carried his jacket over his arm. The Americans were surprised by the slovenly appearance and laconic manner of the bulky sixty-six-year-old, but it was not done for a Mafia chieftain to show off, either in their clothing or outward behaviour. Don Calò moved slowly through the crowds. Then under the guns of the tanks, without a word, he pulled the handkerchief from his pocket. With his nephew, Domiano Lumia who had returned from the US shortly before the outbreak of war, he clambered up on to the lead tank. He told Mangiapane to return to Mussomelli and report what had happened in Villalba to *Zu Peppi*. The American tanks then whisked Don Calò off to safety behind Allied lines. There he was made an honorary colonel in the US Army, though the GIs referred to him as "General Mafia".

Colonel Salemi had gun batteries 3,000 feet up the San Vito mountain. They overlooked the valleys of the Tummarano and Platani rivers, which the Americans would have to pass through if they were to reach Palermo. Another motorized detachment occupied Mount Polizzelo, stretching as far as the Serra di Villalba and dominating the Vallelunga-Villalba-Mussomelli road, while German tanks were hidden in the pass of Cunicchieddi near Vallelunga. Together they barred the roads from Agrigento and Catania to Palermo. Salemi now waited for the inevitable.

However, when the roll-call was called on the morning of 21 July, two-thirds of Colonel Salemi's men failed to report. "Friends" had visited during the night to persuade them to abandon their positions and avoid useless bloodshed. Soldiers who voluntarily laid down their arms were offered civilian clothes so that they could return to their families unmolested. Others were warned that certain ill-intentioned people might take advantage of the darkness and their superior knowledge of the terrain to seize them and hand them over as prisoners to the Americans. Later that day, Salemi himself was grabbed by the Mafia in Mussomelli and imprisoned in the town hall. At 4 p.m. a column of Moroccan troops under the command of General Juin, who had been halted at the village of Raffi, got a signal from the Mussomelli Mafia to advance. The battle of Cammarata had been won without a shot being fired.

Don Calò was away from Villalba for six days. During that time, Turi accompanied the American column up the road to Cerda, where it met the coast road from Messina to Palermo, and Don Calò travelled with the other claw of the pincer that encircled all the troops on the western slopes of Agrigento and Palermo provinces and cut off the whole of Trapani province. He left the column when it met up with the other claw at Cerba. This was the limit of his home province of Caltanissetta. Although he was considered overall chief of the *Onorata Società*, it was not considered good form to trespass on the territory of others. In any case, he had to get back to Villalba to organize the removal of all the Fascist mayors in the province and replace them with his own men. Don Calò himself was appointed mayor of Villalba by the American occupying force and the Carabinieri barracks in the town were named after him. A group of Don Calò's closest friends cried: "Long live the Mafia! Long live delinquency! Long live Don Calò!" And the Americans granted them permission to carry firearms in case they had any more trouble with the Fascists.

Even without Don Calò, the initial "L" continued to do its job. Some fifteen per cent of the American landing force were of Sicilian birth or descent. They all carried American flags emblazoned with the letter "L". Before the invasion the Mafia had helped smuggle Allied agents in and out of Sicily and Charles Poletti, the governor of Sicily after the occupation, had slipped into Palermo under Mafia protection long before the landings. During the invasion itself, the Mafia conducted numerous acts of sabotage behind the lines.

The "L", of course, stood for Luciano, who was then serving a thirty- to fifty-year sentence on sixty-two counts of enforced prostitution and related extortion. Luciano had been born in Lercara Friddi, just fifteen miles up the Palermo road from Villalba. After Luciano used the Castellammarese War of 1930–31 to rub out the Mafia's old guard in New York, he, Meyer Lansky and the other members of his gang took over the New York crime families with Luciano as the unofficial *capo di tutti capi*. They then ran the Mafia as a national syndicate or cartel.

In 1935, Thomas E. Dewey was appointed special district attorney in Manhattan. Seeking to make his reputation, he took on the racketeers using, sometimes, dubious methods. He went after Luciano on prostitution and extortion charges. Though the case was weak, in the highly charged atmosphere following the gang wars, forty-year-old Luciano was convicted and given what amounted to a life sentence. When World War II broke out, Luciano was in Dannemora, upstate New York, one of the toughest prisons in the system.

Dewey was planning to run for governor of New York State in 1942 as a stepping stone for his presidential bid in 1944. Luciano promised his support to Dewey if he would pardon him when he was elected. However, Luciano's lawyer Moses Polakoff pointed out a flaw in this strategy.

"If you expect to get parole after Dewey becomes governor, just like that, you're making a big mistake, Charlie," he said. "He'd be impeached, that's how serious a mistake it would be. It would kill his chances to be president, and he's not going to jeopardize himself whether you give him political support or not."

But Luciano had a plan. He had just received a letter from Vito Genovese, who had fled to Italy to avoid prosecution for the murder of fellow racketeer Ferdinand Boccia. By then Genovese had become a close friend of Mussolini and was living it up in Rome.

"He made a lot of contacts down in Sicily with guys whose names I gave him before he left," said Luciano. "The most important thing was that in Sicily my name was like a king. Vito said that Mussolini was really pourin' out shit on Americans, but as far as I was concerned, down in Sicily they thought of me as a real number one guy. And that set me to thinkin' how I could give Dewey a legitimate excuse to let me out."

Luciano had read in the newspapers how the US Navy were worried about the large number of Italian migrants who worked in the New York docks. By the end of 1941, with the US at war with Italy, they had divided loyalties. There was a danger of sabotage on the waterfront. The Navy also feared that dockworkers might be giving the enemy details of movements of shipping. Between 7 December 1941 and 28 February 1942, German submarines had sunk seventy-one merchant ships off the east coast. There were strikes in the docks and vital war supplies were being stolen. However, the Mafia controlled the longshoreman's union. So the security of the docks was in Luciano's hands and releasing him to guarantee it could even be seen as a patriotic gesture. But what Luciano needed was a front-page story to bring home to the American public the ever-present danger of sabotage.

On 7 December 1941 – the day the Japanese attacked Pearl Harbor – the American authorities seized the French luxury liner SS *Normandie* which was tied up in New York harbour. Their intention, after making the appropriate deal with the leader of the Free French, General Charles de Gaulle, was to convert the liner into a troop ship. However, Luciano's enforcer and head of Murder, Inc. Albert Anastasia had other plans. He set fire to the *Normandie*.

"It was a great idea and I didn't figure that it was really gonna hurt the war effort because the ship was nowhere near ready," said Luciano. "Besides, no American soldiers or sailors would be involved because they wasn't sendin' 'em noplace yet . . . Later on, Albert told me not to feel too bad about what happened to the ship. He said that as a sergeant in the Army he hated the fuckin' Navy anyway."

On 9 February 1942, the *Normandie* went up in flames. Early the following morning, she capsized and the newspapers were full of stories about the need to prevent further disasters on the New York waterfront. Under the prompting of Frank Costello – born Francesco Castliglia in Calabaria before emigrating to the US at the age of nine – Italian political leaders pledged the loyalty of the Italian immigrants to the American flag. Even Italian and Sicilian gangsters, they said, though criminals were above all patriotic Americans who would rally to the flag in times of crisis. As the Mafia was deeply embedded along the waterfront, the Navy came up with "Operation Underworld", a government-approved plan to get organized crime to support the war effort.

The Office of Naval Intelligence put a young reserve officer named Lieutenant Charles R. Haffenden in charge of the operation. He got in touch with Dewey's office, who put him in touch with Luciano loyalist Joseph "Joe Socks" Lanza, who was the tsar of the Fulton Street fish market. Every boat that landed fish there paid him $100 and every truck that hauled fish away paid him another $50. No one had a stall there without his say-so and he exercised such tight control, through intimidation and murder, that he could even run the fish market from a prison cell in Flint, Michigan, when imprisoned in the Federal penitentiary there for conspiracy in the 1930s.

Lanza agreed to meet Haffenden at a park bench outside Grant's Tomb on upper Riverside Drive at midnight on the grounds that being seen talking to someone in uniform could cause problems for him. When Haffenden asked for his help, Lanza said that he would give him all the help he could in the fish market, but for help in the docks and along the rest of the waterfront he would have to speak to Lucky Luciano, currently an inmate at Dannemora prison. This was exactly what Frank Costello and Meyer Lansky had told him to say.

Dewey's office then put Haffenden in touch with Moses Polakoff. He suggested that, instead of setting up a meeting directly with Luciano who was still bitter with the authorities over his arrest and conviction, they should first have a meeting with one or two friends of Mr Luciano's who might help talk him round. So on 11 April 1942, Commander Haffenden and Murray Gurein from Dewey's office had breakfast with Moses Polakoff and Meyer Lansky in a hotel dining room on West 58th Street overlooking Central Park.

The following day, Luciano was called to the warden's office at Dannemora to take a "confidential" telephone call. It was from Frank Costello who told him that the government wanted him to do them a favour and a guy from the Navy wanted to ask him some questions.

"Listen, Frank, I'm not talkin' to anybody to do favours," said Luciano. "If they're so anxious to see me, let 'em bring me down to New York. I don't feel like doin' favours while I'm up in this dump." As he said this, Luciano said he "kinda smiled at the warden, because I don't want him to think it's nothin' personal".

Frank asked him to hold on. When he got back on to the phone, Costello said that he was with guys from Dewey's office who said that they would arrange to have him transferred to Sing Sing for the meeting. A few days later, the transfer came through.

"It was like goin' from Siberia to civilization," said Luciano. "I got a very nice cell all to myself, a clean one with hot and cold running water. I even had decent toilet paper for the first time in six years. A little thing like that can mean a helluva lot when you're shut up in jail."

That afternoon, he was called into the lawyer's room where Lansky had laid out a spread of all Lucky's favourite food from New York delicatessens. Frank Costello was also there, along with Haffenden and a man from Dewey's office. They had to wait until Luciano had finished eating before they got down to business. Haffenden asked if he would be willing to use his influence to help.

"Why are you fellas so sure that I can handle what you need while I'm locked up in the can?" Luciano asked.

Haffenden said that he had it on "very good authority" that anything Luciano said would be acted on where it counted. Eventually Luciano agreed and, while Haffenden went off to phone Naval Intelligence, Luciano got to talk to Dewey's representative.

"We put it right on the table," said Luciano. "I said that the way I figured it, after Wilkie beat Dewey for the Republican nomination in 1940, Dewey hadda win the governorship of New York in order to get in line for another shot at the nomination. Costello chimed in and said that he'd already gotten word that the Republican big shots had agreed to push Dewey for president ... I repeated my promise that Dewey would get all our support and we would deliver Manhattan, or come damn close, in

November, which would mean he'd be a shoo-in. Then, as soon as he got into office, he hadda make me a hero. The only difference would be, a hero gets a medal, but I'd get parole."

If Dewey did not agree to this deal immediately, Luciano would swing his support against him. Even if he became governor, when the Republican party were building him up to run for president, Luciano would start a campaign for a new trial by smearing Dewey. He would tell the newspapers that Dewey had got witnesses to perjure themselves, that he had put words in their mouths, that he had bribed them to give false testimony. Although he had tried these tactics in an attempt to get an appeal before, with Dewey running for president, a lot of the big newspapers would print all the dirt they could get on him.

While Dewey's representative went to deliver Luciano's message to his boss, Luciano, Lansky and Costello discussed whether a deal with Dewey would allow them a bigger corner of the market in meat and gasoline now that rationing had been introduced. While he waited for Dewey's reply, Luciano refused any more meetings with representatives of the government. Eventually, Polakoff returned with Dewey's reply. He had agreed in principle. But that was not good enough for Luciano. He insisted that he be released on unrestricted parole so that he could go back to New York and pick up the reins of his empire. Dewey said that he could not do that. He could only grant Luciano his freedom once he had won the governorship. Even then, Luciano would have to agree to be deported to Italy and remain in permanent exile from the United States. Dewey wanted Luciano out of the way when he ran for president.

For Luciano, this meant that he would have to stay in jail until the war was over. He could hardly be deported to an enemy nation. To seal the deal, Luciano agreed to pay Dewey $90,000 – $25,000 straight away to his "secret campaign fund" and $65,000 to be delivered in cash, in small bills, when he got on the boat. Luciano later checked and found that the $90,000 never showed up in Dewey's books or tax returns. Nor did it show up in his campaign funds. The money had simply been pocketed.

Luciano was better than his word. As well as stopping sabotage on the docks, Operation Underworld led to the capture of eight German agents who were landed from a U-boat in June 1942. They were carrying explosives, $170,000 in cash, maps and plans for a two-year campaign against munitions plants, railroads and bridges all down the East Coast.

However, Lucky Luciano denied helping in the invasion of Sicily. So did the government.

"As far as me helpin' the Army land in Sicily, you gotta remember I left there when I was, what – nine?" he said. "The only guy I knew real well over there, and he wasn't even a Sicilian, was that little prick Vito Genovese [a Neapolitan]. In fact, at that time the dirty little bastard was livin' like a king in Rome, kissin' Mussolini's ass."

However, Luciano himself had boasted that he had given Genovese the names of a lot of contacts in Sicily, which he later used to run drugs into the United States. And Luciano's name was big enough for the single letter "L" to save hundreds, if not thousands, of American lives.

Dewey was elected governor in 1942, and served three consecutive terms from 1943 to 1955. He won the Republican nomination for the presidency twice, but lost to the incumbent Franklin D. Roosevelt in 1944 and, against all predictions, to Harry S. Truman in 1948.

In 1946, Governor Dewey granted Luciano executive clemency and he was deported. But he was not out of pocket. Though he had given Dewey a $65,000 going-away present, Meyer Lansky gave Luciano a suitcase containing

$1 million on the dockside. They later got together in Cuba, where they ran drugs into the US. Luciano died in Naples in 1962. His body was returned to New York to be buried in the family vault in St John's Cemetery, Queens.

Lansky fled to Israel in 1970 to avoid prosecution for tax evasion, but returned and was eventually acquitted. In 1979, the House of Representatives Assassinations Committee linked Lansky to Jack Ruby, the nightclub owner who killed John F. Kennedy's assassin Lee Harvey Oswald. He died in 1983 and is buried in an Orthodox Jewish cemetery in Miami.

Don Calò went on to set up a sweets factory in Palermo with Lucky Luciano. It was thought to be a front for heroin trafficking. As mayor of Villalba, Don Calò allowed the Communists to hold a rally there, but when the Communist leader spoke out against the poverty of the peasants there, Don Calò shouted out: "It's a lie."

Gunfire broke out and bombs were thrown. Eighteen people were wounded. Don Calò and his cohorts were arrested over the incident. The court proceedings dragged on for fourteen years. Due to various amnesties, pardons and remissions, few of the accused served more than a couple of months in jail.

Seventy-seven-year-old Calogero Vizzini died of natural causes at his home in Villalba with the trial still going on. Thousands of peasants, politicians, priests and Mafiosi turned out for his funeral. The town of Villalba was plunged into mourning for eight days. Over the entrance to the cathedral hung a panegyric which concluded with the words: "He was an honest man."

Don Calò himself had once told a journalist: "When I die, the Mafia dies."

He was wrong.

Show Biz and
Assassination Squads

Vincent Teresa

After Joe Valachi broke the omertà *in 1963, he was followed by Vincent Teresa who testified to the Senate in 1971. With a long career as a swindler and a thief, he was the lieutenant of New England crime boss Raymond Patriarca. In the early 1970s he agreed to be a Federal witness against several Mob figures, including Meyer Lansky who was wanted for income-tax evasion. In exchange for his testimony, he got fifteen years knocked off the twenty-year prison sentence he was serving after being convicted of stealing securities. During his testimony he told the Senate investigating committee that he had begun his life of crime at fifteen and, over the years, he had milked "suckers" of millions of dollars. One of his most lucrative operations, he said, was organizing gambling junkets to London, Las Vegas and the Caribbean. Along the way he would augment his fees by using loaded dice to mulct his rich clients. After testifying in a series of Mafia trials, he was relocated to the West Coast and given a new identity under the name Charles Cantino. He then helped write two books,* My Life in the Mafia, *published in 1973, and* Wiseguys, *published in 1978. In 1977 he was invited to go to Australia to give evidence to a citizens' committee on drugs and gambling, but he was deported when he arrived because on his visa application he had said he had no criminal record. He died of kidney failure in Seattle at the age of 61 in 1990.*

At 10.10 a.m. on 25 October 1957, a short, squat Sicilian hustled his way through the lobby of Manhattan's Park Sheraton Hotel and entered the barber shop. He nodded to barber Joseph Bocchini and slipped into his chair for a shave.

Outside on Seventh Avenue, obscured by the milling crowds, two men stepped from a sedan and strode briskly behind a casually dressed workman who was walking towards the hotel. A man nodded at the doorway as the workman went in, followed by the two strangers. The workman paused briefly in front of the barber shop, pointed a newspaper at Bocchini's chair, and disappeared into the hotel.

The two men reached beneath the collars of their coats to pull handkerchiefs tied around their necks up over their noses. Drawing guns from their coat pockets, they walked into the barber shop towards the unsuspecting figure relaxing in Bocchini's chair. At 10.20, the quiet barber shop erupted in screams and shouts as shots echoed through the room. The man in the chair dived for the floor, but eleven bullets ripped into his body. Then one of the gunmen stood over the bleeding man and applied the *coup de grâce*, a bullet in the back of the head. Lying in a pool of blood before eleven startled witnesses who could never identify the assassins was Albert (The Executioner) Anastasia, the vicious chief of Murder Inc., and the boss of what is now known as the Carlo Gambino crime family.

Anastasia was a victim of his own speciality. For a quarter of a century he had coldly arranged the murders of hundreds of victims with no more emotion than if he were ordering a plate of spaghetti. Fear was his weapon and the source of his power. It was also his downfall. For it was the fear of his cunning and wolf-like savagery that prompted five crime bosses of Cosa Nostra to plan Anastasia's murder. Anastasia was too dangerous and uncontrollable to let live.

The murder of a crime boss involves secrecy of the highest order. It involves promises, compromises, deals and trust between the plotters, whose lives depend on the loyalty of their co-conspirators. The mastermind of this conspiracy was New Jersey boss, Vito Genovese, whose life Anastasia had threatened. Genovese arranged communication between the bosses through his trusted aide and underboss, Anthony [Tony Bender] Strollo. In later years, Strollo was to fall from grace and become a victim of Genovese's cunning himself.

Murders at this level also require an inside man, a person close to the victim whom the victim trusts and confides in. Such a man was Carlo Gambino, Anastasia's own underboss and closest confidant. Gambino's role was to arrange for the absence of Anastasia's ever-present bodyguard, Michael [Trigger Mike] Coppola, during the assassination. He was also assigned to win the approval for the murder from the boss of another crime family, the father-in-law of his daughter, Thomas [Three-Finger Brown] Lucchese. Gambino, an ambitious man who preferred a modest demeanour to the flamboyant violence of his boss, Anastasia, was amply rewarded for his treachery. He was confirmed as the new boss of the Anastasia crime family a month later at the famous Appalachin barbecue attended by more than sixty crime bosses.

Though the conspiracy was put together by Tony Strollo, acting for Genovese, the actual planning of the murder fell to a gang of young toughs headed by Lawrence and Joey

Gallo. The Gallos headed the assassination squad for the Brooklyn Mob, and it is believed that during their careers they were responsible for 500 or more deaths. (Lawrence Gallo died of cancer in 1968, and Joey Gallo was killed in April, 1972, after the unsuccessful attempt to assassinate crime leader Joseph Colombo; he was gunned down in Umberto's Clam House in New York by two men he knew and had trained as gunmen.) The Gallos had handled many murder assignments for Anastasia himself and were close to Anastasia, having grown up with the Anastasia family.

But the Gallos had become even closer to Carmine [The Doctor] Lombardozzi, an Anastasia soldier who was a key man in the conspiracy against Anastasia and who, like Carlo Gambino, was to be elevated for his role in it. The Gallos had frequently worked for Lombardozzi as enforcers in his vast loan-shark rackets. Lombardozzi knew first-hand about their resourcefulness as killers.

The Gallos were daring but not foolhardy. They understood the danger of an attack on Anastasia. They knew that the men assigned to pull the trigger would have to be men whom Anastasia would not recognize, and so they ruled themselves out and all of their regular companions as well. They decided to ask Raymond Patriarca for the use of Jackie [Mad Dog] Nazarian, an expert in murder, as the leader of the assassination team. And they chose one of their own hangers-on, a little-known but vicious enforcer named "The Syrian", to be the back-up gunman on the hit. The Gallos themselves would be present at the scene of the hit, though well hidden, keeping track of Anastasia and making sure everything went smoothly.

"The contract to murder Anastasia involved a lot of people. They were people Anastasia trusted, people he didn't suspect. They were also people who were afraid he wanted to take over the whole Mob, become the boss of bosses.

"People I worked with in The Office told me Tony Strollo approached Raymond Patriarca for the gunman they needed. The New York boys wanted a gunman that Anastasia wouldn't know as well as a guy that wasn't afraid to hit him. Most of New York's hitmen were scared to death of Anastasia. Strollo phoned Patriarca who conferred with the other bosses involved. Then Strollo sent the Gallos to Providence for a meeting with Patriarca. Patriarca assigned Nick Bianco to act as the liaison between Nazarian and the Gallos. Bianco came from Brooklyn and he knew what Anastasia looked like. He was also close to the Gallos. He was a punk at the time, but now he's a captain, a boss with the Colombo crime family.

"The idea of importing gunmen from other mobs isn't new. Anastasia used to send out assassins all over the country to handle hits for other mobs. Today, every mob has its own assassination squads who are available for lend-lease assignments. Whether you go to Chicago, New York, Montreal, Newark or Boston, they have assassination squads made up of men who get a regular weekly salary just to be ready for the day a hit is needed. The members of the squad are hand-picked by a boss. Their talents always include three things. They are experts with a variety of guns and other weapons. They are cool under pressure. They also have no emotion.

"I remember there was one guy I heard about who worked for Anastasia's old Murder Inc., who is typical of what I mean. They called him Ice Pick Barney. His technique was as cold and as calculating as they come. He and other men assigned on a hit would force their victim into a men's room. Then Ice Pick Barney would pull out his ice pick and, while the others held the victim, he'd put the ice pick through the victim's eardrum into the brain. The pick left a tiny hole and would cause very little bleeding. They'd wipe away the blood that trickled from the ear, but the bleeding in the brain would cause the guy to die. When a doctor examined him, he'd rule the victim died from a cerebral haemorrhage. They're a special breed, the assassins. They aren't like the average *made* guy. Every made guy, every member of the Mob, has to make his notch . . . kill someone on assignment. For some it's tougher than for others. But for a rare few, it's a well-paid profession. They handle killings as though they were selling insurance.

"In New England, The Office had its own assassination squad. There was an average of a dozen solid guys who Patriarca could count on to go to the wall for him. They got paid well . . . a regular salary from The Office. Joe Barboza, while he worked for Patriarca during the Irish gang war, got $900 a week just to be available for hits. That was their salary, but they had the right to pick up more money loan-sharking or counterfeiting or whatever they wanted to do as long as it didn't interfere with their main job of killing.

"Rudy Sciarra is a good example of what I'm talking about. He is a short guy, ruggedly built with a rough face and light curly hair. He's a stone-cold killer, but in other ways he's a nice guy. Sciarra was big in the credit-card racket. He had a guy with a machine who could print counterfeits of American Express cards. Everyone in the New England mob used Sciarra's cards. He sold them for $100 apiece to Mob-connected people, but I got them for $15 apiece because I was working for Henry Tameleo. I used the cards in cabarets, men's stores, hotels and motels, and to transport stolen cars to Florida and California. I thought nothing about running up a $2,000 tab at the Fontainebleu in Miami when I was entertaining a group at a Frank Sinatra show. The head waiter knew what was going on. He didn't care. I'd give him $150 to $200 in tips.

"When Sciarra wasn't hustling cards or shylocking, he was out on hits. One of the jobs he had to handle was Nazarian, the guy who hit Anastasia. Now sometimes being a professional hitman means that if you handle a job like the Anastasia hit, you become a big man in the Mob. That's what happened to Nazarian. He became a big man ... too big. He was a miniature Anastasia. He threatened to kill anyone who stood in his way. Patriarca became afraid of him. Everybody on the street was afraid of him. Nazarian was a savage. That's why they called him Mad Dog. He once strangled a witness [Edward Hannan] slowly with bailing wire and dropped him on the city dump so everyone would know he was garbage – because the guy had decided to testify about seeing Nazarian kill George [Tiger] Balletto at the Bella Napoli Café in Providence. There were twenty-two witnesses to the Balletto killing, but only this one guy decided to talk. Nazarian could have killed him quick, but that wasn't the way he did things. He twisted that wire real slow, tortured the poor slob because he enjoyed it.

"But Nazarian wasn't happy just being Patriarca's top gun. He was making a fortune, but he figured he should be a boss. He bragged about killing Anastasia, then he threatened Patriarca. Patriarca did what he had to do. He assigned Sciarra and Lou [The Fox] Taglianetti – he was Patriarca's boss of gambling in Rhode Island – to get Nazarian. That took a lot of guts, Nazarian was a whiz with a gun. He could smell a bad deal a mile away. But he never suspected Taglianetti. He was a boss, the last guy he'd think would go out on a hit. That's why it worked so beautifully. That's why most Mob hits work so well. The victim never expects to be killed by the people who kill him. So on 13 January 1962, they hit Nazarian as he left a crap game in Providence. He was hit by five slugs, but even as he was dying he tried to choke Taglianetti.

"Assassination squads have a variety of roles. They keep discipline in the Mob where they work. They handle local hits when they're needed, and they protect the boss when he's in danger. They're also sent out to do other jobs for other mobs. There's no charge for the service ... it's a favour from one boss to another. That's where Patriarca made his mistake during the Irish war. He didn't use the assassination squads from other mobs to whack out the people who were causing all the trouble. He hired guys that weren't *made* members, like Barboza, to do the dirty work. You can't trust people from the outside. They don't live by the same rules that made people do. Barboza didn't. He killed for the hell of it whenever he lost his temper. He became as hot as a pistol to the Mob. What Patriarca should have done was import hitmen from other mobs to come in and clean the troublemakers out right from the start.

"Our assassins had done the same thing for other mobs. They were used in the Gallo-Profaci gang war in the 1960s to whack some people. I know they were sent to New Orleans to handle a job for Carlos Marcello, the boss down in Louisiana. I don't know who the target was, but I know they had a contract down there. I remember one case where our assassins ... I don't know which ones were used ... were sent to whack out a guy called John [Futto] Biello in Miami.

"Biello was a captain in the Genovese mob. I remember Tameleo telling me that Biello had been a friend of Joseph Bonanno's and that Bonanno had told Biello that he was going to take over the New York mobs by whacking out some of the bosses. Biello was a treacherous bastard. He was one of those who tipped off the bosses about what Bonanno was planning to do. Then, when the Mob kidnapped Bonanno and held him while the old dons decided what to do with him, Biello was one of those who

voted to have Bonanno whacked out. At any rate, Bonanno
never forgave Biello for his treachery.

"That was a Bonanno philosophy . . . never forget.
Tameleo told me one day how Bonanno advised him to put
people who rubbed him wrong to sleep. 'Don't let the guy
know how you feel,' Bonanno told him. 'Just keep patting
him on the shoulder. Every time you see him, notice what
a nice day it is. Pat him on the back. Tell him he looks good
today. Sooner or later this guy will find a hole in his back
when your time is right. Be patient. Never let anyone know
you're laying for a guy because that guy will turn around
and lay for you. Always be a diplomat. Make the guy think
you're his friend until the right time comes, the right setup, and then you make your move like a tiger.'

"That was what Bonanno did with Biello. He never let
him know there were any hard feelings. Then it happened.
It was in March 1967, and I was in Florida with Cardillo
and some other people. A friend of mine called Fungi
phoned me up one day. We'd known each other for years
and were good friends. Fungi was one of Bonanno's
lieutenants. 'You want to go out with me?' Fungi asked. 'I
got to go pick up the boss at the airport. Joe B is coming
in.'

"I didn't ask questions. What the hell did I know? So
I went. Bonanno came in on an American Airlines flight
from Arizona. I'd met him twice before and he looked
good. He got in the back seat of Fungi's car and we drove
to the Dream Bar in Miami, a place that was owned by
Pasquale Erra, a Genovese soldier. About a half hour later,
Patsy [Erra] came in and walked over to our table. Joe
Bonanno got up and the two of them walked over to a
corner table, had a couple of drinks together and talked in
each other's ear. Then Bonanno came back and told Fungi
to take him to the airport so he could catch an eleven p.m.
flight back to Arizona.

"It was either the next day or two days later [18 March 1967] when I read in the paper that they had found Biello's body with four bullets in it in a car left in a municipal parking lot at 71st Street and Bonita Drive, Miami Beach. The car was a rental obtained under a phoney name. Now Biello was a big man. He had interests in a record company and he was the hidden owner of the old Peppermint Lounge in New York and another in Miami that made a bundle out of the twist craze. He was a millionaire with a lot of influence, but he was still a walking dead man as far as Bonanno was concerned. Bonanno had a lot of friends in the Mob even though he was put on a shelf and kicked out of the rackets in New York.

"He still runs things in Arizona and Colorado and some other places. Don't think for a minute he doesn't. Bonanno's still a big man, but he doesn't sit with the bosses any more.

"After I read the paper, I bumped into Fungi again and he told me that the reason Bonnano had come to Miami was to arrange to have Biello put to sleep. I said: 'Look, Fungi, I don't want to hear about it.' I left and went back to Rhode Island. I had an obligation to tell Patriarca what happened right away. Particularly since I'd been with Bonanno. I told Patriarca: 'Fungi told me that Joe B put the X on this guy . . . he gave him the kiss of death.' Patriarca looked at me for a moment, then he said: 'Yeah, well, forget about it, Vinnie. Things will iron themselves out.'

"I didn't understand what he meant until later. I found out that it was Patriarca's assassins who were sent to Florida to handle the job. Patsy Erra set it up because he was a guy that Biello trusted. That shows you what I mean. In the Mob you can't trust anyone. Bonanno was as treacherous as any guy there ever was in the mob. He was always looking to get ahead by stepping on somebody else.

"Probably the best assassination squad in operation was the one in New Jersey under Joe Paterno. Frank [Butch] Miceli was in charge of that one with Frank [The Bear] Basto. They went anywhere on a hit. One of the jobs they handled was Willie Marfeo. That was a job that Patriarca did go out of town to have handled.

"Marfeo was a bookmaker, an independent who worked on Federal Hill in Providence. He and his brothers started running an illegal dice game on the Hill and they weren't kicking in to Patriarca or Tameleo. Now Patriarca was paying for police protection for that, and here this Marfeo was running games in competition with Patriarca's boys and at the same time reaping the benefits of Patriarca's protection. Patriarca told Tameleo: 'Go down and tell these clowns we want a cut. Either they give us a piece or they're out of business.'

"So Tameleo went to see Marfeo, who was a wise punk. Marfeo said he'd pay, but a week went by and nothing was kicked in. Tameleo went back. 'Look, Willie, this is your last warning,' he said. 'Either we get a piece; you knock the game off, or you're in a whole lot of trouble.'

"Marfeo just smiled at Tameleo. Then he slapped Tameleo in the mouth. 'Get out of here, old man,' he said. 'Go tell Raymond to go shit in his hat. We're not giving you nothing.'

"Tameleo was trembling with fury, but he kept his cool. His voice was soft, but as cold as steel. 'Mister,' he said, 'go pay your insurance. You're a dead man.' He walked out. When he came back and told Patriarca about what happened, Patriarca went wild. He was so mad he was almost crying.

" 'Why didn't you shoot him right then?' Patriarca shouted.

" 'I didn't have a gun,' Tameleo answered. That's when Patriarca decided to import some outside hitmen. He knew Marfeo would be looking for one of Patriarca's men and would be careful. Marfeo wouldn't be expecting an import.

"Before you call in outside guns to handle a job for you, you've got to have the whole hit planned to a T for them. You provide the guns, the cars, the best location for a hit and the escape route. Patriarca and Tameleo took care of everything. Then a contact was made with Joe Paterno and Miceli showed up at The Office for a conference. A few days later [13 July 1966] Willie Marfeo was eating pizza with some friends in a place called the Korner Kitchen Restaurant in Providence. A guy he'd never seen before walked in, made everyone in the restaurant lie down on the floor and pushed Marfeo into the phone booth. He closed the door and then he let go with four slugs that went through Marfeo's head and chest, killing him. That was in broad daylight. The guy escaped in the morning crowd and nobody saw anything. Nobody ever saw anything if they knew what was good for them in Providence.

"That wasn't the end of the problem. Two years later, Marfeo's brother, Rudolph, started threatening Patriarca. He was going to get even for his brother's death. This time Patriarca didn't go to New Jersey to handle the job. He used his own assassination squad, Sciarra and Maurice [Pro] Lerner. Lerner was something special. He had worked with John [Red] Kelley and me and Billy [Aggie] Agostino on bank jobs and later he worked with Kelley on some of the big armoured-car robberies. He was a college kid who'd played some professional baseball. You'd never in a million years have pegged him for being a hitman. But he was. He was the deadliest assassin ever to come out of New England. I remember one time he had to kill a guy who'd been screwing the mob. He knew the guy would answer the door when he knocked. For ten minutes before he knocked, Pro practised a swing with a baseball bat so he would groove his swing to exactly the right angle. When he knocked and the guy opened the door, Pro hit him with one swing and smashed his face in, killing him on the spot.

"Patriarca needed someone to plan the job because Rudy Marfeo was very careful. It seemed like he was always protected and never followed a particular routine. Pro suggested Red Kelley, and Patriarca bought it. When it came to smarts, nobody could beat Kelley. He planned a job like he was putting a Swiss watch together. He used to set up armoured-car jobs like ducks in a shooting gallery. He's got the patience of a saint. Kelley studied Marfeo for weeks. Marfeo didn't know him and Kelley had a way of blending into the crowd so you'd never know he was there. He found out there was one time every day when Marfeo visited a particular grocery store. The next thing he did was plan a route from a golf course to the grocery store. Timing was everything in this job and he timed everything on the route over and over and over again. He knew exactly how long it would take to reach the store and how much time they would have to get at Marfeo when they arrived. He even figured how long it would take to drive in traffic on the escape route. He ran practice runs until everyone was sick of them. Then he went to New York, got a sawed-off shotgun and a carbine and some Halloween masks. He even got special Double O buckshot shells because they're best for killing at a short distance. On the day of the hit, he waited with a couple of friends at a golf course for the guys who were to handle the job. So no one would notice them, Kelley and his friends were dressed in golf caps and Kelley bounced golf balls in the parking lot. Then he met with Lerner, John Rossi and Robert Fairbrother who were to handle the actual hit. They caught Marfeo and a friend of his, Anthony Melei, cold at the grocery store and gunned them down at the exact moment Kelley said they should.

"I think Patriarca should have used Miceli's crew on that one. Lerner was a great hitman, but if he'd used Miceli, they wouldn't have needed Kelley to plan the job. Miceli would have worked it out himself rather than have an outsider, a guy who wasn't *made*, plan a job.

"Miceli and Basto had a fantastic operation going. Their squad had ten men in it and they got a regular $500 a week, but that was only a fraction of what they made. They had the best counterfeit business going in the country. There wasn't anything Miceli and his gang couldn't provide. They printed phoney postage stamps, passports, drivers' licences, stock certificates and cash like it was confetti. New Jersey is the biggest centre of counterfeiting in the country. Not only that, but in New Jersey you could buy just about any kind of gun you wanted from Miceli's group ... machine guns, hand grenades, mines. I think he could have supplied you with a tank if you needed it. In fact, that's how I got in trouble another time with Jerry Angiulo ... handling some of Miceli's counterfeits.

"It was in 1963. I had a chance to buy queer $20 bills from Miceli for ten cents on the dollar. I took a couple of samples back to show Patriarca and Tameleo. We met in a hotel in Rhode Island and I went into the men's room with Tameleo and showed him the queers. They were beauties. I told him I could move over a million dollars' worth overnight and sell them for twenty cents on the dollar.

" 'Look, kid,' Tameleo said, 'we don't want any part of it, but you got our okay. Just do one thing. Make sure none of these flood any of our card or crap games and stay away from the racetracks. Don't you pass them!' No problem. All I was going to do was sell them to a contact. In three days, I unloaded $500,000 in queers in the Boston area and made myself a quick $50,000 profit. The next thing I know is that I get a call from Sal Cesario, Angiulo's strong-arm, to come to Jay's Lounge for a sit-down. So I went to the bar and I saw Smigsy, Jerry's brother. I asked him what Jerry wanted to see me about. He said he didn't know, but told me to go downstairs to the cellar.

"Now the cellar of this place is really something. Wall to wall carpeting, a private apartment for Angiulo and in one main room where you entered there was a table about twenty feet long with all kinds of chairs around it. Joe Russo, another of Angiulo's musclemen, told me to sit at one end of the table. I waited about fifteen minutes and out comes Angiulo. I remembered it like it was yesterday. He had grey silk pants on . . . black patent leather slippers . . . a black velvet smoking jacket with an ascot and a cigarette with a holder. He looked like George Raft, the actor, in a gangster movie. So he walked up to the other end of the table, looked down at me and said: 'Oh, so you're the kid.'

" 'I'm the kid?' I said. 'Geez, Jerry, you've known me for years. What do you mean, I'm the kid?'

" 'Don't you lie,' he snapped. 'You brought in some queer twenties into the city.'

" 'I'm not lying to you,' I said. 'Sure I did . . . why?'

"Now he's talking like he's in an old Al Capone movie. 'You may not walk out of this joint alive tonight,' he said.

" 'Whoa . . . take it easy, Jerry,' I answered.

" 'Now you shut up,' he shouts. Suddenly he's wild, loud, raving like a lunatic. 'You're in a lot of trouble . . . you may end up in a box. Your money has flooded all the crap games and the racetracks and we got a lot of beefs from the law and everybody else.'

" 'Wait a minute,' I said. 'I got an okay from Raymond and Henry to bring the stuff in.' By now there's a dozen guys in the room. I don't have a chance and I know it.

" 'From who?' he shouts. 'I'm the boss here.'

" 'I got it from Raymond and Henry,' I said. 'Here . . . here's Raymond's phone number. Call him.'

"So he sends one of his brothers out to call Patriarca and about twenty minutes later he returns and whispers something in Jerry's ear. Angiulo turns to me and shouts: 'GET OUTTA HERE. Don't come back and keep outta my sight.' He didn't mention it, but Patriarca told him I had the okay. I don't know how the stuff hit the games and tracks. The people I dealt with were told to move the money in other places.

"A creature of habits on the street is a complete fool. It can only lead to disaster for him eventually. A man who takes the same road home every night, goes to the same nightclub at the same time every night or the same restaurant, or leaves his office at the same time each day, is a perfect mark for assassins. That's one thing very few Mob guys learn. Change your routine every day. Never do the same thing twice in a row. You'd think they'd learn but they don't. There's always one habit, one routine they follow and that's what can nail them.

"There are other things that help assassinations to come off so successfully in the Mob. The favourite technique in setting up a guy for a hit is through the use of guys you do business with regularly. They might call you up and ask you to meet them at a particular location to look at a trailer-load of hijacked goods they have for sale. They might ask you to meet them at a nightclub or at a house. When you get there . . . wham, bam, you're dead.

"Joe Palladino tried to set me up one night. We'd had a few beefs at Chez Joey's, our nightclub on Cape Cod, but I didn't think it was anything serious. I was home in Medford that night, one of the rare nights I got to be with the family. I was lucky to see Blanche in the morning before I went to work. I used to be on the street eighteen to twenty hours a day, seven days a week. It was a helluva way to live with a family, but that's what happens in the

Mob. For a hustler, a money-maker, there's virtually no time for home life. At any rate, it was two a.m. and there was a knock at the door. Blanche and I were in bed at the time. I said to Blanche: 'There's something wrong. I've had this feeling following me all night.' It was that sixth sense of mine working again. Like extra-sensory perception. I could sense danger. Many times I knew something was going to happen. I just felt it . . . and things would happen. This was one of those times.

"I went to the door and it was Joey Palladino. 'Vinnie, I got a couple of broads down at the club,' he said, 'I'd like you to come down. We'll have a real ball.' Now I just knew he was lying even though he'd come up with broads at the last minute before. I agreed to go. I went back to the room and got dressed, telling Blanche there were some problems at the club that I had to take care of. But before I went I got a gun from the dresser drawer. I don't normally carry a gun, but this time I had a bad feeling. As we drove to the club, I asked Joey why he'd decided to come at this hour. 'They're terrific broads, Vinnie,' Joey said. 'I thought you'd enjoy it.' When we got there I saw Bobby Daddieco standing near the bar, stone-drunk. Bobby and I had had a beef over something minor and I'd forgotten about it. But when I walked into the place, Bobby pulled a gun out and pointed it at me. He was planning to shoot me. I fingered the gun in my pocket. It was pointed straight at his gut, but I tried diplomacy first. Daddieco and I had always been close, so I started reasoning with him. I found out Joey had been working on him all night, convincing him that I was out to kill him and the only way to handle me was to kill me first.

" 'Joey tells me you think you're a real big shot,' Daddieco said. 'You're supposed to be smarter than I am, a big wheel with Providence.'

"I told Daddieco what a punk Palladino was. We talked for an hour. Palladino hadn't realized how close Daddieco and I were. We ended up beating the hell out of Joey for trying to set me up for a hit. But if I hadn't had my wits about me, if I hadn't sensed danger, I'd have been set up by a guy who was supposed to be a friend and killed by another so-called friend.

"Friends are only one of dozens of ways Mob assassins use to set you up. Many times it's a guy's girlfriend. She may not be willing, but they'll make her do it. They'll threaten her life, or her kids, or her parents. Then she'll call the boyfriend and tell him to meet her at a restaurant or a motel or her apartment at a certain time. The assassins will just lie in wait in the dark, whack the guy over the head, carry him to a car and take him someplace where they'll whack him out.

"Sometimes you have some nuts in the Mob who think up pretty weird ways to kill a guy. Take Nicola Giso, an old *made* guy from Boston who used to be close to Joe Lombardo. Giso had lost respect in the Mob in the early 1960s when he'd taken $100,000 of Lombardo's money and blown it with Ralphie Chong in New York. The old dons of the Mob had a round-table on whether or not they'd let him live. They agreed to but he had to pay every nickel back with interest. Because of that Giso tried everything to stay in the good graces of Tameleo and Patriarca. He was in Providence one day at Patriarca's office when a discussion came up about what to do about Angelo DeMarco, a two-bit hood who was going around Boston calling Patriarca a fag and threatening a lot of Mob people.

"DeMarco was an animal, a part-time hitman crazy enough to make a try on Patriarca himself. Patriarca and Tameleo decided DeMarco had to be hit and Giso piped up that he had a good way to do the job. He and DeMarco were pretty close and he said he could get him to meet him in a restaurant for coffee. 'I'll sit down with him,' Giso said, 'and when he isn't looking, I'll put some poison in his coffee. He's too tough to get any other way.' Tameleo called Giso a stupid son-of-a-bitch. He said if Giso ever tried anything like that he'd have him killed. Later on Tameleo had two of the assassination squad catch DeMarco. They left him on the city dump in Everett.

"Now if it's a guy on the lam from the Mob, there are other things used to help the assassin. The Mob has a terrific intelligence system . . . probably better than most police departments. I don't care where you run to hide, as long as you have to work, the Mob is able to find you. They had a connection with someone in the US Social Security office who could check records for them. As soon as the victim used his social security card and . . . you can't work at a legitimate job without one . . . bang, the word got back to the Mob where the victim was working. In a matter of hours the hitman was on his way to case the area and set up the murder.

"They had other ways too. They have doctors. If there is something basically wrong with the victim, like a defect, a scar, a special allergy or a history of a particular disease that needs special treatment, the Mob used connections it had with various medical associations and doctors to check around the country to find the guy with the problem they knew he had. It might take months, even years, but the Mob has so many doctors on the hook, putting their money out with the Mob on loan-sharking, that they had a built-in intelligence system.

"Doctors are big with the Mob. They have so much buried money, money they don't report to the tax boys. They want that money to work for them, but if they invest it legitimately, the tax men will find out. So they invest it with Mob people. In Boston, there were dozens of doctors who provided money to Mob guys for loan-sharking. The doctors got one per cent per week return on the money they gave the Mob and the Mob made another four per cent a week on their money. There were other doctors that Mob guys had set up in compromising situations with broads or queers and they used that to blackmail them. Still others fronted at nightclubs for Mob people or in other business enterprises. Anything to get that under-the-table money that Uncle Sam can't find out about. Doctors are bigger crooks than Mob people, at least the ones I've met and know about.

"Beyond the doctors, the Mob had the cops. They could and do use crooked cops to check anything out anywhere in the country. If the FBI was keeping a guy under wraps that the Mob wanted to hit, they'd use the cops to try and find out where he was hidden. They'd have a high-ranking cop contact the FBI and say they wanted to question the victim for suspicion of a robbery or a burglary. The FBI was too cute for them on this. They knew better than to deal with local cops when they had an informer stashed. They'd just tell the local cops that they didn't have him under their control any more . . . that the Justice Department had taken him over. The FBI would never give local cops a flat no. They'd just waltz the cops around the yard a few times. But even without information from FBI files, the Mob could reach into police files all over the country, even in honest departments, to find out about a guy. All you needed was one crooked cop asking for information, and they had hundreds on their payroll. They still do.

"What they can't get from cops, they get from crooked probation and parole officers who keep track of guys freed from jail on parole. These people usually have a good line on where a guy they've once handled has gone. For the right price, there were guys on probation in New England who would finger their mother. The Mob knew that and used them.

"Don't ever underestimate the Mob. They're smart. They'll run a victim down through insurance company checks. Everybody has insurance, even a guy on the lam. He's got a car, or a house, or life insurance or boat insurance. Whatever it is, it has information on where he is or what he does in the application for the insurance. When he fills out that application, the Mob's guns can nail him. They have hundreds of insurance offices of their own and they start making checks on a target by saying he owes them back premiums or they have to find him to pay off an award. Whatever the reason, if the sucker bought insurance, he's as good as dead.

"The same thing is true of drivers' licences or car registration. They can check through paid-off people they've got in state licence bureaus to find out if a guy took out a new licence in a neighbouring state or anywhere in the country for that matter. And if you think that's bad, think about this. If you've got kids, they have to go to school. Once they do, if they're using the same name, the Mob can trace you through transferred school records. That's why an informer has to change his identity completely as well as his appearance if he wants to stay a step ahead of the assassins. Very few make it. Sooner or later they find you."

But according to Vincent Teresa, life in the Mob is not all murder and mayhem. There is fun to be had too:

"When a Mob guy owns a club, it's a guaranteed success . . . they draw business and broads and entertainers like flies. Don't ask me why, but people seem to want to come to a Mob place. Maybe it's the excitement of mingling with mobsters. Maybe it's something else. Outside of the general public, the Mob guys generate business themselves because they do other business in the club. Take the Ebbtide. It was a goldmine. I operated my loan shark business there. I set up hijacks, bought stolen goods, arranged for stolen stock deals. When I was at my table, maybe forty or fifty guys would come in with their dates to see me. A guy would come to my table, sit down, have a few drinks. Maybe we'd talk fifteen or twenty minutes. Then he'd go to his own table and buy drinks and dinner for himself and his girl. He'd also pay for the drinks at my table. Now this would go on from seven at night till two or three in the morning. So the club had a guaranteed, steady flow of customers. After a guy met with me for business, it was rare for him to get out of the club without running up a tab for $100. You multiply that by forty and you're doing $4,000 a night business just from people coming to see me. That's the way most Mob night-spots operate. That's why they always make money.

"A lot of people came because the girls flocked to places like the Ebbtide. The girls were usually waitresses, secretaries or clerks looking for a night of fun. They loved to be near Mob people. I guess it was the thrill of danger and violence and doing something they knew was wrong. They were all young. Any girl over twenty-three was an old maid. Most of them were eighteen or nineteen years old and they'd do anything we wanted them to. They'd draw the men like flies, the middle-aged men who were lucky to get to their wives once in six months. Now they'd come to the club for a good time and the first thing they ran into was some eighteen- or nineteen-year-old dressed in tight pants, wiggling her tail around, rubbing up against him. Man, he doesn't want to know anything after that. He's a setup, a target for a score. We'd get him up tight with one of those young chicks and before you knew it, Mr Middleage was willing to do anything to bed that broad. We'd get him laid and take him upstairs and knock him out in a card game.

"The Ebbtide was a rock-and-roll place. There had to be ten girls to every guy in the place, and all the girls were just dying to be recognized. They liked to walk into a place and have some Mob guy say, 'Hi, Barbara,' as though they were somebody. They didn't care what you asked them to do as long as you were a Mob guy who gave them a little recognition. If we wanted them to go to bed with a guy – to blow his pipes – they'd do it without question. They couldn't care less. They didn't get money. They didn't ask for it. All they wanted was recognition. Every now and then, when one of them did you a favour, you'd give them a gift. Maybe, I'd have a load of stolen dresses upstairs. 'What size you wear, Julie?' I'd ask. 'Go upstairs . . . tell Richie I said to give you a couple of dresses and slacks.' That was a big thing for her. Or if some creep was bothering one of them, they would come walking over and say: 'Vinnie . . . that guy is bothering me.' So I'd walk over to the clown and tell him: 'Julie's a friend of mine. You go off and mind your business or get out of here.' Now Julie felt very important. It was all a bunch of bullshit. I couldn't have cared less if that guy killed Julie or whoever. But by keeping on the right side of her, by using a little diplomacy, I could call on her to take care of some sucker I was setting up for a score.

"Girls weren't the only people who went nutty over Mob guys. Entertainers are worse. They want to be around Mob people because they know the Mob controls the better places. So they come in, they get cosy with you and then they ask your help in getting them a spot at a place like the Mayfair in Boston or the Copacabana in New York. It was good for our business to have them. We paid them the union scales and for the top names we paid top dollar. But a lot of them were compulsive gamblers and they'd end up losing what they had coming in salary. Like Fats Domino. He was a helluva entertainer. He'd play at the Ebbtide maybe three times a year at $12,000 a week and he'd end up owing us money. I remember one night he ended up not only owing us his salary, but we took his diamond cufflinks as well. We'd take him upstairs and knock him out of the box in a rigged dice game. He never knew what happened. We did the same with Lou Monte at Chez Joey's. I think we paid him $11,000 a week. He'd wind up losing it in a crap game. I felt sorry for him. His kid had an incurable disease and he went all over the world to try to find a cure for him. Lou was a nice guy.

"Some of the entertainers used us. That used to boil me. They'd use us, move up to the top and then ignore you. Like Jerry Vale. Jerry began playing The Frolics, a club owned by Chickie Spar. It became a regular appearance. He was great. Jerry knew all of us. We packed the place for him. But when he got well known and he was working places like the Copacabana in New York or the Ed Sullivan television show, he didn't remember anybody. I bumped into him one night at the Copa in New York City. He ignored me as though he didn't know me. I pulled him aside. I said: "I don't want to embarrass you, now . . . but do I embarrass you by saying hello?" If he'd said anything, I'd have given him a whack in the mouth. All he said was that my face slipped his mind. How could my face slip his mind? He'd seen it every day for months.

"Dean Martin was different. He came to the Mayfair at the recommendation of some of his friends from Ohio. He was just getting started, but he was a barrel of laughs whenever you saw him and he never forgot a face, never forgot to say hello to you no matter where you were. He's just a nice guy and a helluva entertainer and everybody liked him for it.

"The only guy the Boston Mob couldn't stand was Frank Sinatra. Let me tell you a story about him. This was before he made the big time again with that picture, *From Here to Eternity*. He was begging for spots to sing at then. The Palladinos let him do his stuff at the Copa in Boston and they paid him a good buck for it. He did all right, not sensational, but all right. Then he went to Joe Beans and asked if he could borrow some money. He told Joe that he could deduct what he borrowed the next time he came in to play the club. He said he'd be back to play the club in about a month after the movie came out. Joe was glad to help out. Then the picture came out and it was a smash hit. Sinatra paid Joe back what he owed him but he never came back to play the club like he promised.

"Sinatra has a helluva lot of talent, but he's got no class. He picks his spots to be a tough guy with people. I've been in his company in Florida two or three times and I don't like the man. He was close to Sam Giancana, the boss of Chicago. He's always talking about the Mob guys he knows. Who gives a damn, especially if you're a Mob guy yourself? He's very boisterous, loud, but I know Mob guys who idolize him, like Butch Miceli. He used to stick close to Sinatra like glue, and he carried a phone book around with Sinatra's private number on every page.

"Now Sinatra's a big man. Don't get me wrong, he's earned his reputation as an entertainer. He's a real showman on stage. But he's got a lot of Mob friends as well as friends in all walks of life. I don't begrudge him a thing and one thing, he doesn't forget his friends either. But I get a big kick out of these phoney politicians that gravitate around him, like flies. Look at Spiro Agnew, or before they knew better, President John F. Kennedy and his brother Bobby. They used him to help them raise money. Then they turn around and say they're great fighters against corruption. They criticize other people for being with Mob guys. They're hypocrites. They don't criticize Sinatra for the people he knows."

The Last Mafioso

Aladena Fratianno

The third of the triumvirate of informers condemned by Joe Bonanno was Aladena "Jimmy the Weasel" Fratianno. As acting head of the Los Angeles crime family, he was the highest-ranking mafioso to become a Federal witness. Born in Naples, Fratianno was brought to Cleveland as a baby. They lived in the Murray Hill-Mayfield Road district then known as Little Italy or simply the Hill. As a child, he began stealing from fruit stands and earned his nickname "the Weasel" from outrunning the police. Working for the Mob in Cleveland, he established a reputation as a hitman. In 1947, he joined the Los Angeles family and claimed responsibility for at least eleven gangland slayings under Los Angeles crime boss Jack Dragna. Following the death of Dragna in 1956, he rose through the ranks until, in the 1970s, Fratianno learned that the Cosa Nostra had put out a contract on him. For his own protection he turned state's evidence. From December 1977 to August 1987, Fratianno was the Justice Department's star witness, fingering such notorious Mob bosses as Frank "Funzi" Tieri, Carmine "Junior" Persico and the head of his own former crime family, Dominic Brooklier. As a paid informant Fratianno was sheltered by the Federal witness protection programme, which provided him with financial support, bodyguards and a series of phoney identities. But in 1987, Fratianno's government caretakers cut off his living allowance, on the grounds that the Federal witness protection programme "was never intended to be a retirement plan for former mobsters". The Justice Department claimed that Mr Fratianno could take care of himself. He made money by charging hefty fees to appear on TV crime documentaries and as an expert witness in underworld trials. He collaborated in the writing of two autobiographies: The Last Mafioso *with Ovid Demaris and* Vengeance is Mine *with Michael J. Zuckerman. He died in in 1993 after suffering from Alzheimer's Disease.*

It had taken him thirty-three years to arrive at this moment. Early that evening he was brought to a winery on South Figueroa Street and now he waited in a small, dimly lit room for the final act to be played out.

Jimmy Fratianno prided himself on his ability to remain calm under stress, but he could feel the excitement stirring through him. He locked the feeling inside, not wanting to share it with the other four candidates. He could hear the deep rumble of voices in the other room, the scraping of chairs, and he knew that many awaited his entrance. Standing room only, he thought, trying to lighten the feeling that was knotting his nerves.

Then the door opened and Johnny Roselli beckoned to him. "It's time," he said.

They walked down a short hallway and stopped before a closed door. Roselli squeezed his arm and smiled.

"Just a couple things, Jimmy. After you've taken the oath, go around the circle and kiss everybody and introduce yourself. Then join hands with the others. Are you ready?"

He nodded and Roselli opened the door. It was a large room and the pungent odour of fermented grapes was stronger here. There must have been fifty men in the room, many of whom he had met in the seventeen months he had been in Los Angeles. They were gathered in a circle around a long table, their faces grim, their eyes shadowed by the harsh lighting from bare overhanging bulbs.

Roselli led Jimmy to the head of the table where Jack Dragna was standing, a short, heavyset man with horn-rimmed glasses, who reminded Jimmy of a banker. Tom Dragna, as usual in sports clothes, was on Jack's left and Momo Adamo on his right.

"Jimmy, Jack Dragna's the boss of our family," Roselli said. "Momo Adamo's the underboss and Tom's the *consigliere*."

Jack Dragna raised his hand and spoke to everyone in the room. "Everybody join hands," he said.

On the table in front of where Jimmy was standing was a revolver and a dagger crossing one another. The next time Jack spoke was in a confusing mixture of Sicilian and Italian. He spoke rapidly and Jimmy tried desperately to understand what was being said to him in front of all these people.

What he was able to make out went something like this: "We are gathered here this evening to make five new members: Jimmy Fratianno, Jimmy Regace, Charley Dippolito, Louie Piscopo, and Tom's son, Louie Dragna. Now, Jimmy, you are entering into the honoured society of Cosa Nostra, which welcomes only men of great courage and loyalty.

"You come in alive and you go out dead. The gun and knife are the instruments by which you live and die.

"Cosa Nostra comes first above anything else in your life. Before family, before country, before God. When you are summoned, you must come even if your mother, or wife, or your children are on their deathbed.

"There are three laws you must obey without question. You must never betray any of the secrets of this Cosa

Nostra. You must never violate the wife or children of another member. You must never become involved with narcotics. The violation of any of these laws means death without trial or warning."

There was more but, thirty years later, this was what Jimmy Fratianno remembered. The rest of the ritual sermon was a blur.

The next thing Jimmy heard was Jack Dragna asking him to raise the index finger of his right hand. He wondered at the request until Jack pricked his finger with a pin. A small bubble of blood burst forth.

When he looked up, Roselli winked at him. Still speaking in his Sicilian-Italian dialect, Dragna said, "This drop of blood symbolizes your birth into our family. We're one until death."

He paused a moment and then stepped forward and kissed Jimmy on both cheeks. "Jimmy, you're now a made guy, an *amico nostra*, a *soldato* in our *famiglia*. Whenever you wish to introduce a member to another member he don't know, you say, '*Amica nostra*.' In English, you say, 'This is a friend of *ours*.' But whenever you introduce a member to someone who's not a member, you say, 'This is a friend of *mine*.' "

The ceremony was over. Jimmy turned and kissed Roselli. People began talking again and Jimmy was so excited that he could feel his legs tremble as he moved from man to man, kissing and shaking hands, being slapped on the back, hearing words of congratulation. He was now a member of an ancient and extremely exclusive society. It made him a special person, an inheritor of enormous power. It was something he had wanted as long as he could remember.

In a way, it was almost as though a carefully plotted script had delivered Aladena "Jimmy" Fratianno to that room. Born on 14 November 1913, in a small town near Naples, he was brought to the United States by his mother when he was four months old. His father, Antonio, was already in this country with relatives in Cleveland. In 1915, a daughter, Louise, was born, followed by another son, Warren, three years later.

Fratianno's background was classical American Mafioso. Aladena, as Jimmy was christened, was one of thousands of Italian immigrants living in the Murray Hill-Mayfield Road district then known as Little Italy but also called the Hill.

At the age of six, he had seen three men mowed down by machine-gun fire in front of Tony Milano's speakeasy and his reaction had been an awed, "Holy mother of Jesus!"

The conditions in Cleveland's Little Italy were not all that different from those in the old country. Except, of course, that now the Italians were a minority, confined to a ghetto by their language and manners. They laboured long hours in menial, back-breaking work for minimal wages, their crafts for the most part forgotten in their desperate need to provide food and shelter for their large families.

Some, however, were self-employed and could hold their heads up with pride. Among them was Antonio Fratianno, who worked as a landscape contractor and was known as a serious, sober man, a good provider, but also the absolute autocrat of his household.

Aladena's first memory, and one he never forgot, remembering it always with a pleasurable glow, was the horse and buggy his father had bought when Aladena was three years old. They lived on East 125th Street then, and he remembered how the neighbours had admired the buggy with the fringed canvas top. He loved that horse and buggy and the way the fringe would dance happily as the horse trotted down the street. He cried the day his father sold it, harder than he did when his father used the strap on him.

His father was strict and quick to punish. Although he was strict with Louise and Warren, he spared the rod with them, a fact not lost on Aladena, who grew even more resentful. The punishment gradually became a duel of willpower between two determined enemies. The harder he was beaten, the harder he became to handle. He grew obstinate and defiant, determined to have his own way and ready to defy all who contested him.

In school he was rowdy, getting into fights with other boys and teachers, until finally he was sent to Thomas Edison, which was known as a "bad boy" school. There he formed a life-long friendship with Louis "Babe" Triscaro, who later would become an important Teamsters official and the liaison between Jimmy Hoffa and the Cleveland Mafia.

Almost from the time he could walk, Aladena had been preoccupied with the importance of money. Besides having his own paper route at the age of six, he hawked newspapers at the No. 4 gate at the Fischer Body plant, and in front of the Hayden Theater evenings and weekends. At eleven he was working with his father, putting in a six-day week during summer vacations and all day Saturdays during the school year.

During this period he gained the cognomen that would stick to him for the rest of his life. There was a policeman who used to chase him whenever he stole fruit from sidewalk stands, which was often, and one day Aladena hit the policeman in the face with a rotten tomato. The policeman gave chase. People stopped to watch, and an older man said, "Look at that weasel run!" When making out his report, the policeman wrote down the nickname and it became part of his police record, following him wherever he went.

It was just prior to this incident that he had started calling himself Jimmy – Aladena sounded too much like a "broad's name" – and the next thing he knew he was "Jimmy the Weasel". Although at sixteen he entered amateur boxing competitions as Kid Weasel, winning the Collingwood Community Center trophy in the lightweight division, his friends never used the nickname, at least not to his face.

His first experience with bootlegging was at the age of twelve. He was a waiter in a speakeasy owned by a woman called Bessie. For nearly two years he worked part-time for Bessie and saw so many drunks that it turned him against liquor. He would see men come in and drink their entire paychecks, money they needed for their families. At night in bed he would think, "God, people got to be crazy to get drunk." It was the money part that bothered him the most.

His behaviour in school gradually improved and he transferred to Collingwood High School for the ninth grade, but a year later he caught cold, ignored it until it turned to pneumonia, and with a fever of 106 degrees lapsed into a coma. It was two weeks before he regained consciousness and when he did he found a priest giving him the last rites. As the priest touched his tongue with the Communion wafer, Jimmy opened his eyes and said, "I'm better." Then he slipped back into his coma for another week.

By the time he opened his eyes the second time, the pneumonia had turned into pleurisy, which had created an enormous deposit of pus in his left lung and pleural cavities. It got so thick it was pushing his heart against his right lung. When all efforts to remove it with a syringe failed, Dr Victor Tanno decided that the only way to get at it was to remove a rib. Because of his weakened condition, ether was out of the question. They would use a local anaesthetic, but as Dr Tanno warned him, it would freeze the flesh but not the bone. With Jimmy strapped to a chair, facing the back of it, and held by his mother, Dr Tanno made the incision in his back and began cutting into the rib.

The memory of that pain would be with him all the years of his life. Fifty years later he could still remember how he had screamed and cursed that doctor, could still feel the teeth-gnashing pain of the saw cutting into bone, a pain so intense he felt blinded, his brain on fire, every nerve end begging for mercy, and he could still feel his mother's arms around him, hear her cries as if they were coming from a great distance, echoing off the walls and pounding at his ears with his own cries and curses.

When the doctor finally cut through the rib and pulled it out, the pus shot out with explosive force. Dr Tanno laughed and said, "Look, nurse, it's like an oil well erupting."

He never returned to school. Although his grades had been below average, he was extremely quick with numbers, a talent that he had already put to practical use. At the age of fourteen, while hawking newspapers at Fischer Body, he had become acquainted with Johnny Martin, a gambler who operated games at Mike's, a Greek restaurant across the street from the No. 4 gate. Martin, who had taken a liking to the boy, spent hours in a room above the restaurant teaching him all the cheating tricks he knew. He taught him how to shuffle cards, how to deal seconds, and how to mark them during a game by using a small piece of sandpaper hidden in the palm of the hand. Jimmy got so he could mark an entire deck in less than an hour. He learned to use shaded dice, to palm the third dice, to switch, and which numbers were winners and which losers.

By the age of seventeen he had become Martin's partner at Mike's, receiving an even cut of the winnings. Later Jimmy bought a portable crap table and began holding his own games at a friend's house. Booking the game and using shaded dice, he would clear three or four hundred dollars in a matter of a few hours. This money was a far richer reward for less effort than the paltry wage he received from his father for driving a truck each day.

At eighteen he was charged with raping a twenty-five-year-old divorcee. Under cross-examination the woman confessed she had lied because she thought she could extort money from his father, and the case was dropped. But the charge of rape, like the nickname "Weasel", would become apart of his police record, a blemish irrevocable for all time.

A few days before his nineteenth birthday, on a cold moonlit night, Jimmy and a friend went ice-skating at Elysium Park. Jimmy could do just about anything on skates. He played hockey, was an agile figure skater, and could even dance on ice while wearing his long-bladed racers. This made him popular with the girls, which was all the incentive he needed to strut his stuff.

On this particular evening, he showed off for a girl who was with three other girls and five tough-looking Polish boys. When he was leaving the Elysium, the five boys attacked him. The next thing he knew fists and feet were coming at him from all directions. He tried to fight back, but he was pounded into the ground. He was groggily crawling around on all fours, when a heavy boot caught him square in the nose. Bone shattered, blood spurted out, and he flopped over on his back in time for the boot to catch the side of his nose. He rolled over on his stomach and tried to protect his face and head with his arms. He was vaguely aware of blows raining against his body but he was soon beyond pain.

He came to in a receiving hospital. The bridge of his nose was hopelessly crushed and they had to rebuild it with gristle taken from the lower part of his chest. After the operation, he was advised to return for plastic surgery when it had healed, but he never went back.

With the help of his friend, Anthony "Tony Dope" Delsanter, a husky six-footer, Jimmy went out looking for the Polish boys. He caught four of them, in the dark of night, when each was alone, and after knocking them to the ground, Jimmy had gone to work with a blackjack, breaking noses, knocking out teeth, fracturing jaws, and cracking skulls, even breaking the arm of the boy whose boot he suspected had broken his nose. All the boys required hospitalization and all needed many stitches in their heads. The fifth boy had moved away, but Jimmy continued looking for him for a whole year before he grudgingly acknowledged defeat.

For Jimmy, it was something that had to be done, a wrong that had to be righted, a vendetta in the best Italian tradition. While working the boys over with the blackjack, he had realized how easy it would be to kill. He had hit hard enough for that, he had thought at the time; it had not bothered him in the least. For Jimmy, it was an important realization.

When Jimmy was twenty, Jack Haffey, the boss of the 26th Ward, who worked as a state inspector on highway construction, confided to Jimmy that he had top political connections and if they worked together they could make some money. The first opportunity was a contract calling for 25,000 yards of fill for a reservoir. Jimmy's father had two trucks, and Jimmy suggested that he lease six more. The state was paying fifty cents a yard and, with sideboards, they could load two and a half yards in their one-and-a-half-yard trucks. His father was interested until Jimmy told him it would cost $500 to get the job.

"I don't want to get in no trouble," his father said.

"You ain't going to get in trouble," Jimmy replied. "This guy's a pal of the governor."

"I don't want to do nothing crooked."

"Ah, forget it," Jimmy cried. "I can't make no fucking money with you. I'll lease some trucks and do the job myself."

The next day he became his own boss. He leased eight trucks and gave Haffey the $500 payoff. When the first truck arrived at the reservoir, Jimmy said, "Jack, measure this truck coming in. All my trucks are the same size."

Haffey looked the truck over. "What do you think, Jimmy?"

"Three and a half yards, Jack. We're stacking them up high."

From then on, Haffey wrote down three and a half yards, which meant that Jimmy was making fifty cents extra on each load. With eight trucks making six and seven trips a day, it meant that he was earning an extra $25 to $30 a day, besides the ten cents a yard broker's fee he was making from the truck owners.

About this time, Jimmy also started booking at the local racetracks and hanging around the clubhouse of the Italian American Brotherhood (IAB) on Mayfield Road. Run by Tony Milano (who would later become the underboss of the Cleveland family), the IAB was the hangout for all the local big shots, who sat outside in the summer, talking quietly among themselves and watching people walk by.

"Big Al" Polizzi was the boss. There was Johnny DeMarco and "Johnny King" Angersola, with his brothers, Fred and George. Jimmy also got to know the leaders of the Jewish mob, known as the Cleveland Syndicate. These men – Louis "Lou Rhady" Rothkopf, Moe Dalitz, Morris Kleinman – operated gambling joints in Cleveland, as well as in Newport and Covington, Kentucky, all with the blessings of Big Al's Mayfield Road Gang. Others in the syndicate included Ruby Kolod, Sam Tucker, and, in later years, Lou Rhody's nephew, Bernard "Bernie" Rothkopf, who would grow up to become president of the MGM Grand Hotel in Las Vegas. They also were involved in Buckeye Enterprises, which controlled various gambling concessions, and was the hidden link between the Mayfield Road Gang and the Cleveland Syndicate.

Even as a young boy, Jimmy had suspected that there was some kind of a secret Italian organization that was more cohesive and powerful than the Jews or Irish with whom they worked, but in those days the words Mafia or Cosa Nostra were never used even on the Hill. The only reference to any crime organization ever mentioned was "The Combination". And it was The Combination which then controlled organized crime in Cleveland.

In 1934 Jimmy bought a two-year-old Marmon limousine and began chauffeuring customers from the East Side to The Combination's gambling joints around Cleveland. Lou Rhody paid him seven dollars a load. Jimmy drove the limousine himself for a while and then hired a driver.

With money rolling in from the gambling, the chauffeuring and the trucking, he bought himself a new Chevrolet coupe and began having his clothes tailor-made. He wore a broad-brimmed Capone-style hat, alligator shoes, and carried a couple thousand dollars in his pocket. Life was sweet in the midst of the nation's worst depression.

With more leisure than he knew how to handle, he turned to golf and met Bill McSweeney, a big, tough Irishman who broke heads for the Teamsters union when he was not belting golf balls out of sight. McSweeney's boss was Tommy Lenahan, a man in constant need of head breakers because the Teamsters was a small, struggling union in those days.

Jimmy's first involvement with the union was in their effort to organize the parking lots in Cleveland. With the "Neanderthal" McSweeney and others at his side, five-foot-nine Jimmy, who weighed a hundred-fifty soaking wet, would march into parking lots and throw muriatic acid on cars while his partners slashed tyres and broke windshields.

The pay was fifteen dollars a day, plus ten dollars a day for every man Jimmy could induce to work for five dollars a day on his crew. During the Premier Aluminium strike, Jimmy had a crew of nine, recruited from the Hill, who fought against scabs and cops, both private and public, with lead pipes, baseball bats, blackjacks, and tyre chains.

Jimmy's old friend from bad boy school, [Louis] Babe Triscaro, was also cracking heads on the picket lines. From the Premier it was on to the knitting mills around Seventy-ninth Street and Euclid Avenue. And from there to the transportation drivers, with special instructions from Lenahan as to whose head to break.

By the end of 1935, after an exhausting four months of hand-to-hand combat on picket lines, Jimmy came into his own. He went to Florida with the rest of the big boys on the Hill. That was the year The Combination opened The Plantation, its first gambling casino in Miami. He bought a new Oldsmobile, a flashy wardrobe, had $2,500 cash in his pocket, and some expertise in bookmaking.

Johnny Martin had long ago explained the fundamentals which had proved profitable at the local racetracks. Hialeah would be no different. "Booking at the track," Johnny had told him, "is the easiest, safest way to gamble in the world. If you know what you're doing, you'll never lose a nickel. Just balance your book and never refuse a bet. Drop all the long-shots in the box – but when you go to the window don't let the bettor know. The reason they bet with you instead of going to the window themselves is that they don't want to reduce the odds. Get yourself a runner. And at night when you go to bed, pray that your bettors get their horses from the racing form and not from some fucking hot tips. Stay away from hot horses."

On his first day at Hialeah, Johnny King introduced him to "Lucky" Luciano, who looked pretty relaxed for a man who was then the subject of the hottest investigation in

New York history. Two of Luciano's boys began giving Jimmy their action, going a hundred and a hundred, win and place, on each race, each selecting a different horse from the racing form. It could not have been more perfect. The meet was fifty-five days and in that time Jimmy took them for $24,000.

When he returned home, Jimmy started booking at the World Exposition, which had moved from Chicago to Cleveland. He made his headquarters in the midgets' tent, most of whom were avid horse players. He liked their company, enjoyed their sense of humour, their ability to ignore the misfortune that had made them objects of curiosity. And they were good customers.

In the evening, Jimmy and his friends made the rounds of nightclubs, getting the best tables and hobnobbing with the owners, who showed their pleasure at meeting these rising Young Turks by introducing them to their friendly chorus girls. The friendliest girls, the ones who flattered their ego by never asking for money, were also introduced to James "Blackie" Licavoli, who was on the lam for the murder of Toledo beer baron Jackie Kennedy and his girlfriend. Blackie's cousin, Thomas "Yonnie" Licavoli, and four others were serving life terms for his crime, while five others involved in the murder had evaded justice by going into hiding. It was through Blackie Licavoli, when Licavoli went to Pittsburgh to stay with Mafia boss John LaRock (*née* LaRocca), that Jimmy and Tony Dope met Frankie Valenti who one day would be the Mafia boss of Rochester, New York, and would, in these early years, teach Jimmy a few tricks.

· At the French Casino Jimmy first met his future wife. He walked into the place, took one look at the hatcheck girl, and immediately sent for the owner to be formally introduced. She was eighteen and her name was Jewel Switzer. She was Irish and German, with blonde hair and big blue eyes, not exactly the kind of girl Italian boys brought home to mother in those days. On 1 August 1936, they drove to Bowing Green and were married. Two months later she was pregnant.

In the summer of 1936 Jimmy and his Cleveland friends discovered that it was a lot quicker and far more profitable to rob gambling joints than to run their own crooked game. Tony Dope Delsanter, who had spent time in a reformatory, was ready for a fast score.

Their first job was a poker game. Jimmy and Tony Dope walked in without disguises, pulled out revolvers, and ordered the nine men in the room to strip down to their underwear and face the wall. They got $5,800 in cash and some jewellery.

The LaRock-Licavoli connection set up the next score. Frankie Valenti had a swanky gambling joint picked out: They went in fast, with their faces obscured by silk stockings, and Jimmy and Tony Dope, who carried sawed-off shotguns, jumped on top of crap tables and screamed, "This is a stickup, against the walls, motherfuckers," and two hundred people ran to obey their command. The take was $70,000.

It was the kind of easy score that encouraged them to try others. One was a customer of the Cleveland Trust Bank, which was just around the corner from the home of his parents on Earlwood Street. Every two weeks, this man, whom he had met at Mike's, used to draw $25,000 from his bank to cash cheques at Fischer Body.

Jimmy had parked his brand new Buick, which was to be the crash car, on St Clair Avenue, about a hundred yards away, but with an excellent view of the bank. A friend, Hipsy Cooper, in the getaway car, was about fifty yards ahead of him, and both were watching as Valenti and Tony Dope held up the man at gunpoint as he emerged from the bank and ran down the sidewalk toward the corner of Earlwood where Hipsy was supposed to pick them up. Except that he was not moving. Jimmy gunned the Buick, pulled up alongside Hipsy, and screamed at him to get going. But Hipsy appeared to be in a state of shock. Cursing and threatening dire retaliation, Jimmy knew that he had no alternative but to use his own car to help his friends escape. The theory of a crash car is to obstruct whatever pursuit there may be of the getaway car, regardless of the risk involved.

Jimmy skidded around the corner. He knew his friends, fleeing on foot, would head down the alley behind the bank to Blenheim, take a right, run up Blenheim about ten houses, jump a fence and dash through back yards to his house. Jimmy hit the alley, slammed on the brakes, and threw the Buick into a spinning skid, coming to a stop sideways so that it completely blocked the alley. Behind him was the man who had been robbed, standing on the running board of a car he had commandeered to give chase. And behind him was a police car, with siren blaring.

Jimmy jumped out of his car and started waving his arms in an hysterical fashion. "They've got guns," he cried. "They've got guns, I saw them, they're armed and dangerous, duck down, they've got guns and they're dangerous."

"Get the hell out of the way," the man on the running board screamed. "Let us through here."

"Oh, my God, this is terrible. They've got guns," Jimmy continued to cry, waving his arms like a man who has lost his senses.

"Get that car out of there," a policeman, hanging out the opened window of his car, shouted as he waved his hand, signalling Jimmy to move out.

Jimmy jumped into his car, spun the wheel around, threw it into reverse, and slammed on the brakes inches from the other car's front bumper. He threw up his arms in desperation, stalled the engine, turned the motor over with the ignition off, ground the gears, and finally roared out of the alley when he was sure that his friends had had ample time to reach his house.

They were sitting in the parlour, gulping steaming cups of coffee his mother had just served them, and they were livid. They wanted to kill Hipsy. "Where's the cocksucker?" Tony Dope wanted to know. "He left us there to die."

Valenti was angry but less emotional about it. "Where'd you get that *cretino*?"

"It's his first score," Jimmy said. "He panicked, froze at the wheel."

"I'm going to kill that prick," Dope promised.

"Fuck him," Jimmy said. "Let's cut it up three ways and forget him."

Jimmy's daughter Joanne was born on 24 June 1937, a beautiful, happy baby, but Jimmy had little time to spend with his family. Exactly one month later he pulled his last job for a while. The victim was Joe Deutsch, a layoff bookmaker who was too slow in paying off. When Jimmy called to ask why he had not been paid, Deutsch said, " 'Listen, punk, you'll get paid when I get good and ready to pay. No sooner, understand." Jimmy started screaming and Deutsch slammed down the phone in his ear.

For the next few days, Jimmy was like a demented man.

He told Tony Dope and McSweeney that he wanted to hurt Deutsch, and they suggested that they might as well get some money while they were at it. For a while they followed Deutsch as he made the rounds of his drops. Jimmy decided to use his Buick and Tony Dope stole some plates which they attached to the Buick's plates with clothes pins painted black.

They struck at nine-thirty on a Saturday night at the downtown intersection of Ninth and Superior, with people five rows deep along the sidewalks. McSweeney was behind the wheel of the Buick and Jimmy and Tony Dope were in the back seat, each armed with a .38 revolver. When the light turned red, they were right behind Deutsch's car. They jumped out of the Buick and came at Deutsch from both sides, with Jimmy on the driver's side. They opened the doors and Jimmy said, "Joe, move over. Don't make no dumb plays and you won't get hurt."

The moment Deutsch saw the guns, he began screaming for help. "Hit him in the fucking mouth," Jimmy told Tony Dope as he tried to shove and push Deutsch out of the way so he could squeeze in behind the steering wheel. He heard the dull thudding of Tony Dope's gun as it repeatedly smashed against Deutsch's head. Blood spurted on Jimmy's new grey gabardine suit and he screamed at Tony Dope, "Pull him away from me." The light turned green and he frantically shifted into gear. He meandered up side streets, getting away from the commercial district, until they were on a quiet residential street.

Deutsch was unconscious and Tony Dope had cleaned out his pockets. Jimmy pulled to the kerb and McSweeney stopped behind them. While McSweeney removed the hot plates, Jimmy looked for a sewer to dump the plates and guns. But McSweeney had borrowed his gun from a friend and refused to throw it away. Instead he put it in the glove compartment, and with him behind the wheel, with Tony Dope at his side and Jimmy in the back seat, they decided to go to McSweeney's house for Jimmy and Tony Dope to clean up and to divide the 1,600 dollars found on Deutsch, which was a long way from the 10,000 they had expected.

"We nearly got in the shit," McSweeney said. "That sonovabitch screamed loud enough to wake the dead."

Jimmy laughed. "As long as he don't wake the Cops."

Before he could finish the sentence they heard a siren. Seconds later a squad car pulled alongside and a policeman waved them to the kerb.

They waited in the Buick as two policemen approached from both sides of their car. The officer on Tony Dope's side played a flashlight on Jimmy in the back seat.

"What happened to you, buddy?" he asked.

"I was in a little fight at the poolroom," he said, with a note of apology in his voice. "They're taking me home so I can clean up."

"Oh, yeah? Get out of the car, all of you."

What happened next was inevitable. They found McSweeney's gun and later they found Deutsch, who refused to identify his assailants, but the police lab matched the blood, and that was it.

The judge handed down ten-to-twenty-five-year prison sentences to all three. Jewel screamed when the verdict was pronounced and his mother and sister held on to each other and wept. There were tears in his brother Warren's eyes when Jimmy turned to wave to his family, refusing to walk to the railing to touch or speak to them. His father's eyes were dry as he stoically gazed at his son. He shook his head, once or twice, as if to say, "Why didn't you listen to me," but it was too late.

In 1937 the nation's second oldest penal institution was the Ohio State Penitentiary. Its forty-foot high grey stone wall covered four square blocks in downtown Columbus, an awesome, soul-chilling sight. Passing through its massive steel gates at the age of twenty-three, Jimmy knew he would have to spend some of the best years of his life behind that forbidding wall. For the first time in years, he felt weak and powerless, vulnerable in a world that could crush him like a bug.

All that he had to draw succour from was the advice an old con had given him: "Jimmy, remember one thing when you walk through that gate. Once you're in that joint, you're going to do that time. Nothing can stop that. So do good time. Learn how to relax. Forget your family, forget your friends on the outside. Pretend they don't even exist. Don't worry about nothing. Don't count the days, throw out the calendar. Sleep all you can and dream about sexy movie stars. When your pecker gets stiff in the night, think about Jean Harlow and whack it. Stay away from punks. There's nothing they can do for you that you can't do with your palm. Get involved in prison activities. Keep your nose clean but don't take no shit from nobody. Grab a club and break their fucking heads in a minute. That way nobody's ever going to fuck with you again. When you don't know what to think about, try to imagine what you're going to get for breakfast or dinner or supper. Get involved in team sports. Don't worry about cockroaches or bedbugs and rats.

"Face up to the reality of prison life. Don't talk to screws, you've got nothing to say to them. They've got nothing to do with what happens to you in there. Remember that it's the cons that run the prison. They're the clerks, they do all the paperwork, keep the files, assign the good jobs, the good cell blocks, they see that you get extra privileges. Screws don't do nothing but watch. Go to school, you won't learn nothing, but you'll get to see other cons, for that joint keeps everybody under lock and key twenty-four hours a day.

"It's a hard place and it's killed lots of good men, young and old, but it can't kill nobody that knows how to do good time. That, my boy, is the secret of surviving in that joint. Do one day at a time and let the outside world go fuck itself."

Jimmy never forgot that advice, and recites it verbatim forty years later. It served him well through the many years of time he would do.

He soon learned that it really was the cons who ruled the prison, and that the most important one at the Ohio Penitentiary was Blackie's cousin, Thomas "Yonnie" Licavoli. Yonnie got Jimmy a job in the kitchen, a prize assignment, and had him transferred from a cell block to a dormitory. For the three years that he was there, Yonnie was his protector.

In the spring of 1940, Jimmy's father brought him both good and bad news. The good news was that he had met a man who could get him transferred to the London Prison Farm for $1,500. The bad news was that Jewel, who had moved to Los Angeles with her parents, had divorced him. "She still loves you," his father said, "but they made her do it." Jimmy wanted to laugh – not that he was happy about the divorce, but because it was so unimportant at this point in his life.

There were no grey walls at the prison farm in London, Ohio. There was a cyclone fence, dormitories, freedom to talk, no marching to the dining hall, plenty of windows with no bars, and lots of fresh air and outdoor sports. From early spring to late fall, Jimmy spent most of his time playing softball. Warden William Amrine was a softball freak. He had an all-star team called Amrine's Angels which played games all over the state and the players lived in the honour dorm. Jimmy made Amrine's Angels his second year there. He was a good player, quick on the bases, slick with a glove, and the best line-drive hitter on the team. His batting average led the league for three consecutive years.

Not neglected, however, was his talent for gambling. Shooting craps on top of their bunk beds, without a backboard, Jimmy was soon an expert at a pad roll. By rolling the dice with the two sixes facing each other it was impossible to crap out on the first roll.

For a while Jimmy was the farm's fire chief and he used to sleep days. Late one afternoon he reported on sick call.

Jimmy knew the doctor, who was a softball fan. He said, "Doc, this's probably going to sound awfully funny to you, but I think there's something wrong with me."

"What's the problem? Getting headaches?"

"Doc, I had four wet dreams this afternoon. I took four showers and scored four times for sheets. That ain't normal."

"I never heard of that," the doctor said. "What have you been eating, for Christ's sake?"

"Well, doc, when I get off work, I have a quart of half-and-half, a couple eggs, you know, and some vanilla extract, and I stir it all up like a milk shake."

"My God," the doctor said. "I've got to try that. Four? Are you sure?"

"I usually get a couple, you know, but never four before."

"My advice is stop drinking that stuff until you get out of this place."

The solution, Jimmy decided, was a three-day pass, which he arranged by having his sister send a telegram that his mother was too ill to visit him. Deputy Warden Jay Young accompanied him to Cleveland. Jimmy gave him a $250 bonus, free and clear of all expenses. When word got around the prison, officials began competing with each other for the privilege of taking him home. In all he had five three-day passes.

Jimmy was released from the prison farm on Washington's Birthday 1945. A month earlier, he had found an opportunity to visit Yonnie Licavoli at the Ohio penitentiary and had told him of his plans to remarry Jewel and move to Los Angeles.

"Jimmy, if you go to Los Angeles, get in touch with Johnny Roselli," Yonnie had advised him. "He's in the federal joint at Leavenworth right now. He got caught in that movie extortion rap with some of the top guys in the Chicago outfit, but I hear they're working out some deal to spring them. When he gets out, he'll come to L.A., and you give him my regards. Tell him I'd appreciate it if he got you straightened out with the right people." It would be two and a half years before Jimmy would finally meet Johnny Roselli.

Following his release from the prison farm, he went back to pulling jobs with Frank Valenti, trying to build up a nest egg for his California venture. To satisfy his parole officer, he managed canteens at three factories for Babe Triscaro who was now the business agent for the truckers' local, with plush offices in the new Teamsters building.

Managing canteens looked like a legitimate job to Jimmy's parole officer, but it was a black market operation and a gold mine. He sold nylon hose, cigarettes, liquor, food and gas ration stamps – anything that was hard to get. He bought from hijackers, burglars, and hustlers, and sold at mark-ups of two and three hundred per cent. From time to time, to improve his mark-up, he would personally venture into the hijacking business, with the deals set up by Teamsters officials.

Jimmy and Jewel were remarried before moving to Los Angeles in June 1946. Unknown to Jewel, Jimmy had nearly 90,000 dollars stashed in the truck of his new Buick, the money he had been collecting to launch his California career.

His first large-scale operation in Los Angeles was as a bookmaker at the Chase Hotel in Santa Monica. He rented a three-room suite on the third floor and opened a cigar stand in the lobby. He formed a friendship with Salvatore "Dago Louie" Piscopo and gradually became friendly with the Dragnas and some of their associates. Over pizza and coffee at Mimi Tripoli's pizzeria on the Sunset Strip, and over some of the best Italian food in town at Naples, he met Giolama "Momo" Adamo, and his brother, Joe; Charles Dippolito and his son, Joe, who owned a vineyard in Cucamonga; Leo Moceri, who, like Blackie Licavoli years earlier, was on the lam from the Jackie Kennedy murder in Toledo; several Matrangas, Frank, Joe, Jasper, Leo, and Gaspare, who was not related to the other four and had once been the boss of Calumet City, Illinois, but now lived in Upland, California; Pete Milano, Tony's son; Frank "Bomp" Bompensiero, who was from San Diego and was in partnership with Jack Dragna in a couple of bars in that city, including the Gold Rail; Tony Mirabile, also from San Diego, who owned dozens of bars; James Iannone, who under the alias of Danny Wilson had acquired a reputation as a muscleman but was in fact terrified of violence; Louis Tom Dragna, who was Tom's son; Nick Licata and his son, Carlo; Frank DeSimone, who was an attorney; Sam Bruno and Biaggio Bonventre, both of whom always looked ready for action, and were; and Simone Scozzari, who years later would be caught at the Apalachin, New York, Mafia meeting with DeSimone and deported.

It was in September 1947 that Jimmy went to Dago Louie's house to meet Roselli. He found him to be a gentleman in every sense, which pleased Jimmy because he had heard so much about this man from Yonnie and Dago Louie. Jimmy noticed that the cut of Roselli's suit was far more conservative than anything he had ever worn. Everything was subtly colour-coordinated and Jimmy resolved to discard his own wardrobe which looked flashy and cheap by comparison.

Looking at Roselli only confirmed that old saying about not being able to judge a book by its cover. Some of the toughest guys he had known had often appeared more gentlemanly than the rough-looking punks who fainted at the sight of blood. Here was Roselli, looking like a man of distinction in his conservatively tailored suit, his blue eyes gently amused as he spoke in soft, modulated tones. Who would have guessed that as a kid he had been tough enough to make it with Capone at a time when tough guys were dying like flies. Later when Capone went to prison, Roselli took his orders from the new Chicago boss, Frank Nitti. Roselli was then dispatched to California, where his job was to protect Nationwide, then the only horserace wire service in the country. He also was a "labour-relations expert" in the motion picture industry, keeping an eye on Willie Bioff, who Nitti had placed in charge of the International Alliance of Theatrical Stage Employees and Motion Picture Operators. Then, in 1944, on the testimony of Bioff, the top hierarchy of the Chicago Mob was convicted for extorting a million dollars from the movie industry and sentenced to ten-year prison terms. Then, following his release from Leavenworth Penitentiary on 13 August 1947, Roselli had rejoined Jack Dragna in Los Angeles.

At this very moment, Roselli and his Chicago cohorts were the subject of a congressional investigation that charged they had been prematurely released from prison in a scandal that cast suspicion on the Justice Department and the White House.

But here he was, a month later, talking pleasantly in Dago Louie's parlour. The contrast and subtlety of it made a deep impression on Jimmy. Having paid his dues, Roselli could sit back and live on his reputation. The organization would take care of him. He would never want for money or power. He had it made. That was what Jimmy wanted, what was missing from his life, what made him feel like he was standing still. He needed that feeling of accomplishment, to be separated from the multitude of hustlers he worked with every day, the punks of the world. Roselli was a gentleman, a man of respect, and Jimmy Fratianno was a hustler in search of an identity.

Later in the evening, Dago Louie excused himself and Jimmy had an opportunity to relay Yonnie's message about straightening him out with "the right people". When Roselli asked if he knew what Yonnie had meant, Jimmy said, "Johnny, I've been wanting this since I was a kid. I knew the Italians on the Hill had something special going for them, but it's so fucking hard to crack."

Roselli smiled. "That's right, Jimmy, and that's the way it should be. When you get the wrong guy in there, you've got to clip him. There's no pink slip in this thing."

Following the initiation ceremony at the winery, Jimmy and Roselli went to Dago Louie's house to celebrate. Roselli lifted his glass and offered a toast to the two men he had sponsored. "*Amici nostra*," he said, "may we all live long and prosperous lives."

"I'll drink to that," Jimmy said, laughing happily.

"Christ, that was really something tonight." He paused and looked at the two men. "You know, Johnny, this'll probably sound crazy; but for a while there I felt like I was in church."

Roselli nodded gravely.

"I felt like Jack was going to make me a fucking priest."

"Well, Father Fratianno," Dago Louie said, "how about a blessing?"

They laughed and both started asking Roselli questions at the same time.

"Hold it," he said. "Why don't I lay it out for you guys. You know, tell you what you should know about our thing." He paused and looked at them. "You are soldiers. In the old days they called you 'buttons'." This is a special kind of army. It's made up of a boss, the commanding general; an underboss, who may or may not be important, depending on the family situation, but most times he's there to back the boss's play. The *consigliere*'s the adviser, the guy who's supposed to know all the ins and outs of the organization. Then there's *capiregime*, captains or skippers; and finally, *soldati* . . . See, it's really an army of captains and soldiers.

"But there's soldiers and then there's soldiers. It's like a democracy, some are more equal than others. Certain soldiers carry more respect than others. But any soldier, no matter who he is, carries the power of the organization with him wherever he goes in this country. And no other family can touch him without the approval of his boss. See, all families, no matter how big or how small, have separate but equal power. Oh, yes, going back to what Jack was saying about made guys. Whenever made guys get together to talk family business, everybody that's not made has to leave the room no matter how much they're trusted.

"Now, the commission. It's made up of the bosses from ten families. The five New York families, Buffalo, Philadelphia, Cleveland, Detroit, and Chicago. The point is that these bosses don't have an ounce more power than any other boss. It makes no difference whether the boss is Tommy Lucchese, who's on the commission, or Jack Dragna, who's not. The power is equal. The only purpose of the commission is to settle disputes that come up between different families. It has nothing to do with the business of individual families. If Jack wants to clip somebody in his family, or somebody else in his territory, he clips him. He don't need the commission's permission. This is his country and he runs it any damn way he sees fit. No other family can fuck with him here. If they do then it's a problem for the commission.

"Let's say we have a problem with Colorado. Jack would go see Joe Batters (*né* Anthony Accardo) in Chicago. He's the arbitrator for everything west of Chicago. He straightens it out. That's what the commission's all about. All bosses on the commission also have equal power. There's no boss of bosses, never has been. That's all bullshit. Some bosses, maybe because they are older and wiser, command more respect than others, but that's all.

"Now you also hear a lot of bullshit about being paid for hits. Forget it. That's against the rules. You kill when you're given a contract by your skipper or sometimes it might come directly from the boss. If you're given the contract, you've got to do the hit. Most soldiers are under skippers. And it stops right there. Take Bompensiero in San Diego. He's the skipper down there and he runs the show in that town. He takes orders directly from Jack, but his soldiers take their orders from him. If Bomp says you clip somebody, you do it. You don't ask no fucking questions. You'll never make money doing work for the family. That's just part of your responsibility as a member.

"But there's another angle to this. The fact that you're a member gives you an edge. You can go into various businesses and people will deal with you because of what you represent. See, you've got all this power. Nobody fucks with you. We're nationwide. We can get things done nobody else can. And that means you can make a pretty good living if you hustle."

The Ice Man

Richard Kuklinski

Richard Kuklinski was not a Sicilian or an Italian. His father was Polish; his mother Irish. He came from the projects of Jersey City. His father was an alcoholic who beat his children savagely. Richard's older brother died as a result of these beatings. Kuklinski himself took to torturing cats. He claimed that his own first murder victim was Charley Lane, a gang leader in the projects. At the age of fourteen, he beat Lane to death. After disposing of the body, he tracked down the other members of Lane's gang and beat them to within an inch of their lives. He came to the attention of the Mob when he started selling pirated pornographic films to the Gambinos. A large man, they used him as a debt collector and he built up such a fearsome reputation that they employed him regularly as a hit man. He claimed to have killed over a hundred people, including the Gambinos' other feared executioner Roy DeMeo and Teamster's boss Jimmy Hoffa, whose disappearance in 1975 remains an enduring mystery. Experts in the field have expressed doubts about both these claims, but there is no doubt that he was an habitual killer. In 1988, he was convicted of five murders and given two life sentences. In 2003 he pleaded guilty to murdering New York police detective Peter Calabro which earned him another thirty years. He admitted to Calabro's murder in

*the second of two HBO documentaries made about his life.
He also participated in the writing of two biographies* The
Iceman: The True Story of a Cold-Blooded Killer *with
Anthony Bruno in 1993 and* The Ice Man: Confessions
of a Mafia Contract Killer *– quoted here – by Philip Carlo
in 2007. In the books, he lists the many ways he liked to kill
– using firearms, including a miniature derringer; ice picks;
hand grenades; crossbows; chain saws; and a bomb attached
to a remote-controlled toy car. His favourite weapon, he
said, was cyanide solution administered with a nasal-
spray bottle in the victim's face. He gained his nickname
"Ice Man" from his practice of freezing the bodies of his
victims to disguise the time of death. He claimed to have
kept Hoffa's body in the freezer of a Mister Softee ice-cream
truck for two years. He also claimed to have lived the "all-
American family" life in suburban New Jersey with his
wife Barbara and their three children, but Mrs Kuklinski
told author Anthony Bruno that her husband had tried to
smother her with a pillow, pointed a gun at her, tried to run
her over with a car and, on three occasions, hit her so hard
that he broke her nose.*

Carmine Genovese was out of jail and needed another man
killed, though this time, he told Richard, the mark had to
suffer before he died and the body had to "disappear".

"This guy," Carmine said, "did something to a friend
of mine's wife. Something very disrespectful. You make
sure he suffers, understand? Do it good and I'll pay you
double . . . OK?"

"OK, sure, no problem," Richard said. He did not ask
what the man had done, why he had to suffer. That was
irrelevant, none of his business.

Again, Carmine gave Richard a photograph of the mark,
and the address of the place he worked, a used-car lot on

Raymond Boulevard in Newark. In the picture, the mark was standing in the lot next to a woman who looked kind of like him.

"You do this right, I pay you very well, *capisce*?"

"*Capisce*," Richard said.

"Maybe you can bring me a little piece a him so I can see for myself and tell my friend how he suffered."

"A piece of him?" Richard repeated, a little confused.

"Yeah, so I can show my friend."

"How big a piece?" Richard asked.

"Not so big. Maybe like his hand . . . some toes, OK?"

"Yeah . . . sure, OK," Richard said. "No problem. I aim to please."

"Good," Genovese said. They shook hands. The contract was sealed. Glad Carmine was giving him another "piece of work", Richard left his place, his mind suddenly filled with the job before him. This was, he would later reveal, the part he liked the most: the stalking of a victim. Richard instinctively knew how to do this, and he looked forward to it. Clearly, Richard had grown into a psychotic sadist, one who had discovered a way to hurt and kill people and get paid for it. Life was good.

It was a sprawling used-car lot. Colourful flags were strung across it every which way. Richard quickly found the mark. He was tall and thin and was often walking about the lot with customers. He even went on test drives with people. Before Richard made any kind of move, he surveyed the place for two days, found out when the most people were there, when the mark arrived and when he left. When Richard had a clear plan in his mind, he parked his car a few blocks away, on a quiet street lined with broken-down warehouses. There were fewer people shopping for cars about 11 a.m., just before lunch, and that was when Richard walked on to the lot, straight up to the mark, a friendly smile on his high-cheekboned face. It was late March, the weather had become mild, Richard wore a baggy jacket. In one pocket, he had a .38 derringer; in the other, a jawbreaker – a kind of cosh consisting of a piece of solid lead the size of a cigarette packet encased in black leather with a short, thin handle – perfect for knocking people unconscious with one blow. Smiling, Richard told the mark he needed an inexpensive car quickly, that his car had been stolen and he needed wheels for work.

"Something reliable," he said. "I'm not handy with engines, and I don't want to get stuck, somewhere at night," he explained, his face suddenly grave. Richard was, in fact a consummate actor. He had natural ability, no doubt acquired on the street, to look someone square in the eye and lie through his teeth.

"Got the perfect car for you," the mark said, and led him over to a two-door Ford. Richard looked it over carefully, kicked the tyres.

"Can I take it for a spin?" he asked.

"Of course," the mark said. "Let me get the keys." He walked into the little office on the left. Richard had set the trap; soon he'd spring it. They piled into the car. Off they went. Richard drove a few blocks, talking about how well the car handled, then headed directly towards his car. Completely unaware of what was about to happen, the mark was no doubt calculating his commission. Richard pulled up to his car and stopped, said he wanted to check under the Ford's bonnet.

"Is that OK?" he asked politely, smiling.

"Sure, no problem. Got nothing to hide here, clean as a whistle." The mark was caught up in the moment, having no idea about the hatchet, rope and shovel in the boot of Richard's car. Richard slid out of the Ford and opened the bonnet. The mark, of course, followed. As he was looking down at something Richard had pointed to, Richard struck him with the jawbreaker just above the ear. He went right down, out cold. In seconds, Richard put him in the boot of his car, taped his mouth shut with industrial duct tape and tied his feet and hands behind his back. Calm and cool, Richard got to the freeway and drove south to the Pine Barrens, desolate forests that were perfect for what he had in mind. This was where he had disposed of Charley Lane – the projects' bully – so many years ago. Richard had already scoped out a good spot, where he hid his car behind a thick stand of pines. Here he opened the boot, dragged the panic-stricken mark from his car and tied him to one of the trees, his back tight up against it. Richard took a length of rope, forced it into the mark's mouth and tied it tightly to the rough pine tree, forcing the man's tongue up against the back of his rapidly constricting throat. The mark was crying now, trying to talk, to beg, to plead, but he made only muffled unintelligible grunts. He seemed to know why this was happening, as if, in a way, he had expected it. At this point, Richard actually told him that he had to suffer before he died. He went back to his car and retrieved the hatchet and shovel, very much enjoying the whole thing.

He made sure the mark saw the hatchet and shovel, watched the reality of their meaning in Richard's enormous hands sink in. The man began to scream, to try to break free, but it was impossible. He wet himself, a thing Richard would see many times in years to come. Richard proceeded now to smash the mark's ankles and knees with the hatchet. Then he chopped off his fingers, one at a time. Richard stepped back to see the degree of pain the mark was suffering. He'd been planning to take fingers back to Genovese as proof of suffering, but he suddenly got a *better idea*, as he put it . . .

When Richard had finally killed the mark, he dug a hole in the pine-needle-covered ground, threw what was left of the hapless man into it, retrieved the proof Genovese had asked for, and returned to Hoboken, carrying it in a plastic bag he'd brought along, listening to country music as he went.

He found Genovese at home.

"Did you do the job?" Genovese asked.

"Yeah, it's done," said Richard.

"You bring me something good?" Genovese asked.

"Sure did," Richard said, amused, placing the bag on the kitchen table.

Curious, Genovese looked inside, and there was the mark's head. A big smile spread over Genovese's large, round face.

"Son of a bitch! Beautiful . . . you did good, son of a bitch." Genovese said, realizing he had found a rare man in this giant Polack. "Very good! *Molto bravo . . . molto bravo!*" he added.

"Want me to get rid of it?" Richard asked.

"No . . . leave it here. I want to show it to my friend. Did he suffer?" asked Genovese.

"Yeah, he suffered good," Richard said, and Genovese paid him 10,000 dollars cash on the spot for, he said, "a good job well done".

The cash in his pocket making a pleasant bulge, Richard left Genovese, knowing his reputation as an efficient contract killer was assured.

Richard still frequently thought about killing his father, Stanley. He'd start thinking about him, remember the brutal, callous treatment he'd meted out, get all mad inside and want to beat him to death. On several occasions, he actually went to a bar near the projects where Stanley hung out, looking to put a bullet in his head, but his father wasn't there.

It was like a spur-of-the moment thing, Richard explained. *He was lucky because when I was looking for him he wasn't*

*around. Even now, I mean sitting here and talking about him,
I regret a lot not capping him – the prick . . . the sadistic prick!*

Stanley never realized how close he'd come to being
killed by his second son.

Joseph, Richard's younger brother, was also extremely
violent, and in frequent difficulties at school, always getting
into trouble, stealing things, drinking excessively. Richard
wanted to reach out to him, give him advice, put some
money in his hands, but he loathed his mother so much
by this time that he wouldn't even go near their apartment
any more.

After being given the head of the car salesman, Carmine
Genovese took a shine to Richard. Carmine had a lot of
money on the street, and he began to use Richard as his
chief collector and enforcer, or bagman. Had Richard
been Italian, Genovese would surely have sponsored him
for induction into the family, but he was Polish, so that
could never happen. Still, Carmine gave him a lot of work.
Richard was collecting money for him from people up and
down the East Coast. He was reliable, honest and very
violent when necessary – sometimes too violent. Richard
was always knocking on Carmine's door with brown
paper bags of money in his hand. He never stole a dime
from Carmine; indeed, he never even thought about it,
which only made Carmine that much more fond of him.
Everyone who borrowed money from Carmine Genovese
knew the ground rules out of the gate and paid it back
quickly, as agreed. Nor to do so, everyone also knew, could
be fatal.

For the most part, Richard enjoyed working for
Genovese. He made money – most of which he pissed
away. People respected him and showed him deference,
and his reputation as a dangerous "mob-connected guy"
spread all over Jersey. Nobody fucked with him. Even other

Mob guys stayed clear of Richard Kuklinski. He became known as "the Polack". That became his street name.

Richard took to carrying two guns and a knife whenever he went out. If he wasn't armed to the teeth, he felt naked. He was fond of over-and-under .38 derringers, double-barrelled, with the barrels one on top of the other rather than side-by-side. They were so small that they could readily fit in the palm of a hand, and at close range they were lethal. Richard enjoyed killing up close and personal, and to kill someone with a derringer you had to be right on top of him; that is why, he said, he also enjoyed killing with a knife.

It's intimate. You can feel the blade going in, the bones breaking, see the shock on the guy's face and watch the lights go out.

When asked if he believed in God, believed that it was a sin to kill a human being, he said: *The only God I believe in is a loaded pistol with hair trigger. Funny how, before I killed a lot of guys they'd call me God. 'Oh God, no! Oh God, no!'* he said, smiling, amused by the memories.

Richard's wife, Linda, gave birth to a baby boy whom they named Richard. Richard senior felt no love for or emotional attachment to his child. He was a natural extension of a sex act – nothing more. Richard didn't even go to the hospital when Linda gave birth, nor did he help bring her home. He acted as though it were someone else's child, not his; but it didn't take long for Linda to become pregnant again.

Linda saw all of Richard's weapons but never questioned what they were for. She knew how violent and psychotic Richard could be and acted as if she were blind. She knew too that if she questioned him, demanded information, he might very well explode and hit her. In this, Richard was a carbon copy of his father – the man he hated most in the world – but he did not, never would, hit his son, or strike any of the five children he would eventually have.

Richard was, for the most part, fond of children; he saw them as put-upon innocents and became enraged when he saw an adult hitting a child. One time, he beat the hell out of a man he saw hitting his kids in a parking lot; in years to come, he'd kill a friend of his because the man asked him to murder his wife and eight-year-old son.

I don't kill women and I don't kill children. And anyone that does don't deserve to live, explained Richard. As cold and completely indifferent as Richard was to the suffering of men, he could not stand to see a child harmed. He also hated rapists – *tree jumpers* he called them – and was always on the lookout for sexual predators. He viewed them as *vermin that need immediate eradication.*

Richard was still taking trips to Manhattan's West Side, where he killed anyone who got in his way, who was pushy or rude. He very much enjoyed killing aggressive beggars, usually so quickly that they didn't even realize what had happened until they hit the ground.

One night, Richard came upon two burly, leather-clad men raping a young boy behind a red eighteen-wheeler parked close to the Hudson. He was walking along, admiring the way the lights on the Jersey side of the river played on the water, the giant piano keys of light they made, when he heard a plaintive cry, moaning and meaty thumps. He slowly walked round behind the truck, and there he saw the rape: a boy was being forced to fellate one man while the other sodomized him. The men were laughing. They were drunk. They were now in trouble. Richard pulled out a .38 derringer and without a word shot both the rapists dead.

"Thank you, mister, thank you!" the boy said, pulling up his trousers, wiping blood from his nose.

"Get the fuck out of here," Richard said, and proceeded to cut open the stomach cavities of the two leather-clad men, silently cursing them, before dumping them in the river. Richard knew that if the stomachs were eviscerated, gases could not build up, so the bodies would sink and stay down.

He took great pleasure in killing these two rapists.

Richard had become addicted to killing people. After he committed a murder, he felt relaxed, whole and good – at peace with himself and the world. Richard was very much like a junkie who needs a fix to soothe the pangs of addiction. Murder, for Richard Kuklinski, became like a fix of pure heroin – the best high ever. And the NYPD never suspected that a huge man of Polish extraction from Jersey City was killing the men they kept finding. There were no witnesses, no clues; no one knew anything.

Retired NYPD captain of detectives Ken Roe told me: *Back then there were no citywide records of homicides being kept, as there are today. The local precinct had a file, but that was it, and because most all these killings were of bums, people no one really gave a fuck about, there was no incentive to properly work the case. You see, because he was killing in all different ways, the cops didn't think one guy was doing it. In a sense . . . in a very real sense, they were inadvertently giving him a licence to kill. Hell of a thing.*

Richard's mentor, Carmine Genovese, had another special job for him. A man in Chicago named Anthony De Peti owed Carmine 70,000 dollars and wasn't paying as promised, had stories instead of the money. After Carmine explained the facts of life to him, De Peti promised he'd have the money in two days, "on Wednesday".

"OK, I'll send Richie to come and get it," Carmine said, and called Kuklinski.

"You go to Chicago Wednesday. This guy is going to meet you in the lounge bar in the Pan AM terminal, give

you the money he owes, seventy Gs, you bring it right
back, OK?"

"OK."

"Be careful. He's slippery like a fuckin' wet eel," Carmine
told him.

Richard enjoyed going out to Newark Airport and flying
to Chicago. It made him feel like a successful businessman.
These days, Richard sported a Fu Manchu moustache
and long sideburns that tapered off at sharp angles just
above his jaw line. Stern and forbidding to begin with, he
looked even more scary and unsettling with the curved
moustache and long, dagger-like sideburns. Already his
hair was thinning on top, highlighting his high, wide brow
and the severe planes of his Slavic cheekbones. He had,
of course, a .32 and a knife with him, as well as one of
his beloved derringers. Back then, there was no problem
carrying weapons on to a plane.

Richard arrived at Chicago's sprawling, very busy
O'Hare Airport, went straight to the lounge, sat down
and waited for De Peti to show himself, not expecting any
bloodshed. This was a simple pick-up, he thought. He sat
and looked around, wondering where the hell De Peti was,
becoming a little annoyed. Finally, he stood up and walked
all over the lounge, making certain every man there saw
him. He was hard to miss at 6 ft 5 in and 250 lb. Nothing,
no recognition from anyone. Hmm. He was about to call
Carmine when a man who'd been sitting not ten feet away
from him all along stood up and said, "Rich?"

"Yeah."

"I'm Anthony De Peti – "

"Why the hell didn't you say something? You saw me
sittin' here?"

"I wanted to make sure you were alone," De Peti said.

Richard didn't like that answer. It immediately made
him suspicious. He looked at De Peti with a jaundiced eye.

"You got the money?" he asked.

"Yeah, right here," said De Peti. He was a head shorter than Richard, though wide in the shoulders, with a long, narrow hatchet face and buckteeth. Hairs, like the antennae of an insect, protruded from his narrow nose. He handed Richard a black attaché case.

"But it's not all there," he said.

"How much is here?" Richard asked.

"Thirty-five. Half."

"He's not going to like that."

"I'll have the rest in a day or two."

"Hey, buddy, I'm here now, and you're supposed to have it all, here now. I gotta get on a plane back to Jersey soon. He ain't going to like this."

"I swear I'll have it in a day or two."

"Yeah, well, I gotta call him. Come on," Richard said, and led De Peti over to a nearby bank of phones. Richard got Genovese on the line.

"You find him all right?" he asked.

"Yeah, he's right here, but he don't have it all."

"Son of a bitch. How much does he have?"

"Half, thirty-five, he says. He says he'll have the rest in a day or two. What do you want me to do?"

"Put him on the phone!"

Richard handed De Peti the phone. Smiling, De Peti explained how he'd have the money soon. "In a day, the most, I swear," he proclaimed, making sure Richard saw his smiling face, like all was OK, no problem here – Carmine was his friend, what the hell? He gave the phone back to Richard as flight announcements boomed from a nearby loudspeaker.

"Yeah," said Richard, not liking De Peti. Richard had an uncanny ability to read people, like some kind of animal-in-a-jungle thing, and he did not like this guy, did not trust him.

"Rich, you stay with him, don't let him out of your sight. He says people owe him money, that he'll definitely have the money real soon."

"All right. What do you want me to do with what he gave me?"

"You hold on to that! Don't let him out of your sight, understand?"

"Yeah," Richard said, hanging up.

"See, I told ya," said De Peti. "It's all OK."

"It'll be all OK when you give me the rest of the money," Richard said.

With that, they left the airport, and De Peti took Richard from bar to bar, looking for various people he could never seem to find. After ten hours of this, in and out of different bars, Richard was thinking this guy was trying to give him the slip, buying time De Peti could not afford. They ended up in a crowded place on the South Side called the Say Hi Inn. It was filled with a rough clientele. They ordered drinks. De Peti went to use the phone; Richard kept an eagle eye on him and saw him talking to a big, burly guy whose face was so pockmarked it looked like gravel. Richard clearly saw something he did not like in the big man's eyes. In his right hand, in his pocket, Richard held the white-handled, chrome-plated .38 derringer. There were two hollow-nosed rounds – better known as dumdums – in the gun, bullets which spread out on contact, making horrific wounds. De Peti came back to the bar, drank some of his drink. "He'll be here soon," he told Richard.

"The guy with the money," Richard asked.

"Yeah, guaranteed."

Soon, though, Gravel Face made his way over to the bar. Purposely, he shouldered Richard, looking, Richard instinctively knew, to start a fight with him so De Peti could slip away. Richard slowly turned to him.

"You like your balls?" Richard asked.

"What? What da fuck?" the guy said.

"If you want to keep your nuts, get the fuck outta here," Richard said, now showing him the mean little derringer pointed directly at his crotch, "or I'll blow them both the fuck off here and now."

Gravel Face turned and left. Richard turned to De Peti. "So you're looking to play games."

"No games – what're you talking about?"

"If I start playing games, you are going to end up very hurt. I'm losing my patience. You think I'm a fool?" Richard asked.

"He'll be here with the dough," De Peti said.

But nobody showed up. The bar was closing. Finally, De Peti said they should rent a room in a nearby hotel, that he'd definitely have the money "in the morning".

"In the morning?" Richard repeated.

"I swear."

Reluctantly, Richard called Genovese, who said it was OK to wait. They checked into a nearby hotel. Richard washed up and, tired, lay down on one of the two beds, as did De Peti. But Richard was wary and sleep did not come easily. He didn't know how long he'd been lying there, but he sensed, in his half-asleep state, movement nearby. He opened his eyes. As they adjusted to the dark, he could just discern De Peti skulking through the room, moving towards him, past him and to the window. De Peti slid it open and began to creep, snake-like, out onto the fire escape. In two swift movements, Richard was up, grabbed him and yanked him back into the room, where he pummelled him. Richard moved shocking fast for such a big man, which caught many people off guard. Richard turned on the light.

"You slimy motherfucker, you been playing me all along." Richard kicked him so hard he moved across the floor. Oh, how Richard wanted to kill him, shoot him in the head and throw him out the window, but those luxuries were not his, he knew. This guy owed Carmine a lot of money, and Richard couldn't just go killing him. Instead, Richard called Carmine in Hoboken.

"The fuckin' asshole tried to fly," he said. "I caught him sneaking out on the fire escape."

"Son of a bitch. Put him on'a da phone!"

Blood running from his mouth, De Peti told Carmine that he was only looking to get some fresh air, not escape . . . certainly not trying to get away. "I swear, I swear on my mother," he cried, histrionically holding his hand over his heart for maximum effect.

"Where's the money?" Carmine demanded.

"Tomorrow, tomorrow, I swear!" De Peti pleaded.

Richard got back on the phone. Carmine said, "Give 'im until tomorrow. He don't come up with the money, throw him out a window with no fuckin' fire escape, OK?"

"OK," Richard said. "Gladly."

The next day, it was the same story, running around different bars and lounges, looking for various people who had the money. It was as if, Richard was thinking, De Peti was playing a shell game, a three-card monte shuffle. Again, De Peti went to use a phone. There was a door near the phone, and Richard could see De Peti eyeing it. He hung up, came back, said they had to go to a pizza place. They waited there an hour, and then went to two more bars.

Richard was tired of De Peti's bull. "He'll be here, he'll be here," he kept telling Richard, and no one showed up.

Pissed off, Richard took De Peti back to the hotel and, without another word, hung him by his feet out of the window. Begging, De Peti now said he'd get him "all the money", that it was in a place he owned over on the South Side.

"You lying to me, I'll kill you on the spot," Richard promised.

"I ain't lying, I ain't lying," he pleaded, cars and trucks and buses moving on the wide avenue ten storeys below.

Richard pulled him inside. "Let's go."

It was a kind of go-go place. Half-naked girls who had seen better days danced around, wiggling their breasts and shaking their ample asses in Day-Glo red lights. De Peti took Richard straight to a rear office, opened a safe hidden in a cupboard wall, grabbed a pile of notes, and gave him the thirty-five Gs.

"My God, if you had the money, all the time, why didn't you just give it to me?" Richard asked, really annoyed now, anger rising in him.

"Because I didn't want to pay," De Peti admitted sheepishly.

That made Richard see red, his balls, as he described it, were all twisted already, and this was the straw that broke the camel's back.

"Really?" he said, smiling slightly, making the soft clicking sound out of the side of his mouth.

"Let me get one of the girls in here to clean your pipes out," De Peti offered.

"Naw, that's OK," Richard said.

After counting the money, Richard suddenly pressed the little .38 derringer hard to De Peti's chest and pulled the trigger. Boom. The report of the gun was muffled by De Peti's chest and drowned out by the music coming from the club.

With a horrific hole in his chest, De Peti hit the ground hard and was soon as dead as a doorknob.

Calmly, Richard left the club, hailed a cab a block away, went to the airport and caught a flight back to Newark. As soon as he hit the ground, he went to see Carmine Genovese.

"And what happened?" Carmine asked as he opened the door.

"I got two things to tell you."

"Yeah?"

"First, I got the money – all of it. Second, I killed him. All he did was play me," Richard said, nor sure if Carmine would get mad. After all, he had killed a customer of Carmine's after getting all that was due.

"Good, bravo. We can't be letting these fuckin' assholes play us for fools. That gets around on the street, we're out of business. You did the right thing," Carmine said, patting Richard on his enormous back. "You're a good man, Richie. Mamma mia, I wish you were Italian. I'd sponsor you in a fuckin' minute," he said, and paid Richard well.

Carmine, a very rich man, tended – like most Mafia men – to be cheap and greedy. For them, nothing was ever enough.

Content, Richard soon left.

Back in Chicago, one of De Peti's strippers discovered his body. The police were summoned. They questioned everyone in the club and got a vague description of a big man seen leaving the office.

Another unsolved homicide.

Casino

Tony Spilotro

In 1971, Tony Spilotro took over in Las Vegas. He had been associated with the Mob since childhood. His parents were from Bari in southeast Italy and ran a restaurant in Chicago that such celebrated gangsters as Frank Nitti and Sam Giancana used for meetings. From an early age, he got involved in petty crime. In 1962, he pleaded guilty to attempting to fix a basketball game. He became a debt collector for the Chicago Outfit, the local branch of the Cosa Nostra. With the Outfit's enforcer "Mad" Sam DeStefano's heavy mob, Spilotro was sent to kill two gangsters. He quickly gained notoriety when he crushed one of the victims' heads in a vice. In 1963, he was "made" and assigned to bookmaking with his childhood friend Frank "Lefty" Rosenthal. After running the mob's betting operations in Miami, he was sent to Las Vegas. As he took control a series of murders took place. Victims were tortured and dumped out in the desert. In 1973, Spilotro was indicted for murder alongside DeStefano, but was acquitted after DeStefano was slain. The following year he was indicted a second time, this time alongside reputed Mob boss Joseph Lombardo. Again they were acquitted when a key witness was murdered. Things began to turn bad in Las Vegas for Spilotro when he was barred from entering casinos by the Nevada Gaming

Commission. So he diversified into burglary and protection.
The situation deteriorated further when his burglary gang
were arrested and rumours circulated that Spilotro was
sleeping with Rosenthal's wife. The Outfit decided to have
him killed. They lured him back to Illinois when Spilotro
and his brother Michael were beaten with baseball bats, then
burned alive in a cornfield. In his book Casino, *Nicholas*
Pileggi – author of Wiseguy *which was adapted for the*
screen as Goodfellas *– used interviews with Spilotro's*
enforcer Frank Cullotta and Bill Hall, the FBI agent who
bugged him, to tell the tale of Spilotro's time in Las Vegas.

When Tony Spilotro got to town in 1971, Las Vegas was
a relatively quiet place. The bosses had been making so
much money from their own illegitimate enterprises,
such as illegal bookmaking, loan-sharking, and casino
skimming, that there was a concerted effort by the Mob to
keep the town clean, safe, and quiet. The rules were simple.
Disputes were to be peaceably settled. There were to be no
shootings or car explosions in town. Bodies were not to be
left in car trunks at the airport. Sanctioned murders took
place out of town or the bodies disappeared forever in the
vast desert surrounding the city.

Before Tony arrived, Mob matters were so benignly
administered that Jasper Speciale, the biggest loan shark in
town, operated out of his Leaning Tower of Pizza restaurant,
and his waitresses moonlighted as collectors after they
finished work. The town's petty criminals – the drug dealers,
the bookies, pimps, even the card cheats – were operating
for free. Las Vegas was an open city: mobsters from
different families around the country needed no permission
to wander into town, extort money from high rollers, work a
credit seam on a casino, and go home. The kind of street tax
imposed by the outfit back home was unheard of.

"Tony stopped all that," said Bud Hall Jr, the retired FBI agent who spent years eavesdropping on Spilotro's life. "Tony changed the way business was done in Las Vegas. He took over. The first thing he did was bring in some of his own men and impose a street tax on every bookie, loan shark, drug dealer, and pimp in town. A few, like a bookmaker named Jerry Dellman, resisted, but he wound up shot dead in a daylight robbery in the garage area behind his house. Nobody tried to hide the body. It was a message that there was a real gangster in town.

"Tony understood very quickly that he could run Las Vegas any way he wanted, because the bosses were 1,500 miles away and didn't have the same kind of street ears in Las Vegas that they had back in Elmwood Park."

"When Tony first moved to Las Vegas, very few people even knew who he was," Lefty said. "I remember we had this really arrogant guy, John Grandy, in charge of all construction and purchasing. Nobody fucked with John Grandy. If people asked him for anything, he'd say, 'Why the fuck are you bothering me? Get lost!' I handled him with kid gloves.

"One morning Tony was coming in to see me. Grandy was there giving orders to three or four workers who were putting together some blackjack tables for dealers. He had a bunch of construction material in his arms, and he looked over and sees Tony coming up to me, and he says to Tony, 'Hey, come here! Hold this! I'll tell you what to do with it later.'

"I'll never forget this. The stuff weighed about thirty or forty pounds. Tony was so surprised he held it a second before shoving it right back.

" 'Here,' Tony said, 'you hold it, not me. Who the fuck do you think you are? The next time you talk to me that way, I'll throw you out the fucking window!' Quote unquote.

"Grandy looks at me. I look at Tony. Tony is fuming. And Grandy does what Tony says. Grandy takes the stuff back and doesn't say shit. Tony says he'll meet me down in the coffee shop and he leaves.

"When Tony's gone, Grandy says, 'Hey! Who the fuck's that guy? Who's he think he is?' I said, 'The guy doesn't work here. Never mind who he is.'

"But Grandy knows something's wrong. He goes down into the casino and spots Bobby Stella and drags Stella to the coffee shop to look for Tony.

" 'Bobby, who's that fucking guy over there? Who the fuck does he think he is?' Grandy's getting all riled up now.

"Bobby saw he was pointing to Tony and tried to calm him down. 'Slow down. Take it easy.'

" 'What do you mean, "slow down"?'

"Bobby says, 'That's Tony Spilotro.'

"Grandy just stood there and said, 'Holy shit! Holy shit!' He apparently knew the name but not the face. He went right over to Tony and apologized four or five times. 'I'm very, very sorry. I really didn't mean to insult you. Things were a little bit busy and I didn't know who you were. Would you accept my apologies?' Tony said yeah and looked the other way. Grandy ran."

Frank Cullotta got out of prison after doing six years for a Brinks truck robbery, and Spilotro flew to Chicago for his coming-out party. "I had 'Free At Last' on my birthday cake," Cullotta said. "Everyone came and they all gave me envelopes, and at the end of the night I had about 20,000 dollars, but mostly it made me feel great that so many guys were with me and liked me. I was still on paper [on parole], so I couldn't leave Chicago right away, but Tony said that as soon as I got off paper I was supposed to come to Nevada.

"By the time I got there, Tony was already running the town. He had everybody on the payroll. He owned a couple of guys in the sheriff's office. He had guys in the courthouse who could get him grand jury minutes, and he had people in the telephone company to tell him about phone taps.

"Tony had the town covered. He was in the papers all the time. He had broads coming around in Rolls-Royces who wanted to go out with him. Everybody wanted to be around a gangster. Movie stars. Everybody. I don't know what the fuck's the attraction, but that's the way it was. I guess it's a feeling of power, you know. People feel like, well, these guys are hitters, and if I need something done, they'll do it for me.

"He knew I was a good thief, and he said we could make good money. Tony always needed money: he went through cash fast. He liked to bet on sports and he never stayed home. He was a sport. He always picked up the cheque. No matter if there were ten, fifteen people with us, he'd always pick up the cheque.

"He told me, 'Look, get a crew together. And, whatever you gotta fucking do with the guys, you got my okay. Just give me my end. You've got carte blanche out here.'

"I sent for Wayne Matecki, Larry Neumann, Ernie Davino, real desperados like that, and we started putting the arm on everybody. Bookmakers. Shylocks. Dope dealers. Pimps. Shit, we'd strong-arm them. Beat them. Shoot their fucking guard dogs. What did we care? I had Tony's okay. In fact, half the time Tony'd told us who to grab.

"Then, after we'd rob them and scare them, they'd run to Tony for protection to get us off their backs. They never had any idea it was Tony who sent us over to rob them in the first place.

"We made good money turning over houses. It was all cash and jewellery. I'm talking about thirty, forty, fifty thousand dollars in twenties and hundreds laying in dresser drawers. One time I found fifteen thousand-dollar bills next to a guy's bed. Now, where the fuck am I gonna get rid of them? Thousand-dollar bills are hard to get rid of. Banks want your name if you try and cash them. So I pushed them at the Stardust. I handed them to Lou Salerno, and he shoved them in the drawer and gave me back fifteen grand in hundreds.

"How do you think I put up the money for my restaurant, the Upper Crust? I got the money in two days. Me and Wayne and Ernie hit two maitre d's' houses and got over 60,000 dollars. Maitre d's take twenty-dollar bills from people looking for good tables all night. Well, we took the twenties back. One of the guys also had a 30,000-dollar Patek Philippe watch, and we sold it to Bobby Stella for three grand. Bobby gave it away as a present.

"We'd get our information from the casino people. Bell captains. The registration desk. The credit clerks. Travel agency people. But our best sources were the insurance brokers who sold the people the policies of the stuff we were robbing. They'd give us the information on everything. What kind of jewels the people had and how much they were insured for. Where in the house the stuff was located. What kind of alarm system. The people had to put all that info down on their policies when they got insured.

"If the doors and windows and alarm systems were a pain, we'd go right through the wall. Going through the walls was my idea. I invented it. It's very simple. Almost all the houses out in Vegas have stucco exterior walls. All you need is a five-pound sledge to make a hole big enough so you can get in. Then you use metal shears to clip away the chicken wire inside the wall they use for lathing. Then you bang away a little more until you break through the interior dry wall, and you're inside the house.

"You could only do this in Las Vegas, because the houses were stucco and they have high walls around them for privacy. People have pools and things outside, and they like to live private lives. Nobody knows their neighbours. Nobody wants to know their neighbours. It's that kind of town. It's the kind of place, if people hear a noise from the house next door, they tune it out. We did so many of these jobs that the newspaper started calling us the Hole in the Wall Gang. The cops never knew who we were.

" 'Mean fucking pigs,' Tony'd say, proud of us. 'Look what I have created out here.'

"We had it down. We'd be in and out of a house in three to five minutes tops. And whenever we did a job, we had a guy in a work car outside with a scanner picking up police calls. We even had a descrambler so we'd get the FBI. Tony gave us the descramblers and the police frequencies.

"But no matter how well we were doing, we always needed more money. Burglary money goes quick. We always had to divide it four ways – me and my two guys, and then Tony would always get his end. On a $40,000 job, Tony would get ten grand. For sitting home. He got an equal end every time.

"Sometimes, if we needed cash and things were slow, we'd do straight robberies. We took the Rose Bowl out like that. At that time the Rose Bowl was owned by the guy who owned Chateau Vegas, and Tony gives me all the information and then says, 'You're gonna need a guy with a clean face.' So I imported a kid from Chicago with a clean face, a guy that nobody knew. We couldn't use a known guy because we weren't supposed to be doing robberies like this in the first place. If the bosses found out Tony was doing armed robberies in the middle of town, he wouldn't have been here long. But nobody back home knew we were doing burglaries and robberies. That was our little secret.

"The old broad who ran the Rose Bowl and her bodyguard came out into the back parking lot just like Tony said they would, with a bag of money. She walks toward her car. The bodyguard is just standing there watching her. The new kid I brought to town walks right up to her, flashes a gun, and grabs the bag out of her hand.

"The guy she had watching her tried to be a hero, and my kid whacked him with the back of his hand and the guy's on his ass. My kid was real rough. He's in jail now on something else. He's doing forty years.

"The kid runs the block parallel to the Strip. There's a chapel over there. Ernie Davino was waiting for him. Larry Neumann was in the parking lot, right nearby, as a backup if the kid needed help. When the kid jumps into the car with Ernie, Larry has already gotten in back. And as they're coming off the street, I'm coming off the street. We were four blocks away cutting up the money when we could hear the police just starting to show up at the Rose Bowl parking lot.

"Looking back I see how crazy we were. Here we were in Las Vegas with a million ways to make a dishonest buck, and Tony's got us out here doing house burglaries and armed robberies and 7-Elevens. It was dumb."

All booming industries create jobs, and the Spilotro operation was no exception. Within a year Spilotro was providing work not just for his own crew but for dozens of law enforcement officers who tailed him, bugged him, and attempted to ensnare him in elaborate stings. At one point, Spilotro was betting $30,000 a week at a bookmaking operation that was actually an IRS sting; he was attracted by the fact that it offered better odds than any other book in town. When the IRS agent operating the sting had the nerve to ask Spilotro for collateral, Spilotro greeted him with a baseball bat. "Do you know who I am?" Spilotro asked. "I run this town."

Spilotro had moved his jewellery storefront from Circus to West Sahara Avenue, just off the Strip. The Gold Rush Jewelry Store was a two-storey building complete with platformed sidewalk and fake hitching posts.

"We got the necessary probable cause and dropped a mike in the ceiling of the back room of the Gold Rush," said Bud Hall. "The front room was strictly for selling rings and wristwatches. Upstairs, Tony had anti-surveillance devices, telephone scramblers, battleship binoculars so he could see if he was being watched from a mile away, and shortwave radios that picked up police calls and were even able to unscramble the bureau's frequencies. Tony got our frequencies through some Metro cops he had on his payroll. He also had an electronics expert from Chicago, Ronnie 'Balloon Head' DeAngelis, who would fly into town every few weeks and sweep the place for taps and bugs. We always got our best stuff right after DeAngelis left. 'Balloon Head says the place is clean,' Tony would proudly announce, and everyone would relax.

"Tony was a totally focused human being. He woke up in the morning knowing exactly what he was going to do that day. He'd get dozens of calls at the Gold Rush. He had all kinds of financial deals going on at the same time. He had different groups, hundreds of people, a million schemes, all of them in various stages of development. And even though most of them never panned out, he still had to put in a sixteen- to eighteen-hour day trying to put the deals together.

"It would have been difficult doing what Tony did if he had secretaries, a filing system, Xerox machines, and the free use of a phone. But Tony did it all off-the-cuff and kept it all in his head. The only things he ever wrote down were telephone numbers, and he used to write them down in the tiniest little handwriting that made them unreadable without a magnifying glass, and when we'd get ahold of them, we found he would transpose the numbers or write half or three-quarters of each number backwards.

"Listening to someone on a wire every day," Bud Hall says, "is different than being around them all the time socially. It creates a strange relationship between the person listening and the subject. You're listening to their lives, and pretty soon you're inside their lives. I don't mean that you get to like them, but you get to be able to tell by the sound of their voice what their moods are and where in the room they might happen to be. There are times when you can almost lip-sync what they are going to say before they say it. You come to know them so intimately that you almost become a part of the person.

"Tony was the smartest and most efficient mobster I had ever seen. I think he was a genius. His biggest problem was that he was surrounded by people who were always screwing up. That's all we kept hearing him say over and over. He'd harangue his crew about their incompetence and how he had no choice but to do things himself if he wanted them done right.

"If you talked to him on the phone, all you had to say were three or four words and he would have digested the purpose of the call, and the call had better be about business and it had better be in his interest.

"Tony had no capacity whatever for casual conversation. He could be congenial. Cordial. Likeable. But you couldn't waste his time. He lost his temper faster than anyone I ever knew. There was no slow burn. He went right from being nice to being a screaming violent maniac in a second. There was no way to prepare for him. I think the speed with which you were suddenly under attack was as terrifying as the thought of having Tony mad at you. However, once it passed, it passed. He forgot it. He went back to business.

"He lived a completely separate life from Nancy. They shared their son, Vincent, but that was about it. He slept in his own room on the ground floor of their house behind a locked steel door. When he got up in the morning, around ten thirty or eleven, Nancy stayed out of his way. He'd make his own coffee, and when he picked up the paper on the front step or off the walkway, he'd look up and down Balfour Avenue for surveillance.

"When he was ready to leave, there was no 'good-bye' or 'see you for dinner'. He'd just get in his blue Corvette sports car and routinely go around the block a few times, checking for tails. It could take him forty-five minutes to drive the ten minutes between his house and the Gold Rush because Tony would automatically dry-clean himself of tails by driving through shopping centres, stopping at green lights, moving through red, making illegal U-turns, and then checking his rear-view mirror to see if anyone was following.

"After all that time I spent listening in at the Gold Rush and at his house, I decided that he had what we called in the marines 'command posture'. When he talked, people listened. When he entered a room, he was always in charge. But in charge of what? That was his problem.

"One day we picked up that Joe Ferriola, one of the Chicago street bosses, was trying to get a relative a job as a dealer at the Stardust. Tony asked Joey Cusumano to take care of it. Cusumano, one of Spilotro's top guys, hung around the Stardust passing Tony's messages back and forth so much that many of the casino's employees thought he worked there.

"A week passed and Tony got another call from Ferriola's people that she was still unemployed. Tony had a fit. Cusumano checked back and found the casino wouldn't hire her as a dealer because she had no experience and would have to go take a six-week course at dealer's school.

"Tony then tells Joey to ask Lefty, who was pretending to be the Stardust's food and beverage director at the time, to get the kid a job as a waitress.

"A few days later, Joey comes back and says that Lefty doesn't want to hire her because he doesn't think she's good-looking enough to be a Stardust cocktail waitress, and besides, she's got bad legs.

"Spilotro exploded and he did something he should have never done – he called the Stardust himself. He got hold of Joey Boston, an ex-bookmaker Lefty had hired, to run the Stardust Sports Book.

"Tony shouldn't have called the Stardust himself, because now we at the FBI had a tape of Spilotro asking a top executive of the Stardust casino to get a job for a Chicago *capo*'s relative. That's exactly what we had been waiting for. It made for the kind of direct link between the Mob and a licensed casino that neither side would ever want made public, the kind of connection that could jeopardize a casino's licence and call into question just who really owns the casino and who might be serving as a front."

Ferriola's relative eventually went to work as a security guard at one of the other Las Vegas hotels. But the story of how Tony Spilotro, the most terrifying mobster in Las Vegas, could not manage to get a job at the Stardust for the relative of a Chicago *capo* did not help his reputation back home.

"I was around Tony all the time and he was always worried about people listening in," says Matt Marcus, a 350-pound illegal bookmaker who took a lot of Spilotro's action. "We'd be in the Food Factory on Twain Street, a place he had a piece of, and he'd communicate with body language. He'd lean back and shrug and twist his head and frown. He drank tea all the time. Not coffee.' He always sat with the tea bag hanging out of the cup, leaning and shrugging and twisting and frowning. He was positive the next person passing by would be the FBI. He was always changing cars. The intel unit was always checking his licence plates. They'd go right up to the cars and take down their numbers."

"Tony seemed to get a real kick out of matching wits with the FBI, but he wasn't stupid," Frank Cullotta said.

"Whenever he had anything to say we'd go for walks in empty parking lots or on the side of the road in the desert. When you said something to him, mostly he'd just make faces, or frown, or smile and get across what he meant for you to do. Even when he did talk, he'd always cover his mouth with his hand, in case the feds were using lip-readers with binoculars."

At one point, the FBI became so frustrated with its telephone taps and its once-promising Gold Rush microphone that they installed a surveillance camera in the ceiling of a back room behind Cullotta's restaurant, where they suspected Spilotro was having some of his key meetings.

"We got a tip something was up there," Cullotta said, "and we went up behind the false ceiling and tore it out. It was like a small TV camera and it said 'United States Government' or something, and its serial numbers had been scraped off. I got really pissed. I wanted to trash the damn thing, but Tony made us call Oscar [Goodman, Spilotro's attorney] and give it back. I think he liked the idea of the feds coming over with their hats in their hands to get it back."

When the FBI saw that over two years of electronic surveillance had failed to snare Spilotro, they sent an undercover FBI agent, Rick Baken, into the Gold Rush, using the name Rick Calise.

As part of the ruse, Baken had first curried favour months earlier playing cards and losing to Tony's brother John. During their card games Baken let it slip that he was an ex-con and jewel thief who desperately needed cash and was looking to unload some stolen diamonds at a great price. The bureau had, of course, given Baken the backup necessary to verify his criminal past in case Spilotro checked. But even after meeting Spilotro, Baken found that Herbie Blitzstein, Tony's gofer, always kept him away from a direct conversation with Spilotro.

After eleven months of this futile and dangerous undercover work, the feds became so frustrated that they tried a desperation move. Wearing a wire, as usual, Baken approached Spilotro directly and said that he had been picked up and questioned by the FBI and threatened with prison unless he talked about Spilotro's illegal activities.

To Baken's surprise, Spilotro suggested they visit his attorney, Oscar Goodman.

The next thing Baken knew, he was in a defence attorney's office wearing a wire and pretending to be a crook. Goodman listened to Baken's story for about fifteen minutes and gave him the names of several lawyers to call.

Goodman later had a great time playing up the incident just enough to make it appear as if the FBI had tried to violate the attorney-client privilege by eavesdropping on a potential defendant and his attorney.

As time passed, Spilotro spent less and less time with his wife, Nancy. When they were together, they fought and the FBI listened. She complained that he had lost interest in her. She accused him of affairs. He was never home. He never talked to her. In the morning, the FBI recorded the sound of silence as Tony made his coffee and Nancy read the newspaper. Then he would leave for the store without even saying good-bye.

Sometimes Nancy had to call him at work to relay a message; according to Bud Hall, Tony was always rude. "She'd say, 'I don't know if this can wait, but so-and-so called.' 'It can wait,' Tony would say, sort of sarcastically, and just hang up. Or he'd say, in an exasperated tone, 'Nancy, I'm busy,' and hang up. He was never gentlemanly with her, and she'd whine to Dena Harte, Herbie Blitzstein's girlfriend, who managed the front of the Gold Rush. Nancy would tell Dena whenever Tony beat her up or whenever she suspected Tony was fooling around with this one or that one, and Dena kept Nancy informed about what Tony was doing.

"There was one time when Dena called Nancy at home and said, 'The bitch is here.' Nancy jumped in the car and tore over to the place and started screaming at Sheryl, Tony's girlfriend, calling her a no-good cunt right there in the middle of the store.

"We could hear the screaming on the wire, and then Tony comes out, and then we hear Nancy screaming for Tony to stop hitting her. He was really beating her up. We got worried that he was going to kill her. It was a mess. So we called nine-one-one and said we were in the Black Forest German Restaurant next door, and said someone was being assaulted in the Gold Rush. We couldn't tell the cops who we were because at that point it looked like Tony owned Metro, and we didn't want to blow our surveillance. The police got there in a few minutes, and everything calmed down."

"Nancy had her life and Tony had his," said Frank Cullotta. "Hers was mostly playing tennis and running around in white outfits. She had Vincent and Tony's brothers and their families. Once a week Tony'd take her out to dinner or something. But she wasn't afraid of him. She would scream and yell at him and drive him crazy.

"Once, he told me, she tried to kill him. They were having an argument over something and Tony knocked her across the room. She came up with a loaded thirty-eight cocked at his head. 'I'll kill you if you ever hit me again,' she said. Tony said, 'Nancy, think of Vincent.'

" 'I saw death,' he told me after. 'We talked until she put down the gun and then I hid all the guns in the house.' "

"Sheryl was about twenty, but she looked younger," said Rosa Rojas, who was her best friend. "She was a Mormon from northern Utah, cute and fresh. When Tony first met her he used to call her his country girl. She was so naive that when he asked her out, she said she'd only go if she could bring her friend.

"Sheryl and I were both working in the hospital where he was going for his heart problem, which was how they met. They'd go to restaurants, but he never put the make on her. He held her at a distance for a long, long time.

"Before he got too close he found out everything there was to find out about her. He had Joey Cusumano ask about where she was from, who her friends were, how long she lived where she lived. He wanted to know everything he could know about her before he got involved or felt he could trust her.

"It was a long time before she knew who he was. She began to suspect something was strange, because every time they went out, they were tailed by cops in plain clothes. Tony's brother told her that there were some legal problems and that Tony was being trailed because of the legal stuff. Tony used to tell us that we were going to read things about him in the newspapers, but he said the newspapers weren't always right.

"It was only after a long time that Tony and Sheryl started going to bed together. He was a gentleman always. Very quiet. Very reserved. I would see him mad sometimes, but I never once heard him curse or use bad language.

"Eventually, he bought her a two-storey condo around Eastern and Flamingo, a two-bedroom place for about $69,000. It had everything. Refrigerator. Blinds. A washer–dryer. There was a garage and small patio and a sliding door that led into the downstairs, and upstairs they had the bedrooms and a large room that had all of the stereo and TV equipment you would want. That's where they spent most of their time – watching ball games and listening to music.

"Tony was very generous. He used to leave $1,000 a week in a bear-shaped cookie jar in the kitchen. He never mentioned money and it was never mentioned that he was keeping her, but when he bought her a full-length mink coat Sheryl felt he had finally committed himself to her. She had really fallen in love with him.

"She didn't know he was married for quite a while. When she found out, it was very hard. She believed the only reason she and Tony weren't married was because Tony was a very strict Catholic and would have trouble leaving his wife. For a while, Tony even had Sheryl learning to be a Catholic. He gave her religious books to read. He knew the Bible.

"He never ever said anything bad about his wife. They had been married in the church and it was a difficult situation. On top of that, Tony loved his son. Vincent meant everything to him. Vincent was his soul. Tony would always get home at six-thirty in the morning so he could be there to make breakfast for Vincent. Sheryl said he would do that even if he was in bed at her place.

"Eventually, Tony bought a car for her. It was a new Plymouth Fury. It wasn't a showy car.

"When Nancy found out what was going on, things got a little tough. Sheryl had stopped by the Gold Rush to see Tony. She was wearing a diamond-studded S necklace that Tony had given her, and when Nancy came in and saw Sheryl wearing the S necklace, Nancy went wild and she reached for it.

"I got there just at that time and I found the two of them wrestling on the floor. Sheryl managed to hold on to her S. Tony came out of the back room and broke up the fight so Sheryl and I could get away.

"In the end, when it was over between Tony and Sheryl, he wouldn't return her calls. Sheryl was really crazy about him, but maybe she pushed too hard. He was having a lot of problems with the cops when they broke up, and maybe he was trying to spare her.

"His brother John used to tell her not to try and reach him. 'Don't call him,' he'd say. 'Spare yourself.' But she'd see him making his court appearances on TV and she saw that he was gaining weight and didn't look good, and she used to blame Nancy for not taking care of him. Sheryl used to make sure he ate the right food, and her refrigerator was always filled with fruits and salad and the kinds of healthy food that were good for people with heart problems.

"After she and Tony broke up she got a job doing cocktails at night. Tony wasn't happy about it. But she had grown accustomed to his lifestyle. She needed the money. Then she got into dealing blackjack. She worked in the old MGM, at Bally's. She had a prime shift and made excellent money. She started meeting high rollers. She wised up. She learned and started looking around for another rock to stand on."

"One day we're in the back of the My Place Lounge, in the parking lot, and Tony tells me to kill Jerry Lisner," said Frank Cullotta. "Jerry Lisner was a small-time drug dealer and hustler.

"Tony said: 'Frankie, you gotta take care of this guy. He rolled. He's a rat.'

"I told Tony that Lisner would be hard for me, because I had just beaten him out of 5,000 Quaaludes and he and his wife didn't trust me.

"And Tony got all mad. 'I'll go kill the motherfucker,' he says. 'Just get him over here.'

"I told him it wasn't that I didn't want to do it; it was that Lisner was worried about me. It would be hard to get close enough to get him.

" 'I want it done now!' he said. 'Now and quick!'

"That was all he said. He walked inside the joint. We were all being followed all the time, so I got in my car, went home and packed a bag, drove all the way from Las Vegas to Burbank airport in L.A., where I took the next flight for Chicago. Nobody even knew I had left town.

"In Chicago I got ahold of Wayne Matecki. We left the next night using fake names on a flight for Burbank, got in my car, and drove back to Las Vegas.

"We went from the airport to my condo, the Marie Antoinette, where I thought I'd take a chance and call Lisner. I say to myself, 'Let me give it a shot. See if he's home.' He is. I say, 'I've got a mark, a real good one. Somebody we can take for a lot of money.' I tell him the guy is in town. I'm talking a great score.

"He tells me to bring the guy over. We use a work car where we've got a police scanner and a twenty-five-calibre automatic. I didn't have a silencer so I made half loads – I half-emptied the bullets so they wouldn't make as much noise.

"I left Wayne in the car with the scanner and I went inside. I told Lisner I wanted to talk with him before the guy came in. I want to make sure that there's nobody in the house. I know his old lady works. I know he's got two sons, but he was always complaining that they were pains in the ass.

"As we're walking into the house I'm asking, 'Are you sure nobody's home? You positive? Where are your kids? Where's your wife?' He's telling me that there's nobody home, and I'm telling him I want to make sure before I bring the guy inside.

"We're walking around inside and I say, 'I hear a noise,' and he's saying it's nothing. I looked out the living room toward the pool and I closed the blinds. We're walking together and we're coming out of the little den area and I pulled the stick out and popped him two times in the back of his head.

"He turns around and looks at me. 'What are you doing?' he says. He takes off through the kitchen toward the garage.

"I actually looked at the gun, like, 'What the fuck have I got? Blanks in there?' So I run after him and I empty the rest in his head. It's like an explosion going off every time.

"But he doesn't go down. The fuck starts running. It's like a comedy of errors. I'm chasing him around the house, and I've emptied the thing in his head.

"I catch him in the garage. And as I catch him in the garage, he hits the garage door button, but I hit him before it goes down. I can see he's getting weak. I drag him back into the kitchen.

"I've got no more bullets. I'm thinking, what am I going to do with this guy? I grab an electric cord from the water cooler and I wrap it around his neck and it breaks. I was going to the sink to get a knife and finish this thing when Wayne walks in with more bullets.

"Lisner is still gasping. He says, 'My wife knows you're here.'

"I emptied the gun into his head. In the eyes. And then he just went down, like he deflated, and I knew he was gone.

"Now I wanted the house to be clean. I had blood all over the place. Blood was all over him. My worry was that I'd leave a print in the blood somewhere on his body or clothes.

"I hadn't worn any gloves because Lisner wasn't dumb. He wouldn't have let me through the door if he saw me wearing gloves. So I made sure I didn't touch anything. The only thing I knew I touched was the wall, when I hit him near the water cooler. And there, right away, as soon as he went down, I wiped everything clean real fast.

"But there was the danger of my prints on his body, so I grabbed him by the ankles and Wayne opened the sliding door, and I dragged him to the pool and slid him, legs first into the water. He went in straight, like a board. Like he was swimming.

"I knew by soaking him in the pool the blood would dissolve and any of my prints on the body would disappear. I looked down as he floated there and I saw the blood starting to come up.

"Then Wayne and I looked through the house. I wanted to make sure the guy wasn't recording my conversation with him in the house. I looked downstairs and Wayne went upstairs. I found his phone book and took it.

"We got back to my place and I took a shower with kitchen cleaner to get rid of any blood trace. Then we got rid of our clothes. We cut them into shreds, put them in a bunch of bags, and drove out into the desert, depositing them all over the place.

"Wayne took a taxi to the airport and went back to Chicago. I then drove by the Lisner house, but there was no activity. So I drove over to the My Place Lounge. As I was pulling up, Tony pulled up with Sammy Siegel.

"I asked him if he had a minute.

"We walked to the side.

"I said, 'It's done.'

"He said, 'Done?'

"I say, 'I just took care of it.'

"He said, 'Did you get rid of everything?'

"I said, 'Yeah. I put ten into him and I threw him in the pool.'

"He looked at me and said, 'Fine. As of this day we'll never talk about this again.' We never did."

"I was driving Tony to a place about sixty miles out of town for dinner, because between his heart and my licensing problems we didn't want to be seen together in town. All the way out he's telling me about how he's under constant surveillance and how he's just trying to make a living and live a quiet life. All I can do is 'yes-yes' him. Tony wasn't telling me all this because he wanted an argument. He didn't seem to put together the fact that he might have been making enemies of various people with the fact they would secretly pass the word around about what he was or wasn't doing. I don't think he understood, right or wrong, that when you're as hot as he was, every cop in the state had your picture up on their bulletin boards. Later, his lawyers found that the federal strike force had pictures of Tony and his whole family, and friends, even their lawyers. The agents and prosecutors had Tony's picture on a dart board and nasty comments written in under most of the snapshots. That's what happens when you're the target. There isn't a cop in the state that doesn't know who you are and isn't looking to either put you in jail or shake you down.

"When we got to the restaurant outside town, two of his guys were already waiting. They had taken a booth in the back.

"We had just sat down when a guy comes over to the table. 'Mr Rosenthal,' he says, 'let me introduce myself to you. I'm the owner of this property. I've seen your picture in the paper and I wanted you to know we're all rooting for you. How's the service? I hope you enjoy your dinner.'

"I told him everything was fine and thanked him, except I felt awful that he spotted me. Then, instead of going away, he turns to Tony. 'And Mr Spilotray' – he pronounced Tony's name with an A – 'can I introduce myself to you?'

"Tony stands up and puts his arm on the guy's shoulder and sort of walks him about twenty feet away, just out of earshot.

"I can see Tony's shaking the guy's hand and I'm watching the guy's smiling face and then I see he goes white and turns around and walks into the kitchen.

"When Tony sits down he's all smiles.

" 'What the hell did you tell that guy?' I asked him.

" 'Nothing,' he says.

"What happened was that Tony walked the guy away

and said: 'My name isn't Spilotray, you motherfucker. You never saw me in your life. And Frank Rosenthal wasn't here either. And if I hear you telling anything to anybody, this place is going to become a bowling alley and you're gonna be in the fucking racks.' "

Spilotro was wired, he was tailed, he was harassed, he was arrested, he was indicted. But he was never convicted. In his first five years in Las Vegas, there were more murders committed than in the previous twenty-five. He was indicted in the murder of a Caesar's Palace box man named Red Kilm, but the case never got to trial. He was suspected of killing Barbara McNair's husband, Rick Manzi, who was involved in a drug deal that went sour, but nothing ever came of it. Spilotro would walk into court waving and smiling, with his lawyer, Oscar Goodman, as the television cameras ground away. Says Frank Cullotta: "The more reporters Oscar saw, the further away he'd park his goddamn car so he'd have more time to be interviewed. Tony swore by Oscar. In all the years he was out there, he never spent more than a couple of hours in jail waiting for bail. When I'd warn him about Oscar, who as far as I was concerned was a publicity hound, Tony'd just nod and chew on his thumb. He used to chew on the cuticle of his right thumb. If you looked at it sometimes it was all raw and chewed away.

Later on, when Oscar got rich, Tony'd look up at the big brick building Oscar built on Fourth Street and say, 'I built that building.' Like he was proud of it. But I never understood why Tony liked Oscar so much. The guy was a lawyer. He made a fortune off Tony. I could never trust a man who wears a fake Rolex."

Joey the Hitman

Joey Black

In the 1970s, author David Fisher was introduced to a man named Joey who purported to be a numbers king and loan shark who also worked as a hitman for the Mob. Although as a Jew, he could not become a made man, he knew the Mafia from the inside. They had been introduced by a highly regarded crime reporter. Fisher had Joey checked out, as far as he could, and became convinced that Joey was the real deal. Fisher relates an occasion when he was dining in a restaurant in Los Angeles with Joey and a friend. Fisher's friend asked Joey what he would do if someone doubted he was what he said he was. Joey grabbed a fork and jammed it against the man's neck, forcing his head back. "I'd ask him to say it again," said Joey.

"It was a nasty moment," said Fisher.

Joey sat down with Fisher to write the book Joey the Hitman: The Autobiography of a Mafia Killer. *His motivation, he said, was to debunk films like* The Godfather.

"Members of organized crime have been made to look like animals," he said, "and actually we're not such bad people. We are the caterers of society. We just give people what they want. We don't set out to hurt anybody. I want people to understand that."

This came from a man who admitted to thirty-eight murders.

Joey kept in touch with Fisher after the book was published. Years later, he heard from a reporter in San Mateo, California, that Joey had been killed, shot in the back with a shotgun – Mafia style – when on his way to the nearby race track. After his death, a detective showed Fisher Joey's rap sheet. There was little doubt he was, as he claimed, a hitman. He had been picked up a number of times on suspicion of murder and was well known to the New York City Police Department and the FBI. However, he had always been released after a few hours, without charge. It turned out that Joey was, in fact, an informant for the FBI. He did not volunteer any information, but he would confirm what the FBI already suspected or give broad hints about things that detectives might like to look into.

It turned out that Joey – real name Joey Black – had also engineered his own murder. In fact, he had put out a contract on himself. Shortly before he died, Joey had been diagnosed with terminal cancer. He took out an insurance policy that would pay double if he died of unnatural causes. The beneficiary would be his sister. On the application, Joey had said that his occupation was "construction worker". If that was not true, the application was fraudulent and the insurance company would not have to pay out. Fisher told the claims investigator that he only knew what Joey had told him. Whether he was really a hitman or a construction worker he couldn't say.

Maria Puzo's book *The Godfather*, and the movie they made from it, did for the organization what silicone does for tits. They both make their respective subjects stand out. We needed *The Godfather* like Joey Gallo needed another portion of clams. Many people think because they saw the movie or read the book they know everything there is to know about organized crime. This is like saying you know everything there is to know about politicians because you watch "Let's Make a Deal". One thing has absolutely nothing to do with the other.

Don't misunderstand me, I thoroughly enjoyed *The Godfather*. I thought it was a very entertaining, very funny movie. It was also a wonderful piece of fiction. Things just don't happen in real life like they did to Marlon Brando and family.

Let us begin at the beginning. The whole thing starts when Sollozzo goes to see Don Corleone to get financing and political protection for a narcotics operation. He's got the whole fucking Mob backing him up, so what does he need Corleone for? The political connections? Any man in his business who is politically connected will help anybody else. That's why it's called an organization. What does this mean to Corleone? The politicians on his payroll do what he tells them to do. Why such a big deal? Besides, Sollozzo did not need Corleone's contacts that badly, he could have gone out and bought his own.

Second, all of a sudden Corleone gets some morals and decides that he doesn't want to deal in narcotics. Ridiculous. When you are controlling a family there is no such thing as not getting involved. Isn't it kind of stupid? Here's a man into bookmaking, shylocking, numbers, fixing, a man who will kill everybody and his brother, and yet he's not willing to sell narcotics. These people are in business to make money, and any man that is a big boss, a controller, he doesn't give one fuck where the money comes from. He'd love narcotics because there's more money being made there than in anything else.

Third, assuming he didn't want to sell narcotics, which no one with his head on his shoulders will believe, he is simply not going to go against a commission meeting, a meeting of the Board of Directors. If a certain thing has been decided there is no reason in the world he's gonna go out of his way to cross them. The commission is too powerful; if it wants something to happen, believe me, it happens.

Next, the shooting of Don Corleone. In every instance I have ever known that a boss was shot, it is because his bodyguard double-crossed him. And a bodyguard does not double-cross him by calling up and saying he is sick. He is there when you get killed. All he does is step aside. He does not leave himself in a position where he will be killed by his own family. Any boss that I've ever known got killed because his bodyguard helped to get him, because he had been offered an improvement in his financial status.

Fifth, the bit about the hired guns "taking to the mattresses". That just doesn't make any sense at all. I couldn't stay locked up in a room with eight other guys for one day, and neither could anybody else. You've got eight tense personalities crammed together waiting for a gunfight, how long can you play gin rummy or poker without going crazy?

During a gang war most people live at home. They just kind of lie low and stay as close to the house as possible. During the Colombo-Gallo War, for example, I met this old friend of mine who was hooked up with the Colombo people. He said, "Why don't you come out to the house for dinner this week? I'm home every night now. But I hope you don't mind if I don't walk you to your car." The home is a sanctuary. You can hit people outside the house, but you can't go inside; it's just not considered proper etiquette.

Even more, no family can afford to keep hired guns locked up in a room for any length of time. An organization that is not earning cannot afford to pay its people, and in order for you to earn you've got to be out on the street.

What do you think is going to happen if they stop working and stop earning money? Listen, if people can't earn they leave you. Now, in this so-called gang war they had, these people who "hit the mattresses" were not earning any money. And – there is just not enough money to continue paying these men.

Another thing, you are not gonna kill a cop, no matter how crooked he is, and get away with it. No matter how bad he is. There is simply no way in the world the police department is going to allow it. They will hunt you down, they will get informers on the street, they will pay money, they will get you no matter how long it takes. You are not going to kill a cop; believe me, you are not going to do it and get away with it. The cops who get gunned down in the city are hit by crazy addicts, black-power people and other nuts.

Now we come to the murder of Sonny Corleone. To refresh your memory they drew him to a deserted tollbooth area and then about a dozen guys all armed with submachine guns popped out from behind the booth and killed him. Wrong. No way in the world you're going to have that many guys there when a murder is committed. You want as few people as possible to know you're connected with the crime to begin with. Then, if you're going to set up a guy you don't have to go through all that planning, like taking over an entire roadway. There are so many different ways to hit a man. Any professional will pick his time and place; he can sucker you out, find you out or seek you out. You don't have to go through an elaborate plan to hit a man. It's very simple to catch him leaving a barbershop, or catch him coming out of his girlfriend's house or catch him having dinner in a restaurant. Nobody is going to be able to stay behind walls forever, and when he comes out you've got him.

If you remember your book and movie, after Sonny got it the Corleone family killed all the other bosses. No way. It cannot be done. As ruthless as you want to be, you wouldn't last. I don't care how careful your plans are, it is a physical impossibility. And no one can afford to hire an entire army of killers to do the job. The price is just prohibitive. The planning is incredible and the undercover work, getting to every bodyguard, is impossible. When that many people know something is going to happen, it doesn't happen. In 1931 the young turks eliminated many of the old bosses in one day and night. That was more than forty years ago and simply could not happen again today.

I thought the most convincing character was Sollozzo, the guy who tried to force the issue of narcotics. He epitomized what a man is in this business, completely ruthless, he doesn't give a fuck.

The character of the Godfather himself, Don Corleone, was a composite of a number of people I know. (I personally thought Brando was good despite the line going around that "The Italian who played Marlon Brando did a good job.") But there were some problems in his portrayal. No boss wants to be referred to as a Godfather. Most people prefer to be anonymous. The men in this business who have gone to prison are men who have allowed themselves to become too well known. The quieter a man lives, the better off he is. And when a boss does have an affair, like the Corleone wedding, he tries to hold it in an out-of-the-way place. He does not invite public figures to these affairs, because he knows the embarrassment it would cause them.

Even the relationship between Corleone and his button men, in particular Clemenza, was ridiculous. A button man is in control of an area and he may see his boss once a week, if that often.

I rated it three stars, a great comedy, and almost everybody I know in the Mob agreed. For a while the movie was the main topic of conversation. Everybody was running around threatening to "make you an offer you couldn't refuse". The most popular joke in the Mob had this guy Funzi asking his friend Tony, "Have you seen *The Godfather*?"

And Tony answered, "No, I went over to his place but he wasn't home." A big game that everybody was playing was trying to figure out who the different characters were supposed to be. There was one character I had no problem recognizing: the horse who had his head cut off. I think I bet on him out at Aqueduct the day before I saw the movie.

We shall now see how it is done in real life.

Everybody loves gang wars whether via television, radio, newspapers, magazines or movies. Everybody, that is, except the gangs. While the general public finds gang wars exciting and fascinating, the gangs find them expensive and dangerous. They could live without them, so to speak. But they do erupt, and when they do there is little anyone can do but try to finish on his feet.

Gang wars are caused by many things: young hotshots trying to push older people out, personal dislikes and, most of all, territorial disputes. In most cases these wars can be settled relatively peacefully, but sometimes both honour and money are involved, and then you have people shooting other people. The biggest war of all time, the one which set the standard by which gang wars are judged, was Chicago's Al Capone–Bugsy Moran War during Prohibition, which lasted until the entire Moran organization was destroyed. In reality there have not been too many real out-and-out fights since I've been in the business. The last big one, the Colombo-Persico-Gallo War, had all the elements of the classic gang confrontation and made headlines all over the country. As far as I know, the entire story has never been told from beginning to end.

I was there, I was approached by all three parties and I know exactly what happened.

This thing had been building for years and there had been some fighting a few times earlier. It actually started in 1957 when Joey Gallo killed Albert Anastasia under a contract let out by Joseph Profaci. As a reward Profaci gave Joey some territory in south Brooklyn. But Joey was very ambitious and wanted a bigger area. In 1959 the Gallo group, headed by Joey and his older brother Larry, broke away from the Profaci organization and started to fight. Although the Gallos were badly outnumbered they fought pretty tough, and bodies kept turning up until 1962.

Actually Joey and his eventual enemy, Joseph Colombo, had started out together in the Profaci organization. They even worked together on a few hits. They both did good work and climbed up the ladder until they split into different factions and organized their own small groups. In 1959 Colombo stayed loyal to Profaci when the Gallos split with him.

At the same time Carmine (the Snake) Persico was also starting to get some power. He was known as a man who could be depended on, even though he blew one of his biggest jobs: Profaci gave him the contract on Larry Gallo and he messed it up. He had suckered Larry into a bar in Brooklyn and was strangling him when a police sergeant happened to accidentally walk in. This was the biggest break I ever heard a man getting. But this attempt caused a great deal of bitter hatred between the Gallos and the rest of the Profaci organization.

Normally the police don't care what happens in these things, unless innocent people get hurt, but they brought this one to a halt by getting Joey on an extortion rap. Peace was more or less made before Joey went to the can, and the shooting stopped. I always felt that Colombo and Persico could have avoided a lot of problems by hitting Joey at this time, which they could have done because he just didn't have that many people. They would have saved themselves a lot of grief.

Of the three of them, I knew Joey Gallo best. Joey was one of the shrewdest and funniest people I ever met, and he was far from crazy. He knew rackets. He knew what made money and what didn't make money. He knew what he wanted to control. And he knew how to convince people that his way of thinking was best.

He once kept a lion in the basement of his social club on President Street in south Brooklyn. If a guy was giving him a hard time, or if someone defaulted or came up short, he would bring them into the cellar where the lion was tied. He would explain what solution he had in mind and then say, "If it doesn't work out, guess who's coming to dinner?" and laugh like crazy.

Joey was short, about five foot six, and had a medium build, and he was a very violent man. But it was controlled violence; he always knew what he was doing. And he was funny, a lot of laughs to be with, what you'd call good company. Years ago, when I was just getting started, we ran some muscle together. I remember one day I was driving along and I look at him and he's staring into the rear-view mirror. He kept contorting his face into the meanest looks he could make. "Hey, moron," I said to him, "what the fuck do you think you're doing?" He looked at me with a sneer splitting his face and said, "What do you think I'm doing? I'm practising to look tough!"

He didn't have to practise too hard, he was tough. But his problem was that, from the very beginning, he wanted power. He needed it desperately. When I left New York to go to California he was just on his way up. A few years later he made a big splash when he killed Anastasia. He never talked about the killing, but I knew he had done it.

He had one thing in him that somewhere along the line I've lost: Joey could hate. He was a brutal ruthless man when he hated somebody, and he found it easy to hate anybody who got in his way. I once saw him work a guy over. He really put his head and his muscle into it. He just kicked this guy until his eye popped out of his head, and then he kicked him in the balls maybe thirty times. He just made himself hate this poor sucker.

We were friendly until the day he died. One of the last times we had dinner together he seemed very wistful. I think he knew he didn't have long to live. "I wish you had thrown in with me," he said. "We could have done some great things together."

I said, "Joey, you went your way, I went mine. You've done good and I've done good and everybody's happy." Joey never really made it as big as he wanted to; he didn't really control too much when he died. But right up until the very end he was trying. That's the thing you always remember about Joey, he never knew when to lay off.

When Joey went to prison in 1962 Larry took over the President Street Mob and the south Brooklyn area. Larry could have handled things until Joey got out because he was tough and smart and people respected him. Unfortunately, he died of cancer and the third brother, Albert, took over. Albert just didn't have the power or strength or the smarts to keep control. When he first took over they called him Kid Blast . . . after a while it became Kid Blister.

Meanwhile, sitting quietly on the sidelines, carefully watching all this, slowly gathering the real power, was Carlo Gambino. He had been in competition with Profaci and when Profaci died in the summer of 1962 he just kind of eased in and took it. He took over whatever he wanted and consolidated his gains because there was no one to stop him – everybody was busy fighting within the Mob.

Finally it got to a point where it was a toss-up who was more powerful, Gambino or Vito Genovese.

Vito Genovese was the most ruthless man I have ever known. He desperately wanted to be the Boss of Bosses and was willing to kill anybody who got in his way. He set up the Albert Anastasia hit (which helped Gambino, an Anastasia lieutenant, move into power) and also tried to get Frank Costello. Chin Gigante did the job, but his shot just wounded Costello and he recovered. It didn't matter, Frank knew enough to take the hint and he retired, leaving Vito in the top spot.

Even after Vito went to prison for fifteen years on a narcotics conspiracy rap he wouldn't give up any of his power. Anthony Strollo, better known as Tony Bender, tried to take a little and one night he went out for a newspaper and never came back. Vito gave the order from his cell.

Anyway, Genovese and Gambino were the big bosses of the New York area in the early 1960s. Between the two of them they controlled everything there was to control. They also had enough influence to make things happen anywhere else in the country, but even they had to first receive the permission of whoever the boss of the territory was.

The period just after Joey went to jail saw a lot of power changing hands. Colombo was busy building an organization out of what had been the Profaci family, Persico emerged as the most powerful group within the Colombo organization, with his own men and area, and Vito Genovese went to jail, leaving the active control to Carlo Gambino. Although there was some manoeuvring for power, things generally stayed quiet while Joey was in prison.

In April 1970 Colombo's son, Joseph, Jr, was arrested by the federal government and charged with melting down silver coins, a federal offence.

This is where it all started again. Claiming that his son was innocent and his entire family was being persecuted because they were Italian, Joe Colombo announced the formation of the Italian-American Civil Rights League. This idea, this "League", had been discussed beforehand with Gambino, with Buster Alai (Alloy), Carmine Tramunti, Tony "Ducks" Corallo, and almost anybody else of importance in the New York organization. The deal was that Colombo would be the titular head of the whole thing. The income was to be derived from memberships, which cost ten dollars per person. The idea was to get every Italian in New York to join, which could come out to be a couple of million people, or $20 million.

The $20 million was what the whole thing was all about. The League was more or less a shakedown operation, and a lot of people were convinced to join and pay their ten dollars. The money was to be split among the New York families.

Mr Colombo's problems began when he forgot that there was a Carlo Gambino, Buster Alai, Tramunti and Corallo, and he put the money in his own pocket. The newspapers wrote that the Mob was angry because the Civil Rights League was attracting publicity to its operations, but that was bullshit. The League was a laughing fucking joke. Nobody cared about the publicity; organized crime had gotten publicity for years, whether we wanted it or not. Anyway this was good publicity, you might say. What got them mad was they weren't getting their fair shares. They were getting double-crossed, and they kept warning Colombo that there was going to be serious trouble if he didn't come through with the coin. While this was going on, Joey Gallo got out of jail.

In public Gallo said he had been reformed in prison, that he had read a lot of books and learned a great deal, and that from now on he was going to play it straight if the

Mob would let him. In private the first thing he did was go to see Carlo Gambino. "Listen," he told him, "south Brooklyn is mine and I ain't giving it up." He wanted the dock area, the President Street area, the bookmaking, the shylocking, the muscles, everything he had before he went to prison. The old man agreed, and Joe Colombo agreed. Colombo was not thrilled but he had no choice. Gambino said that was the way it was going to be, and you do not go against Gambino and live too awfully long.

The final straw with Colombo and Gambino came when an audit of the League's books showed it was bankrupt. Everybody knew there was plenty of money around and it was obvious that Colombo was keeping it. A meeting was held at Buster Aloi's house and word filtered back to me that Carlo sat there and said very explicitly, "I want Joe Colombo hit in the head like a pig."

Guess who they offered the job to? Joey Gallo would have given anything to set this deal up and so he was given the contract. Joey did not instigate this at all, he didn't have the power. Only bosses can approve the killing of another boss. But Colombo had to go because he had gotten to the point where he believed he was bigger than the Mob, that he was indestructible. Wrong.

Hitting a boss is a very complicated undertaking, if you'll excuse the expression. In order to get him you have to have people within his own organization who are willing to double-cross him. Joe Colombo's chief bodyguard at this time was a man by the name of Gennaro (Fat Jerry) Ciprio, and he was the man who had to be gotten to put Colombo in a position where he could be assassinated. He agreed – I assume he was promised more money and power – and the arrangements were made through him. Colombo was to be killed at his own giant Civil Rights League rally in Columbus Circle, right in the middle of Manhattan. They decided on the rally because it was the perfect place to cause mass confusion, which was exactly what they wanted.

Gallo also had to find a man to pull the trigger. He didn't want to use one of his own people because he knew there was no way the killer could get away after the shooting. Through the connections Gallo made while he was in prison he was able to find a black man stupid enough to believe that he was going to get $100,000 or so for committing this particular crime. In reality all he was going to get for his efforts was a bullet in the head. He was dead the minute he agreed to do the job. The Mob couldn't afford to let him live, he simply knew too much. It was a real sucker job.

Ciprio, Colombo's bodyguard, was responsible for the actual details of the plan. It took about a month to set the whole thing up. Ciprio had to get press credentials for Jerome Johnson, the killer, to get through the dozens of cops that were in the area. Again, these credentials had to be provided by someone with the organization. And Ciprio had to manoeuvre Colombo into a position where Johnson would have a clean, clear shot at him. Usually, if you're a bodyguard you shield your man with your own body. If you are out to let him get hit you step aside. Ciprio stayed up on the grandstand and watched the whole thing happen. Colombo should have been killed but he wasn't – although for all practical purposes he's dead because he isn't anything but a vegetable now. Johnson blew the job (the consequences of hiring an amateur) but he didn't live long enough to know that.

The minute he pulled the trigger Ciprio leaped off the stand and headed for him. A New York City cop, who had no knowledge of the plan, wrestled the gun away from Johnson and had him on the ground. The cop never saw Ciprio come up from behind and blow Johnson's brains out. If that cop had been a little quicker, or Ciprio a little slower, Johnson would have lived to tell a very interesting story.

When the shooting took place both Gallo and Gambino were miles and miles away from Columbus Circle. All they had to do was sweat it out that everything went right. Fortunately for them, it did. But there was no doubt who set the whole thing up, and had Gambino not backed Gallo, Joey would have been dead within forty-eight hours. There is no doubt about that. But the fact that Gallo was seen with Gambino after the shooting was enough to stop everybody. No matter how much people would have liked to take care of Joey they didn't dare. It was obvious he had the old man's approval and therefore had to be left alone.

That didn't mean there wasn't going to be a fight. As I said, some potential wars are settled peacefully, but this one didn't have a chance once Joe Colombo got hit. Forget about it. Blood had to run. It had to.

But not right away. Gang wars are expensive and people go out of their way to avoid them. So a very uneasy peace settled over the New York organization. Joey, of course, started getting more powerful. He was busy pretending he had gotten out of the rackets, he was on parole at the time, which had something to do with that act, and was getting chummy with show-business people. According to newspaper columnists, he was also writing a book. As he should have realized, the worst thing you can do in this business is become publicity-conscious. Unfortunately, Joey Gallo liked to read about himself in the newspapers.

Businesswise Joey started to consolidate his gains. Now he had had a hard-on for Carmine Persico ever since Junior (the Snake) had tried to kill his brother. So Joey cried no tears when Carmine got fourteen years in a federal penitentiary for hijacking. Now the positions were reversed, Joey was out and the Persico Mob was being run by Alphonse Persico and Lenny Dell. Joey simply told them he was taking over. The Persico people realized there was nothing they could do, they weren't strong enough to hold the organization together without Junior. So they went to see Carlo Gambino.

Gambino owed Joey something, so when Dell and Persico went to see him he just shrugged his shoulders and said that this was between Gallo and them. That was his way of protecting Joey, his way of letting the Persico people know that he wasn't going to help them, that Joey would be allowed to do whatever he was strong enough to do. He didn't believe for a second they would be strong enough to knock Joey off and he figured, like everyone else, that they would have to capitulate and give it all up. It didn't work that way.

The Persico people went to Tony Colombo and Joe Colombo, Jr, and acting boss Joseph Yacovelli and explained the situation. The way I understand the conversation, they told the Colombo people that if Gallo took over Persico's organization he would be strong enough to take over the Colombo people next. This made a great deal of sense all around, and both groups went back to the old man. If Gallo took them over, they said, he would eventually have to go after Gambino. And everyone knew Joey was a very ambitious man. They finally told the old man that they were going to fight Joey Gallo and, if they did, they would fight him too. That's when Carlo decided he could live without Joey. Colombo and Persico were threatening all-out war, and since he, Gambino, was fighting extradition at that moment, all-out war was something he could do without. So he agreed to let them kill Gallo.

But the Colombo people wanted more than permission. They knew they were now doing Gambino a favour and, in return, wanted the names of the people within the Colombo organization who had set up Joe Colombo to be killed. This was their price, and Carlo agreed it was a fair one.

I was told Joey Gallo was going to be killed about three weeks before it happened. I was sitting in an Italian restaurant on 86th Street in Brooklyn, and Lenny Dell said to me, "There's going to be an open contract on Gallo. Do you want it?"

I said, "No, I'm not thrilled about it."

He said, "Okay, but then we're gonna need guns, you like to come to work?"

No way. "Look Lenny, let's be realistic," I told him. "I know you and I know Joey and I know the Colombo people. I've been doing business with you people in one form or another for years. I don't want to offend nobody. If I take sides now, that means I got to take sides for the rest of my life. I just don't want to do it." I had the right to refuse the job, which I did. But it is also understood that I must keep my mouth shut; I can't discuss the fact that the contract was out with anybody. An open contract means that anybody who has the balls can do it, and anybody with brain shuts up about it.

I wasn't afraid to see Joey Gallo, even though I knew there was a contract out on him, because when Joey went out in public he always had at least one bodyguard with him who could be trusted. Number two, I always carried a cannon, and number three, the man was my friend. So what was I going to do? I had dinner with Joey twice between the time I knew the contract was out and the night the actual hit took place. I never even felt an urge to tell him what was happening. I didn't have to, he knew something was up. I just looked at him and thought, "Well, sucker, you took your best shot, now they're going to take theirs." I never even thought about telling him. I figured he had to know they were looking to hurt him, but he made the same mistake Colombo made, he figured he was Joey Gallo and nobody would dare do anything to him.

His real mistake was not keeping closer tabs on Gambino. He figured Carlo was his man, and he was, but Carlo just didn't want a big war breaking out. What Joey should have done was, instead of talking with Dell and Persico, he should have killed them. Had he done that he would have eliminated all his problems. Their people would have either walked away or come into his organization. Remember, all most men want is a chance to earn a living and he really doesn't care much who gives it to him.

Again, if you are going to hit a boss you have to have help. Even if you are going to hit Joey Gallo. Now, when Joey was killed his bodyguard Pete the Greek was with him and made a legitimate attempt to guard him. Pete used to be with Colombo, but since he himself was wounded and did some shooting trying to defend Joey, it's obvious where his loyalties were. But there was a second bodyguard, a guy named Bobby, who had also been to the Copa with Joey and Pete and Joey's family that night. When he was asked to go along to Umberto's Clam House he refused, saying he was going with some broads. I would have to say this was probably when the phone call was made telling where Joey Gallo would be.

To this day I really don't know who did the job. The story seems to be that this guy Luparelli saw Gallo going into the restaurant and went to the social club where he picked up Carmine DiBiase. They contacted Yacovelli, who was running the Colombo Mob and making the payment, and he said go ahead. DiBiase, or whoever, then walked into Umberto's, killed Gallo, and shot Pete the Greek. After finishing the job, he ran out and hopped into the car Luparelli claims he was driving. They drove to Nyack, New York, and laid low. Eventually Luparelli got the idea that they were trying to poison him in his hideout and split.

I can't buy this whole story, there are just too many contradictions in it. I'm not saying DiBiase didn't pull the trigger, I just doubt it happened like Luparelli says it did. Believe me, I'm not trying to defend DiBiase. He and I almost had it out in a social club on Mulberry Street one sunny afternoon.

I didn't really know Carmine very well, but we had both been involved in a business deal and it annoyed him that I kept the best piece for myself. When we were making the cash split he made some nasty remarks about my ethnic background and I smacked him in the mouth. Then I went home.

The next day I got a message that Carmine was sitting around his social club threatening to kill me. I could see that if he tried to follow through it would put a terrific strain on our friendship, so I decided to beat him to the punch, so to speak. I picked up my .357 magnum, which is one mighty big cap gun, and I drove down to the social club. I walked in and pulled the gun out of my belt and stuck it right between his eyes. "I understand you don't like me," I said.

One look at Carmine's eyes told me he was upset that this rumour had gotten around and he felt this was the proper time to dispel it. "Like you?" he replied. "Like you? I love you!"

It was nice to know the rumours were unfounded. "Fine," I said, "and if I were you, I'd make sure the romance lasts."

So you understand I never received my membership card in the Carmine DiBiase Fan Club. But let us assume you have a hit going. I'm sitting in my social club and you come and tell me so-and-so is in such a place. Now, I have to get permission before I can go ahead, so I'm gonna pick up the phone and call a man at his home or at his girlfriend's, right? Wrong. Wherever he is, no two ways about it, that phone has got to be tapped. Second, I'm not gonna have you sitting in the car while I go inside and shoot it out myself. Third, I'm not gonna take you to a hideout I got and, all of a sudden, try and kill you. And if I was going to kill you, why would I bother poisoning you? What the fuck do I want to do that for when I can just as easily pull the trigger? I mean, the whole story doesn't hold water with me. But I don't know a better version. It doesn't really matter anyway; the end result was the same. So long, Joey.

The newspapers made a big deal out of the fact that Gallo was hit in front of his wife and daughter, which is a clear violation of Mob rules. But they forgot that Joe Colombo was hit in front of his family. Tit for tat. One thing about the Mob, they'll even things up, one way or another.

The shooting really started after Joey was killed. I met with one of the Gallo people who asked me if I wanted to throw in with them until the shooting was over. "I turned the other people down," I said, "why should I join you?" I wanted nothing to do with it. What did I need it for? I'm not some young punk looking to make a reputation.

Normally it is easy to recruit guns during a war. First of all, you know the people who have worked with guns before and you contact them. You offer them X dollars to remain with your people for the length of the shooting. It's not going to last more than a couple of months because there is nobody that can afford it; it's a physical impossibility. You hire a good gun and you're going to have to pay him a minimum of $5,000 a week plus a bonus for everybody he shoots, $20,000 or so, just to keep him there. No professional will risk his life – which is what he is doing – for less. And business is severely curtailed during the fighting. You have to send someone around to protect your people as they make their rounds, and even then they may see only half their regular customers. And you've got to have some people patrolling the neighbourhood, riding around making sure there are no strange faces in the area. A gang war is when you find out who your friends are.

During a war everybody in the organization automatically becomes a gun, even though they really can't handle anything. But on paper they are considered a gun. Plus you have whatever you can grab. You try to have thirty or forty people who can pull the trigger, and if you're paying them $5,000 a week it is going to get very expensive. So it won't last too long.

Once the war breaks out it's easy to see who is siding with who. Just take a ride through their territory and see who's hanging out in the area. And as for the people who have been paying off one boss, if they stop he knows they can't be working with him. That only leaves one other side.

As it turned out the Gallo people couldn't get enough men together to make a fight of it. You have to have something to pay people with, and they evidently didn't have it. There is no longer a Gallo organization. It was completely destroyed when Joey died. It was taken over by Colombo-Persico. The people in Joey's group were drafted, almost like they do in sports, first one family making a selection and then the other and so on. The Gallo people had two choices: either do business with the new people or be completely cut out. Albert Gallo, for example, threw in with Colombo. Business, as they say, is business.

In all, a total of about twelve people went down. They were turning up in car trunks and vacant lots all over the city. Once they had the names, it was a simple process for the Colombo people to eliminate those men within their own organization who had double-crossed Joe Colombo.

The day before Gallo was killed Thomas Edwards (Tommy Ernst) was shot to death on his father-in-law's porch.

That same day Bruno Carnevale was shot in Queens. He had $14,000 on him when the cops found him.

Ciprio was shot three days after Gallo died. He owned a restaurant in Brooklyn and he walked out one night and was gunned down.

Richard Grossman, who I never heard of and who I doubt was involved in this thing, was found the same day, stuffed in a trunk of an abandoned car in Brooklyn.

Frank Ferriano went down the same day. William Della Russo went down five days later.

Rosario Stabile was shot in his car a day after Della Russo.

I think you get the point. Gang wars are about as much fun as walking through a plate-glass window. There is no excitement, no adventure, only a lot of time spent laying low. It always seemed to me that, if your average citizen finds them so exciting, he should choose up sides and go at it himself. But please leave me out of it.

Contract Killer

Donald Frankos

*Donald "Tony the Greek" Frankos was a freelance hitman
for the Mafia for forty-five years. This put him centre stage
in the underworld. He claimed to have killed union leader
Jimmy Hoffa, the former president of the International
Brotherhood of Teamsters in 1975. In 1964, Hoffa had been
convicted of attempting to bribe a member of a grand jury
and sentenced to fifteen years in jail. However, President
Richard Nixon commuted his sentence. Hoffa was last seen
in the parking lot of the Machus Red Fox Restaurant in
Bloomfield Township, Oakland County, Michigan, a suburb
of Detroit, where he was expecting to meet two Mafia leaders,
Anthony "Tony Jack" Giacalone from Detroit and Anthony
"Tony Pro" Provenzano, vice president of Teamsters Local
560 in Union City, New Jersey. Daniel Sullivan, a former
Teamster official and reformer, remembers that some time
before, Hoffa had told him: "Tony Pro threatened to pull
my guts out or kidnap my grandchildren if I continued to
attempt to return to the presidency of the Teamsters."*

"I pumped two slugs into Hoffa's forehead," said Frankos.

*Tony the Greek was brought up in a violent home in
Pennsylvania. After a stint in the US Navy, he went AWOL
in Manhattan, hooking up with a prostitute with a long-
term heroin habit. He murdered a troublesome pimp. In jail,*

his reputation as a tough guy and his ease at death-dealing brought him to the attention of the Mafia and Frankos was soon making big money as a hit man. Along the way, he met a Who's Who *of crime including John Gotti, Joey Gallo, Frank Costello, Harlem kingpin Nicky Barnes, crime boss Fat Tony Salerno – who, Frankos says, ordered not only the hit on Hoffa but also an aborted one on Frank Sinatra – and legendary Irish mobster John Sullivan, who Frankos billed as "the outstanding contract killer of his generation". Finally Frankos was sentenced to twenty-five-to-life. In the penitentiary at Attica, upstate, he turned government witness and began writing* Contract Killer: The Explosive Story of the Mafia's Most Notorious Hitman – Donald "Tony the Greek" Frankos *with William Hoffman and Lake Headley. In the book, he details the day-to-day life of a hitman.*

The phone rang early on this summer 1973 afternoon, and right away I recognized the gruff voice of John Sullivan, an important Irish mobster and a contract killer for Genovese crime family boss Fat Tony Salerno.

"You free today?" Sullivan asked.

"Yeah," I said.

"Meet me at Wolf's Deli in an hour."

At this time I maintained two residences: an apartment reserved for privacy on 15th Street; and a suite to conduct business at the Hotel Wilson. Sullivan phoning me at the apartment boded an urgency not normally associated with our business together, since we saw each other three or four times a week in the regular course of affairs. I suspected he wanted somebody hit.

I pulled on a fresh pair of slacks, topped them with my favourite grey silk shirt, and decided to walk the forty-two blocks from my apartment to the deli at 57th and Sixth Avenue.

Sullivan waited for me at a corner table, wearing a dark business suit, starched white dress shirt, and maroon silk tie. He'd started his lunch: a corned beef sandwich and a bottle of imported beer. About 5'10" and blocky, in his late forties, John never smiled, never lightened up. He asked me how I was doing, and whether I wanted something to eat.

"No thanks. I'm trying to lose a few pounds."

"I need you for a job," Sullivan said. He didn't fool around much, a quality to my liking.

"Who?" I asked.

"Buster DellaValle."

"I know Buster."

"Makes no difference."

"Right," I said.

"So you'll do it?"

"Yeah." I took pride in giving definite answers. No maybes or I'll think it over.

This normally would have ended our conversation, except for Sullivan suggesting likely places for the hit, maybe supplying a picture or two of the intended victim (not necessary here), and providing whatever helpful intelligence he had gathered.

Not the case today. John wanted me to know the pressing reason for the murder contract, so I would act accordingly. I soon sat entranced listening to this veteran gangster explain the twisted course of events leading to the decision that Buster DellaValle had to die.

Buster had been a bodyguard, drug dealer, and hit man for Joey Gallo right up to the time Joey had been killed on 7 April 1972, at Umberto's Clam House in Little Italy. Buster bought the heroin he'd sold for Gallo – and later for himself – from Philip John Manfredi and Philip D. Manfredi, first cousins who operated out of Fat Tony Salerno's neighbourhood in East Harlem. The Manfredis, each in his early twenties, filled in while their uncle, narcotics kingpin JoJo Manfredi, did time for the Feds.

"You know what happened to JoJo's nephews," Sullivan said.

Yes, I did. On the night of 9 August 1972, they had driven their Oldsmobile to a deserted parking lot in the Clasons Point section of the Bronx, where police found their bodies early the next morning. P.D. Manfredi rested in the front seat of the car, shot three times in the head from a distance of less than six inches. P.J. Manfredi, also hit three times, sprawled on the pavement twenty-five feet from the Olds.

I didn't need to see a police reconstruction to know how the murders came down. Someone those kids trusted had sat in the backseat of the vehicle and without warning had opened fire on P.D. Manfredi. Undoubtedly the killer considered him the more dangerous of the two and eliminated him first. P.J. Manfredi had run for his life, but hadn't made it far before a .38 bullet shattered his hand and two more slammed into his back.

"That cocksucker DellaValle whacked them," Sullivan said. The police professed to have no idea of the killer's identity, and they probably told the truth, but John knew who did it.

DellaValle, like other members of Joey Gallo's crew anxious to avenge the death of their beloved boss, had known the Manfredis were close to Fat Tony Salerno, one of the key players in Joey's assassination, and had waited patiently for the right time to strike. He had continued to purchase heroin from the cousins, as if nothing had changed, until he'd won such a degree of trust that they'd let him sit in the back of their car in that isolated Bronx parking lot.

JoJo Manfredi, seeking his revenge, had reached out from prison to Fat Tony Salerno, who in turn had called on John Sullivan. It seemed pretty straightforward for a Mob contract – DellaValle whacking the Manfredis as vengeance for Gallo's death, and allies of the drug dealers striking back. But then John Sullivan added a twist that cast a whole new light on the situation.

"Junior Persico and Jerry Lang," he said, "have already taken a shot at Buster."

Then why wasn't he dead? Carmine "The Snake" Persico, known as Junior, boss of the Colombo crime family, and Jerry Langella, his underboss, ranked among the most dangerous Mafiosi who ever lived. I'd met Junior Persico, who ran his gang from a prison cell, and knew he hated everything about Joey Gallo. It was Persico's gang of top-of-the-line killers who had waged a bloody war against Joey's crew in the early 1960s, and won.

"You heard about that restaurant," Sullivan said.

The Neapolitan Noodle. A fancy, newly opened place at 320 East 79th Street. Yes, I knew about it, just like every New Yorker and, no, I didn't have an insider's view of what had happened there. On 11 August 1972, less than two days after the Manfredi murders, four legitimate businessmen, standing at the Noodle bar, had been gunned down in a hail of bullets. Two of them, Sheldon Epstein and Max Tekelch, were killed, and the event became the talk of the town. A lone gunman had blazed away with a pistol in each hand, and police brass speculated that these had been mistaken-identity murders. The cops had it right.

The killings inflamed much of the citizenry and became a hot topic for politicians, none more prominent than Mayor John Lindsay. It was one thing for criminals to kill one another, but quite different to murder ordinary people. The usually staid *New York Times*, under the headline "Run Gangsters Out of City, Angry Mayor Tells Police," quoted Lindsay: "The recent murder of innocent citizens – allegedly the result of mistaken identity – by gangland executioners is an outrage which demands that the romanticization of the Mob must be stopped and gangsters run out of town."

The Mafia hated this type of publicity, which focused attention on its activities and guaranteed hundreds of harassment arrests. Even police officers the Mob had in its pocket, bought and paid for, were forced to bring Mafiosi in, albeit with profuse apologies, for questioning. Many criminals had to alter the rhythm of their extremely lucrative rackets until the heat cooled.

"Junior passed the order from the joint to Jerry Lang," Sullivan said, "and Jerry was at the restaurant to see that everything went right. Instead, everything went fucking wrong."

The hitter, Sullivan explained, was a guy who'd opened fire before adequately identifying his targets. The intended victims – DellaValle and Bobby Bongiovi, a Gallo soldier – had agreed to a meeting at the Neopolitan Noodle with Alphonse Persico, Sr (Carmine's older brother, known as Allie Boy), Alphonse Persico, Jr (Carmine's son, known as Little Allie Boy), and Jerry Langella, who as an underboss should have performed better. DellaValle and Bongiovi had been told to wait at a specific spot at the bar; they never showed up. Those businessmen had sat down in the wrong place.

The police never solved the Manfredi murders, nor those at the Neapolitan Noodle, nor scores of other hits through the years that a single good informant could have put them wise to. Not nearly as many rats existed then. Savvy detectives admit that a knowledgeable snitch is worth a battery of computers and an army of cops.

John Sullivan ordered a slice of cheesecake and a cup of coffee. Whether planning it or committing it, murder made him hungry.

"You gotta be careful with this guy," John said. "He always packs a pistol."

"Right," I said. I had done time with DellaValle at Dannemora and knew him as a dangerous character. "You might look for him on Lafayette Street. There's a bank there, and two small Greek restaurants. Buster does business out of those restaurants. In the afternoons."

"Okay." I already had plotted how to do it.

"Fat Tony don't want no delays. This Buster situation's been agitating him for a long time. He couldn't move till now because of the pressure over the Noodle."

Sullivan handed me a package. "That's half," he said. When I later opened it at my apartment I found $5,000, which meant, with Sullivan keeping 50 per cent for himself, this was a $20,000 contract. Big money for a hit.

Often a crime boss paid an independent hitter like me $5,000 total, or less. Sometimes he wanted it done for nothing, and I obliged – a professional courtesy, so to speak – to open up other avenues of making money.

"The heat's on," Sullivan concluded, getting up from his chair. "Don't make no mistakes."

The next morning in my suite at the Wilson I carefully prepared for the kill. I spread a yellow-tinted makeup on my face and neck, stuffed cotton balls inside my cheeks, and donned a medium Afro wig. I put on a tank-top undershirt, then applied makeup to all the exposed skin of my upper torso. Next I placed a sawed-off shotgun in a large hollowed out radio I intended to carry. Wearing a faded pair of Levis and dirty high-top sneakers, I was almost ready to hunt for Mr John "Buster" DellaValle.

First I went to see a friend who owned a vegetable store near 12th Avenue, which served as a repository for a wide variety of hijacked merchandise and stolen goods, especially cases of guns swagged off the docks. When I walked in, my friend didn't recognize me, nor did he stare as if startled by a bizarre apparition. Good. I needed to be disguised, without calling attention to myself. I greeted my friend and told him I once again wanted to use the back of his store to chop up a body, then handed him a thousand dollars, the agreed-upon price. He didn't want to hear a name and I didn't give one.

For six straight days I repeated the same prey-stalking routine: don the disguise; drive the stolen Buick with the phoney licence plates to Lafayette Street; park a block away from the Greek restaurants; unload the bicycle I'd folded on to the backseat; place the hollowed-out radio on the handlebars; and pedal by Buster's supposed hangouts. He was never there.

I hated having to psyche myself a mile high each day, then crash down. It was like getting ready to play the Super Bowl and learning the other team hadn't shown up.

John Sullivan, furious, came to my place at the Wilson. "What the fuck is the delay, Greek?" he wanted to know.

I got hot. For years I had maintained my independence, anticipating times exactly like this, and I didn't have to answer to Sullivan. "Fuck you," I said. "You don't talk to me that way."

"Fat Tony wants this guy dead."

"Tough shit! Buster ain't where you said he'd be."

"Well, he's gotta be there," John said. "Fat Tony talks about nothin' else."

"Fuck Fat Tony, too," I groused. Ever since I'd started running with Mob people, more than a dozen years earlier, I'd recognized that freelancing held the secret to maintaining sanity, and I insisted they respect my independence. In return, I did hits the Mafia considered too risky, didn't want their soldiers to handle, or had botched miserably in the first place. Like this one, the DellaValle contract. I showed the wiseguys respect when they showed it to me, and didn't worry that *I* might become a hitter's target. I had a rule about that sort of thing: if the killer didn't get me, I'd go after his boss.

"I have to tell Tony what you're doing," Sullivan said, cooling down.

"Tell him I'm working on it. That it's all I'm working on."

"You want a machine gun? I can get you a machine gun. You know, don't you, that whoever's with Buster, they go too."

"Right. No, I don't want a machine gun." Years before I had practised with one but hadn't felt comfortable with it. Too often the gun misfired, which could mean bye-bye Greek. I would have no second chance with DellaValle.

John finally said, "What the hell, do it your own way. Just *do* it."

I already had everything set up in the Buick: twenty large black garbage bags, surgeon's gloves, chainsaw, and goggles to shield my eyes from flying tissue, blood, and bone chips. I knew there would be a mop and bucket in the vegetable store.

On my second trip to Lafayette Street after John's visit, my luck changed. As I pedalled by the first Greek restaurant, there sat Buster, stationed in a booth with his back against the wall, gazing at the door. I pedalled back to the car and got in, but in my haste I left the bike on the sidewalk propped against a parking meter. I drove directly toward the Greek restaurant, double-parked the car just out of sight of anyone looking through the front window, and stepped on to the street.

That's when I felt a nervous spasm in the pit of my stomach. My hands grew cold, clammy. It always happened this way, when I went after another killer, when I knew it would be his life or mine, no other result possible.

I told myself, *you have the advantage, you're the offence*, a true enough appraisal; but a single mistake with the guy who had killed the Manfredi nephews and I'd be as dead as they were.

Then another feeling, only present when I went to kill someone who might kill me: a powerful wish to be back in the protection of my "mother's" arms. The desire then vanished as suddenly as it had appeared. The time had come.

I entered the restaurant and locked my eyes with Buster's for just a second. I looked away, and with the radio on my shoulder walked straight to the men's room. My heart quickened as I checked the sawed-off shotgun. I calculated the distance from where I sat on the toilet to where Buster sat in the booth as thirty feet. Placing the shotgun back into the radio, which I left slightly ajar for quick access to the weapon, I was momentarily startled by my reflection in the mirror. I didn't recognize me, so surely Buster hadn't. *You got the offence*, Greek. *Take him. Calm and fast.*

I came out of the restroom at a normal pace, picking up speed on my way toward DellaValle. *Goddamn!* I thought, *someone's sitting with him!* A guy about sixty-five years old, his back to the front door, previously obscured from my view by the high-back booth. *This old man could be dangerous*, I told myself. I had known hitters in their seventies, unstoppable tough old cobs, much harder to ice than their young counterparts.

But now, charged with excitement and determination, I could not consider turning back. Not even heroin supplied a rush as powerful as the moments before a kill, adrenaline pumping, senses transmitting messages of astounding clarity, and *fear*. I had reached the top of my profession as a contract killer, living a luxury-filled existence, receiving respect from the crime families; and bone-deep I was afraid of losing it all, a guaranteed denouement if only once I hesitated, lost my nerve, or just plain fucked up. Every time I went on a job I had to psyche myself up, whip my mind and guts into an internal frenzy. Always, acute fear provided the motivating, driving force.

I set the radio down on Buster's table, pulled out the shotgun, and pressed it against his head. We weren't even noticed by the few late-lunchers still scattered in the restaurant. Buster himself had watched me approach, but his warning system had failed him.

"You make the slightest move, you fat piece of shit," I told him in a heavy New York wiseguy accent, "and I'll blow your head off your shoulders. Old man," I growled to Buster's companion, "you keep your hands on the table, or my partner will blow your brains out."

I said all this in a low, calm voice. I didn't want a panic that would necessitate doing the killing here; killing in public is always bad. The newspapers would cover a restaurant murder – as they had the killings at the Neapolitan Noodle – forcing the cops to react more energetically than usual. Mayor Lindsay, grandstanding with that "run gangsters out of the city" order (a command impossible to carry out, given the thousands of threads connecting the "upperworld" – judges, politicians, police, prosecutors, businessmen – to the underworld) could make life uncomfortable for Fat Tony and his ilk, and the mobsters would blame me.

"There'll be no problem," I said, "if you do what you're told. All I want is your money and jewellery."

Although his instincts screamed at him that I lied, DellaValle *wanted* to believe me. I never met anyone who accepted that his life was moments away from ending. I saw the calculating going on in Buster's fearful eyes, watched him convince himself that maybe I told the truth.

"Get up slowly and walk out the front door," I said. "I'll be right behind you. Do what I tell you and you live. Make a break for it and you die right here."

I placed the shotgun against my right side, so it was hidden by the radio, and escorted Buster and his companion out to the sidewalk. From the corner of my right eye I could see a waitress looking at me, but I knew she'd never be able to make an identification. Buster and I had been close at Dannemora, and *he* hadn't recognized me.

I paraded the men the few yards to the car. "Keep moving, motherfucker," I told the old man. "My partner will meet you up the block." To hell with Sullivan's warning – "whoever's with Buster, they go too" – this guy was no threat. I hated leaving the bike behind, but had no choice. I wasn't going to drive back to retrieve it.

Opening the Buick's door on the driver's side, I ordered Buster to get in, then slid him over to the passenger's side with my body, maintaining constant pressure on his rib cage with the shotgun. I reached over, opened the glove compartment, and removed a set of handcuffs. Seeing them, DellaValle's face turned white. I assured him they were only a precaution.

"Where you taking me?" he asked.

"Someplace quiet. Where I can check what you're carrying."

"I can give you everything I've got right now. No problem."

"I'll do the looking, cocksucker, when I want." It was good to throw in the bad language: it let him know he didn't deal with an amateur. The speech of a professional gangster, including his tone, deliberately sets him apart. Cops have *their* way of talking. So do doctors.

I pushed the shotgun hard into his ribs. "*This* I'll take right now," I said, reaching inside his belt and snatching out a .22. "Now lean forward, you motherfucker, and put your hands behind your back." I handcuffed him, pushed him down on to the floor, and felt my breathing start to return to normal. It was virtually all over now, though I reminded myself to remain alert for the unexpected.

My hands nevertheless trembled as I inserted the key into the ignition, started the car, and drove off toward the west side of Manhattan. We travelled perhaps a half-dozen blocks before it dawned on Buster. "I know you," he said. "From upstate. You're the Greek, aren't you?"

It didn't matter if he knew. "Yeah. I'm the Greek."

This terrified him, but also somehow provided hope. "Donald . . . you're Donald . . . Donald . . ."

"Frankos."

"Right! The Greek Frankos. Tony the Greek. Jesus Christ, Greek, we were friends."

"Business is business, Buster. Just stay calm. I won't hurt you if you do what I say."

I could sense DellaValle thinking this over as I drove. He was recalling what he knew about me, and found none of it encouraging. He had been in my shoes when he'd worked for Joey Gallo – there could be only one reason I had him stuffed on the floor of a car.

I let myself imagine what he felt, wondered what would go through my mind in the not unlikely event that I got shanghaied on a similar ride. I didn't think I would beg, as I expected Buster would, but who could know?

"What's going on, Greek? What are you up to? Please. Tell me."

"I already told you."

"You're going to kill me, aren't you, Greek?"

"Where do you get that, Buster? I'm going to rob you."

But DellaValle had been around too long, knew my reputation too well, to buy any nonsense about robbery.

"What are they paying you, Greek?"

"Shut up, Buster. Nobody's paying me." I pulled on to the Westside Highway.

"Greek, please. Listen to me. I got a lot of money. Stashed away nice and safe. It's all yours. I'll take you to it. You can have it all. Just let me go. Please, Greek."

I reached down to my right ankle where I kept a .22 Beretta. I placed the gun in my lap so Buster couldn't see it.

He started to cry. Sobbing and shaking, he pleaded for his life.

"I'm not going to kill you," I repeated. If he died expecting to live, just all of a sudden went to sleep, then he'd die happy. Besides, I wanted him to calm down.

He offered me his loan-shark business, his drug business, "tall stacks" of money he had hidden away. "I'll leave town, Greek. Nobody will ever know you didn't do the job, and you'll be a rich man. Be smart, my friend, tell them you whacked me and take everything for yourself."

A few guys had saved themselves this way: gave up all they had and moved far away. But it was too risky for the individual with the contract; too many things could go wrong. Anyway, the offer had no appeal to me. At this time my reputation as a good fellow, as a stand-up guy, a hitter (and none ranked higher in the eyes of mobsters than a hitter), meant more than anything in the world to me.

At 30th Street I pulled over to the right and stopped. Traffic was light, and the tension in the car was unbearable. Buster defecated all over himself; the sudden, awful stink filled the car.

DellaValle's last words were an apology for shitting in my car. I shot him twice behind the head, and his head bounced back up and almost tore off the dashboard. Then he slumped down, real peaceful, dead.

I pushed Buster's body down closer to the floor, covered it with a blanket I kept in the backseat, and drove the reeking vehicle to 12th Avenue. Too many people were milling about, so I ran the Buick over the kerb on to the sidewalk and parked the passenger side against the vegetable-store entrance. The proprietor and I carried DellaValle to the back.

"It's done," I told John Sullivan over the phone.

"Where you at?"

"Swanee's." A code name we used for the produce market.

"I want to see."

While I waited for John to arrive, I stayed busy. I uncuffed and undressed Buster, an unpleasant job; checked his pockets for money; got help hoisting him on to a table; carried the garbage bags, gloves, goggles, surgeon's smock, and chainsaw in from the car; and, finally, reparked the car. I permitted myself a smile, knowing that when I finished no one could ever put Buster back together again – and the cops would have a helluva time identifying him, if by some odd chance they found any of the body.

A knock on the back door. "Who's there?" I asked.

"Me. John."

When I let him in, he took one look at the naked body and almost knocked the wind out of me. He grabbed me, pounding my back, hugging and kissing me. "*Nobody* can do it better than you," he said. "You're a master at killing. You're the best, Greek. Even Trigger Burke in his grave is smiling at your killing."

Trigger Burke was John's hero. An infamous West Side Irish gangster who went unrepenting and swaggering to the electric chair at Sing Sing in 1957, Burke reputedly murdered more than 100 people. The highest compliment John Sullivan could pay was comparison to Trigger Burke, who had been his mentor.

John then noticed the plastic bags and chainsaw. "Fat Tony decided he don't want Buster chopped up," he said. "He wants the world to see him, as a warning to anyone who tries to kill a member of his own crime family."

Technically, I suppose, John Sullivan was right. Joey Gallo's crew (including DellaValle) belonged to the Colombo organization, with which the Manfredis had been associated, though mainly Gallo had warred against the gang Junior Persico now headed. Fat Tony's connection was the cut of the drug profits his Genovese organization received for permitting access to its territory.

John said, "Just cut Buster's arms off at the elbows and tape them to his stomach." The message: if you kill one of your own with your hands, then you lose the hands that once picked up the pistol.

That night, we dumped DellaValle's body in a shallow grave in the farming community of Jewett, New York, about 150 miles north of Manhattan in Greene County. It took longer than we expected for someone to discover the body. Hunters stumbled upon it 7 March 1974.

John paid me the second part of the contract, $5,000, the night after the hit, plus I had another $3,000 I'd lifted off Buster.

We went to a belly-dancing joint, stuffed ourselves with Arab food, and drank heavily as we watched the dancers undulate in perfect rhythm with the intense Middle Eastern music.

I thought about Buster buried upstate as I left the nightclub with one of the girls. John followed me outside and gave me one last hearty hug. "Fat Tony slept good last night," he whispered into my ear. "You satisfied his thirst for blood."

"I'm happy for Fat Tony," I said. *And for you too, Greek*, I thought. *Your belly is full and your pockets are stuffed. You've come a long way*.

Illustrious Corpses

Tommaso Buscetta

While Mafiosi in America began to speak out, the Sicilian Mafia maintained its silence – until Tommaso Buscetta broke the omertà. *His testimony led to numerous Mafiosi going to jail on either side of the Atlantic. Once known as the "Godfather of Two Worlds", Buscetta knew the inner workings of the Sicilian Mafia, as well as its connections to the Five Families of New York.*

Born to a poor family in Palermo in 1928, Buscetta was the youngest of seventeen children. In 1945, with the Mafia riding high in Sicily again, he joined the Porta Nuova Family under Giuseppe "Pippo" Calò and went into the lucrative business of smuggling cigarettes. By 1957, Buscetta had climbed high enough up the tree to attend a meeting between the American Mafia bosses and the Sicilian godfathers in a Palermo hotel. Both Lucky Luciano and Joe Bonanno were there.

After the death of Lucky Luciano in 1962, power struggles developed between the Sicilian crime families. The result was the First Mafia War, which claimed the lives of sixty-eight Mafiosi. It reached its bloody climax with the Ciaculli Massacre. A car bomb was intended for the head of the Sicilian Commission and godfather of the Ciaculli Family, Salvatore "Ciaschiteddu" or "Chichiteddu" Greco

– the epithet means either "little bird" or "wine jug". It went off, killing seven police and military officers sent to defuse it after an anonymous phone call. This turned the Mafia War into a war on the Mafia. Some 1,200 Mafiosi were arrested. There were massive show trials – one with 114 defendants. Most walked free. Even those convicted of multiple murders rarely spent more than a few years in jail.

Many had fled the country to Argentina, Brazil, Venezula, Canada and the United States. Buscetta, who was wanted for a double murder, turned up in New York where the Gambino Family helped him set up a pizza business. In 1970, he was arrested, but the Italian authorities did not ask for his extradition and he moved on to Brazil. In 1972, he fell foul of the authorities there, who tortured him. He was then extradited back to Italy where he faced a life sentence.

Out on parole, he found that a Second Mafia War was brewing and fled back to Brazil. After two years on the run, he was arrested again and was returned to Italy in 1983. By then many of his Mafia allies – including Stefano Bontate and Salvatore Inzerillo – were dead and two of his sons were dead, along with a number of leading policemen, prosecutors, judges, prominent businessmen and investigative journalists who had all become "illustrious corpses". To avenge his murdered family and friends, Buscetta began talking to the crusading anti-Mafia judges Giovanni Falcone and Paolo Borsellino and became the first of the pentiti. The result was the "Maxi Trial", held in a specially constructed bunker next to the Ucciardone, Palermo's prison. Built from reinforced concrete, it was designed to resist rocket attacks and had a 24-hour air defence system. The accused were held in cages flanked by armed guards. There were 474 defendants, though 119 had to be tried in absentia. They were charged with drug trafficking, extortion and 120 murders. In all, 360 were found guilty and sentenced to a total of 2,665 years in prison plus nineteen life sentences handed out to *the top Mafia bosses and killers. However, there were a large number of successful appeals. Michele "the Pope" Greco was sentenced to life. He died in prison in 2008, still protesting his innocence. Giuseppe Marchese also got life, but in 1992 became a* pentito. *He admitted twenty murders, including those of Stefano Bontate and Salvatore Inzerillo. Like other* pentiti, *he suffered again when members of his family were murdered in revenge.*

Salvatore Riina and Bernardo Provenzano were sentenced to life in absentia.*While a fugitive, Riina arranged the murder of former allies who were trying to unseat him as head of the Sicilian Mafia. He also had Giovanni Falcone and Paolo Borsellino killed. Eventually he was betrayed by his driver Balduccio Di Maggio, whose brother was then killed. It is also said that Bernardo Provenzano "sold" Riina in exchange for compromising material he held in his Palermo apartment. Although he already had two unserved life sentences, Riina was tried and convicted of over a hundred counts of murder, including sanctioning the slayings of Falcone and Borsellino. In 1998, he was also convicted of the murder of Salvo Lima, a politician in league with the Mafia who had been shot dead in 1992 for failing to prevent the Maxi Trial. In 2006, he was tried for the murder of journalist Mauro De Mauro who disappeared in 1970.*

With Riina in jail, Bernardo Provenzano took over as head of the Sicilian Mafia. After forty-three years in hiding, he was arrested in April 2006. Having already been convicted of numerous murders – including those of Falcone and Borsellino – he was sent to serve out his life sentences with Riina and other convicted Mafiosi in the high security jail at Terni in central Italy.

With Provenzano in jail, another power struggle broke out between Salvatore Lo Piccolo and Matteo Messina Denaro. A gang boss from the Resuttana district of Palermo, sixty-

three-year-old Lo Piccolo was the closest to Provenzano and considered "old school". Denaro was just forty-six. From the impoverished western Sicilian provincial city of Castelvetrano, he was known as the "playboy boss" because of his passion for gold watches, fast cars and beautiful women. Like Riina and Provenzano, they had both been on the run for some time – Lo Piccolo since 1983 and Messina Denaro since 1993. Other key players in the power struggle were Totò Riina's physician Antonio Cinà, builder Francesco Bonura, pioneer of the heroin refineries Gerlando Alberti and Nino Rotolo, a henchman of Luciano Liggio and convicted gangster who was kept under house arrest due to a medical condition.

Liggio himself had been acquitted in the Maxi Trial of running the Corleonesi Family from behind bars and ordering the murder of prosecutor Cesare Terranova in 1979. However, he was already serving life sentences for murders stretching back to 1979.

When it was clear that the "Pax Mafiosa" which had held since Provenzano took over in 1993 was falling apart, the police swooped on fifty-two bosses and forty-five "capimandamento" (district bosses) and acting bosses – including Rotolo who had passed a death sentence on Lo Piccolo and his son, Sandro. In September 2005, Rotolo was heard saying he was looking for barrels of sulphuric acid to dispose of their bodies. The two families had clashed over the remnants of the Inzerillo family who had been exiled in the US since the Mafia war of the 1980s, where they had become involved with the Gambinos. Now they wanted to return to Sicily. Lo Piccolo was for their return, Rotolo against it.

Rotolo was sentenced to twenty years for drug trafficking, though faces further charges. Lo Piccolo and his son Sandro were arrested in November 2007. They are currently in jail in Milan.

Buscetta then gave testimony in the New York "Pizza Connection"Trial. He gave evidence on drug trafficking and money laundering, resulting in the conviction of twenty-five Mafiosi. They were largely Sicilian-born and many could not speak English. One of them was the former boss of the Sicilian Mafia Gaetano Badalamenti, who was sentenced to forty-five years in jail. He died in a prison hospital in Ayers, Massachusetts in 2004, aged eighty.

As a reward, Buscetta was allowed to live in the US under the Witness Protection Programme.While the Pizza Connection Trial was going on, Buscetta sat down with authors Tim Shawcross and Martin Young to write Mafia Wars: The Confessions of Tommaso Buscetta. *It gives a shocking insight into the Mafia at work on the lawless streets of Palermo.*

Once the Mafia had recovered from the chaos of the wars of the 1960s, the Commission came back into operation led by the triumvirate of Salvatore Riina, representing the Corleone family, Stefano Bontate, boss of the Santa Maria de Gesù family and a close friend of Tommaso Buscetta, and Gaetano Badalamenti, *capo* of the Cinisi family. Representatives of the different families were given a place on the Commission under the title "district bosses".

While Buscetta had been in Brazil, Liggio had murdered his way to the top of the Sicilian Mafia, investing heavily in the kidnapping industry and the heroin trade. A stockily built man, with a taste for large cigars and dark glasses, his reign was frequently interrupted by bouts of illness caused by Pott's disease (tuberculosis of the bone). Despite this he managed to hold on to power even when in prison. He took care to appoint district bosses who would support him, a move which was deeply resented by Bontate and Badalamenti.

Badalamenti was appointed head of the Commission but, for reasons that have never been explained, he was ousted and his place as head of the Cinisi family was taken over by his cousin Antonio. This coup d'etat was almost certainly orchestrated by Liggio and the Corleonesi. Although Buscetta has not revealed why his friend was expelled, he has this to say about the procedure:

"A Man of Honour can be expelled for reasons relating to the family he belongs to or the Mafia organization as a whole. It is considered a very grave mistake for a Man of Honour to continue to deal and even to talk to a member expelled for not being worthy."

Badalamenti's seat on the Commission was taken by Michele Greco, a close friend of Liggio and a relative of the Grecos who had been caught up in the first Mafia wars. His Ciaculli family became, along with Liggio, the dominant power in Sicily, with connections to the highest political and financial circles. His nickname was appropriately powerful – "the Pope".

The Commission guarded its powers of life and death jealously, and there were many rows over the way decisions were being reached on assassinations.

One of the first state officials to be murdered was the *procuratore generale* – the chief public prosecutor – of Palermo, Pietro Scaglione. Scaglione's career was riddled with allegations of corruption, and although he was investigated for links with the Mafia, the tribunal declared him innocent. He had custody of numerous dossiers relating to Mafia crimes which were mysteriously shelved or lost. One of them was a report from the *carabinieri* on the involvement of all the Mafia families in the narcotics trade. Nothing was done for four years until the *carabinieri* agitated for a Mafia trial, and the entire Mafia from Castellamare, Joe Bonanno's birthplace, was charged, including Bonanno's lieutenants Frank Garofalò and

John Bonaventre and his associate Frank Coppola. After a long and tedious trial, all were acquitted for lack of proof. Scaglione's position was a powerful one, from which he could threaten those he chose to protect. But when he chose no longer to serve the Mafia's interests, they decided to kill him.

On 5 May 1971 he made his daily visit to his wife's graveside in a Palermo cemetery. As he turned to leave, he and his driver were shot dead. No one saw anything, though of course plenty of people knew what had happened.

"The murder in question took place on Via Cipressi in a section controlled by the Porta Nuova family, whose head was Pippo Calò. No murder, in particular the murder of Pietro Scaglione, chief public prosecutor, could have been committed in that area without the consent of the family boss – and this is not just for reasons of prestige, but because this sort of murder inevitably arouses strong pressure from the police authorities in the territory where the crime has taken place and that may have repercussions on the family's operations in their territory."

In this case the rule was observed and, according to Buscetta, Calò's power and status grew after the murder.

Scaglione's death came almost a year after the Milan summit of July 1970 which Liggio and Buscetta had attended. As well as discussing the drug trade, the meeting may have been held to authorize that murder. It may also have arranged for the murder of Mauro de Mauro, a journalist who worked for Palermo's crusading newspaper *L'Ora*.

The disappearance of de Mauro remains a mystery. No one doubts that he was murdered, but Buscetta claims it had nothing to do with the Mafia. The mystery is further clouded by the fact that de Mauro was mixed up with the neo-Fascist movement. He had been investigating the mysterious death of Enrico Mattei, the Italian oil magnate whose plane crashed in Sicily, possibly as a result of sabotage. At the time, Mattei was seen as a threat to the American oil companies and it was alleged by some that the Mafia was contacted to carry out his assassination on behalf of "political interests". The disappearance of de Mauro and the death of Mattei were the first of the long list of what have become "*cadaveri eccelenti*" – the "illustrious corpses".

Over the next decade the Grecos and the Corleonesi eliminated anyone who seemed to threaten their interests, from the most insignificant Palermo villains to the highest officials of the state. Corpses, illustrious and not so illustrious, would become an everyday sight on the streets of Palermo.

Giuseppe Russo, a dedicated *carabinieri* colonel, was drafted into Sicily from northern Italy in 1977 to investigate into the murder of Pietro Scaglione and the disappearance of Mauro de Mauro. But Russo was to die. As Buscetta has now revealed, he was shot by Pino Greco.

After Russo the murders became more frequent – frequent enough to establish a pattern. They usually took place in broad daylight in Palermo, and involved anyone who threatened the Mafia's heroin trade. Their monopoly of the business had been confirmed when they built a number of refining laboratories. Anyone who knew about these laboratories and was foolish enough to broadcast the fact was effectively signing his own death warrant. And anyone trying to investigate the millions of dollars which were being "laundered" back and forth from Italy to America was also likely to be killed.

The powers of investigation available to the judiciary were very limited. The Mafia's political protectors had ensured that their bank accounts, like those of the law-abiding citizen, remained strictly private. The power to investigate finances would inevitably lead to discovery of the drug traffickers. It might also reveal the politicians and financiers who supported them. Those who were brave enough to attempt investigation into the sources of finance and the location of the refineries realized that they were no longer dealing with a Sicilian problem. The narcotics trade was international, and the police and investigating magistrates would require major assistance from overseas in order to tackle it.

Boris Giuliano, the leading detective in Palermo's *escuadra mobile* – flying squad – was one of the first to realize that law-enforcement agencies throughout the world had to co-operate if they were going to defeat the Mafia. In particular he recognized the value of working with the Americans, and was involved in the investigation of a major heroin case with the US customs and the DEA [Drug Enforcement Agency].

On 19 June 1979 a cheap blue plastic suitcase had arrived at Palermo's Punta Raisi airport, twenty-five kilometres outside the city. The case had come via Rome from New York. When Giuliano intercepted it he found $497,000 in small denomination bills – the currency of the narcotics trade. The money was wrapped in several pizza aprons. They were later traced to a pizzeria in New Jersey run by a Sicilian called Salvatore Sollena.

Sollena was the nephew of the recently deposed Palermo Commission boss, Badalamenti. When the DEA in New York infiltrated the operation they discovered that Sollena had not only lost the money confiscated at Punta Raisi, which was payment for drugs he had already received, but that he had recently suffered another blow when a twenty-four-kilo shipment of heroin had been seized at John F. Kennedy airport in New York. His supplier had been his uncle.

Badalamenti was not the only Mafioso to suffer from the

attentions of Boris Giuliano. In the months before his death Giuliano and his associates were getting dangerously close to the centre of another smuggling ring. It could implicate not only criminals in Sicily but respectable leaders of society in Rome and elsewhere.

From 1976 to 1980 the heroin trade between Sicily and New York was dominated by the smuggling network controlled by the Inzerillo-Gambino-Spatola ring. Between 1977 and 1979 the Italian police tracked $4 million which had been transferred from New Jersey to a bank in Palermo. They also discovered a $1 million transfer made by Frank Castronovo, owner of the Roma restaurant in New Jersey (who in 1985 would be one of the principal defendants in the Pizza Connection trial). The money was used by Salvatore Inzerillo for a property transaction, the favoured method of recycling Italian drug money – the "*narco lira*". This operation was easy because Rosario Spatola ran a construction company as a front. Among the public contracts he was awarded was the building of a local school. Inzerillo's company specialized in porcelain and lavatories.

But other connections were about to cause problems. In the 1970s, Michele Sindona had been a useful man with his skill in setting up front companies, but when his Franklin National Bank crashed the reverberations ran deep into the Mafia. As the shattered pieces of his financial empire were put into receivership, traces of the recycling of heroin money from the Inzerillo-Gambino-Spatola ring were uncovered in Italy. It was "black" money, which ran into billions of lire. Shortly after the seizure of the suitcase at Punta Raisi, Giuliano met Giorgio Ambrosoli, the government-appointed liquidator of Sindona's financial network. It is thought that Giuliano provided Ambrosoli with proof that Sindona was laundering heroin money through Swiss banks. Three days after their meeting

Ambrosoli parked his car outside his Milan apartment, got out and locked it.

"Are you Giorgio Ambrosoli?" asked a voice from behind him. He turned around and said, "Yes."

Three gunmen then shot him five times in the chest . . .

On 21 July 1979, Giuliano left his apartment for his usual early morning cappuccino in the Bar Lux. It was eight o'clock on a Saturday morning and there were not many people on the street. He had received a phone call from someone he knew and arranged to go down to meet him a little earlier than usual on this particular morning. According to the only witness in the bar who came forward, this is what happened:

"I noticed a man who was trembling. He was white in the face. He must be ill, I thought. My first impulse was to offer to help. When the Commissario Giuliano went towards the door the man followed him. He drew a pistol and shot him three times in the neck. Signor Giuliano fell face downwards, and the man then shot him four more times in the back."

Giuliano did not even have a chance to pull his own gun.

The killings went on. Michele Reina, the Provincial Secretary of the Christian Democratic Party, was murdered in 1979. A political murder such as this was clear evidence of involvement between the Mafia and the local Christian Democrats. It is suspected that Reina refused to make the necessary accommodations to the Mafia. Someone more amenable would have to be found. Cesare Terranova, a crusading judge who had devoted himself to the fight against the Mafia, was the next victim in the same year. He had single-mindedly pursued Luciano Liggio, whom he branded "Public Enemy No. 1". Like Giuliano, he realized that the only way to defeat the Mafia was to attack their money. He told his wife: "If only I could have the power to investigate, to go into banks and investigate the finances of the people I know three months ago were pushing a cart and are now millionaires – then I could really do a lot."

It was Terranova's courageous stand against Liggio which sealed his fate. Signora Terranova recalls an occasion when her husband had gone to the Ucciardone prison to interrogate Liggio:

"He was told that Liggio was ill and couldn't come down. He realized that Liggio – which means Little King – the Little King of Corleone – couldn't accept the concept that he would come down to be interrogated by a magistrate. It had to be that the magistrate would go up and interrogate him. Just to make doubly certain, he asked the guard, 'Well, is Liggio in bed? Has he been in bed? Is he ill?' And the guard answered, 'No, actually, he's been out in the yard to take air in the courtyard up until ten minutes ago.'

"So at this point, of course, he insisted that Liggio be brought down. He said, 'I don't care how he's brought down but he's got to come down to be questioned.'

"So he sees Liggio arriving on a stretcher on which he is being brought down. The judge starts questioning him – going through the purely bureaucratic things, like 'What is your name?' And Liggio answers, 'I don't remember.' 'Who is your father?' 'I don't remember.' 'Who is your mother?' 'I don't remember.'

"So without batting an eyelid, the judge turns to the person who is taking all this down and says, 'Right, this man does not remember his name; he does not remember who his father was and he doesn't remember who his mother was.'"

Terranova was insulting Liggio. He seemed to be implying that Liggio was admitting he was a bastard. Such was Liggio's rage that he was on the point of spitting at Terranova. He restrained himself, but did not forget:

Judge Terranova was shot at point-blank range less than a hundred yards from his apartment.

As Buscetta has revealed, assassinations, especially those which produced "illustrious corpses", could not be carried out independently by individual Mafiosi. They had to be approved by the Commission:

> "The Commission will then form the team that is to carry out the decision. They have the power to choose the executioners from any family without informing its boss; organizing the crime is, therefore, the exclusive province of the Commission and it is supposed to remain a secret from all the others; with the exception, of course, of the executioners themselves. In practice, however, it usually happens that a Commission member will inform his most trusted colleagues of the decision – but this has very little impact either on the planning or on the execution of the murder."

In the case of Terranova, however, Liggio himself was out for blood. He steamrollered the decision through the Commission, bypassing the members who would have opposed him. Buscetta is keen to stress the lack of "propriety" in Liggio's haste to carry out murder. His lack of consultation with the other members of the board caused great resentment and would in the end help to precipitate the second Mafia war. This is what Buscetta told Falcone about the murders of Reina and Terranova:

> "I know for sure, because I heard it from Salvatore Inzerillo, that these murders were decided upon by the Palermo Commission, without any knowledge on the part of Inzerillo himself or of Stefano Bontate ... These murders further widened the breach that already existed between Bontate and Inzerillo on the one

side and the rest of the Commission on the other. In particular, Salvatore Inzerillo told me that the killing of Cesare Terranova had been committed on orders from Luciano Liggio. He didn't indicate the reasons, but it was quite clear that the motive for the killing was Terranova's legal activity against Liggio."

The police investigation into the murder of Terranova was pursued with about as much vigour as if it had been a traffic offence. Although Liggio was charged with the murder, the prosecution in the trial was hopelessly inadequate. As so often in Sicily, witnesses' memories miraculously faded once they appeared in court. Although the shooting had taken place in the centre of Palermo, no one had seen anything and no one had heard anything. The law of *omertà* was again invoked to shield the assassins . . .

Boris Giuliano's investigation into the Mafia's finances was taken over by a captain of the *carabinieri*, Emanuele Basile. He had been investigating links between the Mafia and Sicily's top bankers and financiers, some of whom were "washing" millions of dollars of heroin money from the United States. By the early 1980s laundering money for the Mafia had become a major industry. There were more banks in Sicily than in any other part of Italy. In the town of Trapani in western Sicily, with a population of only 70,000, there were more banks than in Milan, Italy's financial capital. Between 1970 and 1980, banks in Sicily increased their turnover by 400 per cent. Even the smallest towns in the most remote parts of the Sicilian countryside had their own banks, while in Palermo they competed for customers on almost every street corner. It was an unedifying display of greed by the banking fraternity attracted like sharks to a city awash with money from a trade based on blood.

Although still deprived of the legal powers he needed

to investigate bank accounts, Captain Basile became far too persistent for the Mafia Commission. On 1 May 1980 three gunmen put an end to him and his inquiries by shooting him on the street as he was returning home with his wife and young daughter. Within minutes the police picked up three Mafia soldiers for questioning. They had found two of them racing away in a car belonging to the third, who was arrested a few hundred yards away, trying to climb a high wire fence. He was "searching for lemons", he explained to the police. The three men were already suspects in the murder of another police officer, and while none of them could account for their flight from the scene of the crime, they all gave identical alibis. They were, they said, returning from secret romantic liaisons with young married women. They could not possibly disclose their names as they were all "Men of Honour". One of them was from the Ciaculli family of Michele Greco, and the other two were from Inzerillo's family, the Passo di Rigano. It appears that Inzerillo and Bontate had opposed this killing, and the presence of two of Inzerillo's men suggests that they had been given the contract without his knowledge.

Inzerillo and Rosario Spatola were already being investigated and many arrest warrants had been issued against members of their organization. Inzerillo was so outraged by the warrants that he became almost deranged. Without consulting the Commission, he ordered the execution of the chief public prosecutor of Palermo, Gaetano Costa. On 6 August 1980, as the sixty-four-year-old prosecutor was preparing to abandon the heat of the city for his summer vacation, a young man approached him in the street, pulled out a .38 revolver from beneath the newspaper he was carrying and shot him five times at point-blank range.

Inzerillo's manic reaction was designed to show the

Grecos and their allies on the Commission that he was as tough and ruthless as they were, but it was an act of pure insanity and it broke one of the fundamental rules of the Commission . . .

In 1979 a new killer had joined the Commission – as if they needed one. He has acquired a reputation as the most bloodthirsty psychopath that even the Mafia has ever seen. His name was Giuseppe "Pino" Greco, known as "*Scarpazzedda*", meaning "Fleet of Foot". He delighted in being present at Mafia executions. On one occasion he got so carried away that he chopped a man's arm off. He was a frequent visitor to a dingy basement room just outside the centre of Palermo. It was the Mafia's torture chamber, where victims would be garrotted and their bodies either cut up or dissolved in acid. Michele Greco was the head of the Commission and his protégé Pino Greco, although not related, became head of the Ciaculli family. The Greco-Corleonesi faction was assuming áll the positions of power, and Bontate and Inzerillo, fellow members of the Commission, found themselves increasingly isolated and humiliated. For example, to talk to Michele Greco they were forced to go first to Pino Greco, the newest and most junior member of the Commission. It was a calculated insult.

At the beginning of 1980, the Corleonesi, now fully in control, began to step up their challenge to the power of the state . . .

At the end of 1979 Tommaso Buscetta was released from prison on the Italian equivalent of parole. He went to live in Turin, and took up his old trade of glass engraving once more. Although he had to report to the local prison every night, he still managed to make frequent trips to Palermo and Rome. The seven years that he had spent in Ucciardone prison had greatly increased his stature as a

Man of Honour. He had been treated with tremendous respect. Fellow prisoners would actually bow in his presence or kiss his hand, and on one occasion his word was sufficient to avert a potential riot.

The Mafia virtually control Ucciardone. Many inmates have their food delivered from Palermo's finest restaurants, and carry on their business and personal affairs almost uninterrupted. When Buscetta's daughter Felicia was about to get married she visited her father in prison. He arranged for her to see Pietro lo Iacono, Stefano Bontate's deputy, who ran a shop selling fabrics and trousseaus. Lo Iacono gave her a trousseau for her wedding free of charge. Buscetta himself married, for the third time, in 1979, shortly before his release. Christina had been both loyal and patient.

On his release Buscetta emerged into a different world. Sicily and the Mafia had been radically changed by the profits from the heroin trade. One kilo of morphine base could be bought for $6–9,000 depending on the total quantity; once refined by the Mafia in one of their laboratories, the same kilo at 90 per cent purity would be worth $40–50,000. When sold in New York its wholesale price would be $200,000; its street value would be over $2 million. The Mafia would deal on average in shipments of between twenty and a hundred kilos, each transaction being worth between $4 and $20 million dollars.

According to a secret DEA report a major supplier of morphine base from Turkey, much of it destined for the Pizza Connection, was the Yasar Musullulu organization ... Musullulu would guarantee delivery of morphine base, usually in 500-kilo consignments, to an area within seventy nautical miles of Sicily. He would dispatch his representative to Mazzara del Vallo, a village near Trapani in Sicily, where Michele Greco's refining laboratory was hidden. The morphine base would arrive on a Turkish freighter and be transferred to a speedboat, which would in turn rendezvous with a fishing boat sent from a remote part of the Sicilian coastline. One of the favoured transfer points was the island of Marittima between Sicily and Sardinia. Payment for each shipment would be made in Zürich. Mafia cashiers would make regular flights to Switzerland to settle with Musullulu. The two men he dealt with most frequently were Nunzio la Mattina and Antonio Rotolo, known as "Carlo".

Early in 1983 Nunzio la Mattina was murdered. He had arranged for $1.5 million to be "stolen" en route to Switzerland. Despite his claims that it really had been stolen, his fellow Men of Honour decided not to afford him the benefit of the doubt and he was duly eliminated. His place was taken by Rotolo, who proved to be much more efficient and, perhaps noting the fate of his predecessor, more than anxious to convince his colleagues of his honesty. On his regular visits to Zürich, Rotolo was always accompanied by "six Sicilian-looking males" – who, true to Sicilian tradition, remained silent throughout each meeting with Musullulu. Rotolo brought suitcases with him containing between $3 and $5 million in $50 and $100 bills. He attended at least fifteen meetings of this nature, dealing in a minimum of $45 million worth of morphine base. At a conservative estimate that was worth $500 million wholesale in New York. Street price: an astronomical $5 billion.

It was a serious business.

Rotolo commuted back and forth to Zürich until April 1984. One of the last deals he did with Musullulu took place there in the spring of 1984. He arrived as usual in Switzerland with his escort and suitcases. This time he was paying the Turk $5.2 million for 500 kilos of morphine base. The Sicilians were actually in credit for $1.3 million and were buying the base at $13,000 a kilo. Shortly after the meeting Musullulu disappeared – taking with him over $6 million of Mafia money. He is now in hiding, although he is keen to get back to Turkey and is known to have offered a bribe of $750,000 to an official of the Turkish secret police for a safe passage back to his own country. Shortly after his flight from Switzerland he went to Bulgaria. There, in a bizarre incident, one of his henchmen set fire to him and he was badly burnt. Somehow he managed to survive the attack and is probably still in Bulgaria.

The fact that the Musullulu organization was only one of a number of major suppliers of morphine base to the Mafia laboratories in Italy gives some idea of the sheer scale of the trade. No wonder that, as Buscetta reveals, everybody wanted to get in on the act:

> "When I arrived in Palermo, as well as this incredible amount of wealth, I also found a great deal of confusion among the various families and their Men of Honour, so that I soon realized that the principles that inspired the Cosa Nostra were definitely a thing of the past and that it would be best for me to leave Palermo as soon as possible, since I could no longer see myself in the organization that I had believed in since I was young."

His first contact in Palermo was Giuseppe Galeazzo, whom he had met in prison. Galeazzo approached him on behalf of the head of their family, Pippo Calò . . . Calò operated from a base in Rome, where he was known as "Mario". In one of his several apartments he kept millions of lire in cash and precious works of art which other Mafiosi would sometimes buy from him. In his other apartments he would store heroin and explosives. His influence in Rome, especially his financial contacts, allowed him to act both as the Mafia's ambassador in the Italian capital and also as their chief accountant.

In Rome he had developed contacts with some of the leading gangsters and financiers, including men linked to Roberto Calvi, whose Banco Ambrosiano was used by the Mafia and by Michele Sindona to launder millions from the Mafia's narcotics trade. Calò also had "business" interests in Sardinia with one of Calvi's associates, Luigi Faldetta, a wealthy building developer. Two men who were common to both worlds were Ernesto Diotallevi and Danilo Abbruciati, gang bosses of Rome's underworld. They were on good terms with Flavio Carboni, a millionaire property developer from Sardinia with an extensive network of friends ranging from government ministers to gangsters. Carboni was a leading member of P2 and close to the P2 grand master Lido Gelli. He was also a close friend of Roberto Calvi. When the Banco Ambrosiano became embroiled in a series of scandals involving the Vatican, during which it was discovered that Calvi had made a series of highly suspicious loans to Carboni for millions of dollars, there was an attempt to kill the deputy chairman of the bank, Roberto Rosone. The assailant was shot by a security guard. He turned out to be none other than Danilo Abbruciati, underworld associate of Carboni and Calò. As for Calvi, a few days after Carboni organized his secret flight to London, the banker was found hanging beneath London's Blackfriars Bridge.

Through friends like these, the head of the Porta Nuova family had acquired power, influence and money. He had become a multi-millionaire while Buscetta had been languishing in prison. Buscetta was resentful because Calò had apparently done nothing to help his (Buscetta's) family, something a *capo* was obliged to do under the Mafia code.

When Buscetta abandoned his semi-parole in Turin, he responded to Galeazzo's message and received word from Calò to contact him in Rome, which he did. Calò suggested that they forget about the past, saying that he had not realized how hard up Buscetta had been. Buscetta should stay in Italy, where they could make a lot of money together. The reason, he confided, was that the Mafia had the mayor of Palermo, Vito Ciancimino, in its pocket. Luciano Liggio's deputy, Salvatore Riina, who had taken over the leadership of the Corleone family after Liggio was imprisoned in 1974, had total control of the mayor. Calò explained that there would be another massive redevelopment of Palermo which would make a lot of money for everyone – and that Buscetta could share in this bonanza with Calò, without having to go through a *capodecina*. Buscetta would deal directly with Calò and no one else. It was an offer that most Men of Honour would not have refused.

In addition, Buscetta was offered a house in Rome so that his children could go to the best schools. The offer made, Calò turned to "family" business. He told Buscetta that Stefano Bontate was behaving badly; he had formed an alliance with Salvatore Inzerillo against the rest of the Commission.

Back in Palermo Buscetta met Bontate and Inzerillo to hear their side of the story. The Grecos and the Corleonesi, they claimed, were undermining their power on the Commission. Bontate told Buscetta that for his own self-preservation he was planning to kill Riina. He claimed to have the support of an unaligned Commission member, Antonio Salamone, but he admitted that Salamone would not publicly declare his support for Bontate until after the event, at which point he promised to confirm in front of the Commission that Bontate had acted "with right on his side".

It worried Buscetta that Bontate would fall for such an empty promise. He warned him that to all intents and purposes it was a worthless agreement. Bontate was effectively on his own. Buscetta asked how he was going to kill Riina and Bontate replied that he was personally going to shoot him at a Commission meeting. Buscetta must have wondered about his sanity . . .

His violation of parole seems not to have been taken very seriously. He was able to move around with a minimum of anxiety – as he explains in his confession, it is a well known fact that between 1.30 pm and 4.30 pm in Palermo it is impossible to find a policeman! . . .

Although Buscetta is understandably reticent on the subject, his sons had become involved with some of his criminal associates. Benedetto had already got mixed up with his father's dealings in New York and South America, and although there is little evidence that they committed any crimes, an incident involving Antonio occurred in the late summer of 1980 which gives some indication of the life they were leading.

Pippo Calò, who was still waiting for Buscetta to reply to his offer, told him that he had heard that Antonio was getting into trouble locally by paying for supermarket groceries with suspect cheques. Calò was annoyed, either because this was happening in an area controlled by the Porta Nuova family, or simply because petty crime of that nature was frowned on by senior Mafiosi. In front of Buscetta he called Antonio "a swindler". Buscetta was surprised and angry. That same evening Antonio was summoned to see his father in the presence of Calò. Buscetta told his son in no uncertain terms what he thought of his behaviour. Antonio apologized but pleaded that he had been in such desperate financial straits that he had been forced to pawn his wife's jewellery. Calò seemed to relent. In a gesture of sympathy, the Mafia boss pulled out a wad of notes from his pocket and peeled off 10 million lire in 100,000 lire bills. He pressed the money on the grateful Antonio, saying that, as it was his birthday the following day, this was his present. Antonio went next day to the pawnshop in Palermo and paid 5,400,000 lire to retrieve the jewellery.

A few days later he was arrested as an accomplice in a kidnapping case: Calò's bills had been part of the ransom. When Buscetta found out he was furious. He confronted Calò, demanding to know how he could have done something as stupid as that. Calò attempted to justify himself with the excuse that he had been paid for a shipment of smuggled cigarettes and had no idea it was traceable ransom money. Buscetta did not believe Calò's story. He deduced that his _capo_ had probably organized the kidnapping and then set up Antonio.

For Buscetta it was the last straw. He turned down Calò's offer and told him that he was now finally convinced that the best option for his family and himself was to leave Palermo and return to Brazil. Calò accepted Buscetta's decision and promised that he would pay for Antonio's defence. Buscetta remained in Palermo for the rest of 1980.

Before he left, his old friend Bontate threw a grand farewell dinner for him at his $500,000 villa. The house was protected by electronically controlled gates and closed-circuit television cameras monitored by soldiers from his family. The dinner was a grand affair with the finest Sicilian wines and local dishes. Among the guests were Antonio Salamone, Salvatore Inzerillo and Salvatore Contorno, one of the toughest and most loyal members of Bontate's Santa Maria di Gesù family. In January 1981, equipped with a false passport, Buscetta look a car-ferry from Palermo and drove overland to Paris. From there he flew to Rio de Janeiro. Christina and the children travelled separately by air from Rome.

Once again, Buscetta had got out just in time. Three months after arriving in Rio he read in the newspapers that Bontate had been murdered. It really had been a farewell dinner.

Sorrow at the death of a friend was tempered by the

knowledge of what the cost of that friendship might now be. Buscetta arranged to visit Salamone, who was also in Brazil. Salamone was head of the San Giuseppe Iato family, which included some of the most important Italian and American operators of the Pizza Connection – Alfredo Bono, Giuseppe-Ganci and Salamone himself. Salamone must have had some of the same misgivings as Buscetta. He was the man who had made the tentative alliance with Bontate to kill Salvatore Riina of the Corleone family.

The two met in San Pedro, Brazil. Salamone told Buscetta that he had already telephoned "the Pope", Michele Greco, who claimed to know nothing about Bontate's murder. Salamone had also taken the precaution of contacting Inzerillo, who told him that he was in no doubt that the killing had been arranged by the Corleonesi and that Michele Greco's claim of ignorance was utter nonsense. Inzerillo was highly suspicious of Greco, but he was not too worried about his own safety. He was in the middle of a major heroin deal involving fifty kilos, which he had obtained from Riina. He still owed Riina the money. No one, he was sure, was going to kill him until he'd paid up.

Inzerillo had told Salamone about the circumstances of Bontate's murder. Shortly before he was killed, his deputy, Pietro lo Iacono, the man who had provided a wedding dress for Buscetta's daughter, had been to see his boss. Bontate mentioned to lo Iacono that he was planning to go to his country house that same evening and stay the night there. It was his birthday. Armed with this information, lo Iacono left and alerted Giuseppe Lucchese, a soldier in Michele Greco's family who was waiting outside in a car. Lucchese relayed the message by walkie-talkie to the occupants of another car, which lay in wait further up the road.

A few minutes later Bontate emerged from his house on

Via Villagrazia and set off for his country retreat. He was preceded by an escort car driven by Stefano de Gregorio, his bodyguard. When they reached the intersection of the Via della Regione Siciliana, the lights were just changing to red. De Gregorio sped on, failing to notice that his boss had been caught at the lights. Bontate was a sitting target. The killers opened fire. Although Bontate was armed, he never had a chance to use his gun. His car and his body were riddled with bullets from the automatic fire of a Kalashnikov assault rifle. He was mortally wounded but he still managed to steer the car for a few yards down the street. It crashed into a wall. De Gregorio got all the way to Bontate's country house before he realized that his boss had not caught up with him. He drove back six kilometres to the scene of the assassination. He took one look at the bloodstained body – de Gregorio knew that there was nothing he could do – except get out fast before the police arrived . . .

Bontate's funeral was poorly attended. The only two women who turned up wearing the customary black veils were the wives of Michele Greco and Tommaso Spadaro, Bontate's godfather. Another mourner was Salvatore Contorno. Although not well educated in the formal sense, Contorno was an intelligent and resourceful mafioso who was respected by his friends and feared by his enemies. He had a reputation as a "man of courage", a euphemism for a Mafia soldier who has become an expert killer . . .

The low turnout at Bontate's funeral confirmed his [Contorno's] suspicions that his boss had been set up. One man whom Contorno felt he could still trust was Mimmo Teresi, the *sottocapo* of the Santa Maria di Gesù family. Teresi had been told by Michele Greco that he had nothing to fear and should continue as if nothing had happened. Teresi then had a secret meeting with Inzerillo at an iron warehouse in Palermo, on the Via della Regione Siciliana

– the same street on which Bontate had been ambushed. The next time Teresi saw Michele Greco, "the Pope" asked him why he had gone to the iron warehouse. Teresi realized that he was under surveillance by the Corleonesi. He admitted to Greco that he had met Inzerillo. Greco warned him not to meet Inzerillo again. He also told him that Pietro lo Iacono would now become the regent of the Santa Maria di Gesù family . . .

On 11 May 1981 Inzerillo was driven in his new bullet-proof car to a rendezvous with his mistress, who was installed in a block of flats on the Via Brunelleschi which had been constructed by one of his companies. As soon as he entered the house his driver, Giuseppe Montalto, signalled to a group of men parked across the road. When he came out of his mistress's apartment, Inzerillo was killed by a burst of rifle fire before he even had the chance to dive into his car. The murder weapon was the same Kalashnikov that had killed Bontate. Inzerillo's body was found with a loaded .357 Magnum in his pocket. His sense of security because of his heroin deal with Riina had proved to be false. To the Corleonesi the loss of a few hundred thousand dollars was a price well worth paying for the elimination of their most powerful enemy. In the event, they had not even had to shoot him through the bullet-proof glass.

As with Bontate, the Corleonesi had accomplished the murder of Inzerillo by ensuring his betrayal by one of his own family. They had now killed the two leaders of the opposition and installed their own men in their place. They then set out to dissuade those loyal to Bontate and Inzerillo from entertaining any thoughts of revenge. High on the list was Mimmo Teresi, who had ignored Greco's instructions and had arranged to meet Inzerillo at the exact spot where he was killed. His late arrival saved his life. Later, when he met Salvatore Contorno secretly and told him about his narrow escape, Contorno replied that Teresi was a "dead man" and that he must not make any move which would make the situation worse.

In Brazil, Buscetta knew that he too could be a candidate for the Corleonesi death list. He was in considerable danger as both he and Antonio Salamone had known about Bontate's plan to kill Riina . . .

Mimmo Teresi and Salvatore Contorno were invited to a "peace" meeting by Pietro lo Iacono. Contorno was suspicious and immediately sensed a trap. He decided not to attend and advised Teresi not to go either. Teresi was never seen again. It was the beginning of an orgy of bloodletting which claimed the lives of many of those who were thought to be supporters of Inzerillo and Bontate, or enemies of the Corleonesi. Presiding over the bloodbath was the psychopath Pino Greco.

Inzerillo's son, Giuseppe, was top of his list. Although Giuseppe was only seventeen years old, Pino Greco considered him a threat, having heard that the teenager had boasted, "I will kill with my own hands that dog Salvatore Riina!" Pino Greco could not allow such open boasts to go unchallenged. He personally supervised the murder of Giuseppe Inzerillo. Before he killed him, he tortured him. As a final moment of horror, Greco cut his arm off and jeered at him, "With this arm you will no longer be able to kill Totò Riina!"

The vendetta spread from Palermo to New York. Inzerillo's brother, Pietro, was discovered dead in the boot of a car with dollars stuffed in his mouth and his genitals cut off. These Mafia trademarks suggested that he might have been running around with the wife of another Mafioso (a capital offence) and had been too greedy into the bargain.

Pino Greco next set out to hunt down Contorno, who was in hiding both from the police and the Corleonesi. But

Greco's intelligence network p... was going to visit his parents. He m... an ambush.

On 25 June 1981, at 7.30 in the evening, Co... off from his parents' apartment in the Via Ciaculli, dri... his mother-in-law's Fiat 127. In the car with him was a cousin, Giuseppe Faglietta, who had insisted on coming with him. His wife and son had left before him in a separate car. They drove down the Via Ciaculli and approached the overpass that leads to the Via Giafar. As they did so, Contorno saw someone he knew, Pino d'Angelo, driving in another Fiat 127. Contorno waved at him and let him pass. D'Angelo waved back, overtook and then started to slow down. Contorno was puzzled by that. He was now driving along the highest point of the overpass running parallel with the top floors of the apartment buildings by the roadside. Ahead and to the right, Contorno noticed another familiar face behind a top-floor window of a building beside the overpass. It was a man called Vincenzo Buffa. Contorno began to get alarmed. Alarm turned to fear when a few seconds later he saw a powerful motorbike racing towards him. The rider was Giuseppe Lucchese, one of the team which had killed Bontate. Another man was riding pillion.

It was Pino Greco.

The motorbike pulled in front of Contorno's car. Greco raised his Kalashnikov, took careful aim and opened fire, emptying a full magazine in Contorno's direction. Contorno threw himself against Faglietta to protect him. Miraculously, they survived the hail of bullets. Faglietta was hit in the cheek; Contorno was totally unscathed.

The motorcycle raced off down the road. Greco needed time to reload his magazine.

A few moments later, Contorno saw in his rear-view mirror that the motorbike was coming back at high speed.

Reacting quickly, he stopped the car, pushed Faglietta out and crouched beneath the car headlights. In his hand was a .38 calibre revolver with five rounds. Greco opened fire again with the Kalashnikov and Contorno aimed carefully at his would-be executioner. He was sure that he hit Greco in the chest because the second burst of automatic fire went wild and Greco recoiled. Behind the motorbike was a Volkswagen Golf containing a back-up for the hit-team. Contorno recognized only one of them. Badly outnumbered and outgunned, he decided to make a run for it. Amazingly, both he and his cousin escaped.

Later, Contorno's cousin told him that he had seen Pino Greco on the beach in a swimsuit. His body showed no trace of any bullet wounds. He had been wearing a bullet-proof vest.

Contorno escaped with nothing more than a scratch from a splinter of glass and a shock of hair torn out by a bullet. He had had the narrowest of narrow escapes. He fled at once to Rome. There he thought of contacting Pippo Calò until he remembered that Bontate, shortly before he had been killed, had become increasingly uneasy about Calò's friendship and that Calò's visits to Bontate's house had noticeably diminished immediately before the murder. Contorno decided to lie low and let as few people as possible know where he was.

Soon after arriving in Rome, he received some disturbing news. His wife's uncle had been murdered. A bricklayer unfortunate enough to have been with him at the same time was also killed. Contorno was shocked. This was not some fellow member of the Bontate faction but a distant relative who was not connected with his Mafia activities. Contorno realized that the senseless killing could have only one purpose – to draw him out of hiding and turn everyone against him. There followed a series of brutal murders of his friends and relatives. Contorno continued to hide until he was arrested by the police. The arrest probably saved his life. He emerged as one of the few survivors of the Mafia war. He would follow Buscetta's example and write his own confessions. By the time they talked, both men had seen their families brutally murdered ...

Partly because of increased pressure from the police in Italy, partly because of the growing trade in cocaine, much of the Mafia's trade in narcotics was now being run out of South America. Because so many Latin American countries had major cities with large Italian immigrant populations, it was an ideal location for Mafia activity. It was also easy to fly from South America to New York or back to Sicily. With false passports readily available and hardly any police surveillance, the mafiosi could move around undetected. Now that the French-Corsicans were out of the picture, it was a free market for the Sicilians. Also, the deadly conflict in Palermo could be more or less ignored in South America – there was no Commission to enforce loyalty and execute contracts ...

In the autumn of 1981 Buscetta received some ominous news from Italy. Mariano Cavallaro, the brother of his first wife, Melchiorra, had been murdered in Turin. It looked as if Buscetta's worst fears were coming true, and that he was now implicated in the Sicilian power struggle. Desperate for news he called Pippo Calò, but Calò claimed to know very little about the killing. He tried to reassure Buscetta that it was just a local matter involving Turin and had no connection with events in Palermo. Calò invited Buscetta back to Palermo, offering to pay for the flight since Buscetta said he had no money ...

Salamone had warned Buscetta that Badalamenti might contact him ... Badalamenti was still a man of considerable stature. His message to Buscetta was simple:

"I am here to try and convince you to come back to

Sicily because you are the only person who has enough influence to be able to direct a counter-attack and lead a revolt against the Corleonesi."

Buscetta was unmoved. As far as he was concerned the situation in Palermo was beyond redemption . . .

Badalamenti confirmed that "mopping up" operations by the Corleonesi were continuing. Amongst the victims was his cousin, Antonio Badalamenti, who had been installed as head of the Cinisi family after Gaetano was ousted. Another friend of Bontate and Inzerillo, Alfio Ferlito, the head of a family in Catania, eastern Sicily, had also been murdered by his sworn rival and a staunch ally of the Corleonesi, Benedetto "Nitto" Santapaola.

Santapaola was involved in a bitter feud with Ferlito, who had been a close friend of Inzerillo. It was a friendship which caused great tension and suspicion between the two. When Ferlito was arrested Santapaola planned his revenge. On 16 June 1982 an armed escort of the *carabinieri* accompanied Ferlito as he was being transferred by car from prison in Enna to one in Trapani, but they were no match for the professional killers of the Corleonesi. Ferlito and his escort were wiped out in a carefully planned ambush – the latest victims of the Kalashnikov.

Blood Oath

George Fresolone

*George Fresolone was one of a new generation of mafiosi.
The son of a bookmaker and numbers runner, he was born
in Newark, New Jersey in 1953. From an early age he knew
he wanted to be a gangster.*

*"It was really simple," he said. "In that kind of working-
class world, everyone else broke their backs at some job they
hated, trying to make a buck. But the wiseguys just hung
around, and the money seemed to roll downhill into their
pockets. And they were respected. Next to the parish priests,
they were the most respected guys in the neighbourhood."*

*While still at high school, he began hanging around with
Pasquale "Patty Specs" Matirano, a made man with the
Philadelphia Crime Family. As Matirano's driver, he learnt
the ways of the Cosa Nostra. By the mid 1970s, he had his
own bookmaking and numbers business, and did business
with Joe "the Butch" Corrao, a Gambino family captain and
an important member of John Gotti's crew. On Wednesday
nights, he and Matirano would go to Manhattan to pay
Corrao off. That was the night the Gambinos threw dinners
at Taormina, a restaurant on Mulberry Street across from
the club where Gambino boss Paul Castellano hung out. A
couple of hundred guys from various crews would usually
be there. They would eat and drink, and Fresolone met a*

lot of guys he would work with later. After dinner Fresolone would hand Corrao or one of his men a very fat envelope with anywhere from $20,000 to $50,000 in it.

Through Matirano, Fresolone got involved with the Cosa Nostra in Philadelphia which was run by Angelo Bruno. His consigliere was the ambitious Antonio Caponigro – "Tony Bananas". Fresolone was in a crew with Joseph "Scoops" Licata and Anthony "Slicker" Attanasio, both made guys. After Bruno and Bananas were killed, Nicodemo Scarfo took over. When Fresolone was arrested, he became disillusioned with the Mafia as they did not look after his family. The New Jersey State police put pressure on him to turn state's evidence. They wanted him to rat on Matirano, but he refused to do so. However, it became clear to Matirano that the heat was on. He fled to Argentina. Fresolone then received a phone call from Matirano, saying that he wanted to move to Calabria but was afraid that he would be arrested entering Italy. Fresolone made a deal with the police. He would co-operate provided they did not put out an international warrant on Matirano.

By the time Fresolone became a made man, he was wearing a wire to meetings. The evidence he gathered led to the indictment of thirty-eight mobsters, including "Little Nicky" Scarfo. In 1994 his autobiography, Blood Oath: The Heroic Story of a Gangster Turned Government Agent Who Brought Down One of America's Most Powerful Mob Families, *written with Robert J. Wagman, came out. In it, he explained how Nicky Scarfo took over the Mob in Philadelphia.*

Under most circumstances Patty was about as easygoing and as nice a guy as you would ever want to meet, but if you pushed him too hard, he would push back even harder. He was "willing to do what had to be done" on occasion.

It was near Christmas when a friend of ours who ran a numbers bank for Patty was being hassled very hard by a guy who wanted to muscle in. He knew the numbers bank operator was around Patty, but he pushed anyway. This was a major affront to Patty and something he had to deal with strongly and immediately. One day we were over at the Upstairs-Downstairs Club when Patty heard that this guy had just come into the 3-11. Patty called me and told me to take a couple of the guys over to the 3-11 and hurt the guy, hurt him real bad. "Georgie, don't kill him," Patty said, "but make sure he don't walk too good anymore." So four of us got into the car and went speeding over to the club. I ran in, and this guy was sitting there. I jumped him and started to bang on him real good. I remember I used a bat on his legs, and then I was banging his head against the jukebox for what seemed like ten minutes. The other guys finally came in and pulled me off him. I guess I lost my head and went too far. They took the guy to the hospital.

The guy then ran to Bananas. By this time Bananas had become the Bruno family *consigliere*, the number three man in the organization after the boss and the underboss. Patty was an important man among all the families operating in northern Jersey, but he was under Bananas and had to answer to him. Bananas had long commanded respect and fear – even when he was only a made guy – because of his power and because he was a stone-cold killer. He had started out in the early days as a killer with Albert Anastasia in Murder Inc. Over the years he had built up his own mini-family, guys who were loyal to him first and foremost. In time he became a multi-millionaire, but he still liked to kill people and did it as a kind of hobby. He killed people for all the New York families, and he was the one guy who was feared by even the most powerful bosses. So when Bananas sent Joey Scoops to bring Patty and me to him, all the way over I was quaking. Patty kept telling me not to worry, that everything was square; but I honestly didn't know if I would be coming back alive.

Bananas was really angry. He screamed at me, and he screamed at Patty. He wasn't so much angry that we had beaten on this guy, because he agreed with Patty that that was business, but he was angry that Patty had not cleared it with him. He was even angrier that I had done the beating in what he considered "his" club – the 3-11. Coming into his club to do that kind of business made him look bad. I remember him screaming: Would I go into his house, into his living room, to do that kind of crap? If not, why then did I think I had the right to do it in a joint he owned? Patty ended up calming him down, and the whole thing eventually blew over. I found out later that Bananas actually liked me, and I ended up doing a lot of things for him. But his temper and his habit of killing people to solve problems would eventually catch up with him.

As 1979 passed into 1980, things could not have been going better as far as I was concerned. I was making good money. I had a wonderful wife and son at home. I wasn't a made guy yet, but when I was, I knew I would be set for life.

Then on Friday night, 21 March 1980, Angelo Bruno was whacked in Philly, and Mob life would never be the same. According to many so-called Mob experts, the hit was done because the New York families were feuding with Angelo over Atlantic City. That is completely wrong, exactly 180 degrees backward. Angelo was not killed because he was keeping the New York families out of Atlantic City. He was whacked because he was letting them in.

Patty and I had seen it coming. As soon as we heard the news on the radio, we knew it was Bananas who had whacked Angelo, and we knew why. Bruno was never a strong leader. During part of the 1970s he had spent three years in jail for refusing to testify before the New Jersey State Commission on Investigation. Then, too, it was simply not in his nature to be aggressive. Known as the "Docile Don", Angelo hated violence and valued negotiation and peace above all. So Bananas was pretty much allowed to do his own thing in northern Jersey. Bruno simply did not bother to worry about his *consigliere*'s empire building. Any of the other bosses would have seen it for what it was – a direct threat – and would have had Bananas killed, but as long as money continued to flow down the New Jersey Turnpike from Newark, Bruno let Bananas have his way.

In 1976, Bananas went to jail for assaulting an FBI agent. Ducking a federal warrant, he had been an absent figure, hiding out with his girlfriend in New York City for almost a year. I used to drive Patty into the city to meet with him, and sometimes Patty would send me with messages or money, or to pick stuff up. Finally, during the Christmas season in 1975, the FBI staked out his house, guessing correctly that he would try to visit his family during the holidays. He came out, and when he saw the Feds, he tried to run. A car chase ensued, and it ended when he crashed his car into an FBI car. That's how they got him for assaulting an agent.

When Bananas got out in 1978, Bruno did not simply make him a captain, he promoted him to *consigliere*, the third most powerful position in the family. For the first time Patty and our guys officially had to report to him. Bruno hoped that the promotion would buy Bananas' loyalty. It didn't. Bruno's low-key ways frustrated any number of the powerful family members. Bananas was constantly angry, and so was Bruno's underboss Phil Testa. And there was one thing in particular that really made them mad: Bruno was renowned for his dislike of the drug trade. He even gave interviews and said that all he did was make gambling available to people who wanted to bet and that he would do almost anything to keep drugs off the streets of Philadelphia. A lot of people thought that Testa and the other "young turks" in the family were angered because

Angelo wouldn't let them go into the drug business. Well, not exactly. Angelo was personally against drugs, and he would never personally profit from the drug trade, but if drugs were going to be sold, he saw no reason why some people in his organization shouldn't profit.

What actually was happening was that, with Angelo's permission, a number of Carlo Gambino's blood cousins – including three brothers, Rosario, Giuseppe, and Giovanni Gambino – opened pizza shops in Cherry Hill, Philadelphia, and Delaware. They were actually fronts to move heroin, and many of the sales were to Bruno family members in Philadelphia. They in turn sold the drugs to non-Mafia distributors who sold it to street dealers. The problem was that the Gambinos were making huge profits on the transactions. Many of the Bruno family members, especially those buying the drugs from the Gambinos, believed that if our family had been in the drug trade in an organized manner, we would have developed our own lines of supply directly through the old country and be making two or three times the amount.

That was at the heart of Bananas' problem with Bruno. He was simply too complacent, too willing to go along with what Gambino and the rest of the New York families wanted. That was especially true about what was happening in Atlantic City. The Bruno family had long controlled Atlantic City when it was a down-at-the-heels resort town not worth much Mob interest. But then along came legalized gambling, and suddenly Atlantic City was a prize. Bruno realized that he did not have the muscle to keep the New York families out, so he closed his eyes and let them in, and asked almost nothing in return. To Bananas, this was cowardly, and he believed being spineless was in Bruno's genes. Bananas was a Calabrian; Bruno was from Villalba. Generations of old-country feuds required that Bananas look down on Angelo, so finally he had enough.

But you don't kill a boss like Angelo Bruno without permission.

Patty told me that Bananas had told him he went to Frank "Funzi" Terri, the head of the Genoveses, to get the Commission's permission for the hit. He did not move until he got it, and for the last weeks before the hit, Bananas was telling Patty that he was going to become the new boss and that Patty would become his underboss. Patty said if this happened he would straighten me out first thing and make me the youngest captain our family had ever had. But in the meantime we should keep a very low profile.

Actually, a couple of days after Bruno was whacked, something happened that confused both Patty and me. The night that Bruno was killed, he had had dinner with three other guys at Cous' Little Italy, a small, but popular restaurant in South Philly. Bruno never drove himself, of course; he arrived with Raymond "Long John" Matirano, a family associate who owned a large vending machine business that carried Angelo on the payroll as a salesman. A lot has been made of who ended up driving Angelo home that night, as if it was somehow a part of the grand scheme, but the reality was that Angelo's driver that night was the result of absolute happenstance. Angelo went to dinner knowing that Long John had an appointment after dinner and would not be able to drive him home. He assumed that one of the other guys at the table would, but they begged off, saying they wanted to get home to listen to a live opera broadcast on the radio. An opera lover like Angelo understood that, and it said a lot about his docile personality that he would not think twice when a guy in the family said he had somewhere else to be and could not take him home.

Actually, Angelo knew all he had to do was ask and half the guys in the place would fall all over themselves to drive him. What happened was that Long John went out to the bar to see who was there who could drive Angelo. Several guys volunteered, but Long John chose John Stanfa, who had just come in and was having a drink. Stanfa was relatively new to Philadelphia, having arrived a few years earlier from Sicily where he had been connected. He had come to Philly because he was being sponsored by a relative who lived there. Carlo Gambino, who apparently knew Stanfa's people back in the old country, had personally called Angelo and asked if we could take him in. Angelo said sure, we would be happy to, so Stanfa came, began a small home repair business, and was starting to be with our guys.

The two drove away in Stanfa's old Chevy. After making a stop to let Angelo buy a paper, they pulled up in front of Angelo's brownstone at 934 Snyder. John later told me that they sat there for a few minutes talking about Sicily when suddenly the shooter came up behind the car, stuck a double-barrelled shotgun through the window, put it to the back of Angelo's head, and pulled both triggers. Some of the pellets passed through Angelo into John, but the moment he heard the shots, John was out of the car and running. He was young, and I guess he had really good reflexes. In any case, the shooter did not go after him, and John spent a day or two in the hospital and was questioned by the police.

Much was made later out of the fact that the window had been open, it being a cold March night and all. Stanfa had supposedly been in on the hit and had lowered the power window on Bruno's side with the controls on his side. This was a nice theory, but the problem with it is that Stanfa's car did not have power windows, and the window was not wide open. It was down only a few inches, but that was enough. As anyone who had ever driven with Angelo knew, he had a habit of lowering the window a few inches and then hooking his fingers over the top. I'm sure that is exactly what happened that night.

Despite the fact that Patty and I were sure Stanfa was not involved, a day or so later Patty got a call from Bananas telling him that Stanfa and Frankie Sindone, a family captain in Philly, were coming up. He told Patty to bring them to him, and they would go together into New York to meet with Paul Castellano. The Gambino boss had been close to Angelo and, we were told, was very angry about his being whacked.

That made no sense. Based on what he had been hinting at for weeks, we just assumed it was Bananas who whacked Angelo. It was natural to suspect Stanfa, because he was driving; as for Sindone, if I hadn't known what Bananas had been saying the past weeks and had to guess, Sindone would have been among the top two or three guys I would have picked to have made the hit. Logic does not always rule in the Mob, and reasoning can get very cockeyed. But I picked Sindone because he was very close to Angelo and might be considered the best choice to succeed him.

The family had been badly fractured for a long time. Angelo had not spoken with his underboss, Phil Testa, for almost two years. Testa was the leader of the faction that was not happy with the way Angelo had been running the family. That obviously would make Testa suspect number one; but right behind him would be Sindone because if the Bruno faction retained control, he would likely be chosen the next boss.

Given what we knew about the hit and our assumption that Bananas had cleared it with the Commission, Patty and I could not understand why Castellano would now be leaning on Stanfa and Sindone. Even stranger was that Patty told me to be prepared to do some "work" that night. "Bananas says that if Paul does not believe these guys, they ain't going back to Philly," he told me. "We'll have to do it, so I want you to be ready by the time we get back."

The two of them drove up from Philly and met Patty and me at the 3-11. Then the four of us went over to a diner on South Street owned by a guy who was with us. (At that time the diner was still under construction and not yet open for business.) There we met Bananas, and I stayed behind while the four of them got into one of Tony's cars – with one of his guys driving – and they all headed for New York. I went back to the 3-11 and got a couple of heavy plastic tarps, the kind house painters use, and I went to Happy Bellini, a guy who was connected to us, and picked up a couple of guns. I waited for Patty to call. Several hours later they all came back laughing and carrying on like no one had a care in the world. We had a couple of drinks, and they headed back to Philly. Patty later told me that Castellano had been ready to have Stanfa and Sindone killed, but Bananas saved them by assuring Paul that neither of them had been involved. So I returned the guns to their owners and put the tarps away for another day. John Stanfa is now the boss of what is left of the Bruno-Scarfo family. I wonder if he knows how close he came to dying that March day in 1980.

As for me, I had come pretty close to spending probably the rest of my life in jail. I later found out that the Feds were following Stanfa that day because they, too, thought he was connected with the hit. They followed him up from Philly right to the door of the 3-11. They had surveillance photos of Patty and me coming out with them, and they followed us to the diner and then tailed Bananas' car into New York. The plan Patty and I had made was that, if Castellano ordered it, when Stanfa and Sindone came back to the diner, we would kill them right there, roll up their bodies in the tarps, and dump them somewhere. If we had done it – and I'm sure I would have been one of the shooters – the whole thing would have been played out almost in front of the FBI cameras.

But Stanfa and Sindone went back to Philly, and I kept wondering what was going on. I half-wanted to ask

Bananas, but Patty had long ago warned me, "When one of our friends leaves us suddenly, don't talk about it, and above all don't ask questions of nobody. You can keep your ears open and take in everything that is said, but don't ask questions because you never know who you are talking to and whether he might think you're butting in where you don't belong." I remembered that and kept my lips buttoned. But keeping your nose out of things did not mean that you were prevented from speculating quietly about what was happening. Two things didn't make any sense to Patty and me. Number one, why would the Commission okay the whacking of Angelo when he had opened Atlantic City to them? He was so easy to get along with, and he never stepped on anyone's toes. The New York families would have to be crazy to want to have to deal with Bananas as boss. And number two, if they had given Bananas permission to make the hit, why call Stanfa and Sindone in and rake them over the coals? We couldn't figure it out – that is, until we saw how it all ended, and then it made perfect sense.

On the night of 17 April, when I heard over the radio that the cops had found an unidentified body in the trunk of a car in New York, I knew right away it was Bananas. It was a Thursday, and I had spent the morning at the 3-11 playing gin rummy with him. In those days Bananas may well have been the richest gangster in the metropolitan area, richer than most of the big bosses. But even though he was a man worth millions, he loved playing cutthroat gin, and he revelled in winning. He loved to beat me, and although I often saw him carrying $50,000 or $100,000, he would collect every cent I lost to him – and then he loved giving it away in front of me. That morning I lost $200 to him. Then he asked me to drive him to the train because he had to go to New York. On the way to the station he explained that his no-good brother-in-law Freddy Salerno was in some kind of trouble over a jewellery booth he owned in the diamond district, and he was going into the city to meet with some guys and straighten it out. The last thing Bananas said to me as he got out of the car was "I'll call you about what time I'm coming back so you can be here. And take the $200 you owe me and give it to the barmaid back at the 3-11 from me."

Bananas always hosted a major Mob dinner at the 3-11 on Thursdays. Guys would come from Philly, Atlantic City, and New York for an evening of good Italian food and drink, and sometimes we fed forty or fifty guys. It was the high point of Bananas' week, and he wouldn't miss it for the world. But he did miss it that Thursday night. We sat around waiting for him to call for his ride from the train, but he never did. When I heard on the car radio, driving home from the dinner, that a body had been discovered, shot gangland style, I just knew it was Bananas, but it would be almost two weeks before anybody knew for sure. For reasons that have never been entirely clear, the FBI identified the body almost immediately but didn't notify the family for eleven days. All we knew was that Bananas had disappeared. We were reasonably sure it was his body that had been found, but there was some possibility he had simply gone underground.

We later learned from the undertaker, who was a friend of ours, that as many as a half-dozen guys must have opened up on Bananas the minute he walked into that meeting. But the FBI guessed that the initial barrage had not stopped him. He was in terrific shape for a man over sixty, and he went after some of his attackers. That accounted for numerous stab wounds on the body as well as the dozens of bullet holes. Bananas had been shot so many times, his body was almost not identifiable. Then they had stuffed money in his mouth and other body cavities, the sign that the murder victim was too greedy.

And to wrap things up, they shot Freddy, too, and stuffed him with money. They were sending a strong signal.

Actually, Freddy getting whacked along with Bananas was quite an irony. Even years later a lot of people thought that it was Freddy who was the shooter in the Bruno hit, and that was why he was whacked. That's nonsense. Angelo Bruno was personally whacked by Tony Bananas. Tony himself was the shooter. That's how he grew up. He loved that kind of stuff, and he wasn't about to let anyone else do something he wanted to do so badly. Besides, as he told me more than once, Tony absolutely hated his brother-in-law. The guy was always getting into scrapes that he had to bail him out of. Time and time again Bananas had to call some guy or go to New York, to get Freddy out of some jam or another. About the last thing in the world he would do was trust Freddy to whack Angelo. In fact, as we drove to the train the day he was killed, Tony was bitching about having to save Freddy once again. "I'm going to whack that son of a bitch one of these days," he told me. "I'm getting tired of him screwing up." It was ironic that in dying, Bananas got his wish. Freddy was killed, I'm sure, just because he was there. And he was there because they needed him to lure Tony.

I was scared to death the night I heard that Bananas had been whacked and for the week or so following because we still didn't know what had happened. Since Patty and I assumed Bananas had the Commission's permission to whack Angelo, then Bananas' death in New York could only have meant that one of the New York families was moving in on us and perhaps was trying to take over the entire Bruno family as well. If that was true, then Patty was a prime target. In times like this a family is supposed to stick together, but I began to get an inkling of exactly how many of the guys around us thought of themselves above all else.

Basically, most of them simply disappeared. They should all have gathered around Pat, but instead they went into hiding. Patty and I armed ourselves and went into hiding, too, but only for a couple of days. Finally, Patty said the hell with it; if they want us, they're going to find us. So we went back to the club and resumed our normal schedule. Truthfully, we were not as calm as we wanted to appear, but we began to relax after Patty was ordered down to Philly about three weeks after Bananas was whacked.

This meeting of all made Bruno family members had been called by the Commission – the heads of the five New York families – so no one dared miss it. It was held in the back of a restaurant – with no little irony, Cous' Little Italy, the same South Philly joint where Angelo had eaten his last meal the night he was whacked. Everyone tried to appear calm and casual, but the tension in the air was thick. Since I was not yet made, I couldn't get into the back room for the meeting itself, but Patty told me what had happened as we drove back to Newark.

The meeting was run by Bobby Manna, the *consigliere* of the Genovese family. He first tried to settle everyone down by guaranteeing that none of the New York families was trying to make a move against the Bruno family. He indicated that the killing of Bananas had been a personal thing and that nothing extended to the people who had been around him. He said that the Commission approved of Phil Testa assuming the role of boss and that as far as the Commission was concerned all other matters were a closed issue. There was some grumbling among the old-timers that it was up to us and not the New York families as to who should be our boss. If it had been left up to them, they probably would have chosen Sindone. But since Testa had been underboss and this naming of him by the Commission prevented any kind of war breaking out over succession, it was grudgingly accepted.

A short time later Patty and I found out how Bananas had effectively been tricked into signing his own death warrant. He had gone to the Genoveses and told them of his problems with Angelo. The answer he got was "Take care of your problem." Bananas understood this to mean that he had a green light to kill Bruno. But after he did it, the Commission met, and Funzi Terri said he had told Bananas to work things out with Angelo. So as far as the Commission was concerned, Bananas had made an unauthorized hit on a boss, and that was an automatic death warrant. The bottom line was that the New York families knew Bananas was a danger to them and would be even more so as the boss of the Bruno family. But he was simply too powerful to hit without a reason. He had a hundred soldiers in his crew, and there would have been an ugly war. So Funzi simply let him have more than enough rope to hang himself.

Bananas' whacking of Angelo had a big impact on our family. Maybe Angelo wasn't aggressive enough for Bananas, but everyone was making money and there was peace. Now peace was something we would be without for quite some time.

Once Testa took over, he moved quickly to cement his hold. First he had Angelo's cousin, Johnny DeSimone, whacked. Then in a move that almost anyone could have predicted, he had Sindone killed. A lot of people speculated that these two guys were done in retaliation for Angelo's hit, that somehow they were involved. Again, that was exactly backward. DeSimone and Sindone were hit because they had been close to Angelo and now might pose a threat to the new leadership. Phil Testa was simply house cleaning.

He might have expanded this to other guys who had been close to Angelo, but they got him first. Just a week short of a year after Bruno was killed, Testa was also killed. He was whacked by his underboss Pete Casella. Casella had served a seventeen-year prison sentence for drug dealing. He had done his time in a stand-up fashion, not ratting on anyone, not agreeing to any of the many deals he had been offered by prosecutors. He thought this entitled him to some consideration, including being named boss instead of Testa for whom he had little good to say. He was also a friend of John McCullough, the longtime head of Local 30 of the Roofers' Union. Testa had McCullough whacked when he tried to organize in Atlantic City and wouldn't take no for an answer. Casella planted a bomb on Testa's front porch and blew him up late one night as he returned home from making his rounds. The killing threw the family into turmoil, and it looked as if a war was in the offing.

Actually, when Testa was killed, Patty and I were hiding out in Florida. The New Jersey Crime Commission had gotten it into their heads to investigate Bananas' murder, so they issued a subpoena for Patty, who didn't want to talk to them or appear in front of any grand jury. So he ducked the subpoena, and we screwed to Florida where we were sitting in the sun at the Thunderbird Hotel when the call came telling us that Testa had been whacked.

Several weeks went by with not much news out of either Philly or Newark. We heard that "Harry the Hunchback" Riccobene, an oldline Bruno captain and ally, was pushing to succeed Testa. Harry, who was heavily into the drug trade, had started to talk with other family captains, drumming up support. We assumed since Testa had left no clear-cut successor that the family captains would meet to select the new boss. It looked as if the Hunchback was gathering the necessary votes.

Then suddenly the phone started ringing. Another meeting had been called in Philly by Bobby Manna. Patty considered going, but he assumed the meeting would be staked out by the Feds and by local police, and that he would be picked up if he showed his face. He considered sending me as his emissary, but since I wasn't made yet, this would not have been well received. So we sat in Florida and waited. Within minutes after the meeting we got a call with the startling news that Little Nicky, Nicky Scarfo Sr, was our new boss.

Manna had told the meeting that the Commission was extremely unhappy over the whacking of Phil Testa. Given the abrupt nature of Testa's leaving, there was no clear-cut successor. This was a bad situation, and the Commission was therefore stepping in to prevent a war. Manna told the gathering, just as he had with Testa a year before, that he was there to indicate that the Commission was "recommending" Nicky as the new family head. A lot of guys thought this was wrong. It was the second time in a row that a new boss was being named from New York, and it was starting to look as though the Bruno family was being run by the New York families. But things were so unsettled they didn't feel they could challenge Manna. And in a way he was correct: If things were left to work themselves out, there probably would have been a war between Scarfo and Casella. But they were angry because they believed that Manna had manipulated the whole thing with the Commission. He and Nicky were very tight.

In a show of good faith and out of deference to the stand-up way he had served his time, Casella was allowed to retire to Florida (where he died of natural causes). His brother Tony, also involved in whacking Testa, was allowed to retire, too. He became a virtual recluse, rarely leaving his house in South Philly. The guys who actually planned and carried out the hit, including Chickie Narducci, were told they owed their total loyalty to Nicky, or else. So it was now the era of Little Nicky, and things were never the same.

★　　★　　★

In a way Nicky Scarfo became Angelo Bruno's worst mistake. His parents were Calabrian; they had emigrated to Brooklyn, where Nicky was born. Shortly thereafter they moved to Philly, and Nicky and his two uncles, who were actually about his age, grew up in the Bruno family. All three were made while they were still in their twenties. About the kindest thing you could say about Nicky was that he was completely crazy. Maybe it was because he was so small, but he was deeply paranoid and liked to kill people, which made for a bad combination. Bananas liked to kill people, too, but at least he was rational.

Bruno learned about Nicky one day in 1963 when the then thirty-two-year-old Nicky walked into a crowded diner in Philly. All the seats at the counter were taken, so Nicky marched up to one Joseph Duggan and demanded that he give him his seat. Duggan quite naturally said no. Nicky then reportedly screamed, "Don't you know who the fuck I am?" Duggan said he couldn't care less. Nicky pushed him. Duggan threw a punch. Nicky pulled out a knife and plunged it into Duggan's heart, killing him instantly.

Bruno was enraged when he heard of the incident. You simply did not kill civilians in public for no reason other than their resisting your throwing your weight around. But since Nicky was a made member, Angelo felt he owed him some measure of help. Strings were pulled, and the case landed before a very friendly judge. Nicky's plea of self-defence was rejected out of hand, but he was allowed to plead to a lesser offence and received three years. When he got out, Angelo effectively banished him, sending him to Atlantic City, which in those days was a virtual wasteland. Angelo could have saved himself and the world a lot of grief – and a lot of guys would still be alive today – if he had simply had Nicky killed back in 1963 when it became apparent how out of control he was.

Nicky was gone and all but forgotten in his exile. He had put together a small crew aided by his nephew, "Crazy Phil" Leonetti, and the Merlino brothers, Salvatore, called "Chuckie" by everyone, and Larry, called "Yogi". These guys eked out a small living by charging protection to bar owners, running some gambling operations, loan-sharking, and labour racketeering. But then Nicky caught a break by going to jail.

At the same time the New Jersey State Commission on Investigation called Angelo to testify about his knowledge of organized crime, they also called others from various families active in Jersey, including the Genoveses, the Bonannos, and the Gambinos. Among the guys dragged before the SCI were both Nicky and Bobby Manna. Like Angelo, they also refused to talk, and they, too, were sent to jail. At various times a total of nine guys went to jail for contempt of the SCI. The assumption was that they would serve only a year or so, but the state meant business, and all of them ended up serving anywhere from three to seven years. They did their time housed at Yardville, the New Jersey state prison system's reception centre in Trenton. Although nine men were eventually sentenced for contempt, only seven were in Yardville at the same time. A newspaper story of the day dubbed them the "Yardville Seven", and they have been known by that handle ever since.

All of the Yardville Seven grew very tight, and being a member of that elite group boosted Nicky's standing in the eyes of almost everyone else in the family. And because Nicky did his time in a stand-up fashion, Angelo was forced to allow him back into family affairs even while keeping him in Atlantic City. Quite probably Nicky would have abandoned Atlantic City and gone back to Philly if legalized gambling had not been on the horizon. On the day in 1977 that it was approved, Nicky emerged as a major player, not only in our family but in organized crime on the East Coast.

Nicky was quick to respond to this newfound stature. After years of keeping a Bruno-enforced low profile, he and his crew began to act the part of Mob big shots right away. First they killed a local judge, Edwin Helfant, whom they had paid off to give a light sentence to one of the crew and then saw him throw the book at the guy. Then Crazy Phil Leonetti whacked a guy who owed him loan-sharking money and was refusing to pay. The cops had an eyewitness, and they put Crazy Phil on trial. But he walked when the witness suddenly had a serious and complete memory loss. Then Nicky ordered a Philly dope dealer who owed him money killed, with the hit carried out by Chuckie Merlino and Salvy Testa, Phil Testa's son.

Finally, Nicky got into a beef with a guy who was associated with the family, Vincent Falcone. It got back to Nicky that Falcone had called him crazy – actually an astute observation. Nicky went nuts. He called and invited Falcone to a Christmas party, and he sent Philip Leonetti and Yogi Merlino to pick him up. When Falcone got to an apartment in Margate, just outside Atlantic City, he found out that he was the party. Crazy Phil shot him in the head while Nicky stood there laughing and screaming at the guy. Then when it looked like Falcone was still breathing, Nicky tried to take the gun away from Philip and finish the job himself. But Philip pulled away and shot Falcone again in the chest. Philip later told me he had looked down at the guy and shouted, "If I could bring the motherfucker back to life, I'd kill him again."

People have always tended to write Little Nicky Scarfo off as a stupid thug. Sure, he was a thug, a killer utterly without conscience, but he was not dumb. I first met him one night at the 3-11 in Newark in the mid-1970s. He had come to town to meet with some union guys. He cut quite a figure, a cocky and dapper little man always dressed in a very expensive suit. You knew right away that this guy was no dummy. Nicky was quick and he was cunning, and he proved it by the way he outsmarted the New Jersey Gaming Commission.

When legalized gambling was first suggested in the state legislature, there was an immediate outcry that it would be taken over by organized crime. So the legislature went to extraordinary lengths to protect against the Mob through a complex and rigid system of licensing and oversight. If the Mob had tried to go into Atlantic City through the front door, it would have been met with force, and the effort would likely have failed. Nicky was smart enough to realize that it was probably fruitless to buck the system head-on, so he decided that if he couldn't go in through the front door, he could find a back door. The back door Nicky found into the Atlantic City casinos was through the labour unions.

Nicky reasoned that within a short time there would be thousands of workers in the casinos and hotels, and these workers could be quickly organized. He also reasoned that if he controlled the union that controlled these workers, he could hold the work stoppage sword over the heads of the casino owners. And as a plus, he would get access to all the health and welfare funds that would be flowing through the new union.

The key was Frank Lentino, a retired Philadelphia Teamsters' Union executive who was an associate of the Bruno family and for years was involved in the systematic shakedown of contractors in Philadelphia. At seventy Lentino retired and moved to Atlantic City. There he was recruited by Nicky, and it was arranged for him to sign on as a consultant to the existing Bartenders' Union, which was run by Al Daidone and closely allied to Bartenders'

Local 170 in Camden, which was run by Ralph Natale, a Bruno family member. Within short order the small Atlantic City local was expanded into Local 54 of the Hotel Employees' and Restaurant Employees' International Union, and when membership climbed from about 4,000 hotel and restaurant workers in the pre-gambling days to more than 30,000 with the arrival of the casinos, Nicky was on his way.

Nicky was not subtle. With control of the union he had the power to call hotel or casino workers out on strike. Since one night's wildcat strike could cost a casino a million or more, the owners were very anxious to avoid any labour problems. Nicky was anxious to accommodate them. But he wanted a few things in return, service contracts foremost among them. In exchange for labour peace, hotels and casinos made Mob-connected companies the providers of everything from garbage hauling to supplying meats, poultry, and liquor.

Nicky also made another decision, and that was to stay out of the construction trades. With the coming hotel-building boom, it would have been a natural to try to tie up the building trades unions. But Nicky knew that the New York families were into the construction trades, so he left these for them. Obviously millions could be made from construction contracts and shakedowns, but in showing deference to the New York families in the area, he won for himself the right to be left alone with the employees' union. And as Nicky told me once, "The employees' union is going to be around long after all construction has been completed."

But Nicky was not left out of the building boom altogether. He owned and Phil Leonetti ran a company called Scarf, Inc., that was in the cement business. Much of the cement that was poured in the new hotel and casino construction came from Scarf. Then Nicky had a big piece of two other companies, Batshore Rebar and Nat Nat, Inc., that were in the steel and steel-reinforcement business. They were run for Nicky by the Merlino brothers, and these companies provided the structural and reinforcing steel for most of the new casino projects.

When Angelo Bruno made the decision in 1978 to allow the New York families into Atlantic City, Nicky made a big scene of being enraged. He complained to Bananas and Phil Testa. But here again Nicky showed how cunning and smart he was. He effectively played both ends toward the middle. If the New York families were going to be allowed in, they would have to come to him if they wanted into the unions. He used his old Yardville Seven connection with Bobby Manna and his Calabrian heritage to set up a working arrangement with the Genoveses and the Gambinos.

As Nicky explained to me and Patty, this move was crucial to winning over the Commission to back him for boss of our family. He told us this a few days after the Philadelphia meeting when he and Phil Leonetti went down to Florida to pay a courtesy call on Patty. He explained that the moment he heard Testa was dead, he was on his way to New York to meet with Manna. Through Manna, Nicky posed a question to the heads of the New York families: Did they want to risk a new boss of the Bruno family declaring Atlantic City a closed territory? The New Jersey Gambling Commission had gone to such lengths to try to protect against organized crime that the last thing the families needed was some kind of war over Atlantic City. The New York families would undoubtedly win, but at what price? Back me, Nicky said, and the arrangements we have been working on will continue. Manna agreed, and the Commission agreed with Manna. Little Nicky was now the man.

Donnie Brasco

Joseph Pistone

Joseph Pistone was brought up in Paterson, New Jersey. He was of Sicilian stock and learnt enough about the ways of the Mafia to infiltrate the Mob as a special agent for the FBI. Pistone joined the New York truck hijacking squad in 1974. Two years later, he went underground, posing as a jewel thief from Florida named Donnie Brasco. He spent six years working undercover in the Colombo and Bonanno Families. His undercover work also took him to Miami where he worked alongside Joe Fitzgerald, another undercover FBI agent. Through his connections, he got to know the Bonanno capo Dominic "Sonny Black" Napolitano, Michael Sabella, Anthony Mirra and Bonanno soldier Benjamin "Lefty Guns" Ruggiero. The undercover operation ended in 1982 when Napolitano ordered Pistone to murder Anthony "Whack Whack" Indelicato, who was supposed to have been killed along with his father Alphonse "Sonny Red" Indelicato, Philip "Philly Lucky" Giaccone and Dominic "Big Trin" Trinchea in 1981. This forced him to abandon his undercover role and turn evidence he had collected to the FBI. It led to over 200 indictments and over 100 convictions of members of the Mafia.

After Napolitano was told that Pistone, alias Brasco, was an FBI agent, he refused to turn state's evidence and enter the

Witness Protection Programme. He told his girlfriend that he bore no ill will against Pistone and that, if anyone had to bring him down, he was glad it was Pistone. Knowing he was going to be killed, Napolitano went to a meeting in Flatlands, Brooklyn, where he was shot dead by Bonanno captain Frank "Curly" Lino and Ron Filcomo. Bonanno boss Joe Massino was convicted of ordering Napolitano's murder. When Napolitano's body was found on Staten Island, the hands had been cut off. A contract was put out on Ruggiero too but, by then, he had been taken into protective custody by the FBI. Nevertheless, he refused to become a government witness and join the Witness Protection Programme, and the contract on him was cancelled. He was convicted of three counts of murder and drug trafficking in New York, and extortion, planning a bank robbery and illegal gambling in Florida. He died of cancer in jail in 1994.

A contract was also put out on Pistone. With author Richard Woodley, Pistone wrote the book Donnie Brasco, *which was made into a movie in 1997, starring Johnny Depp and Al Pacino. In the book, Pistone writes of the constant battle to maintain his assumed identity when surrounded by suspicious Mafiosi who had usually known each other since childhood.*

One morning not long afterward, I walked into the store. Everybody was there, but nobody was saying much. Jilly took my elbow and said, "Don, let's take a walk."

We went outside. He said, "Look, Don, nothing for nothing, but Patsy and Frankie, they don't feel comfortable around you. They got a beef."

"What's the problem?"

"They feel like they don't know you well enough. They don't want you involved in any more jobs until they know more about you. They want the name of somebody that can vouch for you down in Miami where you said you did a lot of work, so they can feel more comfortable with you."

"Well, how do you feel, Jilly?" I said. "We've done stuff together, right? You know who I am. You got any problems with me?"

"No, I got no problems with you." Jilly was uncomfortable. "But I grew up with these guys, you know? They been my partners for years, since before they went to the can. So they got this little beef, and I gotta go along with them. Okay?"

"Fuck them, Jilly. I'm not giving them the name of anybody."

"Let's just take it easy, okay, Don? Let's go in and talk it over, try to work it out"

Jilly was the made guy, the boss of this crew. I had rubbed these other guys the wrong way, and they had gone first to Jilly and put the beef in with him, which was the right way to do it. He had to respect their wishes because of the proper order – he had known them longer than he knew me, even though he had faith and trust in me. It was their beef, but it was his responsibility to get it resolved one way or the other. He was handling it the proper way. He came to me and talked to me first.

Then, when I hard-nosed it, said no right up front (I couldn't give in right away, I had to string it out and play the game), he said we had to sit down and talk about it. When you sit down, everybody puts their cards on the table and airs their beefs out. And Jilly had to lean toward them in granting their request about getting somebody to vouch for me in Florida. At that point I wasn't worried: because things were being handled in the right way, according to the rules,

We went back in the store. I went over to Patsy and said, "You got a beef?"

"You say you pulled off all those scores down in Miami before you came here." Patsy said. "But we don't know nothing about that. And you seem to want to say a lot around here. So Frankie and me wanna know somebody you did those jobs with, so we can check you out."

"You don't need to check me out," I said. "I been around here five-six months. Jilly and the other guys are satisfied. I don't have to satisfy you just because you were in the can."

"Yeah, you do," he said. "Let's go in the back and sit down." Everybody walked into the back room. Patsy sat down behind the desk. "You could be anybody or anything," he said. "Maybe you're a stoolie. So we want to check you out, and we need the name of somebody to vouch for you."

"I'm not giving you any name."

Patsy opened a desk drawer and took out a .32 automatic and laid it on the desk in front of him. "You don't leave here until you give me a name."

"I'm not giving up the name of somebody just to satisfy your curiosity," I said. "You don't know me? I don't know you. How do I know you're not a stoolie?"

"You got a fucking smart mouth. You don't give me a name, the only way you leave here is rolled up in a rug," he said.

"You do what you gotta do, because I ain't giving you a name." It was getting pretty tense in there. Jilly tried to be a mediator.

"Don, it's no big deal. Just let him contact somebody. Then everybody feels better and we forget about it."

I knew all along, from the time he pushed it to the gun, that I would give him a name. Because once he went that far in front of everybody, he wouldn't back off. But even among fellow crooks you don't ever give up a source or contact easily. You have to show them that you're a stand-up guy, that you're careful and tough in protecting people you've done jobs with. So I was making it difficult for them. I acted as if I were really torn, mulling it over.

Then I said, "Okay, as a favour to Jilly, I'm gonna give you a name. You can check with this guy. But if anything happens to this guy, I'm gonna hold you responsible. I'll come after you."

I gave him the name of a guy in Miami.

He said, "Everybody sit tight. I'm gonna go and see if we can contact somebody down there that knows this guy of yours." He left the room and shut the door.

I was nervous about the name I gave him. It was the name of an informant, a thief in Miami who was an informant for another agent down there. It had been part of my setup when I was going undercover. I had told this other agent to tell his informant than if anybody ever asked about Don Brasco, the informant should say that he and Brasco had done some scores together, and that Brasco was a good guy. The informant didn't even know who Don Brasco was, just that he should vouch for him if the circumstance came up.

So now I had a couple of worries. That had been seven months before, I wasn't absolutely sure that the informant got the message, and if he had been told, would he remember now, seven months later? If the informant blew it now, I was going to get whacked, no doubt about it. The other guys in the crew here didn't care; they were on the fence. But Patsy or his pal Frankie would kill me, both because of the animosity between us and because they had taken it too far to back down.

While Patsy was gone, I just sat around with the other guys playing gin and bullshitting as if everything were normal. Nobody mentioned the problem. But I was thinking hard about how the hell I was going to get out of there at least to make a phone call.

After couple of hours I figured everybody had relaxed, so I said, "I'm gonna go out and get some coffee and rolls. I'll take orders for anybody,"

"You ain't going anywhere," Frankie says, "until Patsy comes back."

"What are we here, children?" I say, "I got no reason to take off. But it's lunchtime."

"Sit down," Frankie says.

If it came to it, I would have to bust out of there somehow, because I was not just going to sit there and take a bullet behind my ear. There was a door out to the front, which I figured Patsy had locked when he went out. There was a back door, which was nailed shut, never used. And there were four windows, all barred. I didn't have many options. I could make a move for the gun on the desk; that was about it. But I wouldn't do anything until Patsy came back with whatever the word was, because I might luck out. And if I could stick with it and be lucky, I would be in that much more solid with the Colombo crew.

We sat there for hours. Everybody but me was smoking. We all sat and breathed that crap, played cards, and bullshitted.

It was maybe four-thirty when Patsy came back. Instantly I could see I was okay, he had a look on his face that said I had beaten him again.

He said, "Okay, we got an answer, and your guy okayed you."

Everybody relaxed. Everybody but me. With what had gone down, I couldn't let that be the end of it. You can't go through all that and then just say, "I'm glad you found out I'm okay, and thank you very much." The language of the street is strength; that's all they understand. I had been called. I had to save some face, show everybody they couldn't mess with me. I had to clear the air. I had to smack somebody.

The gun was still lying there. But now we were all standing up, starting to move around and relax. I wanted to take Patsy first. But Frankie was the one between me and the gun. I circled around, casually edging over to him. I slugged him and he went down. Patsy jumped on me and I belted him a few times. Then the rest of the crew jumped in and wrestled us apart. I had counted on the crew breaking it up before it got out of hand, so I could make my point before the two of them got at me at once.

Patsy was sitting on the floor, staring up at me.

"You fucking punks," I said. "Next time you see me, you better walk the other way."

Guido, the toughest of all of them, stepped in front of me and looked at everybody else. "That's the end of it about Don," he said. "I don't want to hear nothing else from nobody about Don not being okay."

I had met Anthony Mirra in March of 1977. He invited me downtown to Little Italy. He had a little food joint called the Bus Stop Luncheonette at 115 Madison Street. We used to hang out there, or across the street at a dive called the Holiday Bar.

Mirra also introduced me to Benjamin "Lefty Guns" Ruggiero, like himself a soldier in the Bonnano family. Like Mirra, Lefty was known as a hit man. He had a social club at 43 Madison Street, just up the street from Mirra's Bus Stop Luncheonette. Mirra used to hang out there. He introduced me to Lefty on the sidewalk outside the club. "Don, this is Lefty, a friend of mine. Lefty, Don."

Lefty was in his early fifties, about my height – six feet – lean, and slightly stoop-shouldered. He had a narrow face and intense eyes.

Mirra turned away to talk to somebody else. Lefty eyed me.

"Where you from?" He had a cigarette-raspy voice, hyper.

"California," I said. "Spent a lot of time between there and Miami. Now I'm living up at Ninety-first and Third."

"How long you known Tony?"

"Couple months. Mainly the last few months I've been hanging out in Brooklyn, 15th Avenue. With a guy named Jilly."

"I know Jilly," Lefty said.

Prior to that introduction, I was never invited into Lefty's club, and you can't go in without permission when you're not connected. From that time on, I would go down to Lefty's almost every day to meet Mirra. So I got to know Lefty.

I then began dividing my time between Mirra, Lefty, and the Bonanno guys in Little Italy, and Jilly and the Colombos in Brooklyn. Since I wasn't officially connected to anybody, it was permissible, if not encouraged, to move between two groups. But it was also a lot to handle when you're trying to stay sharp on every detail.

Agent Joe Fitzgerald had set himself up with an identity, an apartment, and the rest, just as I had, and we did basically the same thing. Fitz was doing a good job working the street in the Miami area; and he fingered a lot of fugitives for arrest. But for whatever reasons, the operation there didn't catch on as readily. Most of the guys Fitz was able to get involved with were guys that were chased out of New York, small-time dopers, credit-card scammers, and the like. No real heavyweights.

Now that I had some credentials with both the Colombo and Bonanno people, we thought that maybe I could help stimulate some contacts in Miami. So from time to time I would go down there and hang out with Fitz, letting people know that I was "connected around Madison Street" and in Brooklyn.

I had a dual role, hanging out with Fitz. First was to help him if I could, by being a connected guy from New York who he could point to for credibility. Second was to build up my own credentials. I would tell people in New York that I was going down to Miami to pull some sort of job. I would be seen down there hanging out in the right places. Word always gets back. So you always had to stay in character.

One time we were at an after-hours joint named Sammy's, where a lot of wiseguys hung out. We were at the bar. Fitz was talking to a couple of women to his right. I was sitting on his left, at the *L* of the bar, and around the corner of the *L* were three guys talking together. One of them was drunk, and I recognized him as a half-ass wiseguy from New York.

This drunk starts hollering at me. "Hey, you! Hey, you, I know you."

I ignore him, and he reaches over and grabs my arm. "Hey, I'm talking to you!" he says. "I know you from somewhere. Who you with?"

"I'm with him," I say, pointing to Fitz.

Not only is he drunk, but he is also saying things he shouldn't be saying around wiseguys, asking things he shouldn't be asking – such as about what family I was with. I signal to the two guys with him. "Your friend is letting the booze talk," I say. "He's out of line, so I suggest you quiet him down." They shrug.

I call the bartender over. "I want you to know that this guy is out of line here," I say. "And you're a witness to what he's saying, if anything happens."

The drunk keeps it up. "I know you from New York. Don't turn away from me. Who you with?"

I lean over to Fitz. "He grabs me again, I'm gonna have to clock him," I say.

"No problem," Fitz says. He is standing there, all 6'5" of him.

"When you're ready, let me know, I'll take care of those other two guys."

The drunk grabs me by the shoulder. "Hey! I'm talking to you!"

"Okay, Fitz," I say. I reach over and belt the drunk, and he slides off the stool. At the same time Fitz clocks the second guy, and then the third guy, one right after the other. All three of them sink to the floor.

Everybody in the joint turns away. Where wiseguys are concerned nobody wants to know anything.

I say to the bartender, "You saw and you heard, right?"

"Yeah," he says.

"So if anything comes down regarding this, just say how this guy was out of line. Fitz knows how to reach me and my people in New York."

It turned out the guy was a member of the Lucchese family. Word did get right back to New York. Everything was smoothed over. It helped my image.

Fitz and I cruised the Miami-area hangouts that had been identified as likely places for contacts: Sneaky Pete's, Charley Brown's Steak Joint, the Executive Club, Tony Roma's, Gold Coast up in Fort Lauderdale.

But we weren't able to lure the big-timers into conversation.

For several months I went back and forth between the Colombos and the Bonannos, between New York and Florida.

Fitz and I were out one night in a nightclub near Fort Lauderdale. We were sitting at the bar. Fitz introduced me to a lot of people he knew in there. "This is Don from New York." Guys were going into the john to snort coke. I was just sitting at the bar bullshitting with a couple of half-ass wiseguys and their girlfriends.

Then this one guy comes out of the john and comes over to me holding this little open vial. He holds it out to me and says, "Here, Don, have a snort."

I smack his arm, sending the bottle flying and the cocaine spraying all over the place. I grab him by the lapels and hoist him. "I don't do that stuff," I say, "and you had no business offering it to me. Don't ever offer it to me again. I make money off it, but I don't use it. I keep my head clear at all times."

"But look what you did," he whines, "all my stuff!"

"Write it off to experience," I say. "You wanna fuck up your head, that's up to you. Don't bring it around me."

I didn't do these things to be a tough guy. But with things like drinking and drugs, you can't be a fence-sitter around these guys. If you smoke a joint or take a snort the first time – maybe just to show that you're a regular guy – or if you say, "Maybe later," it gives the impression that you do drugs. If you're a fence-sitter, then you're in a bind. You just invite people to keep offering it to you. And if you say, "Not now," and then keep refusing and refusing and putting it off, they begin to wonder: What's up with this guy? But if you draw the line right in the beginning – I don't do it; I ain't ever gonna do it – then that's it, nobody cares anymore.

A lot of people have the misconception that Mob guys are all big drinkers or dopers. Some of them are – a greater proportion of young guys do drugs than older guys. But so many guys don't do anything that you don't stand out by saying no – it's no big deal. Tony Mirra killed twenty or thirty people, and he drank only club soda.

The thing is, even though it's a fake world for you as an undercover agent, it's a real world for the people that you're dealing with. And you have to abide by the rules in that world. And those rules include how you establish your own standards, credibility, and individuality. I know one or two guys that drank or did drugs while they were undercover just because they thought they had to do that to blend in or show they were tough guys. It was an enormous mistake. You can't compromise your own standards and personality. Smart wiseguys will see right through your act. You look like somebody that has no mind of his own, hence no strength . . .

I was down in Miami one time working with Fitz for a week. I had told Jilly and his guys that I would be down there. But I didn't call them back with a telephone number where I could be reached.

As it turned out they had tried to find me because they wanted me in on a big job they were going to pull down there.

They had connections in Florida. Guido told me that he had been dealing drugs in Florida for nine years, especially in the Key West area, where he had the fix in with the police department and the district attorney's office. Vinnie told me that he had a friend who owned a nursery on Staten Island where he was growing a big marijuana crop, and that when it was harvested in August, Guido would take it to Florida for sale.

In this instance they had information about a house in Fort Lauderdale where they could pull off an easy $250,000 cash score. It was a four-man job. When they couldn't locate me, Jilly joined Guido and Patsy and Frankie. When I got back to New York, they filled me in on what had happened. They had pulled off the job and it had been a disaster.

The information their Florida tipster gave them was that an elderly lady kept the cash and diamonds in a safe. Guido bought safecracking tools for the job in Miami. They went to the house, flashed their detective shields to the lady, and said they were on an investigation and needed to come in. They handcuffed the lady. But there was no safe. And there was no quarter of a million in cash.

What they found were bullet holes in the ceiling, bank books showing that a huge deposit was made the day before in a safe-deposit box, and a little cash lying around.

By the time they accounted for plane fares and tools and other expenses, they came out of the job with about $600 apiece.

Their information had been good, but late. Later their tipster filled in the story. The lady's husband had died and left the quarter mill. He had promised a large chunk of that to his nephew. But the widow didn't like the nephew and didn't want to give him the money. The nephew came to collect. He tried to frighten the lady. He pulled out a gun and fired two bullets into the ceiling. But she didn't give up the money. The next day she put it all in a safe-deposit box. That was the day before Guido and Jilly went there to steal it.

"If I'd've known all this ahead of time," Guido told me, "I never would have pulled the job."

Jilly got 1,200 ladies' and children's watches from a job at the airport. He brought samples into the store. As usual, he offered me a piece or all of the load if I could find a market. He gave me a sample to show, a Diantus.

Meanwhile he had located a potential buyer. A couple of guys were interested in part of the load. The next afternoon, we were in the back room when these two guys walked in.

I recognized one of them as a guy I had arrested two years earlier on a hijacking charge, back before I went undercover and I was on the Truck and Hijack Squad.

I had worked on the street only a couple of months up in New York. So it wasn't as if I had arrested thousands of people. When you arrest somebody like that, you usually remember him. I remembered the face; I remembered the name: Joe. Just like the crook, he usually remembers the cop that arrests him. It's just something that stays with you. There we were.

I was introduced. Joe knew the other guys but not me. I watched his face. No reaction. I wasn't going to excuse myself and leave, because something might click with this guy, and if it did, I wanted to see the reaction so I would know. If I left and something clicked with this guy, I could come back to an ambush. I watched his face, his eyes, his hands.

They talked about the watches, the prices. I decided to get the guy in conversation. Sometimes if a guy's nervous about you, he can hide it in his expression, just avoid you. I figured if I talked to him, I could get a reaction – either he would talk easy or he would try to avoid conversation with me. I had to be sure, because there was a good chance I would run into this guy again.

"By the way," I said, "you got any use for men's digitals?" I had one and showed it to him.

"Looks like a good watch," he said. "How much?"

"You buy enough, you can have them for twenty each."

"Let me check it out, get back to you. Where can I reach you?"

"I'm right here every day," I said.

The conversation was okay. There was no hitch in his reactions. They chatted a few more minutes and left. The whole thing took maybe twenty minutes. The guy simply hadn't made me. Those situations occur from time to time, and there's nothing you can do about them, except be on your toes.

A couple days later I asked Jilly, "Joe and that other guy, did they buy the watches?"

He said. "Yeah, they took some of mine, but they didn't have any market for yours."

From time to time somebody in Jilly's crew would ask me if I had any good outlets for marijuana or coke. I was noncommittal. At that time I wasn't trying to milk the drug side, other than to report back whatever I saw and heard. The FBI wasn't so much into the drug business then. We didn't want to get involved in any small drug transactions because we couldn't get authority to buy drugs without making a bust. We were still operating on a buy-bust standard, meaning that if we made a buy, we had to make a bust, and that would have blown my whole operation. So in order not to complicate the long-range plans for my operation, I pretty much had to steer clear of drug deals.

Guido came up to me at the store. "You got plans for today?" he asked.

"No, I'm just gonna hang out. I got nothing to do," I said.

"Take a ride with me. I gotta go to Jersey."

We took Jilly's car, a blue 1976 Coupe de Ville. We drove across the Verrazano Narrows Bridge to Staten Island. We drove around Staten Island for a while, then recrossed the bridge back to Brooklyn.

I said, "I thought you said you had to go to Jersey?"

"I do," he said. "I gotta meet a guy."

We drove up the Brooklyn-Queens Expressway, crossed the Brooklyn Bridge to Manhattan, and headed north on the FDR Drive. Obviously Guido had just been cleaning himself, making sure nobody was following him with the run to Staten Island. We crossed the George Washington Bridge into Jersey. We took the Palisades Parkway north.

A little after noon we got to Montvale, New Jersey. At the intersection of Summit Avenue and Spring Valley Road, Guido stopped to make a call at a phone booth. He got back in the car and we just sat there.

"We wait," he said.

About a half hour later a black Oldsmobile pulled up beside us. The driver motioned for us to follow him. We followed him north for a few minutes, across the Jersey line into New York. We pulled into a busy shopping centre in Pearl River. Guido and the other driver got out and talked. The other guy was about six foot, 180, with a black moustache. Guido signalled for me to get out of the car.

The guy opened his trunk. There were four plain brown cardboard boxes in there. We transferred the boxes to Guido's trunk.

Guido asked, "How much is in there?"

"You got ninety-eight pounds," the guy said. "That's what you gotta pay me for."

We got back in the car and headed for Brooklyn.

"Colombian," Guido said, referring to the marijuana in the trunk. "We should get $275 a pound. On consignment, I got access to another 175 pounds. The guy said he could also supply us with coke, but not on consignment. Money up front for blow."

I unloaded the boxes and put them in the back of Jilly's store. The next day when I came in, the boxes were gone. They didn't keep drugs in the store. Guido handed me a little sample bag. It was uncleaned – stalks, leaves, seeds. "Think you can move some of this?" he said.

"I don't know," I said. "I never moved any of this stuff through my people. I'll ask around."

I held on to the sample for a couple of days, then gave it back.

"Nobody I talked to could use it," I said.

None of these guys used drugs themselves, so far as I could see. To them it was strictly a matter of business. If these guys had been dopers, it might have been a different story. They really might have tested me. But the fact was that the way you proved yourself with these guys was by making scores, making money.

According to the Mafia mythology, there was supposed to be a code against dealing drugs. In the old days there wasn't a huge amount of money to be made in drugs, and they didn't do it. Now that's where the money is, forget any so-called code. Like anything else with the Mafia, if there's money to be made, they're going to do it . . .

Another day I got to the club and Jilly wasn't there. I asked Vinnie, "Where is everybody?"

"Jilly and Guido got a contract," he said, "and they're out looking for the guy they gotta hit."

You don't ask questions about a hit. If they want you to know, they'll tell you. But my job was to get information if possible. When Jilly came back, I asked him, "Where were you guys?"

"Me and Guido had to look for somebody," he said.

"Anything going on?" I asked, as if it might be some kind of score.

He proceeded to talk about an upcoming hijacking. I tried to wrangle the conversation back to the guy they were looking for, but he wouldn't talk about it. It wasn't unusual that he wouldn't tell me. Who was I? At the time I was just a guy who had been hanging around a few months, let alone an FBI agent. You don't just tell anybody if you have a piece of work to do.

I don't know if that particular hit came off or not. Whacking somebody is something that you don't talk about. In my years with the Mafia guys sometimes they would sit around and discuss how much work they'd done in the past – "work" meaning hits. But ordinarily they never discussed openly any particular individual they hit, or an upcoming one. If something went wrong, they might sit around later and laugh about it.

One time I was hanging out with Lefty Ruggiero at his social club in Little Italy, and he and a bunch of guys were laughing about a job. They had gotten a contract to hit a guy. They tailed this guy for a week, looking for the right opportunity. Then they were told the contract's off, don't hit the guy. And it turned out it was the wrong guy they were following. They would have hit the wrong guy. To them it was the funniest thing in the world. "What the fuck you think of that? We're following the guy for a week and it's not even the right guy – ha, ha, ha! We're out every fucking night following this jerk-off. Piece a fucking luck for him, right? Ha, ha, ha!"

All this time I was trying to remember everything. Since I didn't take any notes – didn't dare to take any notes or write anything down, even in my apartment – I had to remember. Anything of a criminal nature discussed in conversation, any new guy that came through the clubs, the different deals and scores and the different guys involved and amounts of everything – I had to try to remember it all. Eventually federal court cases would depend on the accuracy and credibility of my memory.

It was a matter of concentration. That and little tricks. Like remembering licence-plate numbers or serial numbers on weapons in series of threes. The frustration always was that I couldn't ask a lot of questions, which is one of the things I was trained to do as an FBI agent. A lot of the things I had to remember were things I overheard, and I couldn't ask for these things to be repeated, or for what I thought I heard to be confirmed. When swag came in and out, I couldn't ask to look it over more closely, or where it came from, or who it was going to, I had to hope those facts were volunteered. I had to be just a hang-around guy who wasn't more interested than was good for him.

Concentrating on conversations is draining. Most of the talk was idle, simplistic bullshit about the most mundane things – getting a haircut or a new pair of Bally shoes; how the Jets or Giants were doing; how the Chinese and Puerto Ricans were ruining neighbourhoods; how much better a Cadillac was than a Lincoln; how we ought to drop the bomb on Iran; how we ought to burn rapists, each guy would gladly strap the perverts in and pull the switch himself. Most of these guys, after all, were just uneducated guys who grew up in these same neighbourhoods.

But they were street-smart, and the thread of the business ran through everything all the time, and the business was stealing and hits and Mafia politics – who was up, who was down, who was gone. Somebody might be talking about a great place to buy steaks at a cut rate and in virtually the same sentence mention a hit, or somebody new getting made, or a politician they had in their pocket. These tidbits would lace conversation continually but unpredictably, and they flew by. If I wasn't always ready, I would miss something I needed to remember. And I couldn't stop them and say, "What was that about paying off the police chief somewhere?"

What's more, to be above suspicion I had to adapt my conversational style to theirs. Occasionally I would change the subject or wander away from the table purposely, right in the middle of a discussion about something criminal that might be of interest to the government – precisely to suggest that I wasn't particularly interested. Then I would hope the talk would come around that way again or that I could lead it back, get at it later or in another way. It was a necessary gambit for the long term.

And then I would have to remember facts and names and faces and numbers until I could call in a report to my contact agent.

That's why when I would get home for my one day or evening in two or three weeks, it would be difficult to adjust and focus deserved attention on my family. Especially when they didn't know what I was doing and we couldn't talk about it.

One hot August afternoon I was in the store when they came in from a job. Jilly, Guido, Patsy, Frankie, and a couple of other guys, one of them named Sonny. Jilly was nervous as hell. I had never seen him so nervous.

"We hit this house in Bayonne this morning," he told me.

"The guy was a big guy [I wasn't sure whether he meant physically big or important] and I thought I was gonna have to shoot the motherfucker because he wouldn't open the safe. I had my gun on him, and I said I was gonna shoot him if he didn't open it up or if he tried anything. I really thought I was gonna have to shoot him. Finally he opened it and we handcuffed him and the woman and taped his mouth shut."

He was visibly shaken, and I didn't know why, because he'd been out on any number of similar jobs.

They had opened a black attaché case on the desk in the back room, Without making a point of sticking my nose into it, I could see jewellery – rings and earrings and neck chains – some US Savings Bonds, plastic bags of coins like from a collection, a bunch of nude photographs of a man, and a man's wig.

Also in the case were sets of handcuffs of the type you can buy in a police supply house, several New York Police Department badges they probably stole someplace, and four handguns.

"We posed as cops to get in," Patsy said. "Tell him about the priest."

Sonny said, "I was in the getaway car across the street from the house, with the motor running. I happened to be in front of a church. I'm sitting there waiting for the guys to come out, and this priest comes walking by. And he stops to chat! 'Isn't it a lovely day,' this priest is saying to me. And he goes on about it. I can't get rid of him. I don't know how the guys are gonna come out of the house, running or what, and this priest is telling me about the birds and the sky. I couldn't leave. Finally he said goodbye and walked away. I could still see him when the guys came out."

Jilly handed me a small bunch of things. "Get rid of this junk, will you? Toss it in a dumpster in Manhattan when you go back."

It was stuff from the robbery they didn't want, and didn't want found in the neighbourhood: a pink purse, a brooch and matching earrings, the nude photos, a US passport.

What I wanted was the guns. They were stolen property that we could trace back to the score and tie Jilly's crew to it. And we always wanted to get guns off the street.

"If you want to move those guns," I said to Jilly, "I got a guy that I sold a few guns to from my burglaries, so maybe he'd be interested in these."

"We should get $300 apiece for them," he said.

"I'll see what I can do."

He gave me the guns: a Smith & Wesson .45; a Smith & Wesson .357 Highway Patrolman; a Rohm .38 Special revolver; a Ruger .22 automatic. Whatever else the owner was, he was not a legitimate guy. Two of the guns had the serial numbers filed off. They were stolen guns before Jilly's guys got ahold of them. Generally, filing the numbers off doesn't cause us too much of a problem. Most of the time the thieves don't file deep enough to remove all evidence from the stamping process. Our laboratory guys can bring the numbers back up with acid.

The next day I put them in a paper bag and walked over to Central Park at Ninetieth St. My contact agent, Steve Bursey, was waiting for me. I handed him the bag. We decided we would try to get by with offering Jilly $800 for the guns. You never give them all that they ask in a deal. First, it's government money, and we don't want to throw out more than we have to. Second, you want to let them know that you're hard-nosed and not a mark.

The next day I went back to the club and told them that my man offered me $800.

"That's not enough," Patsy said. "You said you could get twelve hundred bucks."

"I said I'd try," I said. "The guy is firm at eight hundred."

"No good."

With some deals I would have just said okay and given the stuff back. But not with the guns. I didn't want to give the guns back. "Look, I got the guns, I got eight hundred on me. You want it or you don't." I tossed the money down on the desk, trusting to their greed when they saw the green. There was some squabbling.

"We could have got more somewhere else," Patsy said.

"Hey, if you can get more, take the fucking guns and bring them somewhere else. But who's gonna give you more than two hundred apiece for guns that are probably registered and have been stolen and the numbers filed off? You think I didn't push for all I could get? There's eight hundred of my own money. You want the deal, I'll just collect from him."

"Okay," Jilly said. He picked the money up and gave $100 each to Guido, Frankie, and Patsy as their share, and $100 to me for peddling the guns. I handed in my $100 to Agent Bursey. So the guns cost the FBI $700.

Guido was bitching about a bunch of people that had recently been made in the Colombo family. He mentioned both Allie Boy Persico and Jerry Lang. Allie Boy was Alphonse Persico, the son of Carmine "The Snake" Persico – sometimes referred to as junior – who was the boss of the Colombo family. Jerry Lang was Gennaro Langella, who some years later would become underboss of the Colombo family and acting boss when Carmine The Snake went to prison.

"I've done more work than half the guys that were made," Guido said, meaning that he had been in on more hits, which is one of the prime considerations in getting made, "and I ain't got my badge. That kid Allie Boy is just a wiseass punk. He never did a bit of work to earn his badge. The only reason he got made is because his old man is boss."

"You better shut up," Jilly said. "People walking in and out of the store all the time, we don't know who hears what. We're gonna be history from that kind of talk about the boss's son."

I was standing outside Lefty Ruggiero's social club on Madison Street in Little Italy when Tony Mirra came by and told me to drive him to Brooklyn.

That set off an alarm in my gut. Although it was known that I was moving between crews of two different families, that kind of freewheeling eventually draws suspicion. Pretty soon, if you don't commit to somebody, they think you can't be trusted. Suddenly Mirra, a Bonanno guy and a mean bastard, wants me to go with him to Brooklyn where I have been hanging out with Colombo guys. Was he taking me there for some kind of confrontation?

In the car Mirra said he had an appointment with The Snake. Recollections came rushing into my head. The guy in Jilly's that I recognized as somebody I had once arrested – had he known me, after all? Guido's remarks about Allie Boy Persico – had those remarks about his son gotten back to The Snake? The recollections didn't make me feel good. Was I going to be grilled about Jilly's crew, things I had heard, what I was doing there?

If The Snake had heard about the complaints, was I going to be pressured to rat out the people doing the complaining? If I were pressured for information, would it be some kind of test?

My mind was racing as we crossed over the Brooklyn Bridge. I tried to sort out the possibilities and options. I definitely would not rat anybody out. That was for sure. If I turned rat on anybody to save my own skin, I would have to pull out of the operation, anyway, because my credibility would be blown. So if I was pressured to rat anybody out, I would just take the heat and see what happened. If they were testing my reliability, I would pass the test, and that would put me in solid.

Unless, of course, they really wanted me to talk, and decided to hit me if I didn't. They could whack me out over there and dump me in the Gowanus Canal where I wouldn't be found until I was unrecognizable. Nobody would know.

Mirra was silent. We drove to Third Avenue and Carroll Street in the Park Slope section of Brooklyn, not far from Prospect Park. We parked and waited. Carmine Persico drove up in a white Rolls-Royce convertible with New Jersey plates – 444-FLA. I recognized him from pictures. A sturdy guy in his middle forties, with thinning hair, a long neck, baggy eyes, and a fleshy nose and mouth. He and a much younger man, maybe in his early twenties, got out of the Rolls and talked to Mirra for a few minutes.

When Mirra got back in the car, he said, "That was his son with him, Allie Boy. He just got straightened out."

"Straightened out" means made. I didn't say anything. "Tommy LaBella's supposed to be the Colombo boss," Mirra said, "but that's in name only, because he's so old and sick. The Snake is the real boss. I had to talk to him about a shylock business we're trying to put together with him."

A shylock business between the Bonanno and Colombo families was all it was. I was so primed, I actually felt a letdown. Given the options, I'll take a letdown.

You could never relax with these guys, because you never knew what would be heavy-duty and what would be light.

       ★   ★   ★

By midsummer of 1977, we had enough information on hijackings, burglaries, and robberies to bust up Jilly's crew any day in the week. But I wasn't moving up. I was making more inroads with Mirra and Ruggiero and the wiseguys in Little Italy than I was with the fences in Brooklyn.

I began to think, instead or concentrating on fences, what about a direct shot at the Mafia?

I brought this up in a telephone conversation with my supervisor, Guy Berada. It intrigued us both. We even risked a rare meeting in person, for lunch at a Third Avenue Manhattan restaurant called Cockeyed Clams, near my apartment.

We re-evaluated our goals. The more we thought about it, the more we thought, if I get hooked up with a fence, that's all I'm hooked up with. But the Mafia had a structure and hierarchy; if I could get hooked up with wiseguys, I had a chance at a significant penetration of the Mob itself.

It would mean a greater commitment from the Bureau, an increase in risks and pressures. So far as we knew, the FBI had never planted one of its own agents in the Mafia.

Finally the opportunities outweighed all other considerations. It was worth a shot to abandon the fence operation in Brooklyn and "go downtown", throw in with the wiseguys in Little Italy.

I would continue to operate alone, without surveillance. Little Italy is a tight neighbourhood, like a separate world. You couldn't park a van with one-way glass on a street down there without getting made in five minutes. I would continue to operate without using hidden tape recorders or transmitters because I was still new, and there was always the danger of getting patted down. The Bureau had informants in Little Italy. They wouldn't know who I was, I wouldn't know who they were. I didn't want to risk acting different around somebody because I knew he was an informant, or having somebody act different around me.

Having made the decision, I couldn't just abruptly drop out of the Brooklyn scene. I still had to use the Brooklyn guys as backup for credibility. In all likelihood, sooner or later the downtown guy would check me out with the Brooklyn crew, and I didn't want any of Jilly's guys to say I just disappeared one day. I wanted to ease out gradually.

I hung out more and more with Mirra and Ruggiero, less and less with Jilly's crew. Gradually it got to where I was just phoning in to Jilly once in a while. By August I was full-time around Little Italy.

Jilly stayed loyal. Agents routinely show up to talk to wiseguys like Jilly, show pictures of people they're interested in, see if you have anything to say, let you know they're keeping tabs on you. One such time, agents came out to talk to him. They showed him several pictures, including a picture of me. These agents didn't know who I really was. They told him that I was a jewel thief and burglar, that they had information that I was hanging out around there, and they wanted to know what he knew about me.

Jilly wouldn't acknowledge whether he knew me or not. Even though I wasn't around there anymore; he wouldn't give up anything about me.

Two years later Jilly got whacked. He was driving his car near his apartment. He stopped for a red light and some guy on a motorcycle pulled up beside him and pumped a couple of .38 slugs into him. It was a regular Mob hit. Our information was that they thought Jilly was talking. But he wasn't.

Underboss

Sammy Gravano

The name of Sammy "The Bull" Gravano came to public attention during the trial of John Gotti in 1992. Gravano had been Gotti's underboss in the Gambino family and had turned state's evidence against his boss. As a result of Gravano's testimony, Gotti was convicted of thirteen counts of murder, along with conspiracy to commit murder, racketeering, illegal gambling, loan-sharking, obstruction of justice and tax evasion. Gotti died in jail in 2002. Ironically, Gravano, a career criminal, himself admitted nineteen murders.

Born in Bensonhurst in 1945, Salvatore Gravano did not do well at school. He suffered from what was later diagnosed as dyslexia. By the time he left school at the age of sixteen, the one thing he had learnt was to assert himself through violence. He began stealing at the age of eight. By thirteen, he had joined the local street gang, the Rampers. He came to the attention of the local mafiosi through his fighting ability and they nicknamed him "The Bull". He was soon in debt to them when they arranged for the return of a stolen bike.

After a period in the Army, he married Debra Scibetta, whose brother he arranged to have killed seven years later. He quickly graduated through larceny, hijacking and armed robbery, and made contacts in the Colombo Family. After Gravano murdered Joe Colucci, Joe Colombo indicated that he would become a made man as soon as the Cosa Nostra's membership book opened again – it had been closed since 1957.

By then, Gravano had fallen out with the family of his sponsor Tommy Spero and switched his affiliation to the Gambino Family. Under the wing of long-time capo *Salvatore "Toddo" Aurello, Gravano went into the construction industry, extracting huge kickbacks for every ton of concrete poured. He also took up boxing and bodybuilding, allegedly consuming large amounts of steroids which resulted in a short temper and a tendency to kill on a whim. Paul Castellano, head of the Gambino family, had to discipline him several times for murdering other made men without permission.*

Eventually, Gravano fell in with John Gotti, an ambitious Gambino captain in Queens. Together they planned the assassination of Paul Castellano and his underboss Thomas Bilotti. This was done against the rules without reference to the Commission. In retaliation the Genovese and Lucchese crime families set out to murder Gotti. However, the car bomb intended for Gotti killed his underboss Frank DeCicco instead. Gotti was soon arrested on racketeering charges, leaving Gravano and Angelo Ruggerio to run the Family, while he called the shots from prison. Gravano and Ruggerio fell out, while Gravano went on an unauthorized killing spree, even murdering his own men. However, Ruggerio fell from favour when he was indicted for distributing heroin on the evidence of Federal wiretaps. He died of cancer soon after.

Gravano was appointed consigliere. *When Louie Milito, a friend of Gravano's since his days in the Rampers, objected, he was killed. He also set up Tommy Spero and* capo *DiBernardo. Even though Gravano had been promoted* consigliere *then underboss, Gotti still used him as an assassin, even having him drive the getaway car on one occasion.*

When Gotti was tried for assault and racketeering in 1986, Gravano paid a juror to find him not guilty. Gotti then earned the nickname "the Teflon Don". The newspapers were also calling him the "Dapper Don" because of his sharp suits, hand-painted ties and expensive haircuts. Members of the Gambino family began to worry that he was attracting too much attention to their activities, particularly as he very publicly held court in the Ravenite Social Club in Manhattan's Little Italy.

On 11 December 1990, FBI agents and New York City detectives raided the club and arrested Gravano, Gotti, Gotti's new consigliere Frank LoCascio and Thomas Gambino. The FBI has wiretaps of Gotti denigrating Gravano, accusing him of creating a "family within a family". It seemed to Gravano that Gotti was going to make out that Gravano was a crazed killer who he had tried to restrain. This impression was reinforced when Gotti told Gravano that he was not to speak to his lawyers unless he was present.

Gravano then turned state's evidence in exchange for a reduced sentence. Gotti was sentenced to life without possibility of parole. Gravano was sentenced to twenty years, but was soon released into the Witness Protection Programme. He left that to relocate to Arizona. There, through his son, he got involved with a white supremacist gang known as the Devil Dogs and began trafficking ecstasy. He was arrested and sentenced to nineteen years in Arizona state prison. More murder allegations were made against him by Richard Kuklinski. But the "Ice Man" died before the case came to trial. Meanwhile Gravano sat down with the author Peter Maas to write Underboss, where they described in detail the art of the Mob hit.

On 19 September 1980, the body of reputed high-ranking member of the Philadelphia family named John (Johnny Keys) Simone was discovered in a secluded, wooded area in Staten Island with a gaping gunshot wound in the back of his head. It was not the first time a body had turned up in Staten Island that was the obvious result of a Mob execution. The mystery was what Simone's body was doing so far from home and why the body was without shoes.

Sammy had the answers.

For decades, the Philadelphia family had been a model of stability, first under Joseph Ida and then the boss who succeeded him, Angelo Bruno. Carlo Gambino and Bruno had been very close. Both had become bosses at approximately the same time and both had seats on the Cosa Nostra Commission. So close was the Gambino/Bruno friendship that the Philadelphia vote on Commission matters was usually sent in via the Gambino family and almost inevitably took the same side. After Don Carlo's death, Paul Castellano continued this relationship. FBI surveillance observed him dining with Bruno in New York as well as in Philadelphia.

Mob dynamics in Philadelphia changed with the emergence of legalized casino gambling in neighbouring Atlantic City. Bruno, wealthy, getting on in years and fearing the federal attention it would bring him, had little interest in Atlantic City. This not only caused unrest in the family but it created a vacuum – the plum of construction deals, of moving in on union organizing, gambling junkets and casino service operations – that especially attracted the Genovese family.

Bruno was shot to death in March 1980. "For the record," Sammy said, "the Genovese family had manipulated a Philadelphia family member, Tony Bananas, to murder Bruno. Then they sacrificed this Tony Bananas. Right away, there was a Commission meeting, and to cover themselves the Genovese people volunteered to track down Angelo Bruno's killer. And soon after, Tony Bananas was found in the trunk of a car."

But peace never returned to Philadelphia. The anarchy was such that Bruno's successor as boss, Phil Testa, was blown apart by a remote-control bomb, packed with roofing nails, that had been placed under his front porch; a method of assassination strictly forbidden under Cosa Nostra rules.

The continuing battle for control of the family pitted the family *consigliere,* Nicky Scarfo, against another faction now being led by a powerful *capo,* John Simone.

Sammy's involvement in the hit on Simone began with a completely unrelated event. "It just shows you," Sammy said, "the reality of an all-out mob, any mob, war, how complicated it gets, all the twists and turns, all the plotting and deception driven by greed and the quest for power, all the murders!"

For Sammy, it began when Toddo Aurello said: "Take a ride with me up by Paul's." Two aging members of Aurello's crew, Nicky Russo and "Pal Joey", operated in New Jersey. "Toddo told Paul that this Nick Russo's son was killed in some dispute by a Frankie Steele, who headed up a powerful Irish gang over there. Russo naturally wanted to avenge his son's murder. One night down around Philadelphia, he comes on Steele, who is alone in a car. He took a shot at Steele and misses. Steele comes back at him and shoots Russo in the leg. When Steele moves in to finish him off, his gun jams. He starts beating Russo on the head with it. He's gonna beat him to death. Somehow Russo manages to get in another shot and hits Steele in the stomach. Steele took off and Russo is still alive by the skin of his teeth.

"Toddo told Paul that Russo and Pal Joey are old guys. They can't win. They are outnumbered, outgunned and out-everything. They need help.

"Paul listens and says, 'All right.' He looks at me and says, 'Sammy, you want to go on this?' I said, 'Of course, Paul, whatever you want.' He tells me to choose anybody I need. Paul said, 'Whack him out and anybody in his gang who gets in the way.'

"I go down to Jersey and meet with Nicky Russo. But Steele wasn't stupid. He wasn't making it easy to find him. I knew he'd been shot and I had all the Philadelphia-area hospitals checked out to help get an address. But there was no record of any hospital admissions. Then I found out that he had made a visit to an undertaker to remove Russo's bullet. Jesus, I thought, this guy has balls. But the most important thing I found out was that some made guys in the Philadelphia family got him to the undertaker. Steele is hanging out with them. This changed everything. If and when I find him and start shooting, suppose he's with a wiseguy? I won't know who's who. I could take some made guys out and this could cause big trouble.

"I report this to Paul and he agrees. In the Philadelphia war, Paul has sided with Nicky Scarfo. He tells me to notify Scarfo of what was going on. I explained the situation to Nicky Scarfo and he says, 'Sammy, let me do this. Tell Paul I'll take care of the problem.' And he does.

"This still don't satisfy Nicky Russo. He says that Steele had a baby son, or a baby brother, I forget which, and he wants the kid killed, like they do in the old country. I told him, 'You got to go back to Paul on this one. I am not killing a baby. I don't give a fuck about what they do in Italy or any of them antique bullshit ways they have there. Not only am I against it, I'm not doing it, period. I ain't killing no kid.'

"When Paul is told about this, he becomes real irritated with Russo. He tells him that it's over with, Steele, the guy who killed his son, is gone. Enough is enough. Case closed.

"I figure that's it. I go back to my business. But before I know it, I'm up to see Paul about some construction stuff. He is fuming. The veins in his neck are popping out. His face is as red as a pepper. He's just been to a meeting of the Commission, which has already voted to back Nicky Scarfo in Philadelphia, and he's told that Scarfo is protesting that his main competition, that this Johnny Keys – John Simone – had been seen huddling with a made member of the Gambino family over in Jersey. And who is it but Nicky Russo and Pal Joey. Scarfo assumed the worst. The Gambino family is secretly supporting a bid for power by Johnny Keys. Talk about how being in Cosa Nostra distrust breeds distrust!

"It's a major, major embarrassment for Paul. The Commission sanctioned a hit on Johnny Keys and gave the contract to the Gambino family.

"Paul wants to see Russo. Toddo and me bring him to Paul's estate. We're out by the Olympic-size swimming pool he has in back. Russo saves his life by convincing him that his meetings with Johnny Keys was innocent. He said they had been friends for a hundred years. He swears that anything they had to do with each other was purely social. No family business was ever discussed.

"Now, deception is at the core of a clean Mob hit. It's absolutely essential. It knows no bounds. And Paul has learned that Johnny Keys had reached out to an old friend, the boss of the Cleveland family, for support. But the old friend betrays him and reports the overture to the Commission. The Cleveland boss is advised to pass the word to Keys that Paul was interested in being on his side against the Scarfo faction.

"Paul is still fuming. He looks directly at me. It's like Toddo is hardly there. He says, 'Sammy, you're in charge. I want this done right.' I should use Louie Milito and whoever else I wanted.

"He told Russo to go back and to repeat to Johnny Keys what the Cleveland boss said, that Paul is looking for ways to help him. But he is going to have to deal with an emissary straight from Paul. Russo is to cite his advanced age and that his memory isn't as sharp as it was. Russo is old. He has to have a cane to get around because of that bullet from Steele. Paul wants a younger set of ears and a mind that remembers everything. So he's sending a newly made member, not especially ballsy but a good talker and listener and a good relayer of messages. The name of the go-between is Sammy Gravano.

"Russo will do this to perfection. But right then he's dying to get this Keys hit over and done with as quickly as possible. His meeting with Paul has left him nervous and flustered. Getting the hit done will prove his innocence.

"Russo says to me that he can set it up right away. His plan was going to be very simple. Him and Pal Joey meet with Johnny Keys a lot at this ice cream place in south Jersey called Friendly's. They always sat in the same booth in the back. Now Keys don't know me and he don't know Louie. The idea is that the two of them will be waiting in a rear booth where they usually are, and I'll be sitting near the front door at one of the fountain stools with my .357 magnum. Louie will be in a booth halfway between where I am and they are.

"They'll wave to Keys when he comes in. That will be my signal. As he walks by me, I get up. I follow him and shoot him as he's walking towards Russo and Pal Joey. Then Louie Milito will jump up, take out a sawed-off shotgun he has hidden under his coat, fire a couple of shots in the ceiling and yell at everybody in there to hit the floor. And Louie and me would stroll out to a waiting getaway car.

"It sounded good, but you never know. I wanted to check this out from every angle. 'Let's do a dry run,' I said.

"The minute I was in this Friendly's, I saw it would be a disaster, it wasn't doable. There was a whole bunch of people in there. Families. And lots of kids. There was no way I was going to jeopardize them. And I'm not going to shoot the guy in front of a bunch of kids. I told Russo the plan was nuts.

"The first meeting between myself and Johnny Keys took place right after that. It was at a luncheonette in the Trenton area. He was ecstatic to be with Paul Castellano's messenger. I was treated to an in-depth recital of all the events preceding, surrounding and after Angelo Bruno was murdered. He was direct. He wanted Paul's approval in his quest to gain control of the Philadelphia family.

"He talked to me alone in the luncheonette. But I saw that he arrived with bodyguards, who stayed outside. He apologized for this and said he hoped that I wouldn't take any offence. He apologized for frisking me, but there was a war going on and he had to take precautions. He apologized again for being armed himself and showed me his gun.

"I could see he desperately wanted to believe that I was Paul Castellano's eyes, ears and mouth. But it was obvious he was also careful and shrewd. And I wasn't careless, either. I didn't have a gun on me. I didn't know what to expect at this first meeting, but I did know I wasn't going to hit him then. When he was sure I was unarmed, he visibly eased. We talked some more. I told him that we should plan another meeting after I reported back his messages to Paul.

"There had to be another meeting if I was to lull him into a complete sense of security. When I left that first one, I told Louie Milito and Stymie, who I also picked for the hit, that this guy was very sharp. We are going to have a tough time here.

"The next meeting was at a very public bar and restaurant in Jersey. He followed the same security procedures and searches as he did the first time. Of course, I was unarmed. He came with bodyguards. This meeting was to put the icing on the plan's cake. So I brought him welcome news. I looked him straight in the eye and told him that Paul Castellano has decided to back his bid to take over the Philadelphia family. I really laid it on thick. I said that the Gambino family support was not limited to moral support. Paul's pledge of support included money, guns and Gambino family shooters.

"Johnny Keys was, like, delirious. He got almost speechless as I went on to tell him that Paul Castellano was going to get the Commission's backing for him once Nicky Scarfo was dead. I was on such a roll that I couldn't stop. I had more good news. I told him to think of a real secure place for another meeting because Paul Castellano wanted a once-only face-to-face meeting with him. At this meeting, Paul would confirm everything I had just related.

"I watched Johnny Keys as he tried to come up with a suitable place. Suddenly his face lit up. He announced that he had the perfect place. It was a country club he belonged to around Yardville, near Trenton, just off the turnpike from New York. Nobody there would recognize Big Paul. I told him that sounded good. I would get back to him.

"Nick Russo was against the country club. He knew where it was. He thought it was too public, plus he warned me about the club's own security staff. I made Nicky Russo take me there, so I could check the place. I argued the other way. The site was good because Johnny Keys would be comfortable there. He had picked it himself. He would drop his guard completely. I contacted him and said the country club would be fine. But I told him he couldn't have his goons around him when he was meeting with Paul Castellano.

"According to the arrangements made amongst us all, me and Nicky Russo and Pal Joey met with Keys in

Yardville before going on to the club. The three of us did not have guns, but I had hidden one deep under the front passenger seat of the car we were in. Keys joined us. Pal Joey was doing the driving. I was up front with him. Keys got in the back with Russo. He went through his usual litany of apologizing because he was armed. He was concerned about Paul's reaction. I soothed him by saying that Paul understood a war was going on. Once again, he apologized for having to frisk us, which he did, patting us down. But I could see that he didn't have no bodyguards with him. Nobody was tailing us.

"This country club had a big parking lot. The clubhouse was some distance away. As we pulled into a parking space, I saw the van parked between us and the clubhouse. In that van I had Louie Milito and Stymie. My crew was in place. As we got out of the car, I looked at my watch and told Keys that Paul should be arriving any minute. I was still unarmed. I hadn't got the chance to grab my hidden gun.

"We walked towards the clubhouse, taking a path that would lead us past the van. We walked in pairs. I was with Keys. Pal Joey and Russo were ahead of us. It looked like nothing appeared out of the ordinary to Keys. But he was keeping his hand on the butt of the gun that was under his coat. And he kept looking around. As we got to the van, he turned his head towards it. Something had attracted his attention. I had slowed down, so I was a half a step behind him. All of a sudden, he said, 'Hey, Sammy, that van's engine is running.'

"He looked back at me, concerned. I leaped right at him and wrapped him in a bear hug. I had caught him by surprise. He didn't have time to react. I was holding him so tight that he couldn't move his arms. For sure, I didn't want him bringing up his gun.

*   *   *

"All this was happening real quick. But in my mind, it was like slow motion. I felt a tremendous surge of power and confidence. This was going to work. The van's side door opened and Louie and Stymie came out and the two of them grabbed Keys' legs. We all lifted together and Keys was in the van. Out of the corner of my eye, I saw a few people on a putting green looking at us kind of curious, like they were wondering what was going on. But it was over so fast; they didn't know what was going on.

"Now my mind wasn't in slow motion. Keys was on the van's floor. It wasn't graceful. I was still holding on to him. Stymie was on top of me, holding down both me and Keys. It was like the three of us were one person. Louie gets in the driver's seat. Pal Joey is next to him.

"I yell to Stymie that Keys is still trying for his gun. Stymie pried his thumb from the butt. He nearly broke it and we got the gun. Louie takes off. The van jumps the parking lot kerb, goes right over part of the club's lawn and out on to the street. Nicky Russo is left behind to bring back the car we came in.

"When we finished tying Keys up with heavy plastic ties, I was feeling pretty smug. Everything looked like it was working according to plan. The original idea was to kill Johnny Keys at an isolated spot near the club. Then Pal Joey reached into his pocket and realized that he still has the keys to the car Russo was supposed to drive away. The car is stranded in the lot and the gun I had hidden was in it. I knew that bystanders had seen our moves, so there were potential witnesses. We had to get Russo and the car out of there.

"I had Louie stop the van. We let Pal Joey out. I gave him specific instructions. He was to make his way back to the country club as best he could, meet up with Russo and get the car out of the lot. They should go to Russo's home and wait for a call from me to determine if everything was clean and there weren't any problems that would cause more changes in the plan.

"After Pal Joey left the van, we got on the turnpike and headed for Staten Island. Along the way, Johnny started having some sort of seizure. He claimed he was having a heart attack. I had to bend close to him to hear him whisper to reach into his jacket pocket for his nitroglycerine pills. He begged me to put a pill in his mouth. 'Don't let me die from a heart attack,' he said. He knows we're going to kill him and he is saying something like this? That's when I realized that we were dealing with a real man's man here!

"His stature got even bigger in my eyes when we got to the toll plaza at the exit for Staten Island. I naturally assumed that he would start some sort of commotion to get the attention of the tollbooth cops, to try and save himself. I was convinced of this. I whispered to Stymie to be prepared in case Keys tried to pull something. But I was wrong. Johnny didn't try a thing. He didn't refuse to try and help himself because he had given up all hope. It was because he was true Cosa Nostra. This was a family matter. There would be no police.

"We get to Staten Island without incident. We drove to a gas station that some guys with Louie Milito own. We lay over there. The hours go by. I'm calling Russo's house. I'm not getting an answer. I got to know that they got away. Because if they're pinched, they'll be pinched for murder if I kill Keys. He ain't dead yet and I would have gone to Paul and said, 'Things got fucked up. Guys have got pinched. It's your decision what to do now.'

"It was the longest wait in that gas station – I don't know, ten, twelve hours. Johnny Keys don't know what's delaying things. He figures he's been kidnapped to be killed. As a cover, I explain that a decision was being made by the bosses about whether he is to live or die. Each time I left the van to telephone the Russo home, I told him I was phoning the bosses to see if a decision had been reached.

"Johnny Keys was a cousin of Angelo Bruno. During that long wait, he lashed out against the Genovese family. He blamed it for all of the troubles the Philadelphia family had gone through, the war that was raging, all the troubles that not only came to him but to the whole family. How he now knows it was the greed of the Genovese people that caused this. How the Chin – Vincent Gigante – had conned this Tony Bananas that the Commission sanctioned the hit on Bruno. How the Chin conned the Commission by volunteering to do an investigation and taking out Tony. It was brutal the way Tony went, shot in the arms and the elbows first. You could feel Johnny's hatred as he talked about how this life we led was being poisoned. How many more good people would die? But there in that van he continued to act like a man.

"He asked that, if he lost with the bosses and was sentenced to die, that a made guy do it. He said he always promised himself and his wife that he would die with his shoes off. If the decision came against him, would I take them off? 'Of course,' I said. I never asked him what the reason was. The more we talked, the more impressed I was. I really respected him.

"When I sent Louie and Stymie out for food and coffee, he tells us to hold the sugar for him! Afterwards, I heard a noise outside the van. I drew my gun. Maybe a cop was nosing around, checking out the van that was parked there so long. He must have guessed what I was thinking. He whispered, 'If it's a cop, shoot him before you shoot me.' His resolve shook me up. It was like at the tollbooth. There would be no police involved in family business. But it wasn't a cop. It was Louie and Stymie coming back from the food and coffee run.

"Louie and Stymie told me later that during one of the times I was trying to phone Russo, Johnny said to them he underestimated me all along. He said this was the first time in his life that he was caught unawares of a plan hatching around him. I'd completely sucked him in. He told them that he'd been responsible for about fifty hits himself, but that Sammy did the best piece of work setting this up he ever saw.

"I finally did make contact with Nicky Russo. Him and Pal Joey were safe. I told them where we were and to come. I was outside the van when they showed up. They said there was a lot of confusion back at the country club. Nobody was exactly sure what happened. Pal Joey was able to return and drive Russo away without any problems.

"This was bad news for Johnny Keys. I went back into the van and told him that the 'decision' had come back against him. He had lost. He had to go. Like the man he was, the man I had come to understand him to be, the man I had learned to respect over the past hours, he accepted this without comment. Me and Stymie and Louie – none of us – were happy with what was to come. I felt terrible that a man with such balls had to be hit. But this was Cosa Nostra. The boss of my family had ordered it. The entire Commission ordered it. There was nothing else I could do.

"We drove to a section of Staten Island that had a back road running along a wooded area. We stopped the van. I remembered his request about his shoes. I took them off.

"Pal Joey went to grab him and pull him out. He kicked out at Joey right in the chest. He said, 'I'll walk out on my own. Let me die like a man.' He took five or six steps away from the van. Without a word, he lowered his head, quiet and dignified.

"I nodded at Louie Milito. As requested by Johnny Keys, he would be killed by a made member. Louie put a .357 magnum to the back of Johnny's head and fired. The shot immediately levelled him to the ground. He died instantly. He died without pain. He died with dignity. He died Cosa Nostra.

"I sent Russo and Pal Joey back to Jersey. Louie, Stymie and me drove away in the van. There was total silence in that van. Nobody spoke a word.

"The next morning it was all over the news that John Simone's body was found by two sanitation workers.

"I went to see Paul Castellano. He knew that the original plan was for the hit to be down in Jersey. I told him why it had to be changed. I explained everything that happened.

"Paul smiled and put his arm around my shoulder. He said he was proud of Sammy the Bull.

"I had to tell Paul that I was literally sick about this. We had just killed a guy who was the epitome, in my opinion, of our life, everything we were supposed to be. I looked Paul straight in the eye. 'This is one hit I'm never going to be proud of,' I said."

Gravano also detailed the planning of the audacious assassination of Gambino Family Boss Paul Castellano. It was to take place in broad daylight in rush hour in the middle of a busy street in midtown Manhattan outside Sparks Steak House on 46th Street between Second and Third Avenue.

"The more we thought about it, the better it looked," Sammy said. "We concluded that nine days before Christmas, around five to six o'clock at night, in the middle of Manhattan, in the middle of the rush hour, in the middle of the crush of all them shoppers buying presents, there would be literally thousands of people on the street, hurrying this way and that. The hit would only take a few seconds, and the confusion would be in our favour. Nobody would be expecting anything like this, least of all Paul. And being able to disappear afterwards in the crowds would be in our favour. So we decide this is when and where it's going to happen.

"The day before, we have a meeting in the basement of my office on Stillwell Avenue. John comes down with Angelo and the entire hit team. John is supplying them, because it's basically his problem. If everything gets fucked-up and the team is killed, whatever it may be, why should we take down our own guys, put them at risk?

"Frankie DeCicco comes down with Joe Watts. Altogether, there are eleven of us. There are the four shooters, all from John's crew. Only one of them, John Carneglia, is a made guy. They'll be waiting for Paul at the front door to Sparks. Another guy with John, Tony Roach Rampino, will be a backup right across the street from Sparks. Sparks is on East 46th Street between Third and Second Avenue, closer to Third. Up the street towards Second as backups will be Angie, Joe Watts and another associate with John, Iggy Alogna. John and me 'Will be in a car on the other side of Third Avenue. If it comes down to it, I'll be the backup at that end.' So we had Sparks Steak House sandwiched in.

"John, Angie, me, Frankie and Joe Watts know who's going to be hit. John just says to everybody else that there's gonna be two guys killed. He says he ain't saying who they are yet, but it's a huge hit. John tells them that no matter what, don't run, even if there are cops around. These two guys have got to go. 'Don't worry about the cops, he says, 'because if you run and these guys ain't dead, we'll kill you.' "

"The following afternoon everyone except DeCicco gathered in a park on Manhattan's Lower East Side. Frankie will be inside Sparks making sure that Jimmy Brown and Danny Marino – all the people there for the meeting with Paul – don't do anything.

"Joe Watts drove me to the park. The shooters were there. The four of them wore long white trench coats and black fur Russian hats. You couldn't tell one guy from the other.

I don't know whose idea that was. I guess John's. But I thought it was brilliant. Nobody would pay any attention to them. I mean, in New York you could practically walk down the street naked and nobody would notice. Besides, Sparks was only a couple of blocks from the United Nations. You saw all kinds of different clothes. But the big thing would be confusing the witnesses. 'Well, what was their weight, their height?' 'I dunno.' 'What did they look like?' 'I dunno, they all looked alike.' And these would be people who don't even know what was going on, who weren't prepared for it. All they would remember were the outfits.

"Walkie-talkies were handed out so we could communicate with one another. Then John told everybody that it was Paul and Tommy Bilotti who were going. We went over real quick what everybody's position would be. I left the park with John in a Lincoln. He owned a Lincoln, but I don't think this one was his personal car. Frankie had told us that after court, Paul was first going to go to the office of his lawyer, Jimmy LaRossa, so we figured he wouldn't get to Sparks before five o'clock.

"I don't think we said hardly anything on the way uptown. Our minds were on what was going to happen. John pulled the Lincoln in on the northwest corner of Third Avenue and 46th Street. People were swarming all around, just like we thought. I could see the canopy that said Sparks. The shooters in their white coats were already waiting by it. I could see Tony Roach across the street. The other guys up towards Second I couldn't see. The problem was our parking spot on the corner wasn't too good. We were sticking out into the crosswalk. So John said he was driving around the block again. There was the chance that Paul would arrive while we were doing this, but a cop might come over to ticket us the way we were parked and might recognize John. Besides, if it went the way we wanted, we were just observers.

"John circled the block. When we came back, the spot was a little better, and we pulled in again. A couple of minutes later, another Lincoln came up next to us and stopped for the light. The dome light was on in the Lincoln and when I looked into it, I saw Tommy Bilotti and Paul. They were talking to each other. Tommy wasn't three feet away from me. I turned and told John. I got on the walkie-talkie and warned the guys outside Sparks that Paul would be there any second. I reached for my gun. I said to John if Tommy turns towards me, I would start shooting.

" 'No, no,' he said. 'We got our people in place.'

" 'Yeah,' I said, 'but if Tommy sees us, maybe they won't go there.' Just then the light changed, and Tommy pulled up in front of Sparks. I didn't see Paul getting out, only the white coats moving towards the Lincoln. But I saw Tommy get out from the driver's side. All of a sudden, he was squatting down, like he was seeing something, which was Paul getting shot. And then I saw a white coat come up behind Tommy, and Tommy went down. The white coat was bending over him. I looked to see if any of the people on the street was doing anything. They weren't.

"John slowly drove across Third Avenue into the block where Sparks was. I looked down at Tommy Bilotti laying in a huge puddle of blood in the street and I said to John, 'He's gone.' I couldn't see Paul. John picked up speed, and we took a right down Second Avenue and headed back to Brooklyn, to Stillwell Avenue. I didn't see any of the shooters or the backup guys.

"We had the radio on, 1010 News, I think. On the way, we heard the report that there was a shooting in midtown Manhattan. And next that one of the victims was the reputed Mob boss Paul Castellano. But I was in such a haze that I don't remember anything else about that ride. If you offered me two million dollars, I couldn't tell you.

"Frankie DeCicco came to my office to meet me and John. He said one of the waiters at Sparks came over to him and Jimmy Brown – Jimmy Failla – and said Paul had been shot. He said Jimmy turned white and told him he could have been in the car with Paul, and Frankie said, 'Don't worry, you wouldn't have been hurt.' And Frankie said when they left the estuarial they ran into Tommy Gambino. Frankie told him that his uncle just got shot and to go back to his car and get the fuck out of there.

"I don't know who shot who. You don't ask. I only heard later from John that one of the shooters, Vinnie Artuso, didn't get a shot off. His gun jammed. Everything else went according to plan. It was, like they say, 'Elementary, my dear Watson.'

"We made an agreement that nobody involved in this from here on out would ever speak to each other about it at any time under any circumstances and wouldn't admit anything to anybody else in our family or in any of the other families."

The manner and place of Castellano's death catapulted him from relatively minor media interest to the sort of coverage reserved for the assassination of a head of state. Not only did the tabloids go all out – "Big Paul, Chauffeur, Take Their Last Ride" – but the *New York Times* featured it on the front page above the fold two days running.

Castellano and Bilotti were each reported to have been shot six times, each also the recipient of a *coup de grâce* to the head.

The city's police commissioner said that according to witnesses it was uncertain whether two or three men had carried out the gangland executions. No one remembered seeing four. What eyewitnesses most recalled was 'that the assassins were wearing identical Russian fur caps and long coats, variously described as either dark- or light-coloured.' They were then seen fleeing on foot toward

Second Avenue. A witness said that one of the gunmen had been holding a walkie-talkie immediately prior to the shootings.

The head of the state's organized crime task force declared that Castellano's violent death would have required the formal approval of the bosses of the other four families in the city.

Bruce Mouw knew better, but he wasn't available for interviews. Sammy owned a quarter interest in Caesar's East, a restaurant on 58th Street off Third Avenue, twelve blocks due north of Sparks.

"We had to have a meeting of the captains in the family," Sammy said. "Frankie DeCicco spoke to me about doing it in Caesar's East. We rushed the meeting. It was a couple of days after Paul went down. After the regular customers cleared out, all the captains met downstairs at a long table. Except Tommy Gambino, who I don't believe we called. The drivers and anybody else that was brought stayed upstairs. The only ones down there who wasn't a captain was Angelo and me. We stayed behind everybody at each side of the table. We had guns. You could say we were there for intimidating purposes. Joe Gallo was at the head of the table. Frankie and John were on each side of him. He was our *consigliere*. With Paul gone and Neil being dead, he was now in official control of the family.

"He was an old-timer, and he's playing this game with the captains. He knew what to say. He knew the ins and outs of Cosa Nostra. He told them that we had no idea who killed Paul. He said he was going to use Frankie and John to help him run the family and to investigate what happened. He told them not to discuss anything with anybody outside our family about the hit and not have any members carry guns or overreact to anything. Anything they heard or found out, they were to report it back through John Gotti or Frankie DeCicco. I think they were all shook-up. They knew we probably did it, but they didn't know for sure and they could see Joe Gallo was not saying, 'Arm yourselves and get ready for war.' He was communicating that they would be all right. Nobody was in trouble. Nobody was going to get hurt. We're going to have an investigation.

"Officially, this is how we went to the other families. We told them we didn't know what happened with Paul, but our family was intact. We weren't in a position that a war would break out. We had no internal trouble. And we didn't want anybody to get involved in our problems.

"A couple of weeks later, all the captains were called in again. The meeting was held in the recreation room of some big housing project in downtown Manhattan. Somebody knew somebody who gave us access to that room. Joe Gallo reiterates that we still don't know what was going on, we're still investigating. But the time had come to put our family together and vote for a new boss. Everybody has got the drift by now. It's all over the newspapers that John Gotti did the hit. And they can see the closeness of Frankie DeCicco, Sammy the Bull, Joe Piney, Joe Gallo.

"Between themselves, before Paul was hit, Frankie and John have agreed that John will be the boss and Frankie the underboss. At the meeting, Frankie gets up and votes for John Gotti. It zips right around the room. Nobody opposes. It's unanimous. At that point, John announces that Frankie will be his underboss and that Joe Gallo will stay on as *consigliere* of the family. He says he's making Angie Ruggiero the captain of his old crew. Frankie's uncle, Georgie, will replace Frankie.

"Now I'm going to be made an official captain, too. But I don't want it announced there and then. Toddo Aurello was at the meeting, and he knew I was part of this whole move. I want to give respect to Toddo and not have anything like that done while he's sitting there. I went to him afterwards and I told him that if he wanted to stay on as captain of the crew, I would start up a new crew. I said, 'It's completely up to you. Whatever you want,' and he said, 'Sammy, I'm tired. I been using you as acting captain. I'd like to step down.'

"I said, 'OK. You have been like a father to me. I'll take the crew, and you'll be dealing directly with the administration of the family.' 'That'll be great,' he said. He shakes my hand and gives me a kiss and says, 'Be careful.' I set up an appointment with John, Frankie and Toddo, where Toddo asks official permission to step down. They give it, and that same night they make me a *capo*.

"John makes some other moves. He appoints his brother Genie a captain. And he breaks Tony Scotto down from being a captain to a soldier. Scotto had been away for payoffs and tax evasion. I happened to be at Paul's when Tony had recommended Sonny Ciccone to be acting captain to run the dockworkers in his absence. Tony had mixed in with a lot of celebrities – politicians, like that guy running for president, Eugene McCarthy, entertainers, whatever – and John wasn't too fond of him. So he replaced him officially with Sonny.

"Now was the point to see if we were gonna get retaliation from any of the other families. If there would be a war. So we sent out committees to notify them that we had elected a new boss, who our new boss and underboss was, who our new captains were. We said, 'This is our new administration. We're still investigating the Paul situation. There are no problems in our family. We don't want no sanctions against us. And we want our Commission seat.'

"We got recognition from every family, including the Genovese family. Except the Genovese people said that there was a rule broken, that this situation "With Paul had to be put to rest, and someday somebody would have to answer for that, if and when the Commission ever got together again. We said, 'Don't worry. As soon as we find out, we will retaliate. Until then, we're just going to run our family.'

"We had our Commission seat, and from what we thought, it didn't seem like there was going to be any war. There wasn't going to be anything. It had gone up as high as the Commission level and there wasn't any opposition in any way, shape or form. Frankie and me had still been hiding out with guns in a safe house set up by Joe Watts. We were still tight, but after about a month, we started to loosen up somewhat. And then, about three months after this, it happened."

On Sunday, 13 April 1986, like politicians rallying loyal supporters, Gotti and DeCicco planned to visit the Veterans and Friends Club in Bensonhurst, the headquarters of the family's private trash-collecting *capo*, Jimmy Brown Failla. Sammy also would be on hand.

"We're doing our little stops," Sammy said, "gathering power and strength, building momentum. Me and Frankie get there. We have coffee, see the boys, do a little 'Hey, how you doing? Good to see you.' And then John gives a call. He can't make it. He'll meet us in the city. Frankie tells me this. So we plan to go to the city in Frankie's Buick Electra, but we stay for a while doing our thing, talking to the boys.

"Then this guy, Frankie Hearts – Frank Bellino – comes over and asks Frankie DeCicco, 'Hey, do you have a card for that lawyer, Alaroni?' And Frankie says, 'Yeah, I think I got it.' He looks through his wallet; all the other cards he's got in his pocket. But he doesn't have it. He says, 'You know what? It's probably in the fucking car, in the glove compartment.'

"I said, 'Frank, you want me to get it?' And he says, 'No, you'll never find it. There's a lot of shit in there. Come on,' he says to Frankie Hearts, 'I'm sure it's there,' and they both walk out of the club.

'I'm still inside the club. From what I heard later, as they walk across the street, they could see a bag under the car. A paper bag. Frankie DeCicco joked with Frankie Hearts. 'Look at that bag. There's probably a bomb under my car.' He don't think anymore about it. It's an absolute rule in Cosa Nostra that you don't use bombs.

"Frankie DeCicco opens up the door and slides in on the passenger side and he's looking through the glove compartment while Frankie Hearts is standing there. That's when the bomb went off. Frankie Hearts goes flying backwards. The blast blew his shoes off. And his toes.

"When I heard the explosion, I didn't think of a car. It was so fucking powerful, it sounded like a whole building blew up, a boiler or something. I came out of the club, and Frankie's car is in fucking flames. And there's Frankie Hearts with the blood shooting out of his feet.

"I go flying across the street. I saw Frankie DeCicco laying on the ground beside the car. With the fire, it could blow again. I tried to pull him away. I grabbed a leg, but he ain't coming with it. The leg is off. One of his arms is off. His uncle Georgie came running over with another guy, Butterass, and a guy named Oscar. They're trying to help me. I got my hand under him and my hand went right through his body to his stomach. There's no ass. His ass, his balls, *everything*, is completely blown off.

"Just then a police van comes by on patrol. It backs in and they lower the tailgate and we pick Frankie up, holding whatever we can of him together, and put him in the van. Then they got Frankie Hearts and put him in the van and they shoot off for Victory Memorial Hospital.

"I was wearing a white shirt. I looked at my shirt, amazed. There wasn't a drop of blood on it. The force of the blast, the concussion, blew most of the fluids right out

of Frankie's body. He had no blood left in him, nothing, not
an ounce. I told my brother-in-law, Eddie Garafola, who
had tried to help me with Frankie, to get going right away
and go to John's club. I said, 'He's supposed to meet us in
the city, but he's in Queens still. Tell him what happened.'
Then I told him to get all my guys to meet at my place,
Tali's, and to come heavy.

"Everybody who was in the club is out on the street. I
looked over and I thought Danny Marino had the strangest
expression on his face. He's with Jimmy Brown's crew and
him and Jimmy were waiting at Sparks for Paul. But I
thought then that he was just scared. I'm telling them all to
go to Tali's. Jimmy Brown said he'd be at home if I needed
him. Danny Marino said the same thing. A guy named
Paulie, a made guy in the family, comes near me and says,
'What the fuck good are they at home?' That remark never
left me. In my head, I was thinking it was true, who needed
them at home? But I didn't even answer. I was too busy.

"My brother-in-law had come back and said, 'John
wants to see you right now, immediately.' I got in the car
and go to this restaurant in Queens, where John is. He
says, 'Well, we got problems.'

" 'I know,' I said. 'I don't know what the fuck is going
on, but we definitely have problems.' For four months,
since Sparks, we figured it was over. No problems. And
here's Frankie, all at once, blown to bits. I'm still at the
restaurant when one of John's people walked in and said,
'John, Frankie's dead. They said he died on the way to the
hospital.' He was already dead on the street, I thought. He
had nothing left in him.

"John said the only thing was to stay on full alert and
see what comes next, what we could find out. It looked
like there could be a war after all. Our first thought was
the Genovese family. But the Chin was a real stickler for
the rules of our life, and one of the rules was you don't use

bombs. Nobody had pulled off a bombing in New York since the beginning of Cosa Nostra. Would Chin break this kind of rule? Was Frankie fucking some guy's wife that we didn't know about? Maybe greaseballs from Sicily did it. Paul had a lot of connections over there, and in Sicily they bomb all the time.

"When I went back to Tali's, I told everybody to keep their eyes and ears open. Report anything they picked up. But there wasn't anything. Not a peep. Everything stayed quiet. It seemed like whoever was behind this was willing to settle for the satisfaction of taking down Frankie.

"It was only a long, long time afterwards that I found out what happened and that it was Frankie and John they were really after. The 'they' being Gas Pipe Casso from the Lucchese family and Chin Gigante. I was shocked. It goes to show how Cosa Nostra was just one double-cross after another. We had reached out and got Gas Pipe's tacit approval about Paul. Maybe Chin don't know this. But after Paul goes down, Chin grabs Gas Pipe – they had a relationship – and says, 'Well, Paul's out of the picture, let's take out John Gotti and Frankie DeCicco. It'll be a real hit parade.'

"They tell Jimmy Brown and Danny Marino what they're gonna do and that Jimmy and Danny will be appointed by the Commission as a committee to run the Gambino family for Chin. Let me tell you what a stand-up guy Jimmy Brown is. If some black guy walked in and said he just killed Paul Castellano and was the new boss, Jimmy would say, 'Gee, great. What do you want me to do, boss?' So basically the Genovese and Lucchese families would control our family.

"Gas Pipe was a couple of blocks away when the bomb went off.

"The mistake was using a couple of West Side guys, meaning they were associated with the Genovese people. I still don't know who they were or even if they're alive. One of them put the bomb under Frankie's car. The other one was on the remote control. When he sees Frankie come out of the club with Frankie Hearts, he thinks Frankie Hearts was John. Frankie Hearts has kind of the same build as John and the same greyish hair. And he presses the button. *Boom!*

"I got along good with Gas Pipe. I still like him. For him, it was business, a master Cosa Nostra double-cross scheme, nothing personal. The only thing I didn't like was the bomb. I would have more respect for him if he used a gun, according to the rules. I think the bomb was probably a devious Chin idea to make us think the Sicilians done it. I heard when my name came up, Gas Pipe said, 'Forget it. We're not gonna kill Sammy.' That would've been another mistake. If John had been in the car and they put in Jimmy Brown and Marino, I would have killed them both. They were the true betrayers. They knew what was going to happen. And then I would've gone after Gas Pipe and Chin. I don't think I could've won, but I would've fought until my death.

"Besides his toes, Frankie Hearts got mangled up a little. But he survived. That was how I found out what was going on just before the blast. I decided one thing. I used to drive myself. I was getting a driver. Not to say that joke line like in the movies, where the old boss tells his wife, 'Go start the car.' But to never leave my car alone anymore, so nobody can fuck with it."

Born to the Mob

Frankie Saggio

Frankie Saggio was born in the Bensonhurst district of Brooklyn on 7 September 1964. The neighbourhood was home to many Castellammerese. His uncle Philip Giaccone – Philly Lucky – had been born in Ridgewood, Queens, but his mother came from Castellammarese del Golfo. It seems that Giaccone had not wanted to join the Mafia, but he had no choice. His father died in the middle of the Depression, leaving Philly Lucky to provide for his mother and sister. He was recruited by John Bonaventre, who ran most of the local rackets for the Bonanno Family. Philly Lucky got to run all the business coming out of Kennedy Airport. He even got Frankie's father a no-show job at the airport, while Saggio Snr ran his own auto body shop. His father did not get involved in the hold-ups and other criminal activities because he was a haemophiliac and was in and out of hospital having blood transfusions.

From an early age, Frankie would sit out on the stoop of his home and listen to the stories Uncle Philly and other wiseguys would tell him. These men were contemporaries of Al Capone who himself had been born in Brooklyn. After school Frankie would play outside the Italian social clubs on 18th Avenue and watch the gangsters go in and out. And Philly Lucky preached violence. "Frankie," he told the young boy, "*if someone bothers you in school or out on the street, you pick up anything you find – a baseball bat, a brick, a garbage can – and bash their skull in.*"

From the age of seven, his uncle would take him over the East River to have a haircut, a shoeshine and lunch in Little Italy. It was there that Frankie got a detailed education in the ways of the Cosa Nostra. Uncle Philly was steeped in the Mafia ethos. His father-in-law was Carlo Gambino, head of the Gambino crime family. If one of his men turned up at his house with his girlfriend, the door would be shut in his face. He would be told to come with his wife, or not at all.

Frankie was warned never to gamble. The idea was to run the games and never to be a player as the house always wins. Uncle Philly knew what he was talking about. He ran a horse room – an illegal off-track betting shop – and a shylock business, loan-sharking. According to Frankie Saggio, it was his uncle who "taught him the value of a dollar and how to steal it from someone else". Young Frankie also noticed that people were always giving his uncle envelopes, including one, he noted, with 25K written on it.

Uncle Philly was from an era when being in a Mafia family meant being bound by blood and honour, but by the time Frankie was growing up, those days were coming to an end. By the 1970s, their only concern was money. One of the most ruthless and ambitious Mafiosi at the time was Carmine Galante, whose parents had been from Castellammarese del Golfo. Carmine was born in East Harlem. At the age of fourteen he had been arrested for petty theft, quickly graduating to grand larceny, robbery and assault. At nineteen, he was involved in a gun battle in the Williamsburg district of Brooklyn after committing an armed robbery. A six-year-old girl and her mother were injured in the shoot out. Galante was arrested and spent eight years in Sing Sing. When he got out, Galante became a made man after assassinating the Italian labour *activist Carlo Tresca in 1943, possibly on the orders of Vito Genovese, and quickly rose to be an underboss in the Bonanno family.*

Over the next twenty-five years, he worked his way up to becoming the biggest drug supplier on the East Coast. This made him enemies. Frank Costello set him up for a drug bust in 1962. After surviving several assassination attempts, Costello died of natural causes in 1973. Still thirsty for revenge, when Galante was released on parole the following year, he ordered the bombing of Costello's mausoleum, blowing the brass doors off.

By then Joe Bananas had been forced to step down as head of the Bonanno family and Philip "Rusty" Rastelli had taken over. Rastelli then went to jail on Federal racketeering charges. Galante seized the opportunity to take over the Bonanno family. At the same time, he was conducting a vicious gang war against the Gambinos, killing at least eight members of the family. Galante's activities were now inviting the attention of the Federal authorities and the Commission decided that he had to go. This was done in true Mafia style. As Galante lit his trade-mark cigar after dining with his two bodyguards in Joe and Mary's Italian-American restaurant in the Bushwick section of Brooklyn, three men walked in and blasted him in the face and chest with a shotgun. After the bodyguards had been taken care of, they blasted Galante's dead body again to show that no one was bigger than the outfit.

As Philly Lucky had not been involved in the assassination, he had been nominated to take over as boss of the Bonanno family. But Rastelli was not going to be pushed aside. From behind bars, he ordered Giaccone's death. The contract was given to Donnie Brasco, the pseudonym of FBI agent Joseph Pistone who had penetrated the Mob. However, the contract was cancelled when Rastelli loyalist Dominic "Sonny Black" Napolitano suggested that they take care of

Alphonse "Sonny Red" Indelicato and Dominic "Big Trin" Trinchara at the same time.

There was an awkward scene at the wedding of Philly Lucky's daughter Corinne to Peter Clemenza. A number of senior Mafia figures turned up. At the reception afterwards, Uncle Philly wanted the guys who had filmed the wedding to video guests saying a few words about the happy couple. Frankie did not understand, at the time, why Paul Castellano, John Gotti, Sammy "The Bull" Gravano, Carmine Persico, Sonny Napolitano, Joey Massino, Stevie Cannone and Sally Farrugia all pushed the microphones and cameras away. They did not want to be caught on camera wishing the bride and groom a long and happy life. By this time, Frankie was known to one and all as "Little Gangster" and the name "the Gangster" began to turn up in FBI files.

On 5 May 1981, Philip Giaccone was called to a meeting concerning a dispute involving Alphonse Indelicato. Philly Lucky knew that they were using Sonny Red to get to him. He was probably going to his death, but he was loyal to his men and would not let one of them face the music alone.

Giaccone, Indelicato and Trinchera turned up at 20/20 Night Club in Clinton Hill, Brooklyn, where they were met by Gerlando Sciascia who handled the Bonannos' drug operations in Canada. He ushered them through into a storeroom where Joseph Massino and other gunmen were waiting. The bodies were taken to a vacant lot near Ozone Park in Queens where John Gotti and his brother Gene had arranged to have them buried. However, a few weeks later some children found something "green and brown" that smelled awful oozing out of some canvas sacks. Their parents identified the odour as that of rotting flesh. The newspapers reported that the bodies had been accidentally uncovered by heavy rain. Frank Saggio says that nothing concerning the Mob ever happens by accident. He believes that the Mob wanted there to be a funeral for Sonny Red in hope that his son Anthony "Whack Whack" Indelicato would turn up, so they could whack him too.

   The death of Uncle Philly did not put Frank Saggio off a life of crime, but he decided that, to avoid the modern Mob treachery, he would not sign up to any single Mob family. Instead he would work freelance for all five. He could do this because he was one of the biggest earners in the business, pulling down millions and kicking a share upstairs to the bosses. He quickly graduated from sticking up drug dealers and stealing cars to bankrupting Wall Street brokers, providing protection for porno rackets and overseeing the Mob forays into movie production. But those in power decided that he could not stay freelance forever. He was after all tied by blood to the Bonanno family – the family that had murdered his uncle.

   Soon after joining the Bonannos, Frankie narrowly escaped an assassination attempt and was busted for a major scam. As he had no loyalty to the Bonannos – who were now trying to kill him – Frankie turned himself over to the Feds on the one condition. He would not squeal on his own relatives.

   Saggio told them everything else he knew. He was protected by the FBI and US Marshals, then handed over to the Federal Witness Security Program. He was a fugitive from the Mob and, later, a fugitive from the government. However, in the early 2000s, he took the time to sit down with the crime writer Fred Rosen. Together, they wrote Born to the Mob, which explains how Saggio had got into a life of crime and what he had learned about the old-style Mafia from his Uncle Philly.

The Warner Brothers crime films of the 1930s – particularly 1931's *Public Enemy* starring James Cagney in his career-making role and any film with Humphrey Bogart or Edward G. Robinson – succeeded in showing the kind of poverty and social conditioning that produced the original group of gangsters that ruled the rackets in the first part of the century to 1931. Reality intruded in 1932.

That year, on the boardwalk in Atlantic City, three men took a walk. What they discussed was a blueprint for organized crime in New York. If executed well, it would ensure that the operation would eventually control a network that would infiltrate all fifty states. The story may be apocryphal, but there is no denying the facts.

At some point in 1932–33, Charles "Charley Lucky" Luciano (aka Lucky Luciano), Benjamin "Bugsy" Siegel, and Meyer Lansky came up with the idea of organizing crime. The "Outfit" was Lucky Luciano's name for this brand of crime that the three men introduced into the US. The two tough Jews and their brilliant Italian counterpart came up with the rather civilized concept of killing only for monetary gain: monetary gain was everything. Eventually, Luciano's "Outfit" would become a nationwide group of well-organized criminals run by the Five Families of New York.

With Mob family ties that stretched back to his great-grandfather Joseph, Frankie's career path was as good as chosen. And while Philly Lucky was dead, his name still translated into respect. Frankie was a restless young man and wanted to start making a name for himself within the Outfit.

Using the juice that his uncle's reputation still carried, Frankie formed his own crew of young independents: Mikey Hollywood ("as handsome as a Ken doll") from the Genovese Family; Larry Zano and his brother Junior, also from the Genovese; and Chris Cappanelli, his brother Anthony, and Mikey Paradiso from the Gambino Family.

"Everyone was tied in and we all hung out and did stuff together," Frankie recalls. "We all had thousands in cash in our pockets from the sale of the [stolen] goods. We started hanging together. We did armed robberies of drug dealers

– never civilians. See, Chris was selling pot, coke – stuff like that. We'd make ten to fifteen K on the sale of the drugs. But it wasn't enough. Why bother buying the shit when we could steal it? Instead of making ten or fifteen, we'd get thirty. We'd rob the dealer and unload the shit ourselves. We didn't care who we robbed, if they were connected or not. And that started it. That was our specialty. That became our full-time job: findin' guys who were buyin' from the dealers, getting their routines down and goin' in when they'd have the most cash or product.

"Our main guy for getting rid of the stuff was Tony Armente, who was a Bonanno soldier. Sometimes, when we didn't have anybody lined up to take off, we'd buy from Tony. You gotta understand; this guy would kill you, stab you in the heart (to stop you from bleeding), cut your throat, hang you upside down in the shower to drain your blood, cut you into ten different pieces, and carry them out in a bunch of American Tourister luggage. Tony would bury you out in this bird sanctuary on Staten Island also called 'Boot Hill'. Tony was on America's Most Wanted. Tony's now doing about 400 years in jail."

Of all the wiseguys Frankie met in this period of his life, the one he formed a lasting friendship with was Michael "Mikey Hollywood" Groak. Mikey had an unusual background for a wiseguy. His father was a New York City detective, first-grade, who became the president of the Patrolman's Benevolent Association, the chief negotiating arm of the NYPD. Mikey had rebelled against his father's life as a lawman. Instead, Mikey chose the fast, dangerous, monied life of a gangster.

"Mikey was as tough as they come. We started scheming, robbing. We got into the cigarette, cigar, and liquor business. Sometimes we'd take a truck down to North Carolina where we'd scam wholesalers outta a $100,000 of cigarettes, then bring it back and sell 'em. Most times we'd place orders at cigarette wholesalers. We'd come up with some phoney name for our restaurant or club or tell them we were opening up a bunch of newsstands, give them an address of an abandoned building, and then have them ship hundreds of cartons of cigarettes to it. We'd pay them with phoney certified checks that we printed up ourselves on a regular check writer."

Through such scams, Frankie and Mikey started racking up the dough and Frankie's criminal career as an independent started to take off.

"Then Tommy D came over. He said he'd heard about how well I was doing, that I was a good earner. The bottom line with these guys is money. He wanted me with him 'cause I had a reputation as a mover. Fuck him – I couldn't stand the son-of-a-bitch!"

Frankie wanted to steer clear of the Bonannos, not just because they killed his uncle but because the politics of the Family were in such disarray. With Rastelli in power, the Family had lost face. The idea of associating with just one Family seemed to have its liabilities.

"I didn't want to end up like my uncle. He had been a Bonanno his whole life; he'd been loyal to them then they clipped him and buried him somewhere. I began to think about going a different way. I wanted to move around freely. I didn't want anybody bustin' my balls. I wanted to do business with any crew. Everyone stuck to their own crew. If I wasn't with any crew, I could move around and not answer to anyone."

Frankie never read any of the self-help books of the 1980s, but he followed some of their best advice: make money doing something you love. Only he didn't quite do it in the way the self-help gurus had in mind.

"Basically, it really was a body shop. Continental Auto Body was the name of it. We started out actually doing collision work in Islip. I used to paint cars. I actually liked it; it was very relaxing. Did that for a while. My firm was doing very well. Then I started seeing there was a lot of money in parts, especially bumpers."

Bumpers?

"Do you remember at the time in the early eighties in New York when there were all these Caddies riding around without front bumpers? It was the biggest thing to rob; people just wanted them – I don't know why. Who cared? I was getting $1,000 just for the bumper. Corvette t-tops [the glass roofs] were also huge at the time. You couldn't park your Corvette anyplace without having the Hap stolen."

Frankie had his own crew of car thieves roaming the night streets, shadows passing through the orange sodium streetlights. Frankie followed the old adage: waste not, want not. These were kids restless to make their way up in the Mob's chain of command. Frankie sold them on his scam as a way of making the bosses sit up and take notice. Working for Frankie was the path of career advancement. The bigger their earnings, the more the bosses noticed.

"The parts business brought in a lot of money but there was a lot of labour involved. It's easier to just sell the whole car. Trans Ams, Camaros, Corvettes – they were real big then. And also at the time, I had a guy. He was a good friend, name of Patty Testa. He was a made guy with the Gambinos. He actually had an auto body place in Flatbush on Utica Avenue.

"Patty was exporting stolen cars out of the country. Patty and his brother Joey were with Roy DeMeo, who ran a crew for Nino Gaggi, a skipper with the Gambinos. My Uncle Jimmy Clemenza was friends with Roy. That's how I met that whole crew. They were my friends since I was a kid. I did a ton of business with Roy, Patty, and Joey – all of them.

"The way it worked, Patty'd call me up and give me an order. 'I need two Lincoln Towne cars, Frankie. I need a black Coupe DeVille. I need a Buick Riviera,' Patty would say.

"We'd agree on the price, which was usually 2,500 a car. I'd get my guys to go out and get 'em at night and the next day I'd go down to the Gemini Lounge where Patty worked. We'd park the cars on Utica Avenue, Avenue M – whatever – and leave 'em with the keys under the mat and he'd give me ten, twenty thousand – whatever it was."

The Gemini Lounge had a reputation.

"The Gemini Lounge. A fuckin' wild joint," says Frankie, laughing. "You didn't want to be in the Gemini Lounge at the wrong time when anybody was on drugs or fucked up. That crew killed a lot of guys: everyone knew they were nuts. I don't think they ever killed anybody for money. When Nino Gaggi needed work done, he went there. They fucked up a lot of guys. Roy was shooting to get his button; if you got in his way, you went.

"The Gemini, it was, like, a lot of knotty pine – that old beamed look. Bar on the right, tables on the left. When I'd walk in, I'd see Joey Testa sitting at one table. He was a fucking homicidal maniac. Sometimes I'd see Richie the Ice Man there. He was another one."

Richie did a lot of "contracts" for the Gambinos.

"There was a door that led to the back; there was an apartment back there. I never saw the Gorton Fishermen outfits [that protected the gangsters' clothes from victims' blood], but I heard the stories. But see, you don't ask questions. There are no daily gangster announcements: 'Who'd you clip this week?' These guys are friends of mine; I never looked at it in a frightening way. I was going to see Joey – we're all friends. And Roy? He was always a gentleman with me. I didn't worry about his temper or any of that shit. I was a kid – what did I know? I thought

I was invincible. If it was today, I would still do business with them, but I'd have a fuckin' pistol on me, safety off."

Frankie's business dealings with DeMeo and his crew came to an abrupt end on 10 January 1983. Skipper Nino Gaggi allegedly clipped DeMeo, then stuffed the corpse in the trunk of DeMeo's own car. The killing had supposedly been carried out at the behest of Gambino boss Paul Castellano, who had grown tired of DeMeo's arrogance and indiscriminate killing, which was bad for business. Castellano had first asked his underboss John Gotti to do the job, but the future "Dapper Don" politely refused. Gotti would eventually kill Castellano and supplant him as boss.

"I fucking hated Gotti and so did everyone else. The son of a bitch brought more attention to wiseguys than anyone did. Every time [federal prosecutor and later NYC mayor] Giuliani prosecuted him, we kept rooting for his conviction."

But that was in the future. Frankie still had to make a living in the present. With DeMeo out of the way, he needed a new outlet for his car theft business.

"I started dealing with a guy on the Island – Bones. He had a Nissan dealership in front and a used body shop in the back. Whatever their suspicion, the legitimate workers at the dealership kept their mouths shut. You didn't have to be brilliant to figure out that if you opened your mouth to the cops, you'd wind up in Gravesend Bay. The water was so foul there, it actually dissolved metal; flesh was no problem.

"Now, I'm dealing with Bones and another guy who worked there – Sally Regina – overheard that I was the guy who got all the cars. He came up to me and started talking to me about cars and shit and I didn't trust him too much. I don't really want to deal with this guy. I really wouldn't talk to him. I just didn't trust him; there was something about him, like he's listening too close or something. But fucking greed takes over. I let Rico handle him. I wouldn't talk to him. But my partner Rico – man, did he talk."

At the time, Frankie's partner in the parts and stolen car business was Rico Marino.

"Rico starts dealing with Sally Regina. I'd go to Regina's house and I really wouldn't talk. But my partner Rico starts asking, 'What do you want? Tell me what you need. We can get you anything.' He put us in such a hole, that kid, with his mouth.

"One time we were over at Regina's house where we'd drop the cars off and we're in the garage. And Regina says, 'Oh, my phone's ringing,' and he runs back in the house. [I find out later] the batteries are fucking up on the wire he's wearing. I find that out later on when my lawyer gets the tapes. The only thing they have me on tape saying is, 'To be honest with you, I really don't want to deal with you, you look like a cop to me.' The guy, of course, denies it."

Six months went by. On a bright July day in 1984, Frankie and Rico went to Sally Regina's house to make a delivery.

"We go to his house with a brand new stretch Caddy with five hundred miles, a T-l Porsche, and a 1984 Riviera. We're in the driveway and the money's about to change hands when all of a sudden this guy pulls up in a white Caddy wearing – I'll never forget – a black Members Only jacket. A grey-haired guy. Regina introduces him.

" 'Oh, this is my partner Terry.' I said, 'Partner? What are you talking about?' "

Frankie was angry. And suspicious. Suddenly, after dealing with Regina for a while, he suddenly has a partner that crawls out of the woodwork? Something just wasn't right.

"I walk away. Rico stays there and he's talking to the guy. I'm telling him, 'Are you out of your fucking mind?

Look at that guy. That guy's a cop!' So after a while, this guy Terry drives off. And I'm standing in the driveway and going to get my car to leave. And I see a squad car come down the street and I'm, like, 'What the fuck? Nah. You know, this can't be.' You know how you get that feeling? 'Nah, this can't be for real.' "

But it was.

"Sure enough the fucking police car pulls right into the fucking driveway. I go to turn and run and all I see are guys coming from everywhere. About ten cops run through a neighbour's yard, destroying his plants, and jump over the back fence and some hedges, and then they jump me – about ten of them – cuff me, and get me up. Unmarked cars pull up."

Usually, when a suspect is arrested in Suffolk County on Long Island, they are taken to the closest precinct for booking. But not Frankie and Rico.

"They take us directly to the District Attorney's Office in Hauppage and right up to the Rackets Bureau. They read us our rights and started questioning us – Rico too. They gotta make a production out of it so we don't think he set us up. They tell us how bad they got us, how they got us transporting stolen cars interstate, which is a federal beef."

The cops were making Frankie out to be the mastermind of a major car ring. Which he was. But at the time, Frankie didn't have the perspective to see that. He simply considered himself a guy on the way up, just trying to make a living any way he could. As far as he was concerned, he wasn't hurting anybody. Everything he stole, he figured, was insured; everything he stole was new. Who cared if the insurance companies had to pay up?

"The outcome was they took us and arraigned us. I had gotten arrested a few years before when I was still a juvenile for a burglary. I got probation. At the time, my

record from my first case was sealed. My father had made
sure it was, because I'd been a minor; I got the [mug]
pictures back and everything.

"So now this looks like my first arrest, not second. I
know my first arrest was a 'B Felony' – I've had a little
experience. And the cops start talking and saying this shit
about wanting to help me and I stop 'em cold.

" 'Listen, I want a lawyer.' Soon as I said that, everything
stopped."

Which is the way it's supposed to be. Once a suspect
asserts their constitutional right to an attorney, by law
the questioning has to cease. But in Suffolk County, as a
state commission would discover, that wasn't always the
case. Suffolk County detectives were infamous for beating
confessions out of suspects, regardless of what rights were
invoked. With Frankie, though, there would have been no
point. Uncle Philly had ingrained the code of *omertà* on
Frankie's soul: there was no way he would talk. The cops,
though, continued to try.

"They'd still come into the interrogation room where
they were holding me – you know, the kind of place with
a battered desk and chairs, and walls painted puke green?
They'd try and scare me into talking: 'Oh, you'll get thirty
years.' Stuff like that. Fuck that. Finally, they take me for
arraignment. We get outside and what do I see out front?
Parked in front of the DA's office are the stretch Caddy,
the T-1 Porsche, and the 1984 Buick Riviera. They were
fucking with us.

" 'Hey, Frankie – does that look familiar? What do you
think of that limo?' one of the cops asked.

" 'That's nice, is it yours?' I asked him."

They drove Frankie and Rico to the arraignment "out
east", as Long Islanders like to say, into the furthest
recesses of Suffolk County, to the drab State Supreme
Court Building in Riverhead – the county seat.

"Listen to this. The judge is Michael Mannone, my father's first cousin. He knows my name; he knows who I am. I go for arraignment and all they get me on was fifty counts criminal possession of stolen property in the first degree. The fucking judge – I got no criminal record now – the judge who's my cousin sets bail at half a million dollars! So my father gets this lawyer, Hal Jordan, a wiseguy lawyer out of the Woolworth Building in Manhattan. He comes back to the bullpen.

" 'Frankie,' he says to me, 'Frankie, what the fuck was in the trunk of these cars?! What did you have, bodies in the trunk?' I tell him the judge must have a hard-on for me. I can't figure it out.

" 'Look Frankie,' he says, 'I got another bail hearing scheduled for next week, so you're gonna have to lay up a little bit.' I go the next week for the bail hearing before Judge Mannone and he reduces my bail to 40,000 cash and I get out."

Frankie was only out for two days before he went back down to the Nissan dealership to talk to the owner, Bones.

"I grab the guy and tell him, 'You got a fucking rat, bro. This guy's wearing a wire and everything.' The guy didn't want to hear it; the guy's blowing me off. 'You gotta be a fucking rat too, then. I come here to do you a fucking favour and you're blowing me off and telling me to be quiet?'

"Now I end up thinking that Bones was involved too. So what happens is, I see that the kid, Sally Regina – he's in the back working in the shop, that muthafucker. Sally wasn't a cop; he was just a guy who got pinched for something and was setting guys up to get out of trouble. I go in there, I got a fucking crowbar, and I beat the fuck out of him. I bashed his skull in."

A person can easily die from being beaten with a crowbar, but Frankie "didn't really give a fuck at the time.

I get home. By the time I get there, my lawyer already called. They were charging me with first-degree assault and revoking bail. I go down to turn myself in. My lawyer tells me, 'We take this to trial; there's no way we're gonna win. They got too much on you.' "

So Frankie did what he's good at: he made a deal.

"It was a score, actually. In return for dropping most of the charges against me [including the assault charge], I plead guilty to three counts of criminal possession of stolen property in the first degree. I went up before my cousin, Judge Mannone for sentencing, and he gave me four years."

Every prisoner in the New York State Correctional System has to go through preliminary processing at the Downstate Correctional Facility in Fishkill, NY. The place is about 100 miles north of Long Island.

"I wait in the Riverhead jail until October – about four months before they took me to Downstate. After I sign in and everything, they assign me to Clinton State Prison. It's in an upstate town called Dannemora; most cons just call the prison Dannemora. So for a non-violent felony, first offence, they send me to a Max A joint with perverts and murderers. There were guys doing 300 years there."

He had merited such unusual first-time treatment because the Rackets Squad – whose chief target consisted of mobsters – prosecuted him. In other words, did Frankie receive a more severe punishment because the cops and court perceived him as a "known associate of organized crime" rather than an independent? Likely. Which is ironic, considering he was an independent. From the time of his uncle's murder he had remained unaffiliated. So far it was working – he didn't have to kick upstairs.

"A month before, I'd had my twenty-first birthday on 10 September. And it's my first time in prison – it didn't feel too good. A fucking twelve- or fourteen-hour bus ride up to Dannemora and stopping at all these jails to pick up guys along the way.

"What they do is they shackle your feet and they have this thing they put around your waist and they handcuff you without any chain so there's no play. Then they take the handcuffs and clip 'em to this little black metal box around your waist. You can't move; you have no fucking movement. So I ride for fourteen hours on a bus like that. Fucking torture, bro – torture. They give you a fucking sandwich, right? Try to get the fucking sandwich into your mouth."

Frankie had been on the bus since the early morning. Even inside the bus with its closed windows, he could tell that the air had gotten colder. When they reached Plattsburgh, which is a little south of the Canadian border, the driver took a hard left. The bus rumbled along a dark, two-lane road – Route 374 – for ten miles through the small town of Cadyville, then climbed the Cadyville Hills. At the top of the hill, the driver looked out his windshield. There, built into the side of a mountain, was Clinton State Prison. With a crackle of gears, the bus descended into hell.

The first building on the right is currently called the Annex. Large coils of razor wire surround it. Not long ago, it was the State Hospital for the Criminal Insane; the town residents called it "The Bug House". Now it's used to house inmates. When the bus finally arrived inside the prison walls at about midnight, Frankie got out and looked around.

The moon was half full and he could make out a series of buildings of all shapes and sizes. At the top of the buildings, silhouetted against the dark night sky, was the unpleasant image of barbed wire, twisted into ugly coils.

"This way," said a guard, and marched the prisoners inside a low-lying building.

Frankie marched, but kept looking around. He saw armed guards patrolling the grounds. He noticed the towers, set up at intervals around the prison; he could see the bare outline of the guards inside of them. He figured they must be marksmen carrying rifles fitted with sniper scopes, in case inmates were stupid enough to attempt an escape. He later found out that he was right.

"They took me in, processed me – name, prints, pictures, shit like that. Then they took me up to the cell block. It was fucking huge: an old maximum security cell block with one-man cells. Looked like something from one of those old movies. I start walking down the catwalk and everyone starts screaming, 'New jack, new jack,' throwing shit. For a twenty-one-year-old, it was a pretty wild experience."

When Frankie got to his cell he stopped for a second and then the guard pushed him in. In the four-by-six-foot cell he saw a bunk and a sink attached to a toilet. The overhead light was just a bare bulb and was so dim, he couldn't see. Basically, it was useless, "fucking dead". Frankie turned and faced the catwalk and that's when he heard the sound for the first time.

"The cells were cranked closed. There was a chain that went through every cell, attached to a wheel at the end of the gallery. The guard turns a crank and you hear 'Crrrrrr,' and the bars start moving, then, 'Bang.' "

The bars hit home, sunk into the three-foot thick walls. Frankie looked around at his new home, out at the other cells, and listened as the screams died down until all that could be heard was snoring. He sat down on his bunk and suddenly, he began to think about his Uncle Philly, who had never been arrested in his life. Yet here he was in one of New York State's worst prisons for a non-violent felony.

"I just didn't get it," says Frankie. "My uncle, he did so many things and never once got jailed. I really needed to figure it out."

Frankie would have time to do just that.

Saggio did figure to stay out of jail, but not how to stay out of trouble. Despite his lucrative career as a freelancer, organized crime has to be just that – organized. The Five Families decided that he would have to join one of them. Frankie did not want it to be the Bonanno Family, but it did not look like he would have any choice.

The first part of the discussion between the rival *capos* Tough Tony from the Genovese Family and Tommy D from the Bonanno Family centred on Philly Lucky.

Despite the fact that the Commission had sanctioned his assassination – only the Commission could authorize the death of a *capo* – and despite the fact that he had been officially disgraced within the Bonanno Family, Philly Lucky, in death, was still a Bonanno.

"Think of it," Frankie says. "The sons of bitches had killed him, chopped his body up. And they still owned him and his family. That was the beauty of the Outfit: once you were in, they owned you and yours for generations."

Which meant it looked like Tommy D had won before the contest even began. And Tough Tony? Tony knew Frankie had held back on the kick with the brokerages. He didn't care; there'd been enough to go around for everyone. Frankie had said he would make money for everybody and he had kept his word.

The conversation would then have turned to Frankie's great-uncle Suvio Grimaldi. Suvio was Castellammarese. He had crossed the Atlantic in the early part of the twentieth century during the same wave of immigration that had brought Salvatore Maranzano and Joe Bonanno to the United States. Maranzano had worked his way up the criminal chain, and became one of New York's two big crime bosses; the other was Joseph Masseria. Both were eventually assassinated by men in the employ of Lucky Luciano, who would go on to create the Five Families with Bugsy Siegel and Meyer Lansky.

Joseph Bonanno worked his way up the ladder from soldier to boss and eventually ran his own Family. During 1965, Bonanno attempted a power play in order to become the most powerful Mafia boss – and lost. He was forced into an early retirement in Arizona where he died in 2002.

And Suvio? He became part of the Profaci Family, which would later be renamed the Colombo Family. Suvio married a woman named Octavia Glaizzo; she had a brother, Joseph.

"My grandfather Joseph was a handsome man with dark hair," recalls Petrina Saggio. "He was stocky and a sharp dresser. My grandfather had a ride, a portable whip."

During the summer in Brooklyn, a man would drive a trailer around. Attached to the trailer was a multi-armed octopus that whirled around with terrific centrifugal force. Kids would pay him a nickel and hop in for the ride. Joseph Glaizzo was the gentle man whose fingers were on the ride's power control.

"He also had an ice business. He carried the ice up the steps into people's homes when they still had iceboxes. He wasn't emotionally demonstrative to my grandmother, but he was a good man," Petrina says.

In 1932, Joseph's brother-in-law Suvio, later Frankie's maternal great-uncle, was charged with illegal possession of firearms. Suvio, however, wasn't about to go to jail.

Petrina recounts Suvio's craftiness. "Suvio told his brother-in-law Joseph, 'Look, Joe, if I'm convicted, I'll get a long sentence.' My grandfather asked him why.

" 'Because I got a record. I'll get a long sentence. But you, Joe, you got no record. You take the rap; you'll be out a year – two, tops.' My grandmother, she loved her brother Suvio, so my grandfather did it for her."

And that's how an innocent, good man named Joseph Glaizzo pleaded guilty to a crime he did not commit and served two years in the same state prison system that would house his great-grandson. In manipulating the situation, Suvio showed that he had mastered the real lesson of the gangster's trade: survival. And Joseph?

Frankie says, "When I heard that story about my great-grandfather Joseph, I thought, 'This guy has got balls. A stand-up guy!' Later I realized he'd been duped too. But by that time there was no way out."

Suvio Grimaldi gave Frankie his first tie to the Profaci/Colombo Family. His Uncle Jimmy Clemenza gave him his second. Outside in Spaghetti Park, Frankie was thinking of his Uncle Jimmy too. He knew Tony was going to mention Suvio and Jimmy; they were his only chance to stay clear of the Bonannos. He didn't want to be put into a situation where he had to constantly be watching his back.

As Frankie waited in the park, he remembered the story the Saggio family told about the one time Uncle Jimmy went to kill somebody and things didn't go right. It was such a famous story that Francis Ford Coppola and Mario Puzo used it for the pivotal scene in *The Godfather, Part II* . . .

The Corleone family has a disgruntled, old-line *capo* named Frankie "Five Angels" Pantangelo. He hates "those pimps the Rissoto Brothers", who have no respect and are butching in on his action. He goes to the Don, Michael Corleone, to ask permission to kill them, but Michael refuses. He's too involved in other business deals with Hyman Roth to want the attention that would result from the Rissoto Brothers' assassinations.

Shortly after Michael turns down his request, Frankie Five Angels is in a bar back in New York when two guys come in and try to garrotte him. They have the piano wire wound tightly around his throat and are squeezing the life out of him when a cop stumbles in and sees what's happening. Before he can react, the two assassins gun him down and flee. Frankie Five Angels recovers, thinks it was Michael who arranged his death, and decides to testify against him before a Senate committee that is looking into organized crime.

Michael eventually discovers that it was Hyman Roth who planned Frankie Five Angels's assassination. Through a series of deft manoeuvres, not only does Frankie Five Angels fail to implicate Michael, he absolves him of any criminal responsibility. He then conveniently takes his own life, which seals his lips forever. Michael is left to rule his criminal empire unimpaired.

The actual story has none of the movie's glamour, but the real drama.

During the Depression, James "Jimmy Brown" Clemenza was a gangster. He wasn't some newspaper hound like Baby Face Nelson, Pretty Boy Floyd, or Bonnie and Clyde, the gangsters who robbed and killed for kicks and headlines. Jimmy was in it for the money: he did his job without the headlines.

To Clemenza and the professional thieves and murderers in the Mob, headlines meant attention; attention meant cops; cops meant prison. Prison was a fate to be avoided if possible – and it was always possible.

Jimmy bootlegged quietly in Cicero, a suburb of Chicago, with another boy from the Brooklyn Mob named "Scarface" Al Capone. While officially attached to what would become the Profaci Family, Jimmy was on loan to Capone's Mob. When Prohibition was repealed in 1932, Jimmy came home to Brooklyn.

Over the next three decades he would do all kinds of jobs for the Profaci Family. Jimmy Brown had served the Profaci Family faithfully since its inception and he would continue to do so until he died. He was a true old-liner, a skipper who believed in keeping your word and your place, which is why he watched with distaste as the Gallo Brothers kept trying to butch in on the Profacis' action.

Throughout the 1950s, Larry Gallo, Joseph "Crazy Joe" Gallo, and their youngest brother, Albert "Kid Blast" Gallo, worked as assassins for Nicholas "Jiggs" Forlano. The New York State Commission of Investigation would later identify Forlano, a member of the Profaci Family, as the biggest loan shark in New York City.

The Gallo Brothers got tired of waiting to move up the Mob ladder. In 1959, they formed their own gang of about twenty with guys in the Profaci Family who were equally dissatisfied with Profaci's leadership. While Crazy Joe was the one to be feared in any encounter – he had been certified as insane by a psychiatrist at Brooklyn's King's County Hospital in 1950 – it was Larry who was the brains. If Larry were out of the way, Joey, Kid Blast, and the rest would fall into the gutter.

Before anything like that could happen, the Gallos, with their ranks swelling to one hundred disaffected, got some of their guys to kidnap four of Profaci's closest advisers. Held for ransom, they were eventually released. Profaci then convinced most of the one hundred insurgents to come back into the fold. The Gallos, though, were a different story. Profaci believed they deserved retribution for the rebellion they had fomented.

The neighbourhood was Flatbush, a mostly Jewish area of Brooklyn. A few Italians lived there too, in real middle-class splendour. Flatbush was a step up from Bensonhurst.

There were fewer attached four-family houses there; Flatbush had mostly semi-detached twos and stand-alone singles. One of the main access roads to the neighbourhood that gangster Larry Gallo walked on was Eastern Parkway, the sedate, tree-lined street designed back in the early part of the century by the famed architect Frederick Olmsted, the same man who designed Central Park.

On 25 August 1961, Larry Gallo went to the Sahara Restaurant – a tavern that served only wine and beer – on Utica Avenue, a busy shopping street in the heart of Flatbush. In the dark interior, Larry lounged at the bar over his Pabst Blue Ribbon draught. Outside and down the block, a white sedan pulled up to the curb. Still drinking in the tavern, Gallo had no idea it was there.

Inside the sedan were three men: Frankie's uncle Jimmy and his brother Peter Clemenza, and an associate named John Scimone. Jimmy Clemenza got out of the car and quietly walked down the street. He approached the Sahara steadily but warily, making sure there were no cops around, no witnesses. Then, he turned and quickly walked in the door, his porkpie slouch hat covering his face.

Gallo was swallowing some of the beer when a rope wound around his throat; one moment it wasn't there and the next, it was. As Gallo reached up to try and pull it off, the person holding it, Jimmy Clemenza, pulled harder and the fibres of the rope sank deeper into Larry Gallo's flesh.

Gallo knew he was being garrotted. He knew the action had to have been ordered by the Profacis, with the Commission signing off on the assassination. He also knew there wasn't much he could do. The person strangling him – he still didn't know who it was – had incredibly strong hands. Despite his struggles, he was dying.

Clemenza was literally choking the life out of Gallo. He knew from having done it before that Larry Gallo would stay conscious for at least the first minute and a half. Then Gallo's brain would suffer oxygen deprivation and he'd black out. Until then, it would be sheer, unrelenting agony.

Even when Gallo went limp in his hands, Clemenza would know he was unconscious, but not dead. If he stopped strangling him at that point, there was a possibility that Gallo could be revived. Clemenza would keep up the pressure until he heard his hyoid or throat bone crack and than apply still more pressure until Gallo was clearly, definitely, absolutely dead.

Larry Gallo was just on the verge of passing out when Sergeant Edward Meagher stumbled on to the scene. Meagher had been in a radio car at 2.45 p.m. with Patrolman Melvin Biel when he decided to go into the tavern for a "routine inspection". Jimmy Clemenza, seeing Meagher coming in, dropped Gallo to the floor and hid.

When Meagher got inside, it took a second for his eyes to adjust to the gloom. Then he saw a man lying motionless on the dirty floor and heard him groaning. Meagher crossed the room and bent down to assess the man's condition. Just then, Jimmy Clemenza raced out of the shadows to the waiting getaway car.

Outside, Biel saw Clemenza running and gave chase. Clemenza turned and ran up the street. The white sedan, the getaway car, followed. Someone inside the car, either Peter Clemenza or Scimone, stuck a revolver out of a window and fired a shot that hit Biel on the right cheek. Jimmy Clemenza jerked open the car door and hustled inside. For a man who weighed over 250 pounds, he moved quickly when he had to.

Hearing the shots, Meagher fled the bar, saw the automobile escaping, pulled his service revolver, and fired two shots as the sedan turned north on Utica Avenue and sped north. He didn't hit anything.

Four blocks away, at the intersection of Snyder Avenue and East 49th Street, the sedan slowed down. As bystanders watched in surprise, John Scimone was pushed out of the car and unceremoniously hit the street. Apparently, the

Clemenzas felt he was expendable. Scimone, who had been arrested thirty years before for assault and robbery, made a good patsy: he could be blamed for the attempted murder.

Larry Gallo survived, though his voice was a little hoarse after that. As for Jimmy Brown, it was the only time he failed to clip someone. No one held it against him, however; it was just dumb luck that the cop showed up. By the following year, Jimmy Brown once again had to adjust to changing times.

On 6 June 1962, the twenty-eighth anniversary of D-Day, Joseph Profaci died in the South Side Hospital on Long Island. The cause of death was cancer. There is always an immediate rush to fill the vacuum created whenever a family head dies. But Profaci had no heirs. His brother-in-law, Giuseppe Magliocco, stepped up to fill his shoes and assumed control of the family enterprises.

Looking on with a gleam in his criminal eye was boss Joe Bonanno. Profaci had been his close friend. Nevertheless, his death gave Bonanno an unbelievable opportunity to become the most powerful crime boss since Maranzano. Bonanno devised a scheme that involved clipping family heads Carlo Gambino and Tommy Lucchese and Tommy's cousin, Buffalo, NY family boss Stefano Maggadino. Unfortunately, Bonanno was relying on the young *capo* Joseph Colombo to take care of the killings.

Colombo was actually in tight with Carlo Gambino. He looked at Gambino like a father; he would never betray him. When Gambino found out from Colombo about Bonanno's scheme, he called the Commission into session. Bonanno was asked to explain himself. The deceitful boss was able to talk his way out of having his body carved up and distributed throughout the New York Metropolitan area and retired to Arizona in the late 1960s.

As for Colombo, with Gambino's backing, he became head of the old Profaci Family, newly christened the Colombo Family. Jimmy Clemenza would continue to do jobs as demanded by his Family and also become a *capo* until he retired to Florida in the late 1970s.

"My Uncles Jimmy and Philly bought in Hallandale [Florida] in 1978," says Frankie. "The building was all Italian and Jewish gangsters – funniest thing you ever saw. They would argue day and night. They had a clubhouse where they played cards. All they did was make Hallandale into Brooklyn. They'd been playing cards back home in New York for thirty years.

"Let's see, who else was there from New York? Scottie DiAngelo; Joe Sausage, who owns GS Sausage in Jersey; Angelo Ponti, who owns Ponti Carting. He just went away on extortion. My Uncle Jimmy used to curse every one of them.

"I remember standing in a parking lot talking to Scotty DiAngelo. I'm eighteen or nineteen and these condos all have catwalks and my uncle yells down, "What you doin' talking to that cheap Bastard?" I was embarrassed. I couldn't understand why Scotty's name was 'Scotty' until someone explained 'Scotty' means 'cheap' in Italian."

Besides Hallandale, Clemenza had a home in Florida, NY, where he raised horses. When Jimmy wasn't at home either at the farm or at the Florida condo, he could usually be found in North Carolina.

"Uncle Jimmy used to go to Duke University in North Carolina for the Rice Diet," Frankie says. "He was a big guy – really fat – and he needed to lose weight."

Lina Saggio, Frankie's sister, takes up the story.

"My cousin Corinne told me about the Rice Diet. She said that Uncle Jimmy went down there for years to lose weight. 'Boy I'd love for you to go,' she said. I needed to lose some weight then, so I went down in 1984 with the agreement that my Uncle Jimmy was there and he'd take care of me.

" 'You're here to do one thing and one thing only: you're going to lose weight and forget about anything else,' Uncle Jimmy said to me as soon as I got off the plane. He was heavy and had a rough voice from all the cigars he smoked. He said whatever he felt like and you just had to take it.

"We stayed at a hotel where he was head honcho. Every day he took my arm and we'd have to walk eight miles a day to get our meals. He had a driver down there too and him and the driver would follow me with the Caddy, to make sure nothing happened.

"Uncle Jimmy, he was respected everywhere. Even when he was doing the diet and went in the hospital to give blood and urine samples, it was always 'Good morning, Mr Clemenza,' 'How ya doin' Mr Clemenza,' from the staff."

But even Jimmy Clemenza's considerable influence was not enough to stop love from blooming.

"What happened was, he used to watch me from his window when I'd go out. He was afraid I'd go and eat something or meet the wrong kind of person. One day, I met my husband-to-be, Kelly Scott, at a convenience store next door to the hotel. I was there buying cigarettes and started talking to him.

" 'Come to the hotel and have lunch,' I suggested.

" 'OK, I'll come over,' he said. When he walked in the front door, he was stopped by Uncle Jimmy.

" 'You go in the dining room,' Uncle Jimmy told me. But I stayed to listen.

" 'Do you know who I am?" he asked Kelly.

" 'No,' Kelly answered.

" 'This is my niece. Leave her alone and stay away from her.'

" 'I like her and I think she's nice,' Kelly said.

" 'See the leather on your shoes? Keep walking,' said Uncle Jimmy and his chauffeur escorted Kelly out.

"I was crying. I called up my father. He talked to Uncle Jimmy. My father told Uncle Jimmy not to hurt him. My brother, he talked to Uncle Jimmy and got him to cool off and leave me alone. But Uncle Jimmy was still giving Kelly the business so a couple of days later, I took off with Kelly and left Uncle Jimmy behind."

Eventually, Lina married Kelly and her family accepted him as one of their own. A few years later, Uncle Jimmy died a peaceful, natural death. He had managed to live his life the way he wanted: as a true outlaw who, in the end, died in bed. But Uncle Jimmy also knew he was one of the few who actually fulfilled such a wish.

After carefully evaluating all of Frankie's family tree, Tommy D and Tough Tony came to the conclusion that, if anywhere, Frankie belonged with the Colombos. Two of his uncles had been in that Family compared with only one in the Bonanno Family. But the Colombos did not have a representative at the sit-down and a Bonanno and Genovese were not about to give the Colombos the Five Families' prime earner.

Tough Tony was forced to admit that he held the losing hand; there was no blood relationship between the Genovese and Frankie. Tony had just taken him in, while Tommy and the Bonannos could show a direct link to Frankie Saggio through Philip Giaccone.

From across the street, Frankie watched as the door to the Parkside Restaurant opened and Tony emerged, grim-faced. Frankie hoped that Tony had won and was just putting on an act for Tommy's benefit. Frankie remembers how Tony broke the news.

" 'You belong with the Bonannos, kid. There's nothing I could do,' Tony told me. Tony felt bad. He knew how much I hated Tommy D. I was being forced to go back to work with the crew that killed my Uncle Philly."

And now, Frankie Saggio really needed to start watching his back.

For the Sins of the Father

Albert DeMeo

Albert DeMeo was the son of Roy DeMeo, ranking member of the Gambino Family. Born in 1942, in Bath Beach, Brooklyn, DeMeo Snr had begun loansharking as a teenager. By twenty-three he became owner of the Gemini Lounge which became the headquarters of his crew. A large number of murders occurred there and bodies dismembered. By the time Albert was five, his father was taking him on some of his Sunday errands. And crime was the family business. One of Roy's crew was his cousin Joseph "Dracula" Guglielmo.

While DeMeo had links to the Lucchese Family, he also worked with Anthony "Nino" Gaggi, a soldier with the Gambinos. He became involved in car theft, drug trafficking, money laundering and hijacking. With the money he made he bought into other businesses. In 1973, Paul Rothenberg, the proprieter of a pornographic film lab DeMeo and Gaggi had a share in, was arrested. Fearing that he may talk, DeMeo invited Rothenberg to meet him at a local diner and shot him twice in the head in the alleyway outside. In 1975, members of DeMeo's crew stabbed Andrei Katz, the owner of a body shop they had a dispute with, and dismembered his body.

Throughout the 1970s, they claimed more victims. Usually the target would be lured in through the side entrance of the

Gemini Lounge, then taken upstairs where DeMeo would be waiting. He would be carrying a gun with a silencer and a towel. He would shoot the victim in the head, then wrap the towel around it to staunch the blood. Meanwhile, another member of the crew would stab the victim in the heart to stop the blood pumping. The body would be stripped of its clothes and left in the bathroom until the blood had congealed. Meanwhile plastic sheets would be laid out on the floor. The body would then be cut up. Parts were put in bags which were, in turn, placed in cardboard boxes that were taken to the Fountain Avenue Dump in Brooklyn. Hundreds of tons of garbage were deposited there every day, so finding body parts was almost impossible. Even when the police tried it once, they had to abandon the attempt when it proved too costly.

DeMeo went into prostitution and pornography. He dealt cocaine and marijuana out of the Gemini Lounge, even though those higher up in the Gambino Family said they did not approve. Even so, Gaggi continued to take his cut.

In May 1976, DeMeo was punched in the face by Joseph Brocchini. As Brocchini was a made man, DeMeo was told he was not allowed to retaliate – or, if he did, he was not to be found out. Soon after Brocchini's used-car dealership was raided. The staff were handcuffed and blindfolded, and Brocchini was shot five times in the back of the head. The office was ransacked. To all intents and purposes, it was an armed robbery gone wrong. The following month, DeMeo shot Vincent Govemara, a young man with no connections to organized crime, after Govemara annoyed Gaggi. In July, DeMeo flew to Florida to murder George Byrum, another man Gaggi had targeted for revenge. He had sawed Byrum's head half off when disturbed by construction workers nearby. An FBI informant who reported that DeMeo was a ruthless killer was murdered.

When Carlo Gambino died and Paul Castellano took over, Gaggi was promoted to capo and DeMeo hoped to become a made man. However, Castellano looked down on DeMeo as a cheap hoodlum. DeMeo then made an alliance with an Irish-American gang called the Westies, doing a hit for them. The Westies then became an arm of the Gambino Family. As DeMeo had set up the alliance, he was formally inducted into the Gambino Family, but warned not to murder anyone without permission and avoid drug trafficking. Even so, he continued selling drugs and committing unsanctioned killings. He did not even hide the fact. He killed car thief Jonathan Quinn, who was a suspected informer and his nineteen-year-old girlfriend Cherie Golden. When taken to task by his superiors, DeMeo said that it was too risky to leave her alive.

By 1978, DeMeo was bragging that he had killed a hundred people and solicited contracts from the Five Families, which he fulfilled for as little as $5,000 – or even for free as a "professional favour". He even killed and dismembered one of his own crew, Edward "Danny" Grillo, after Grillo fell into debt and Gaggi thought he might be susceptible to police coercion. He also killed his second-in-command Chris Rosenberg, after Rosenberg had murdered a Cuban drug dealer who had connections to the Colombian drug cartel. The Colombians threatened to declare war on the Gambinos unless Rosenberg was killed.

Before Rosenberg was killed, DeMeo shot Dominic Ragucci, a student who was paying his way through college as a door-to-door salesman. When he parked his car outside DeMeo's house in Massapequa, Long Island, DeMeo assumed he was a Colombian assassin who had come to kill him. After a car chase, Ragucci's car became too damaged to continue and DeMeo killed him. Gaggi then ordered DeMeo to kill Rosenberg before any more innocent victims were killed. Rosenberg, who claimed he had no knowledge of *the Colombian situation, was then killed and his body left in his car at the side of a road in Brooklyn where it would be found. The Colombians wanted proof that Rosenberg had been disposed off, so his body could not be dismembered and disappear on the Fountain Avenue Dump. According to his son Albert and two of his crew who eventually turned state's evidence, DeMeo was genuinely upset by the death of Rosenberg. He had never exhibited remorse before. But that did not stop him killing. He murdered a car dealer who discovered that DeMeo was selling stolen cars and threatened to inform the police, along with an acquaintance who was not involved.*

James Eppolito and his son James Jnr, two made men in the Gambino family, complained of DeMeo's drug dealing to Paul Castellano. They were members of Gaggi's crew. Castellano gave him permission to handle the situation. DeMeo and Gaggi murdered the Eppolitos in a car on the way to the Gemini lounge. A witness reported the murder and, after a gun battle in which he was wounded in the neck, Gaggi was arrested. He was charged with murder and the attempted murder of a police officer. But through jury tampering, he was only convicted of assault and sentenced to five to fifteen years in the federal penitentiary. DeMeo killed the witness shortly after.

By then, the FBI had a huge file of people linked to DeMeo or the Gemini Lounge who had disappeared. A bug in the home of Gambino soldier Angelo Ruggiero picked up Angelo telling Gene Gotti that Castellano had put out a contract on DeMeo, but was having trouble finding anyone to take it as DeMeo was surrounded by an "army of killers". Gambino soldier Frank DeCicco eventually took the contract, but could not get near to DeMeo. Eventually DeCicco and John Gotti handed it on to DeMeo's own men.

On 10 January 1983, DeMeo went to crew member Patrick Testa's bodyshop for a meeting with his men. On 18

January, his body was found in the trunk of his car, which had been abandoned. He had multiple gunshot wounds to the head. It was thought that Gaggi might have pulled the trigger. Crew-members Joseph Testa and Anthony Senter were there too. However, Iceman Richard Kuklinski claimed to have killed DeMeo, having earlier carried out several contracts for him. He even claimed to have pistol-whipped the corpse.

Gaggi was never charged with the murder and died of a heart attack while standing trial for other murder charges. Testa and Senter were given life for a total of twenty-five murders, plus car-theft, drug trafficking and extortion, on evidence supplied by fellow crew-members Frederick DiNome and Dominic Montiglio. Paul Castellano was indicted for the murder of DeMeo. It was thought that he had ordered the murder because DeMeo was set to be jailed for his stolen-car operation. But Castellano was out on bail when Gotti had him gunned down.

It was thought that at least seventy people had been murdered by DeMeo and his Gemini-Lounge crew, though the number of victims may be as high as 200. For Albert DeMeo, who idolized his father, this was a lot to live down as he explained in his book For the Sins of My Father: A Mafia Killer, His Son, and the Legacy of a Mob Life *published in 2003.*

It was my father himself who slowly began cracking the window to give me glimpses of the world he inhabited outside Massapequa. Just as other fathers took their sons for a tour of the fire station or insurance office, so my father began showing me the way his business functioned, the tools of his trade. Neither my mother nor my sisters shared in the knowledge he began to impart to me. It was a man's thing, passed on from father to son.

I started learning about guns when I was six. My father imparted these lessons as matter of factly as he taught me to build shelves or install decking. My dad bought and sold guns regularly, and he was an educated collector. He particularly liked the antiques, pistols from the Civil War and before. Sometimes he would bring home an entire bag of guns and empty them on to the workbench to disassemble and clean in the garage workshop. The mechanics fascinated me; and by the time I was eight, I could disassemble and reassemble virtually any gun like an expert. Dad was careful and precise when handling a gun, and he made certain I never touched one carelessly. He always wore gloves when he handled a weapon. Isotoner gloves were the best, he told me, for it enabled a person to work efficiently without leaving fingerprints.

My father also taught me utter respect for the power that a gun implied. I learned to assume that a gun is probably loaded, that if I picked one up, I should point it down away from others, that I should never point a gun at anybody unless I was prepared to use it, that using a gun was a serious thing. If it became necessary to shoot someone, the safest thing was to aim for the head and get off at least two bullets.

If you aimed for the torso, the other person might shoot you back before you got off a second shot. I understood the gravity of what he was telling me, and it never occurred to me to aim a gun at a human being myself. I knew that Jimmy's father used a gun at work, and I sensed that shooting must form some part of my father's job. I never handled a gun without my father's permission. I knew that my dad kept a gun under the bed all the time, but it never occurred to me to touch it. It was a given that the weapon was off-limits. My father got me my first gun when I was six, a little .22, and took me upstate to a friend's farm to teach me how to fire it. I was allowed to shoot only at targets. One day I shot a chipmunk while I was practising in the brush, and my father was furious. "What did that chipmunk ever do to you?" he asked me. "You don't shoot nothing without a good reason."

My father began taking me with him into the social clubs in Manhattan, especially in Little Italy, about the time I entered the third grade. His business was taking up more and more of his time by then. I would kiss him goodbye when I left for school in the morning, but I was often in bed long before he got home at night. So the weekends became more important than ever. When there was business to conduct on a Saturday or Sunday afternoon, I would make the long drive across the bridge and into the crowded streets of the city with him.

The first social club I remember going to was in Manhattan. I was about eight years old at the time. I don't remember its name. What I do remember is the sense of overwhelming noise and confusion as the men who guarded the entrance opened its doors for us. The place was crowded with small tables where men were playing cards; in a corner another group watched a horse race on a TV mounted above the bar. They were all screaming at the television, either cheering or cursing the horses they had bet on. Almost everyone seemed to know my dad. Guys called, "Hey, Roy!" as my father shook the occasional hand and said hello. Within moments of our arrival other men started approaching my dad to ask him about balloons. The one who got to us first said, "Roy, how ya doin? I need to borrow fifty balloons. Think you could help me out?"

Dad replied, "Sure, no problem, I got fifty with me. Let's take a walk."

All three of us went back outside and started walking down the sidewalk as Dad and the man chatted vaguely about their families. I stretched my legs to keep pace with them, filled with curiosity. Balloons? Dad had balloons? Where were they? In the trunk? Or were we going someplace else? A few blocks away we came to a small café and went inside to sit down. Dad ordered espresso and pastry for all three of us. I grimaced as I sipped the hot, bitter liquid, proud to be included as one of the men. Dad and the man continued to chat about their families, the weather, how the Yankees were doing that year. Finally Dad said, "The usual arrangement."

The man replied, "Sure, no problem." Dad signalled the waitress for the check, and as he reached in his pocket to peel off a twenty from the roll he carried, I noticed him pulling out some envelopes. As he laid the twenty on the check with one hand, I saw him deftly pass five envelopes under the table with the other. The other man, also without looking at them, slipped the envelopes inside his jacket pocket as we rose to go. Back out on the sidewalk, Dad and the man shook hands good-bye, and we walked back toward the car.

Puzzled and a little disappointed, I reached up to touch my father's sleeve.

"Daddy?"

"What, Son?"

"Could I have one of those balloons?"

My father burst out laughing and then stopped walking and turned to me. Bending down, he said, "We weren't talking about real balloons. We were talking about money. A 'balloon' means one thousand dollars. That man wanted to borrow money." . . .

I was halfway through the fourth grade when I finally put a name to what my father did for a living. The first two *Godfather* movies had been released while I was in kindergarten and first grade, and by the time I was ten, every kid in school had heard of the Mafia. One day during a visit to the joke store, I saw some fake ID cards that said, "Member of the Mafia," with a place to sign your name. I thought it would be funny to buy one and carry it around to show the other kids.

I showed the card to my father that Saturday. I expected him to chuckle and say, "Pretty funny, son," but instead he roared with laughter. My mother didn't seem to think it was so funny. Their reactions puzzled me. That afternoon, when we left for a trip to Mulberry Street, my father told me to take my ID card with me. When we found Uncle Nino at the Ravenite, Dad told me to show him my card. It was the first time I had heard Nino laugh really loud. Something strange was going on. I liked the card, but it wasn't that funny. Nino told me to go show it to my friends in the other room. Every time I showed it to someone, he started laughing like it was the funniest thing he had ever seen and handed the card to a friend. One of the men told another guy, "Hey, Tony, maybe we should get ourselves one of these. Whadda ya think?" An idea started to dawn on me. I had to find out if I was right.

I was reading at the eighth-grade level by then, and I had begun reading the morning newspaper along with my dad that summer. Usually I preferred the comics. Now, however, I started paying attention to what my father read. Each day he pored over the *New York Post* and the *Daily News* religiously. I noticed he always went to the obituaries first, then to the crime section. I began to read the same sections of the paper when I came home from school every afternoon, holed up in my room after I finished my homework. The papers were filled with detailed descriptions of murders and robberies, along with references to "reputed mobsters", sometimes by name. The descriptions of the murders were often frightening. But what frightened me far more was the familiarity of some of the names they mentioned. Some of the men I knew from the social clubs had the same last names. Could they be the same guys? I didn't dare ask anyone, not even my father. Once the idea began to germinate, however, it started putting down roots, deep poison roots of terror. I had to know the truth. And no one could find it for me, but me.

My father was gone more than usual the next couple of days, and he seemed preoccupied. He didn't smile as much as usual, and when I talked to him, his mind seemed to be a million miles away. When he left the house late one afternoon, I saw that he was dressed in a black suit and tie. Every instinct told me that something had happened, and my suspicions were further heightened when my mother abruptly turned off the television in the den before the evening news came on. I was already in the habit of watching the news, but on this night, my mother told me to go to my room and leave the television off. I went through the motions of obeying, but the minute she went back upstairs, I crept down the hall to the den and turned the TV back on with the volume down low. The news broadcast showed a church with tall brass doors and a circular stained window, and the broadcaster's voiceover informed viewers that they were watching the funeral mass of Carlo Gambino, godfather of New York's most powerful Mafia family. While the cameras rolled, the doors opened and the mourners filed out of the church, ducking their heads to avoid the cameras. Suddenly time stopped. My heart rose up and choked me as the camera caught two men emerging from the church: Uncle Nino, wearing his sunglasses like always, and right behind him – my father. My entire body went numb. I hurriedly switched off the television and rushed back down the hall to my bedroom. Images from the newspapers swirled through my head, a kaleidoscope of brutality, of swift and brutal death. Somewhere in the blur of those images, everything I had heard and seen for the last five years came into focus.

My father was a mobster. He was part of the Mafia. I was dizzy with fear.

I had always made a point to tell my father goodbye when he left the house. Each time I would put my arms around his neck to kiss him and say, "I love you, Daddy."

And he would scoop me up in his arms and reply, "I love you too, Al." Now, however, the ritual took on a new urgency. From the night I saw his face on the television set, I lived in constant terror of losing my father. My greatest fear was that I would never see him again, and he would die without knowing I loved him.

I lay alone in the darkness that night, watching the dial on my clock creep around until three in the morning, When my father's headlights finally hit the wall beneath my window, I cried with relief, I would lie awake the next night, and the night after that, always waiting to hear my father's car in the driveway.

I never slept through the night again . . .

I had been in training for my father's death since I was twelve years old. I thought I was prepared for it, and from a practical point of view, I was. What I was not prepared for was the abyss of pain that opened beneath me with his passing. My father's final advice to me had been to forget him and to have a good life. The problem was that I didn't have the faintest idea how to do that. So instead I did what most people do in the aftermath of sudden loss: I carried on in the way I was accustomed to. And that meant taking care of business for my father. Not his Mob business. My father had started down that path at the same age I was, seventeen, and I knew where the journey ended. It was a journey I did not want to take. It was the other business of his life that I shouldered.

I bought my first car that spring, a black Corvette, after getting my first legal driver's licence. My father and I had planned to pick the car out together. My family occupied most of my attention. I made it a point to be home as much as possible. Like a protective father, I brought home videos to keep my sisters occupied, took them and my mother out to dinner and to the movies. I even stopped by my mother's favourite diner now and then, to pick up a hamburger and fries for her as my father had once done. She patted me sadly, unable to eat what I'd brought her, but I knew she appreciated the gesture.

I also tried to take responsibility for people who had depended on my father. I had watched my dad take care of people all his life. It was clear that Cousin Joe could not survive on his own; it was equally clear that he would never be able to stay out of trouble. I knew my father would want Joe to be cared for in his old age, so I told him to pack his things and get ready to leave New York permanently. Then I put a sizable bundle of cash in a paper bag and told Joe I was taking him to the airport for a final goodbye. I told him that I didn't want to know where he was going, but that I wished him well. I also told him that I never wanted to hear from him again. To my surprise, when I started to tell him goodbye at the airport, his eyes filled with tears, and he told me he wanted me to have something to remember him by. It was the only thing he had to give me in the way of a legacy, he said. Then he handed me a battered copy of an old journal, filled with notes and handwritten copies of his special recipes. He knew I liked his cooking and hoped that I would use the recipes and remember him. Along with the recipes were little anecdotes, funny stories and comments about the men he had cooked for. It was the last I ever saw of Cousin Joe.

I also felt a sense of responsibility for Freddy, who was still inside. Freddy was devastated by my father's death. Unable to read and capable of writing only his name, Freddy was like a lost child in the wake of my father's murder. Things got even worse for Freddy when his brother Richie was murdered shortly after my father was killed. Richie had worked for my father on and off for several years as part of Dad's auto theft ring. Richie DiNome was an upscale version of Freddy – dark, handsome, smarter, younger. He was a talented thief who could steal twenty cars in a single night. The FBI was pushing Richie hard to turn informant, offering to make a deal for Freddy if Richie turned. One night Richie disappeared, his body turning up a week later with bullets through the back of his head. Someone in the Mob had gotten nervous. Richie knew too much.

Several weeks after our father's funeral, Debra and I went to visit Freddy in jail to see how he was doing. It was a strange visit, for I knew immediately that something was wrong. In all the years I had known Freddy, I had never seen him behave so oddly. He kept asking me, as though he had memorized the questions, "So Albert, who do you think murdered your father? Do you think it might have been one of his associates?" Freddy never talked like that; it was clear he had been coached. It didn't take a genius to realize that Freddy had made some kind of deal to turn informant, but he wasn't bright enough to carry it off believably. Freddy would have gone to the grave for my father, but with Richie dead and his family in need, I knew it would be simple to turn Freddy if he thought he was helping to catch my father's killer. I told him I had no idea who had performed the hit and cut the visit short. Debra asked me why Freddy was acting so strange. I told her I didn't know. The change in Freddy made me very uncomfortable. If I couldn't trust him, whom could I trust?

From the night I saw my father's blood on my hands, I became obsessed with finding his killer's identity. No ounce of common sense, no pang of conscience, no dying warning from my father's mouth had changed my resolution. I needed a cause, and avenging my father's death gave me one.

Despite my unwillingness to discuss it with Freddy, I knew as well as he did that my father's murderer was probably one of his associates. Everything about the murder pointed to an inside job. The question was, who? In the weeks following my father's death, that question had haunted my every waking moment and often followed me into sleep. Paul Castellano was the obvious choice for sending the order, but who had carried it out? Experience told me someone in my father's crew had been involved, though I didn't want to believe it. The afternoon I went by the Gemini to pick up Cousin Joe for the ride to the airport, Anthony and Joey were sitting around the table with some of the minor players. Anthony was sitting in my father's chair, with Joey on his right in my old spot. I felt my stomach tighten, but the Twins just smiled lazily and said, "How ya doin', Albert?"

While I debated which of my father's old crew, if any, I could trust, they made the first overtures and got in touch with me. They needed to tie up some loose ends, they told me, and they needed some of my father's things to do that. They wanted his "Shylock book", a leather ledger where he kept the information on his loan-shark collections. They told me they were going to collect the additional money owed to my father for "us", but they couldn't do that without the book. I knew they were lying. They had no intention of sharing anything they collected; their primary motive was lining their own pockets. Among them all, my father's crew owed him hundreds of thousands of dollars, which they certainly weren't going to pay my family. The crew always spent more than they made, borrowing against the next big score. And finally, they wanted my father's tagging tools, worth a potential fortune if they continued stealing cars. I knew that none of them had either the brains or the discipline to run the operation without my father, but they hadn't figured that out yet. I agreed to meet with them and discuss the details, hoping it would give me a chance to size them up in person.

I suggested we meet at the diner where they used to meet my father. The diner was a nice, family-style restaurant on the main road through Massapequa. It seemed like a safe enough place for such a meeting. I had no idea where Freddy had kept the tagging tools. The ledger was hidden in the cabinet at home. I'd used it to make collections when Dad was in hiding, but I had no intention of turning it over to the crew.

They were all waiting for me in the parking lot when I drove up that afternoon. The Gemini Twins were there, along with a couple of other guys I barely knew. When they motioned me into the car so we could drive while we talked, I climbed in between Joey and Anthony without a second thought. I assumed they were worried about eavesdroppers in the diner. It wasn't until we pulled out of the parking lot that I realized my mistake. As the driver merged on to the highway, Anthony and Joey pulled their coats back so I could see. Both of them had guns sticking out of their belts. I looked at the back of the driver's head and the man riding shotgun up front, and my heart stopped. I had walked into an ambush. "Holy shit," I thought, "this is a hit, and I walked right into it."

As we drove through the fading Long Island afternoon, Joey and Anthony began questioning me about the tagging tools. I told them I didn't know where they were. They seemed to believe me. But when they asked about the loan shark book, I denied knowing anything about it. "I don't know anything about any book," I insisted. "Dad kept all the accounts in his head as far as I know. He told me who to collect from when he needed me to do a pickup, but that's all I know. I don't know anything about a book."

They knew I was lying. I guess it was stupid, but I was trying to buy some time. And if they killed me anyway, I certainly wasn't going to hand over something worth that much money first.

"We're trying to help you, Albert," Anthony kept saying. He tried to look sad, but he couldn't quite pull it off.

It was nearly an hour later when I realized, with an indescribable sense of relief, that they had decided to take me back to the diner. I'm still not certain why they did it. I think they were testing me, hoping I would come up with what they wanted if they played me right. They reminded me of the police with their good cop, bad cop tactics. As they pulled into the parking lot and stopped to let me out, Anthony looked me right in the eye and said, "Oh, Albert – our deep condolences on your father's tragic death. You need anything, you call us." I felt a chill go through me. I knew I was talking to my father's murderers.

Stepping into the parking lot, I replied, "Sure, guys, take care of yourselves. I'll be in touch."

And with that I strode back to my car as my father had taught me to – confident, fearless, arrogant. It was only when I had pulled out of the parking lot and headed for the relative safety of home that I allowed the relief to wash over me. I knew how close I had just come to being killed.

So began the cat-and-mouse game I played with my father's old crew for weeks to come. We each wanted something the other had: they wanted any money-making tools my father had left in my possession, and I wanted a clearer understanding of who had been involved in my father's murder and how. Trying to stay one step ahead of them, I agreed to continued meetings at the diner, but not in the car. I sometimes met them inside for a meal; usually, though, I stood in the parking lot to speak with them. Only yards away from where we stood, a steady stream of suburban traffic flowed by and women took their toddlers for walks in strollers, blissfully unaware of the negotiations taking place within their view.

I had some extra insurance the next time. I knew that a public setting wasn't enough to guarantee my safety. I'd told my friend Nick what had happened, and he'd insisted on coming with me the next time. Nick was no wiseguy; he was just my friend, and he had been backing me up since junior high school, no questions asked. I didn't try to talk him out of it. I'd have done the same thing for him. I told him to arrive in the parking lot a few minutes before I did, where he could keep an eye on me from a distance. I also gave him a loaded rifle to keep trained on all of us – just in case. I was in completely over my head, but I hadn't realized it yet.

The Mob wasn't the only game I was playing. I was also targeted in an FBI investigation. Someone – probably Freddy – had told them how close I'd been to my father. At this crucial point in their investigation of Paul Castellano and Nino Gaggi, they saw me as a potential gold mine of information about my father's criminal enterprises, someone who could put most of his associates behind bars. And they assumed that, because my father's associates were implicated in his murder, I would be willing to cooperate. They were wrong.

It is difficult to explain to an outsider why I was so reluctant to turn informant. After all, I was infinitely more intent on identifying my father's killers than the government could ever be. But the reality was that my options were limited. To begin with, I did not have much of the information they believed I had. I knew quite a bit about the loan-shark operations, as well as bits and pieces of his auto theft and pornography enterprises. But, except for the murder of the college student and some uncomfortable intuitions that he might have been involved in hits on other mobsters, I knew nothing about the violence they hinted at. The most obvious drawback to cooperating with the authorities, though, was fear for my own safety. If I became involved in their investigation in any way, I knew that the Mafia would murder me long before any case went to trial, and my father's killers would go free.

My refusal to cooperate with the authorities did not sit well with them. In the weeks following my father's murder, they did everything they could to force me to work with them. They couldn't subpoena me, since I was still under age. But they could call me in for "just a few more questions" about my father's death. When I left the house, they followed me, and when veiled threats didn't work, they tried sympathizing with me about my "poor murdered father". They couldn't have cared less about my father. They loathed him. They were glad he was dead, and I knew it. So they continued to question, and I continued to deny knowing anything, always in the politest possible terms. Finally I called a lawyer who'd been on my father's payroll, and the harassment stopped. Until I turned eighteen, there was little else they could do.

As the grey winter days melted away, the internal pressure gradually became intolerable. I continued going through the motions of living, but I couldn't hold anything in my mind but my father's dead face. I considered my options. I had a local mechanic build a hidden compartment into my new car where I could keep a gun and had him supercharge my car in case I had to make a fast escape. If I was going to act, I needed to do it soon, but the one-man army I had formed lacked the firepower to do the job. My entire stock of weaponry consisted of a sawed-off shotgun, a Browning 9mm, two .38s, and a pile of ammunition. It would not be enough, I reasoned, not nearly enough. I considered the vague plan I had formed a suicide mission. If I had asked Tommy and Nick, they would probably have helped me, but I was not willing to take my friends with me to certain death. My only hope of taking out my father's betrayers lay in greater firepower. I had heard my father refer to hidden arsenals that included not only stores of automatic weapons but also C-4 grenades and bullet-proof vests. I needed access to those arsenals now, but I didn't know where he'd kept them. After weeks of agonizing, I decided to make a call to the one person I believed I could still trust: Nino Gaggi. Uncle Nino had been avoiding me for weeks, but I told myself that was for his own safety. After several attempts, I finally got through to him. I told him that I thought I knew who had killed my father, and I needed my dad's old weapon supply to take care of business. Did he know where it was? He told me he'd look into it and get back to me.

Two days after I made the call, I went out on a date with my steady girlfriend. We had become more serious after my father's death, when I needed comfort. I knew it might be our last date, for I was planning to do the hit as soon as Nino got back to me: somehow that knowledge gave me peace, for I believed I was doing the right thing at last. I had nothing more to lose. I savoured every moment with my girl. She was so beautiful, so gentle. We had a wonderful evening: dinner in my favourite Long Island restaurant followed by a long walk on the beach, holding hands and sinking our bare toes into the sand. Moonlight shone on the water, and for the first time since my father's death, I felt like I could breathe. There was a glorious sense of seclusion as we walked together that night, her fingers twined in mine and the taste of salt on my tongue. Afterward I drove her home through the dark, silent streets and shared a lingering kiss on the front porch of her parents' home, breathing her into my heart. Driving down the deserted highway afterward, the lights of suburbia asleep for the night, I rolled down the car windows and let the warm wind blow through my hair. My whole body sighed in the relief of that moment.

I never saw it coming. One minute I was cruising down the darkened highway listening to Frank Sinatra on the tape player; the next, four cars came out of nowhere, surrounding me and forcing me off the road. I saw only a blur of green as my Corvette careened off the highway and down an embankment, coming to rest with a loud splintering sound as it hit the trees. My head hit the windshield, shattering the glass, and in the chaos I instinctively popped the catch and grabbed my gun, rolling out of the car on the passenger side. Hitting the ground shoulder first, I managed to fire two shots blindly into the darkness, in the general direction of my pursuers. I couldn't see anything. Someone stepped on my wrist, pinning it against the ground, and I felt my gun pulled from my hand. Hands reached down to grab me from two different directions, and someone slammed me up against the side of my car. Dark figures were on either side of me, pinning my wrists back against the roof, my arms splayed in a mock crucifixion. Blood ran into my eyes, and I struggled to make out shapes in the darkness.

I think there were four of them. All wore dark clothing and black ski masks pulled over their heads. I could barely make out their eyes, but I knew who they were. The Gemini Twins. A familiar voice said, "We're not going to kill you this time, Al, out of respect for your father. But you make any more threats, we'll do what we have to do." He hit me with the butt of his gun, hard, in my left eye socket. I heard a splintering sound, then felt a blow from the other side. The last thing I remember is confusion and pain as I slipped into unconsciousness.

Several hours later I gradually became aware of someone shouting my name. Hands shook my shoulder, gently but urgently. I tried to blink through the blood caking my eyes. "Dad?" I whispered. I knew that voice. "Nick?" I murmured from a red cave of pain. There was something horribly wrong with my body. I was ice cold, and I couldn't seem to move.

I could hear the panic in Nick's voice, and I knew he was crying. "Al? Al? Are you all right? Al?" Incredibly, Nick had spotted my smoking car on the side of the road on the way home from work, glimmering through the trees. Slowing down to look, he thought he could make out the shape of a familiar vehicle. Slamming on the brakes, he had leapt from his own car and slid down the shallow embankment toward the lights. It was there that he found me, motionless in a pool of blood. My body was stiff and cold from shock and from hours in the night air, and at first he thought I was dead. Dizzy with relief to hear me answer him, he gathered me in his arms and laid me gently in the back seat of his car.

I only wanted to go home, but he insisted on taking me to the hospital. He went by my house to get my mother, and minutes later he carried me into the emergency room, my mother weeping a few feet behind. The last thing I remember is whispering urgently to him, "Don't tell her anything." He had nothing to tell, for I was in no shape to give any information, but he nodded nonetheless. Then I slid into the blessed relief of unconsciousness.

The surgery took over eight hours. My cheekbone, eye socket, and most of the left side of my face had been shattered. The surgeon inserted a small wire cage to replace my eye socket and did his best to rebuild my face. Miraculously, my eye had been spared permanent damage. I would not lose my sight. I was going to need several more operations to restore my face cosmetically, the doctors told my mother, but I would be all right. When I regained consciousness late the next day, the doctors informed me that I had been incredibly lucky. If Nick had come along even thirty minutes later, I would have died from shock and loss of blood. Nick was there when I came out of the anaesthesia and for part of every day afterward, until I was finally able to leave the hospital.

So were the feds. Federal agents had showed up within hours of my admission and stayed in the operating room for most of the surgery, ready to take notes in case I said something under anaesthesia. They came and went regularly from my room, sometimes questioning me openly, other times posing as attendants or orderlies. Their faces swam in and out of my view. I had told no one what really happened that night; as far as anyone knew, I'd had a bad car accident and smashed my face on the windshield. Yet the officers were suspicious and used the opportunity to try once again to secure my cooperation. It was easy enough to evade their questions, in spite of my being a captive audience in the hospital bed. Between the pain, the pain medicine, and the weakness, I slipped in and out of consciousness for days. It was simple enough to pretend unconsciousness when I wanted to be left alone. Besides, it was difficult for me to speak with the extensive damage to my face, so they didn't press the issue.

I had not been in the hospital since I was four years old, for the surgery that helped correct my vision. I thought about that first surgery as I lay there with bandages covering one eye. This time, though, my father wouldn't be there when the bandages came off. The long weeks of recovery in the hospital gradually began to bring a clarity I hadn't had since my father's murder. Pain and immobility served as a kind of truth serum, producing not the truths the government wanted, but the truths I needed. I'd told myself that I owed it to my father to take revenge, but I had been deluding myself. My father's "friends" had murdered him and nearly killed me on behalf of an organization that glorified loyalty. My friend Nick, on the other hand, with nothing to gain but at genuine personal risk, had put himself on the line once again to save my life. When the room swam back into focus following my surgery, his face had been there next to my mother's and sisters' anxiously peering down at me. I owed it to all of them never to put myself in that kind of danger again. They had already suffered enough.

When I finally got out of the hospital, I did my best to leave the past behind. Searing headaches hit me sometimes, but each time one did, I used it to remind myself how useless vengeance was. The crew, their warning delivered, left me alone, and I never contacted any of them again. I even stopped visiting Freddy. It was time to bury the past.

The school year ended while I was hospitalized, and summer came to Long Island. I did my best to return to the business of being seventeen years old, swimming in the backyard pool and boating on the canal with Tommy and my girlfriend. College was only a year away, and I began filling out applications. I did not want to spend the rest of my life as the mobster's son.

Unfortunately, the government had other ideas. The federal task force that had been pursuing the New York Mob under the RICO statute for so many years had reached a crucial point in the Castellano investigation. With convictions multiplying and top mobsters turning informant, they scented victory. District Attorney Rudolph Giuliani and his prosecutors were waging a holy war, and as in all wars, personal rights were expendable in the conflict. I became collateral damage in the all-out assault on the crime families of New York.

With my father gone, I thought the surveillance on our family would fade away. Instead it shifted focus, from my father to me. Every time I left the house, someone followed me. I assumed that once the officers saw I had no further contact with my father's associates or enterprises, they would leave me alone. I was wrong. They followed me everywhere: to school, to the movies, even on dates. Like my face, my car had been restored after the wreck and was almost as good as new. It became a beacon for local police. Cops repeatedly pulled me over for imaginary traffic violations, searching my car for God knows what. It was humiliating. I found myself standing on the side of the highway next to my girlfriend while agents rummaged through my car and passing motorists slowed down to stare. My girlfriend was supportive and patient, but it was deeply embarrassing. The only illegal item I was transporting remained untouched, hidden in its compartment under the dashboard. I still didn't feel safe leaving the house without my gun. The superchargers I'd installed on my car enabled me to escape the surveillance vehicles at times, but they also led to a long string of speeding tickets and a suspended licence. As summer turned into fall and I returned for my senior year of high school, I became increasingly angry and frustrated. Why wouldn't they just leave me alone? I wasn't doing anything wrong.

Driving with a suspended licence eventually landed me in court. Angry and unrepentant, I faced the judge ready to do battle. I knew I was guilty only of driving with a suspended licence. When I was told to approach the bench for a plea, however, I realized that I knew the court officer sitting in front of me. He had been on my father's payroll for years, making cases disappear. About the same time I recognized him, he recognized me. Telling my lawyer I wanted a private conference with the officer, I went aside and said to him, "Now we both know these charges are going to be dropped. Don't we?" The unspoken threat was clear. He would be prosecuted if the authorities knew about the favours he'd done my father.

Shifting uneasily, he nodded and said, "Certainly, Mr DeMeo." The charges were dropped, and my mother was furious. She thought that I was spinning out of control and deserved to be punished. She was right, of course. For me, though, it wasn't that simple. I'd watched the legal system talk out of both sides of its mouth all my life. Many of my father's associates were judges or cops. If the government persisted in treating me as the mobster's son, I thought, so be it. They couldn't have it both ways. They were bending all the rules to get to me. Why shouldn't I bend a few of my own?

As the months went by and the harassment continued, I became angrier and angrier. Any hope of a normal life was long gone. The government would never let me shed my father's identity. I felt like Exhibit A in the court of public opinion. One afternoon I was pulled over again and told that I was wanted for several outstanding traffic warrants; I was handcuffed and put into a police car for the ride down to central booking. They had cuffed me tightly, but the physical pain in my wrists was secondary to the psychological misery I felt during the ride.

"Well, well, well, if it isn't the mobster's son," the officer said as he shoved me in the car. "Don't hit your head!" he cautioned as he cracked my skull against the cruiser's roof.

His partner chuckled as he took his place up front. "What do you say we take a little ride down to the station, you arrogant little piece of shit?"

All the way down to the station, they taunted me about my father as I sat trapped behind the steel mesh of the patrol car. When they jerked me out of the car to go inside, I started demanding my lawyer, shouting. "You can't do this to me! I want my attorney!"

"Can't do this? Who the fuck do you think you are? We're cops. We can do anything we want."

Something burst inside, and blind with rage, I lost control completely. I tried to head butt the officer, kicking wildly as they subdued me. One of them pepper sprayed my face while they shackled me, and I collapsed to the ground, blind and writhing in pain. I felt like a trapped animal.

A few minutes later I was thrust into a jail cell where I was shackled to the wall, still cuffed. The struggle had aggravated my skull injuries, and the pain in my bad eye was agonizing. The rank smell of the man they chained me next to nearly gagged me. There were nearly twenty men crammed in the cell with me, most of them ranting and raving, spitting, and urinating on the floor. It was like being plunged into a nightmare. When a police officer walked by the cell a short while later, a tall black man a few feet from me unzipped his pants and began urinating on the officer. Within seconds a barrage of officers descended on the cell, and all hell broke loose. The man they were after squatted and filled his hands with his own excrement, then began throwing it at the officers. Other prisoners followed suit. I sat against the wall, sickened. How had I ended up in this madhouse? Eventually officers restrained the men they were after, but no one attempted to clean up the pool of urine and bowel movements that littered the floor. The stench was overpowering.

With the troublemakers quieted, I became the main attraction for passersby. Officers and jail workers lined up on the other side of the bars to point me out like I was some bizarre species of animal. "Hey, wiseguy!" they called out. "Having fun, little gangster?" The hours dragged on, and I kept asking for a lawyer, asking why I wasn't being booked or taken in front of a judge. Eventually I started talking to the other men in my cell and found out that some of them were pretty good guys, just frustrated with the way they were being treated. They advised me to be patient, said making a scene would only make things worse for me. I knew they were right, and I settled down to wait as best I could.

I remained shackled all day and most of the night. The arresting officers "forgot" about me for more than twelve hours, finally rediscovering my paperwork shortly before dawn the next day. When I was taken before a judge at last, he informed me that the original arrest was for failing to appear in response to a series of traffic tickets. The odd thing about this was that I had never seen any of the tickets they showed me. God knows, I had been guilty of speeding, but I always paid my tickets. But the pile of citations they put in front of me – these, I had never seen before, and I didn't recognize any of the cars I had supposedly been driving. When I pointed this out to the judge, he sarcastically inquired if someone else had been driving other cars while using my name. I was finally released to my lawyer, but I was very disturbed by what had happened in that courtroom. What was going on here? Who was making up charges against me?

A psychological war was being waged against me, and I was losing. I wasn't yet eighteen, but I had already developed bleeding ulcers. Home once again, I spent over an hour in the steam room and shower trying to feel clean. Afterward, as I lay in bed, I mentally listed every crime I had ever committed. Speeding and carrying a concealed weapon, yes. Collecting packages for my father? Yes, probably a crime, for some of them had undoubtedly contained illicit cash or stolen property, though I never opened any of them. Aiding and abetting a felon? But my father hadn't been a felon at the time; he'd never even been charged. Failing to report crimes I had known about? Was that illegal? Did it make any difference that I was a minor during all of it? I didn't know. Drenched in fear, confusion, and guilt, I struggled to sort out the nature of my misdeeds. I had never thought of myself as a criminal; I had thought of myself as a son helping his father. Had I been wrong? And what if I had? I knew that if given the same choices tomorrow, I would help my father again. Did that make me a criminal, too? I didn't know. How long was this going to go on? How far would they go? Sometimes I wished they'd just sentence me and get it over with. Anything was better than this constant anxiety.

The real question that haunted me, however, was not what I had done, but why they hated me so much – and they obviously did. I knew that in their eyes, I was a junior wiseguy, an obnoxious adolescent with a chip on his shoulder. That much I understood, but it didn't explain the passionate contempt they treated me with. One night, sleepless as usual, I went into the bathroom to rinse my face with cold water and caught my own reflection in the mirror. It startled me. Funny, I thought, I never realized how much I look like my father. And that was when it hit me. It wasn't me they hated. They hated my father, and every time they looked at me, they saw my father's face. In their eyes, I wasn't just the mobster's son; I was the mobster. I had spent a lifetime trying to walk, talk, and dress exactly like my dad. In a moment of wrenching clarity, I realized I had succeeded.